Strategies of Dominance

Strategies of Dominance

The Misdirection of U.S. Foreign Policy

P. Edward Haley

Woodrow Wilson Center Press
Washington, D.C.

The Johns Hopkins University Press
Baltimore, Maryland

EDITORIAL OFFICES
Woodrow Wilson Center Press
One Woodrow Wilson Plaza
1300 Pennsylvania Avenue, N.W.
Washington, D.C. 20004-3027
Telephone 202-691-4029
www.wilsoncenter.org

ORDER FROM
The Johns Hopkins University Press
Hampden Station
P.O. Box 50370
Baltimore, Maryland 21211
Telephone: 1-800-537-5487
www.press.jhu.edu/books/

9 8 7 6 5 4 3 2 1

Library of Congress Cataloging-in-Publication Data

Haley, P. Edward.
   Strategies of dominance : the misdirection of U.S. foreign policy / P. Edward Haley.
      p. cm.
   Includes bibliographical references and index.
   ISBN 0-8018-8397-0 (cloth : alk. paper) — ISBN 0-8018-8413-6
(pbk. : alk. paper)
      1. United States—Foreign relations—2001–   . 2. United States—
Foreign relations—Philosophy.   3. United States—Foreign relations—1989–   .
4. Bush, George W. (George Walker), 1946–   —Influence.   5. Clinton, Bill, 1946–
—Influence.   6. Bush, George, 1924–   —Influence.   7. Post-communism.
8. Balance of power.   9. International relations.   I. Title.
E895.H35 2006
327.73—dc22   2005034665

**Woodrow Wilson
International
Center
for Scholars**

The Woodrow Wilson International Center for Scholars, established by Congress in 1968 and headquartered in Washington, D.C., is a living national memorial to President Wilson. The Center's mission is to commemorate the ideals and concerns of Woodrow Wilson by providing a link between the worlds of ideas and policy, while fostering research, study, discussion, and collaboration among a broad spectrum of individuals concerned with policy and scholarship in national and international affairs. Supported by public and private funds, the Center is a nonpartisan institution engaged in the study of national and world affairs. It establishes and maintains a neutral forum for free, open, and informed dialogue. Conclusions or opinions expressed in Center publications and programs are those of the authors and speakers and do not necessarily reflect the views of the Center staff, fellows, trustees, advisory groups, or any individuals or organizations that provide financial support to the Center.

The Center is the publisher of *The Wilson Quarterly* and home of Woodrow Wilson Center Press, *dialogue* radio and television, and the monthly newsletter "Centerpoint." For more information about the Center's activities and publications, please visit us on the web at www.wilsoncenter.org.

For Elaine

"Oh, I have picked up magic in her nearness . . ."

and

In memory of George F. Kennan

Contents

Foreword

Lee H. Hamilton

To succeed, American foreign policy must enjoy the broad understanding and support of the American people. That cannot be achieved unless Americans have a candid, difficult, and sustained dialogue about our national priorities and how we act in the world. To be effective, this dialogue must address the tough issues and how we should respond to them, including the proliferation of nuclear weapons; the future of political Islam; the increase in demand and the decline in supply of energy resources; the spread of epidemic diseases like HIV/AIDS; and the conflict, poverty, and inequality that fester as the dark side of globalization. Americans must be willing to reconsider deeply held convictions, and we must seek out common ground, even as we head into a mid-term election and the 2008 presidential campaign.

In *Strategies of Dominance*, Ed Haley challenges Americans to embark on such a debate. He argues that for the past two decades, Americans have seen the world through the lens of the "post–Cold War paradigm," a compound of assumptions about the unique virtues, power, and responsibilities of the United States. Those assumptions, in Haley's view, turned out to be deeply flawed. Under their influence, the United States waited too long to stop horrific massacres in Bosnia and Rwanda, failed to notice the shift in global terrorism until it was too late to prevent 9/11, and went to war in Iraq without an effective plan for rebuilding that country.

Strategies of Dominance reviews these major and costly blunders — which took place under both Democratic and Republican administrations.

Lee H. Hamilton is president and director of the Woodrow Wilson International Center for Scholars and former chair of the House Committee on International Relations.

It also carefully revisits some of the remarkable successes of the last fifteen years: Central and Eastern Europe were set free and disarmed to a degree no one could possibly have imagined; for a time, the Middle East peace process was rekindled and gave Israelis and Palestinians a few precious "good years" of relative peace; new multilateral agreements and institutions were created, such as the North American Free Trade Act and the forum for Asian and Pacific Economic Cooperation; and the threat of war among the great powers has been sharply reduced for the foreseeable future.

Through this assessment, *Strategies of Dominance* offers recommendations for how American foreign policy can focus on relations with the great and rising powers: China, India, Japan, Russia, and Europe. While Haley rightly outlines American preeminence in the world, he is also astute in recognizing the limitations of "hegemony" and makes a persuasive case that we must reinvigorate our relations with traditional democratic allies and multilateral organizations. Haley casts a skeptical eye on the unilateral application of American power, arguing that the United States must seek greater international legitimacy and cooperation in its actions and seek foreign policy goals through peaceful means.

Strategies of Dominance comes out at a time when our objectives sometimes appear beyond our capacity to reach them. The challenges abroad—from terrorism, to proliferation, to intractable conflict—are placing an extraordinary burden on the United States. Meanwhile, many people around the world have come to distrust American policies and to question America's motives, while many Americans are growing fatigued at the massive commitment of troops and resources overseas through the war on terror and the war in Iraq. At the same time, however, a reservoir of good feeling toward the United States remains among the peoples and governments of the world, and Americans still generally support a robust view of the role of the United States in the world. The challenge is seeking a new basis for international cooperation, and that effort must begin through a reconsideration of American foreign policy. *Strategies of Dominance* points us in the right direction, inviting the American people and our friends and allies around the world to join in a dialogue on how to use American power in a manner that serves America's interests—and the world's.

Acknowledgments

For their generous support of my research and writing, I thank Claremont McKenna College and the W. M. Keck Center for International Strategic Studies. The opportunity to spend six months in residence from January to June 2004 as a Public Policy Scholar at the Woodrow Wilson International Center for Scholars in Washington, D.C., allowed me to benefit from the extraordinary program put together by its director Lee H. Hamilton, deputy director Michael Van Dusen, and associate director Samuel Wells. The Wilson Center is a marvelous institution, and I am deeply appreciative of the freedom I enjoyed there to think and to write and the pleasure and understanding I derived from meeting and talking with a few of the many scholars, journalists, activists, political leaders, soldiers, and diplomats who come to the Center. I am especially grateful to Joe Brinley, director of the Wilson Center Press, for his encouragement and interest in this book. The staff of the Wilson Center library were quick and helpful in tracking down books and articles from the Library of Congress.

My debts to individuals are many and important. During my research and writing, I interviewed members of the intelligence community, political appointees in all three administrations, soldiers, staff members of the Congress, journalists, and American diplomats. Their knowledge, sheer brain power, and commitment to the best interests of the American people always leave me deeply impressed. Their help was indispensable. I am especially grateful to Harry Cahill, Robert Danin, Douglas Feith, Michael Goldstein, Robert Hathaway, David Hertzberg, Andrew Hoehn, Jonathan Howe, Les Janka, Zalmay Khalilzad, Anthony Lake, Tom Kelsey, Tom King, James Mann, Constance Mayer, John Merrill, Charles L. Pritchard, Condoleezza Rice, Dennis Ross, Adrian St. John, and Brent Scowcroft. Harlan and Linda Robinson read early drafts of several key chapters, provided helpful comments, and sustained body and soul with good wine, great food, and dearly loved friendship. I will always be grateful to Nancy Stidham

Boutin for her thoughtful encouragement when I first began the book. Katherine Griffiths and Diane Gedymin generously gave expert help and hope during the early stages of the book. My research assistants kept me supplied with materials on the three administrations: Lauren Beck, Alexander Benard, Lauren Cameron, Olivia Gonzalez, Jonathan Hill, Grace Michel, and Alexis Orton. At the Wilson Center, Tara Patenaude helped me analyze mountains of articles. Rachel Hernandez cheerfully helped prepare the manuscript for publication.

Strategies of Dominance

Introduction

The most widely read books about America's global dominance since the end of the Cold War justify it as an extension of the past or condemn it as hubris and error.[1] The neoconservatives' appeal for Americans to stop second-guessing themselves and impose democracy on the world was influential in the Bush II White House, but has not won a wide following in the United States or anywhere else.[2] This book presents another, and I hope more persuasive, interpretation.

The present is created when continuities from the past collide with the unexpected from the future.[3] If a Richter scale for foreign policy had existed when the Cold War ended, it would have registered shock after shock as the prevailing view of American foreign policy slammed into a world that was no longer familiar because it lacked the restraint of a balance of power. Seemingly without warning, barbaric ethnic and religious conflicts erupted in the Balkans and Africa. Suicidal terrorism collided with barely formed post–Cold War assumptions and strategies. The melding of past and future, of continuous and contingent, gave birth to a combination of beliefs and assumptions that formed the structure of American foreign policy since 1990 and the theme of this book, the post–Cold War paradigm.[4]

The general outlook of a society's decision makers and opinion leaders about the outside world may be described in a number of ways: worldview, mindset, conventional wisdom, and even "groupthink." I have chosen "foreign policy paradigm," and define it as the most general beliefs and assumptions decision makers possess that enable them to understand and solve the problems they face. Thomas Kuhn observed that a paradigm contains both the problems that must be addressed and the preferred ways to solve them. Paradigms are likely to continue until their flaws become so burdensome that they are replaced by a new understanding of the main problem and new ways of arriving at solutions.[5] When it becomes widely accepted, a foreign policy paradigm allows a government to conduct war and diplomacy for years and even decades without reconsidering its fundamental assumptions. Its influence can become so widespread that it is unlikely to be replaced until circumstances have changed profoundly, as happened in the United States after 1945 and 1990, or setbacks occur that are severe enough to discredit it.

Introducing *Strategies of Containment*, his widely read book about post–World War II American foreign policy, John Lewis Gaddis pointed out that historians can be divided into two groups: "lumpers" and "splitters."[6] Splitters doubt every generalization, regard elegant theories with suspicion, and "carry around in their heads lists of exceptions to almost any rule they are likely to encounter."[7] They glory in making distinctions and "elevate quibbling to a high historiographical art."[8] Lumpers, on the other hand, discover paradigms and linkages that fall comfortably into the categories they have put together. The lumpers' world is one of few accidents and little untidiness. The sins of the two are fairly obvious. Splitters sometimes miss the forest for the trees. Lumpers tend to dismiss people and facts that do not fit into their categories. Both approaches are indispensable to learning about the past and trying to understand and prepare for the future. In this book, I come down emphatically on the side of the lumpers.

This book has two goals. The first is to show that beginning in 1990, American decision makers and opinion leaders adopted a new foreign policy paradigm, composed of assumptions drawn from the past, such as American exceptionalism, democratization, economic sanctions, and coercive diplomacy, and others that came out of the unexpected end of the Cold War, such as American primacy, bandwagoning, and globalization. The strategies and policies adopted by the three presidents differed in many ways, but a very strong, and I hope persuasive, case can be made that they agreed about fundamental assumptions and disagreed over means rather than ends. Partisan differences aside, it would have been remarkable if the three presidents had operated from radically different assumptions. Although Americans disagree about who should be president, they and their leaders share fundamental values. Most believe in democracy, the rule of law, the essential goodness of the United States and the American people, the universal relevance of American ideas about democracy, and the unique international responsibilities of the United States. Differences among the three presidents who have served since 1990 are important, but no greater than those between Eisenhower and Kennedy or Truman and Reagan. It is helpful to consider the three post–Cold War presidents and their advisers through the prism of a post–Cold War paradigm just as it was to consider the pre-1990 presidents from the perspective of a Cold War paradigm of shared values and assumptions. Policymakers bring assumptions and predispositions with them into office and learn others on the job. As William Quandt observed, these are crucial sources of foreign policy decisions.[9] Other factors also play a part as well, including the nature of the issues at stake, pressures from the bureaucracy, domestic politics, and crises and developments in the regions where American power and interests are engaged.[10]

In addition to showing that all three presidents operated from a similar set of assumptions about the world, this book also argues that the post–Cold War paradigm turned out to be deeply flawed. In 2005 for the first time since the presidency of Jimmy Carter (1977–1981), the United States found itself weaker and more isolated than it was four years earlier. The Bush II administration was responsible for much of that outcome. Its barely concealed contempt for allies, its flouting of international opinion, and its unilateral actions in Iraq, particularly when no weapons of mass destruction were discovered and its plans for the occupation of Iraq turned out to be negligent and foolish, alienated hundreds of millions of people around the world and weakened the United States. The two preceding administrations committed their share of mistakes. Bill Clinton always stopped short of the decisive measures needed to destroy al-Qaeda, failed to prevent genocide in Bosnia and Rwanda, and was unable to persuade Israel and the Palestinians to make peace despite years of effort. The first Bush administration ignored great suffering in Haiti, and failed to come to grips with nuclear proliferation and terrorism when these problems had only begun to take on a new and far more dangerous form. This book acknowledges the strengths and weaknesses of all three presidents' strategies, but it also seeks an explanation of the decline in American influence around the world that is broader than the faults and virtues of a particular president and his advisers. I am less interested in blaming presidents and their advisers than in understanding why their plans and decisions were sometimes so detached from the realities on the ground.

The post–Cold War paradigm failed to provide a solid foundation on which to base an understanding of the nature of the world and of threats to U.S. interests. It contributed to the failure of the Clinton administration to stop genocide in Africa and the Balkans, and to the inadequate planning of the Bush II administration for the postwar occupation and rehabilitation of Iraq.[11] It prevented the United States from anticipating important international developments, such as the rising incidence of ethnic and religious conflict and resulting genocide. It offered no new insights into the radically altered nature of terrorism in the late twentieth century. Because it was based on a distorted view of American primacy, the post–Cold War paradigm severely strained relations with the country's closest allies in Western Europe, and threw American strategy out of balance, leaving it with commitments to democratize the world that greatly exceeded its capabilities.[12]

Within the post–Cold War paradigm, three sets of assumptions or operational codes have guided American strategy since 1990: the first Bush administration's prudent, carefully orchestrated "new world order," which took a limited view of American security interests and sought to administer American hegemony through the United Nations; the rhetorically imaginative and noninterventionist strategy of the two Clinton administrations' "engagement and enlargement" of democracy and market economics; and the transformative and interventionist strategy of the Bush II administrations, based on military unilateralism and global democratization. Perceptions of the correct ways to respond to threats and opportunities differ as circumstances and the identities of key decision makers change, without necessarily challenging the dominant foreign policy paradigm. The Eisenhower administration's nuclear strategy of massive retaliation differed in important ways from the Kennedy administration's flexible response. Kennedy, a Keynesian economic expansionist, also disagreed with Eisenhower's notion that the United States must keep government expenditures low to cope with the "dual threat" of communist aggression and bankruptcy from an uncontrolled arms race. Kennedy believed that massive increases in defense spending would strengthen rather than weaken the United States. Despite their very significant differences, Kennedy and Eisenhower, their advisers, and, indeed, virtually the entire country, remained firmly committed to the Cold War paradigm of a bipolar world, anticommunism, nuclear deterrence, and a global zero sum contest between two superpowers. In a similar way, the three post–Cold War presidents chose different strategies, but all remained firmly bound to the post–Cold War paradigm.[13]

Like Woodrow Wilson himself, Bill Clinton and both presidents Bush followed noninterventionist and interventionist approaches in response to the crises they faced. They differed about foreign policy not in principle but regarding judgments as to what was prudent and whether the working of globalization would democratize and thereby pacify the world with or without forceful action by the United States.[14] That Clinton was fundamentally a noninterventionist and Bush II an interventionist should not obscure the similarity of their fundamental assumptions. Clinton was convinced that globalization would soon give democracy and market economics to every country. The world would soon be able to take care of itself; there was no need to give history a push. As a result, he resisted military intervention far longer than he should have in Rwanda and the Balkans, which resulted in the needless loss of hundreds of thousands of lives. The attacks of 9/11 revealed George W. Bush's willingness to give history a push, but did not transform his commitment to the post–Cold War paradigm any more than the immense costs of fighting in Afghanistan and Iraq postponed his tax cuts or plans to restructure the Social Security system.

In some ways, the post–Cold War paradigm was the opposite of its Cold War counterpart: in place of a bipolar world, a unipolar world; and in place of a zero sum struggle between two adversaries kept in check by nuclear deterrence, a world of one global superpower that faced no countervailing pressures. The old assumption about American exceptionalism—the unique virtues of Americans and America—remained. But there were differences that were not easily described as opposites or continuities. A unipolar world existed because of American primacy, a new combination of the presence of enormous American military and economic capability and the absence of countervailing power. American primacy gave the United States unprecedented freedom of action and brought coercive diplomacy and economic sanctions into the paradigm with much greater frequency, and much more ambitious objectives than during the Cold War. Borrowed from the Cold War and Woodrow Wilson was the assumption that the key to war and peace lies in the nature of government itself. Bad governments make war and oppress their people; good governments are peaceful, free, and democratic. During the Cold War, Americans believed that bad governments were communist, and there was little that could be done about it because of the nuclear standoff. In the post–Cold War world, bad governments were rogue dictatorships, but American primacy meant that the United States could do a great deal to bring about change, whether to prohibit state-to-state aggression by rogue dictators (Bush I) or bring about regime change and democratization through globalization (Clinton) or force (Bush II). Clinton's and Bush II's view of democracies as peaceful became the basis for making the democratization of the world a vital security interest of the United States, a decision given special urgency after hijacked airliners struck the World Trade Center and Pentagon on September 11, 2001. In addition, all three administrations assumed that economic globalization and a trend toward global democratization served American interests, and could be counted on to reinforce American strategy.

It should not be surprising that Bush I's strategy contained fewer elements of the post–Cold War paradigm than those of his successors. The institutions of the Cold War lasted almost until the end of the first Bush administration (1989–1993): George H.W. Bush left office barely a year after Boris Yeltsin dissolved the Soviet Union. As a result, the first Bush administration carried into the post–Cold War world the extreme prudence and caution born of four decades of deathly nuclear confrontation with the Soviet Union. Even so, Bush I post–Cold War assumptions and strategy strongly resemble those of Clinton and Bush II, particularly in its view of America as a uniquely virtuous country, a belief in American primacy, coercive diplomacy, economic sanctions, and the importance of global democratization.

The post–Cold War paradigm was not always or completely wrong. Globalization described actual trends, such as dramatic increases in the movement of money, goods, people, and information across borders. Democratization correctly noted the steady increase in the number of states around the world with parliaments and elections, although some were illiberal rather than liberal democracies, and others were dictatorships dressed up as democracies.[15] But there were two problems. Political leaders and analysts who ought to have known better often treated what were really hopes and guesses about the future as if the transformations they forecast had already taken place and could be relied on for short-term policymaking. And, the components of the paradigm came together to predispose the United States and other industrial democracies to intervene militarily and economically again and again in the affairs of less developed countries.

The economic interventions were frequent, deeply self-interested, caused enormous social dislocation and hardship, and often put the needs of creditors ahead of the people in the borrowing countries.[16] Economically, they were unavoidable: otherwise, the damage caused by too rapid globalization might have engulfed the developed as well as the developing world. Clinton's secretary of the treasury, Robert Rubin, described the financial meltdown of the late 1990s in this way:

> What people generally referred to as the Asian financial crisis was actually a global economic crisis that began in Asia in the summer of 1997 and spread for a period of nearly two years as far as Russia and Brazil. Aftershocks were felt across emerging markets and even in the industrialized world. Viewed in its entirety, this event posed an enormous threat to the stability of the global economy and caused great economic hardship in the affected countries.

With capital markets "seizing up," and U.S. Treasury bonds, the world's safest financial instruments, losing ground, Rubin said, "cascading financial instability appeared to endanger the entire global financial system."[17] The wealthy industrialized countries and the governments of the countries spiraling out of control had no choice but to make enormous efforts to overcome the problems of runaway globalization and flawed national and international policy. The military interventions were less frequent and aimed at different problems, from famine relief to putting a stop to ethnic cleansing and genocide, reversing outright invasion, countering terrorism, halting the spread of nuclear, chemical, and biological weapons, and transforming the Middle East into a democratic community. The changing character of military intervention shows the increasing influence of the post–Cold War paradigm: the 1991 intervention in Iraq reversed the conquest of Kuwait; the North Atlantic Treaty Organization's involvement in Bosnia (mid-1990s) and Kosovo (1999) put a belated end to genocide and ethnic cleansing; and the second Gulf War (2003–) brought down Saddam Hussein and attempted to establish a democratic state in his place.

Unless American policymakers, the Congress, and the American people abandon the post–Cold War paradigm, and seek other ideas around which to build an effective, humane foreign policy, the United States will continue to lurch from crisis to crisis, isolating itself further until, without allies or friends, it surrenders its world responsibilities in frustration and bitterness. If this happens, the United States and the rest of the world will have squandered American primacy and the chance it offered to accomplish humane, worthwhile goals. Americans could turn on each other in a frenzy of witch hunting and scapegoating, as they did twice in the twentieth century. Or, they could fall for the seductive appeals of the intellectual and ideological merchants of imperialism who argue for the transformation of unilateralism into world domination, a rebirth of imperialism in the twenty-first century.[18] Domination poses a grave danger to the American people and the world. Imperialism would corrupt American institutions, sap the material and spiritual resources of the country, and inflict the casualties and burdens of empire on Americans and their unwilling subjects. It is hard to imagine a better way to provoke a religious war between the West and the Muslim world. Becoming an imperial power would put the United States in the position of Germany in the first half of the twentieth century when its aggressions brought first defeat and then utter destruction. Commenting on his country's experience in World War I, the German historian, Hans Delbruck, observed:

> We must look the facts in the face—that we have in a sense the whole world leagued against us—and we must not conceal from ourselves the fact that, if we try to penetrate to the basic reasons for this world coalition, we will ever and again stumble over the fear of German world hegemony.[19]

In the pages that follow, the administrations of George Herbert Walker Bush, Bill Clinton, and George W. Bush receive two chapters each. The first chapter lays out key assumptions, strategies, and policies, and the second subjects them to critical analysis. The concluding chapter offers my thoughts about a new foreign policy for the United States in the twenty-first century. In brief, I argue for a strategy that focuses on relations with China, India, Japan, and Europe, the only places where the combination of resources and industrial and human potential is capable of threatening American survival. This strategy recovers ties to the country's democratic allies and reassures rather than threatens nondemocratic countries, an approach that links U.S. interests to the protection of the sovereignty of nondemocratic states rather than the subversion of their governments, and their replacement with the trappings of democracy, without regard for a country's place in American vital security interests or the prospects for the survival of post-reform institutions.

The reforms may appear mild, but appearances are sometimes deceiving. Abandoning the post–Cold War paradigm will require an enormous effort by Americans at all levels of society and probably cannot be achieved without the kind of sustained national debate that typically occurs only after a major foreign policy failure and takes a long time. The United States waited from 1920 until 1947 to develop a coherent strategy for the exercise of its growing power and global responsibilities. Consider just two of the elements of the post–Cold War paradigm—American exceptionalism and American primacy. Americans are accustomed to thinking of themselves as disinterested, as above the narrow national or personal interests that they see at play in other nations' politics and foreign policies. American political leaders and opinion guides continue to justify the global engagement of the United States on the basis of American exceptionalism: no other nation has the capability or is morally qualified to lead. Since 1945, there have been two attempts to provide a new basis for the exercise of American power abroad, and the outcome of both suggests the enormous difficulty of the task. Richard Nixon and Henry Kissinger tried to base American strategy on the careful calculation of national interests, but their approach was defeated by opposition from left and right, the one outraged by what it saw as abandonment of moral values, the other by what it considered surrender to the Soviet Union. Jimmy Carter's effort to use the defense of universal human rights as the basis for American foreign policy rather than American exceptionalism collapsed amidst widespread discontent with what were seen as the excessive burdens and limitations that such an approach imposed on American freedom of action. Neither approach has been revived.

The implications of a correct definition of American primacy also pose major difficulties. The United States is superior to all other nations in military and economic strength, but it is not globally dominant. American superiority is real, and will not disappear for years and perhaps decades. No one could hope to be elected president on a platform of surrendering American superiority. But it is essential to understand what it means correctly. As the difficulties in occupying Iraq have revealed, the margins of American advantage are not so great as to allow the United States to wage unilateral war whenever it chooses. At its best, American superiority allows the United States to set the global agenda and invite other countries to follow. To achieve its international goals, the United States must accept the constraints of working with allies and within multilateral organizations, and must seek legitimacy as well as power as it attempts to protect its vital interests. The distrust with which a very large number of political leaders, legislators, intellectuals, and ordinary Americans view these limits suggests how difficult the task will be.

In thinking about these problems, I have often found myself returning to George Kennan's discussion of the deterioration in relations between the United States and Japan during the 1920s and 1930s that culminated in what Kennan believed to have been a totally unnecessary war. Kennan argued that the United States ought to have cooperated with Japan in dealing with matters of mutual advantage in Asia. When disagreements arose, they ought to have been addressed frankly with an eye to the situation as it appeared when seen from Tokyo as well as Washington. To ensure the protection of its vital interests in Asia, the United States ought to have maintained the naval forces allowed under the Washington and London treaties instead of allowing the American navy to decline. In addition, it ought to have made common cause with Great Britain in opposing by political and, if necessary, military means, Japanese initiatives that threatened British and American interests. This would have enabled both countries to bargain with Japan from a position of unity and strength, and could well have attracted the support of the Soviet Union when Hitler began his assault on the Versailles settlement in Europe. Instead, the American government declined to build a treaty navy or find strong allies in Asia. To Japan's dislike that was generated by racist laws in the United States and what it saw as obstruction of Japan's vital interests, the United States added contempt because its tough talk was unsupported by military strength.

Kennan replied in two ways when confronted by arguments that there was no feasible alternative to the policies followed by Roosevelt and his advisers. If the point was that American public opinion or the way the American government worked prevented their adoption, then steps could be taken to alter both. To those who argued that there was no guarantee that his proposals would have succeeded, Kennan answered that there are no guarantees of success in diplomacy and strategy. Had the measures that he recommended been put into practice, it might have been possible to avoid war and still have protected American interests. Without them, war was certain.

1

Bush I and the New World Order

The Cold War struggle had shaped our assumptions about international and domestic politics, our institutions and processes, our armed forces and military strategy. In a blink of an eye, these were gone. We were suddenly in a unique position, without experience, without precedent, and standing alone at the height of power.

—Brent Scowcroft[1]

The Roman god Janus whose two faces looked backward and forward in time perfectly symbolizes the foreign policy of the Bush I administration. When George H.W. Bush and his advisers took office, the assumptions, operational codes, and strategies of the Cold War still held. Less than two years later the administration was consciously moving into a new era. From 1990 onward, in all their most crucial engagements—struggling with China after the Tiananmen massacre, ending the Cold War in Europe, evicting Saddam Hussein's army from Kuwait, and restarting the Middle East peace process—the administration thought and acted in accord with virtually all of the elements that became the post–Cold War paradigm. But just as Eisenhower's strategy differed from Kennedy's, Bush I's sometimes differed from those of his two successors. There was little difference regarding American exceptionalism. President Bush and his advisers agreed that when it acts abroad, the United States seeks nothing other than its own security and desires only to contribute to world peace and stability. Its unparalleled power and uniquely disinterested motives make it responsible for world peace, justice, and democracy within and among other states. The power of the United States is exercised benignly on behalf of good against evil and in selfless defense of the well-being of others. The United States is a model to all nations and has a duty to spread enlightenment around the world.[2] The administration agreed with its successors that market economics and liberal democracy are universally valid and appropriate for all peoples everywhere and represented the best future for the world. It made full use of coercive diplomacy and economic sanctions, particularly in dealing with Saddam Hussein's Iraq. However, the first president Bush and his closest advisers took a relaxed view of the connection between the security of the United States and the spread of market economics and democracy. The United States could be secure, Bush I argued, so long as most of the world's nations were not totalitarian. That the administration focused on eliminating state-to-state aggression rather than forcing regime change also revealed the hands-off approach it took toward democratization.

The Bush I administration strongly supported globalization and believed that the growing complexity of world affairs made it impossible for states acting unilaterally to solve major problems, many of which crossed national boundaries. The accelerated movement of ideas, people, goods, and money could be kept benign only by building new forms of multilateral cooperation such as the organization for Asian Pacific economic cooperation, and the North American Free Trade Agreement, which joined the economies of Canada, Mexico, and the United States. The Clinton administration but not the Bush II administration agreed. Last, Bush I's view of American primacy differed from that adopted by Clinton and Bush II. By 1990 the administration knew the United States was well on the way to becoming the world's only superpower. Even so, it declined to push the limits of American primacy and elected to work with great diligence and imagination to sustain American alliances and to put the use of American military power within a framework of international law, the United Nations, and the consent of the country's allies. Although a conception of American unilateralism surfaced within the Bush I defense department, the White House quashed it and offered instead the notion of a "new world order," which reflected an emphasis on prohibiting state-to-state aggression through the United Nations. As the extent of American primacy grew more and more obvious, the administration felt confident in making full use of coercive diplomacy and economic sanctions. The failure of the new world order to catch on left Bill Clinton and George W. Bush the task of fashioning a consensus around a new vision of the world, and American interests and threats to those interests that would attract the support of most Americans and allied and friendly governments around the world.

Into a New World

The United States acknowledged its global superiority on August 23, 1990, when President H.W. Bush was on a fishing trip aboard his boat *Fidelity*, off Walker's Point, Maine. Bush and his national security adviser, Brent Scowcroft, spoke of Saddam Hussein's invasion of Kuwait and what it meant for the United States and the world. They knew the American military would drive Saddam's army out of Kuwait. "This will not stand," as Bush would say later. But then what? What kind of world would it be? "Our conversation that day," Scowcroft recalled, "broadened to ruminations about being sure we handled the crisis in a way which reflected the nature of the transformed world we would face in the future. We thought that we were perhaps at a watershed of history. The Soviet Union was standing alongside us, not only in the United Nations, but also in condemning and taking action against Iraqi aggression. . . . If the attack on Kuwait marked the end of forty-odd years of such superpower confrontation, what vistas might open up? . . . Compared to the period we had just come through, the era seemed like a new world order."[3] It was a new world. Alone at the top in 1990, the United States was to increase its margin of military and economic superiority during the decade that followed. By 2002, the gross domestic product of the United States was twice as large as those of its nearest competitors, Japan and China. The U.S. defense budget, at $396.1 billion, was larger than the combined defense budgets of the next 26 countries—19 times that of Germany, 9.4 times that of China, 6.6 times that of Russia, 283 times that of Iraq.[4]

Given the international upheavals that lay ahead, it was odd that foreign policy played almost no part in the 1988 presidential campaign. After the Soviet leader Mikhail Gorbachev launched major reforms at home and abroad, President Ronald Reagan had responded cordially, meeting with

Gorbachev often and concluding a major nuclear arms control agreement with him before leaving office. Reagan made sure that no one could misunderstand his feelings about Gorbachev. Before leaving Washington, he stood with Gorbachev to have pictures taken in front of the Statue of Liberty and strolled Red Square with his Soviet counterpart. George Bush had a great deal of international experience and preferred dealing with foreign rather than domestic issues. Of course, Bush and his opponent, Michael Dukakis, knew that elections are won and lost at home, and voters were preoccupied with crime rates and economic well-being. Perhaps that was reason enough for Bush to behave as if nothing had changed in the world. To the extent that George Bush talked about foreign policy, he leaned to the right in an effort to deny an advantage to his more conservative opponent for the nomination, Bob Dole, and to hold the loyalty of the conservative wing of the Republican Party. At the same time, Bush privately reassured Gorbachev that he would continue Reagan's policy of engagement, and that he should ignore what was said during the campaign.[5]

Once in office, President Bush and his experienced team of foreign policy advisers could act on what they had known all along. Gorbachev's reforms had transformed East-West relations, and he was about to run away with the agenda for ending the Cold War. The new administration's first need was to take the initiative away from him. President Bush understood that Gorbachev had made it impossible to do nothing, and he wanted sensible and credible initiatives of his own that would not only safeguard Western security but keep the loyalty of the European allies, win Soviet consent, and resolve a half-century of deadlock and tragedy in the heart of Europe. No one knew where Gorbachev's changes would lead, but as the administration began its strategic review, the president and at least some of his advisers knew they faced a future full of risk and opportunity. If they could find the right strategy, they might be able to capture great gains in security and freedom for Europe. If Gorbachev faltered or was overthrown, a new round in the Cold War would begin. Somehow their strategy had to cope with both possibilities. It was a huge challenge, but an exhilarating one.

Bush's Foreign Policy Team

The most important national security positions in the administration went to conservatives with years of experience in Washington. Secretary of State James Baker, a Texan, a lawyer, and a close friend of the president, had served in the Reagan White House as chief of staff and as secretary of the treasury. Secretary of Defense Dick Cheney had served a dozen years in the Congress and was known for his conservatism. He had been brought to the Ford White House by Donald Rumsfeld, then the chief of staff, and had succeeded him. Air Force general Brent Scowcroft became national security adviser, as he had been in the Ford administration. That the president and his most senior advisers all saw themselves as men of action rather than reflection played an important part in the development of U.S. policy during Bush I. They were inclined to act, rather than to wait on events, to do something rather than sit still. Not even Margaret Thatcher could persuade the administration to accept her vehement and repeated argument to slow down German unification, not just because of policy disagreements but because inaction ran against the activist and highly politicized instincts of senior officials in the administration, especially the president and secretary of state.

Two other features of the Bush administration help explain the way in which the U.S. government responded to the endgame of the Cold War. Baker usually took the lead in dealing with other governments. But unlike its immediate predecessors as well as the Clinton and Bush II administrations, Bush I's senior political appointees worked cooperatively at the highest levels, with a minimum of turf wars and obstruction. Initiatives taken by one group inside the White House, or the State or Defense Departments were not kept secret from the others, as was the case in the Nixon and Reagan years. Scowcroft, Baker, and Cheney did not try to outshine and outmaneuver one another as their counterparts had in the Carter and Reagan presidencies.

Foreign policymaking in the Bush administration was also highly centralized. President Bush enjoyed dealing with foreign policy and thought he knew something about it. Early in the administration, a small high-level group was formed to deal with fast-moving problems, especially regarding the Soviet Union and Germany. At the State Department, Baker's preferred method of operation was to rely on just three people and no one else to help him launch new initiatives. Robert Zoellick worked as a kind of gatekeeper, and Baker required that every piece of paper sent to him had to be sent to Zoellick first. Dennis Ross specialized in the Middle East and the Soviet Union, and Margaret Tutwiler was in charge of public affairs for the State Department and its principal spokesperson. According to Baker, Ross usually took the lead in writing speeches, with help from Zoellick.[6]

Baker was the most activist and political among all the political activists in Bush's cabinet. He cheerfully admitted his bias on the first page of his memoirs.[7] But that did not make his approach unsophisticated or simplistic. Quite the opposite. Baker was proud of his intensely political approach to diplomacy and negotiation. In his mind, the two were inseparable. To Baker, politics was the means by which philosophical goals were turned into something real.[8] Baker revealed the colder side of his approach to politics in an interview, when he described turkey shooting as "getting them where you want them on your terms. Then you control the situation, not them. You have the options. Pull the trigger or don't. It doesn't matter once you've got them where you want them. The important thing is knowing that it's in your hands, that you can do whatever you determine is in your interest to do."[9] No one missed the political implications of the turkey hunt, particularly since the next thing Baker spoke of was that Israel was divided internally. Bush shared Baker's inclination to seek close personal relations with his negotiating partners. Together the two focused their highly personal approach on Gorbachev and Shevardnadze, as well as German Chancellor Helmut Kohl, British Prime Minister Margaret Thatcher, and French President François Mitterrand.[10] Because President Bush and his advisers arrived in Washington at a time when a frozen international universe was beginning to melt, the need for leaders with exactly their skills at devising face-saving compromises and solving narrow, concrete problems was at a premium. Again and again these activist political operators succeeded in finding ways around obstacles that might have defeated the less agile or more deeply reflective. While the world staggered from one bewildering and momentous event to another, George Bush and his band of tough activists seemed to be just the right people for the times.

Bush I Strategic Assumptions

Long-established Cold War axioms freed Bush I from the need to create a new rationale for American foreign policy at the very start of the administration, something that haunted the Clinton and Bush II administrations. At the outset, therefore, the Bush I administration was able to adjust rather than recreate the assumptions that had provided the core of American strategy since the late 1940s:

- The global balance of power has been restored but remains fragile; until Soviet leaders redefine their country's national interests, the United States and the Soviet Union remain locked in a worldwide military and ideological competition.

- American security interests in Asia will not clash with China's attempt to modernize itself and become a great power; in particular, it is in the security interest of China and the United States to oppose the Soviet Union; forces for positive change in China continue to be more powerful than opposing forces.
- Unless the United States engages at the highest levels in managing the Arab-Israeli and Israeli-Palestinian conflicts the situation will worsen and even spin out of control, radicals will be strengthened, moderates will be undermined, and the vital interests of the United States will be endangered.[11]
- Military force should be used abroad only when the security of the country or the lives of American citizens are directly threatened; the United States will never be indifferent to the suffering of others, but will not use military force in vain and costly attempts to right all wrongs.

With China preoccupied by internal development and the Soviet Union attempting major reforms at home and abroad, the international situation was highly favorable to the United States. What was needed was exactly what the Bush administration had to offer: skillful, cautious management of problems in Europe, Asia, and the Middle East. The virtual prohibition against military intervention derived from favorable global circumstances and some hard lessons that senior policymakers in the administration, particularly those in the uniformed services, had learned during the Vietnam War and the ill-fated intervention in Lebanon. Strict limits on the use of military power had been publicized by Caspar Weinberger, Reagan's secretary of defense, and been widely accepted within the U.S. military. The man who would be chairman of the Joint Chiefs of Staff during the Gulf War, General Colin Powell, and who served as Weinberger's military assistant, had learned the same lessons from the Vietnam War.[12]

Gorbachev's winning personality and his attempts to take control of the international agenda in Europe soon forced Bush and his advisers to recognize that they could not leave their Cold War assumptions unchanged. When they consulted academic experts on the Soviet Union they found them divided over whether Gorbachev's reforms (*perestroika*) were a breathing space (*peredyshka*) or a more profound shift (*perekhod*).[13] Much as Dean Acheson had become impatient with George Kennan's subtle distinctions between Trotskyism and Stalinism, Baker found the experts' nuances about perestroika almost useless. "What mattered to me," he said dryly, "were the actions we could take in the face of these two different possibilities, in order to maximize our diplomatic gains while minimizing risks."[14]

Bush, Baker, and their advisers also sought to build regional institutions, to promote trade, and to impose hard-headed calculations of national interest on all foreign policy issues. Baker believed that the founders of post–World War II American foreign policy had been institution builders, and argued that the administration "should take a leaf from their book."[15] Alongside the North Atlantic Treaty Organization, the General Agreements on Tariffs and Trade, the World Bank, and the International Monetary Fund, the Bush administration initiated the negotiations that resulted in the establishment of the North American Free Trade Agreement and strongly supported the proposal by Australian Prime Minister, Robert Hawke, to create an organization for Asian Pacific economic cooperation.[16] Their hard-headedness and limited conception of U.S. security interests showed in the refusal to intervene in Haiti and Yugoslavia, despite great human suffering in those countries. Haiti rates two brief paragraphs in Baker's memoirs, a book of 687 pages. His verdict on the horrors perpetrated in Haiti could just as easily have been applied to Yugoslavia: "The Bush administration believed that there was a national interest in seeing democracy restored to Haiti, but it was not sufficiently vital (when the security of our country or the safety of our citizens was not at risk) to require using military force."[17]

The much bloodier succession crisis in Yugoslavia also failed to meet the test of vital interest, and the administration chose to follow a nonexistent European lead in the Balkans, and to work for nonrecognition and isolation of the combatants. In reaching his decision, Baker and the president relied heavily on Scowcroft and Eagleburger. Both had served in Yugoslavia as young officers, and both thought that they understood the country and the region. Eagleburger and Scowcroft constantly evoked the difficulties that the Nazi armed forces encountered in Yugoslavia during World War II as grounds for staying out. In addition, the European Community seemed keen to assert a leading role, and no Balkan state came close to Iraq's strategic significance, which derived from the importance of Gulf oil supplies.[18] Although many died before the administration left office, hundreds of thousands of Croatians, Muslims, and Serbs were killed in bitter ethnic and religious strife during the Clinton years. Baker was unapologetic. If the Bush administration had tried to intervene, losses in American lives would have been heavy: "I do not believe [the breakup of Yugoslavia and slaughter] could have been prevented by any combination of political, diplomatic, and economic measures."[19]

Tiananmen and the Bush Administration

In 1989, Cold War axioms continued to apply to northeast Asia, where two close allies of the United States—Japan and South Korea—received American protection against China, North Korea, and the USSR. U.S. relations with China had warmed considerably since the early 1970s, partly because of China's fear of Soviet intervention under the Brezhnev Doctrine, and partly out of the American desire to practice triangular diplomacy as it scrambled to recover its equilibrium after the defeat in Vietnam. President Bush's service in China as ambassador meant that China would receive close and favorable attention at the White House, and all seemed set for further improvements.

Overall, the administration tried to remain engaged with China in order to be able to maximize whatever influence it might have over China's foreign policy and internal development.[20] Bush I also wanted to keep trade and investment flowing in the belief that sooner or later the adoption of market economics would lead to democratization, a view that became part of the post–Cold War paradigm.[21] The Chinese government's deadly repression of democratic protesters in Beijing's Tiananmen Square and around the country damaged U.S.-China relations for years, and the two sides' different perceptions of what had happened led to deep misunderstandings between the two governments.[22] Public and congressional anger over the killings and arrests forced the administration to work very hard just to keep the violent reaction from wrecking the entire relationship. The dark shadow of Tiananmen Square covered U.S.-China relations for the entire four years. Tiananmen even reached into the next presidential election when Bush's challenger in 1992, Bill Clinton, attacked the "butchers of Beijing" and the policy of "coddling tyrants from Baghdad to Beijing."[23] Despite the Chinese government's angry defensiveness and severe criticism at home and abroad, the Bush administration clung to its policies. But little progress was possible in U.S.-China relations. Bush made numerous gestures to China, including a secret visit by National Security Advisor Scowcroft and Deputy Secretary of State Lawrence Eagleburger not long after Tiananmen. China's leaders greeted them with a self-righteous, hard-line defense of the crackdown. Bush publicly denounced the repression, but imposed the most limited form of sanctions that he and his advisers could devise: suspending military sales and contacts between military officers from China and the United States. In addition, he allowed Chinese engineers to continue working with their American counterparts to upgrade the F-8 aircraft that China had acquired from the United States. Barely six months after the massacre, he allowed the sale of three American communication satellites that would be launched by the Chinese. He also authorized the Export-Import Bank to support American business activities in China. A year after the massacre, he renewed most-favored-nation trade status for China. In spite of all these steps, the U.S. Ambassador in Beijing, Stapleton Roy, thought it might take decades to repair the damage caused by the killings at Tiananmen. He sought "opportunities to bring China out of its defensive coil after Tiananmen and to create incentives for Beijing's leaders to continue the processes of opening their economy to the outside world and of expanding the zones of freedom within Chinese society."[24] Slowly, the atmosphere began to clear. The Chinese government purchased aircraft from Boeing for $2 billion. Baker was able to win grudging agreement from the Chinese government to block the export of nuclear capable missiles to Pakistan, and accept the restrictions of the international Missile Technology Control Regime on its export of weapons.[25] Other issues, such as the Gulf War, deflected attention away from China. But the administration left office without having realized any of the president's hopes for improved relations.

Ending the Cold War

Given the bitter history of U.S.-Soviet relations during the Cold War, the administration's initial caution was probably unavoidable. Something extremely precious was at stake: The end of the Cold War would increase human freedom immeasurable and greatly diminish the threat of crisis and war that had haunted the great powers for decades. However, Gorbachev's domestic reforms, his apparent refusal to use force in Eastern Europe, and his daring arms control proposals created a risk as well as an opportunity for the West. It was possible that the relaxation of tension Gorbachev was orchestrating so masterfully could turn into euphoria. The people of Western Europe and the United States might force their governments to dismantle the North Atlantic Treaty Organization (NATO) and the entire network of mutual commitments before the Red Army withdrew from the heart of Europe. A coalition of opponents in the Soviet Communist Party and military might overthrow Gorbachev and turn back the clock in Eastern Europe and the Soviet Union itself. To deal with the risks and opportunities, the Bush administration adopted a set of strategic guidelines that, while not fundamentally departing from the long-standing U.S. policy of containment, allowed them to respond to Gorbachev, capture public opinion, protect vital Western and American interests, and shape and ultimately take control of the negotiating agenda.[26]

The main idea was to propose changes that would keep Gorbachev playing on his own turf and away from vital Western interests. The asymmetry of this is breathtaking. For example, the United States outbid Gorbachev by calling for even more drastic cuts in the numbers of Soviet and American troops in Europe. If Gorbachev agreed, nothing would happen to the democratically elected governments and stable societies that had voluntarily joined NATO, but the withdrawal of Soviet troops could mean the collapse of the communist governments of Eastern Europe. This was so appealing that the administration put encouraging liberalization in Eastern Europe ahead of such traditional Cold War concerns as Soviet-American efforts to reduce nuclear weapons.

The negotiating strategy that Baker followed tied these aims together in a mutually reinforcing way. Again and again Baker would tell Shevardnadze and Gorbachev that Soviet interference with self-determination in Eastern Europe, the Baltic states, or Germany would make it very difficult for the administration to provide economic assistance or cooperate on arms control agreements. Of course, American strategy was not the sole or even the most important reason for the peaceful end of the Cold War, and the great and positive changes in Eastern Europe and the Soviet Union. As the architects of containment had predicted, Gorbachev, Shevardnadze, and their fellow reformers in the Soviet Union were determined to change the basis of their society at home and their relationship with the outside world.[27] At the same time, the role of the United States was extremely important. Through its engagement with Soviet and allied leaders, the administration was able to shape Gorbachev's impulse to reform and to ensure that the changes undertaken by both sides would result in greater freedom for the peoples of Eastern Europe and the construction of a durable international order that all could support.

The administration's single-minded pursuit of rapid liberalization, Soviet withdrawal, and German unification left little room for other possibilities or timetables. Thatcher's approach might have reduced the opposition to Gorbachev within the Soviet Communist Party and military, opposition that culminated in a coup d'état against him two years later. But the administration rejected her arguments. A similar pattern of relentless and rapid movement characterized the Bush I strategy in the Gulf after Saddam Hussein invaded Kuwait. In both cases, the Bush administration argued that it had no other choice. Gorbachev and his reforms represented an historic opportunity, perhaps one that would never come again, a chance that would be lost if the West did not "lock in" the Soviet concessions that allowed self-determination in Central and Eastern Europe. Any delay in ousting Iraq from Kuwait would lead to the unraveling of the coalition needed to make aggression by one state against another impossible in the post–Cold War world.[28]

With these considerations in mind, the Bush administration changed the assumptions about the Soviet Union that had guided American strategy for four decades:

- The domestic and international position of the Soviet Union is weak, not strong; it must be made to pay the price of weakness. However, the success of Gorbachev's reforms is not inconsistent with U.S. vital interests, provided the agenda is the correct one.
- Genuine negotiations are permissible, even unavoidable, but the new arrangements in Europe must be crafted in such a way that all parties support them because they have an interest in doing so, not because they have been imposed. A new order that leaves the Soviet Union or other states feeling victimized will not last, and could result in great harm to the interests of the United States, the West, and the peoples of Eastern Europe and the Soviet Union.
- The withdrawal of Soviet troops is the key test of Soviet intentions and the best way to enhance Western security and promote political liberalization in Central and Eastern Europe. The two are mutually reinforcing: as Soviet troops withdraw, liberalization becomes more and more possible.
- Having gone to war twice in Europe in the twentieth century, and having been forced to run great risks at huge expense during the Cold War, the United States has a vital interest in remaining directly engaged in European affairs; NATO is the vehicle for this engagement.
- In addition to making positive changes in Europe, the Soviet Union must also prove its good faith by withdrawing from Afghanistan and ending its support of Marxist revolutionaries in Central America and Africa.

Scowcroft was undoubtedly correct in saying that these guidelines served the administration well in the tumultuous months ahead. New and unexpected developments—the downfall of one communist government after another, the unification of Germany—required additional strategic calculation. But the original conception held firm: ask a great deal, give little in return, keep the pressure on, and work hard to win the cooperation of all concerned. If it became necessary for the West to make concessions, they should come in matters of style and form rather than substance. Regarding style, it was all right to say that NATO would become more political or that nuclear weapons would be regarded by the Western alliance as weapons of "last resort." Regarding substance, there could be no compromise about German self-determination or membership in NATO. Two world wars and the Cold War had taught the United States the importance of Europe to its security. If Gorbachev's reforms continued, NATO would remain important as a way of expressing U.S. interests in Europe. If his reforms stalled or he was overthrown by reactionaries in the Communist Party and Soviet military, NATO would be of vital importance in maintaining security and stability in Europe. Whatever happened, Germany must remain in NATO, because that is where American troops were stationed on the continent.[29]

In the past, the Soviet-centric approach had made nuclear arms control a major concern. It had also led the United States to support only those Central and Eastern European governments that opposed Soviet foreign policy, such as Yugoslavia under Tito, Romania under Nicolae Ceausescu, and from the early 1970s, China under Mao and his successors. But new developments poured in from the region every day, and the Soviet domestic scene was deeply unsettled. In response, the Bush administration decided to delay direct engagement on major arms control and other initiatives with the Soviet Union and, instead, to offer encouragement and limited aid to Eastern European countries that moved away from communist economic and political dogma at home. It would be necessary to counter Gorbachev's propaganda campaign with bold American proposals, but nothing substantive would have to be accomplished in the short term.[30]

The administration policy reviews for the Soviet Union, Eastern Europe, and Western Europe made it clear to Scowcroft that they ought to be considered together rather than in isolation. This led to the establishment of an informal group of senior policymakers, the "core group," who would carry out what Scowcroft called "practical decision-making."[31] Their discussion ranged over a broad range of questions, including the future of the

Soviet Union, the meaning of European unification for American interests, the nature of U.S. engagement in Eastern Europe, and whether Europe after the Maastricht treaty would be able to contain a united Germany. The unprecedented consideration of German unification followed logically from seeking the withdrawal of Soviet conventional forces from Central and Eastern Europe. The president and his advisers were unanimous about focusing on Eastern Europe. The focus would now be "encouraging moves toward reform and getting Soviet troops reduced or removed."[32] While there was unanimity about the goals, there was sharp disagreement about the methods. Scowcroft wanted the president to make bold proposals that would set the international agenda in Europe and take the initiative away from Gorbachev. He favored the withdrawal of all Soviet and U.S. troops from Central Europe. Cheney was suspicious and pessimistic, as he would be often during the upheavals in the Soviet Union and Eastern Europe: it was far too soon to take such a step, he said, and no one knew what would happen in the Soviet Union. Baker thought a proposal to eliminate tanks on both sides would make a good reply to Gorbachev. Since no one supported Cheney's and Baker's positions, the group was left with troop withdrawals, and they settled on a much smaller version of Scowcroft's original idea. As Scowcroft later observed, the positions of the principals in the meeting reflected their underlying views about how to deal with the rapid changes in Eastern Europe and the Soviet Union. "Cheney was the most skeptical," Scowcroft recalled, "holding the view that the changes were primarily cosmetic and we should essentially do nothing." The deputy national security adviser, Robert Gates, agreed with Cheney. Baker was much more optimistic, a stand, Scowcroft adds, that grew stronger as he and Soviet Foreign Minister Eduard Shevardnadze got to know one another.[33]

Baker called the National Security Council and Defense Department viewpoints the "status quo plus" school. Cheney, Gates, and Vice President Dan Quayle, among others, argued that Gorbachev was so weak there was no need to do anything at all. He would have to make all the concessions that the United States needed. Baker referred to his own approach as the "activist" school. If Gorbachev was willing to make major changes, there was no way to find out the limits of what was possible unless the administration took positive steps of its own. They would have to put forward sensible proposals to counter the Soviet leader's appeals to European public opinion. Zoellick and Ross believed that it might be possible to use the logic of Gorbachev's reforms to bring about changes that served U.S. interests. Among other things, if Gorbachev failed to make good on his promises, he would undermine himself and his program. "Our job," Baker says, "was to hold him to his word."[34] In the early going, Baker's appraisal of Gorbachev's intentions and U.S. leverage was cold-eyed and careful. Gorbachev was trying to split the Western alliance by appealing to public opinion and, in the process, strengthen himself at home. If the administration did nothing, Gorbachev would shape the international environment to the detriment of the United States. The trick was to develop proposals that were advantageous to the West and the United States, and that Gorbachev would have to accept or deny the basis of his reform program.[35]

At least as important is what was not done at these crucial early meetings. Putting the emphasis on Eastern Europe and focusing on the withdrawal of conventional forces instead of strategic nuclear issues had the effect of lowering the priority of U.S.-Soviet bilateral relations. The result was to delay the first summit meeting with Gorbachev, which did not take place until late in the fall of 1989. Meanwhile, the strength and bargaining power of the Soviet Union constantly deteriorated as the people of one Eastern European country after another confronted their communist governments and the ferment began to spread to East Germany. In other words, the Bush administration would not put a floor under a declining Soviet Union. Gorbachev would have to negotiate from a steadily weakening position.

The president chose to make his overall strategy public in April and May 1989 in a series of four speeches on relations with Eastern and Western Europe, the Soviet Union, and military strategy and arms control.[36] In their memoirs, Bush and Scowcroft claim that the speeches represented a fundamental change of position. In fact, they offered the same bargain that the United States had been offering for forty years: If the Soviet Union would change its conception of its national interest and end the confrontation with the West, the United States would accept the changes. What was different was that Soviet leaders now believed that making concessions to the United States in Europe and elsewhere would help rather than hurt their country.[37] Bush worried that Gorbachev was running away with public opinion, especially in Europe. "Time's a-wasting, Brent!" he told his national security adviser in mid-May 1989. "We've gotta push." About conventional arms control, he said: "We've got to get ahead of the problem by the time of the NATO meeting [late May, early June]. We've got to be in the position of making a proposal that is really serious and that is taken really seriously."[38] Even so, something important had changed on the American side. Bush's speeches signaled that the administration took reform in the Soviet Union seriously and was prepared to negotiate with the reformers. The administration's new policy created a structure in which bargaining about fundamental issues could take place. That was unprecedented. Previous American and Soviet leaders had never allowed such a structure to develop.

Soviet leaders were willing to pay a high price to gain the support of the United States, Germany, and the rest of Europe for its domestic and international reforms, so high that it demolished the Soviet Union's strategic position in Eastern Europe, freeing its peoples from the threat of military intervention to prolong communist rule. Ultimately, Gorbachev and Shevardnadze were willing to withdraw the Red Army from its bases in Eastern Europe, allow the unification of Germany as a member of NATO, make deep cuts in nuclear and conventional forces in Europe, and end global competition with the West. The Soviet reformers persisted in paying this price until tens of millions of East Germans, Hungarians, Poles, and Czechs pushed aside the communist regimes that had been installed by the Red Army after World War II, and began to make their way toward democratic self-rule. They persisted until the Soviet Union itself and world communism disappeared from history. All that remained was Gorbachev's smile as he flew from capital to capital in the West looking for financial assistance to sustain his vast experiment in managed economic and political change. The challenge that faced Bush and Baker was to keep the changes coming until the process had become irreversible. The outcome of all the changes immensely strengthened the global strategic position of the United States. Even so, for months the administration continued to fret that Gorbachev's appeals would so fascinate European and American opinion that the unity of the Western alliance would be dangerously weakened. Scowcroft proudly said of the April and May speeches that they had created a "valuable framework for the conduct of policy."[39]

No set of assumptions and axioms could have stayed intact after the onslaught of change in Eastern Europe and the Soviet Union. Usually, however, the administration was able to add to the mix rather than drop anything important. Prime Minister Thatcher took a "reluctant unifier" position. She argued that the West should not move ahead on German unification until the allies had thought through all the connections. Scowcroft said the United States had done so and would support Eastern European governments that were reforming. The administration would be careful not to cause unnecessary problems for Gorbachev, but it would also not surrender its support for self-determination. During a flare-up of tensions in the

Baltic states, for example, the administration quietly backed Lithuanian independence, but gave the demonstrators no public encouragement, counseled negotiations with Gorbachev, and spoke of very gentle sanctions when the Soviets threatened reprisals.

The administration initially decided not to oppose German unification. It continued to repeat what Scowcroft called the "ritual incantations of support for reunification of Germany," but unification was not be on the active agenda.[40] As a result, when the huge changes began, German policy had to be made in an ad hoc rather than strategic way.[41] There was a split within the administration, as the National Security Council argued that Germany should be at the center of the administration's European policy, and the State Department insisting that this was at least premature. The unraveling of East Germany persuaded the administration to follow Kohl, but even Kohl's rapid moves made President Bush impatient: he supported unification early and strongly. The close cooperation between Kohl and Bush annoyed Thatcher and Mitterrand, but they knew there was little they could or would do about it. If the two Germanys decided to unite, the Soviets acquiesced, and the Americans supported the deal, Britain and France could not stop them. Afterward, Scowcroft suspected that the administration had given too little consideration to British and French views.[42] Thatcher pessimistically complained that the United States had not attached Germany to Europe but Europe to Germany.[43] Mitterrand was reluctant from beginning to end, but he sought insurance against calamity by obtaining a commitment from Kohl to merge a united Germany more deeply into Europe.

Signs soon began to appear that Gorbachev's mix of economic and political reform and restrictions on the use of force could lead to the unraveling of the Soviet Union itself as well as the communist governments of Central and Eastern Europe. Within the USSR, fighting broke out between Armenia and Azerbaijan over the Armenian enclave, Nagorno-Karabakh, and Moscow was unable to quell the disturbances. Another Soviet-created minority, the Abkhazians, in the Republic of Georgia sought to secede. In April 1989, demonstrations in Tbilisi, the capital of Georgia, ended in clashes with Soviet troops from the Ministry of the Interior. Anti-Soviet sentiments grew during the following months, and the Georgian Supreme Soviet claimed the right to veto Soviet laws. Thousands of miles to the north the peoples of the Baltic republics made a try for independence. According to Gates, as early as July 1989, a Soviet analyst at the CIA, Grey Hodnett, began arguing that with or without Gorbachev, the USSR faced escalating instability, popular protest, violence, and the breakdown of central authority.[44] In Hodnett's words, these developments would "prevent a return to the arsenal state economy that generated the fundamental military threat to the West in the period since World War II."[45] His forecast had a major impact on thinking at the White House. Fully aware of how tenuous Gorbachev's hold on power had become, the administration still continued to push its international agenda of arms control, German unification, and democratization of Eastern Europe. The president and his advisers concluded that there was nothing to lose by going as fast as possible. If anything, the growing evidence of Gorbachev's vulnerability convinced them to get as much accomplished as they could before the Soviet Union collapsed.[46] In any case, there was little they could do about internal conditions in the USSR.

The American assumptions were borne out remarkably well, but Gorbachev's were not. Gorbachev acted in the mistaken belief that it would be possible to reform the Soviet Union and Eastern Europe without jeopardizing the dominant role of the Communist Party in those countries. He also wrongly assumed that the Soviet Union could be held together, even if he allowed political and economic pluralism and ended the arbitrary use of force. And it appears that Gorbachev and many on both sides of the Berlin Wall believed that West Germany's Social Democrats would win a crucial election in East Germany preceding the decision on unification. The Social Democrats lost; if they had won, their growing neutrality and anti-U.S. positions could have delayed if not halted unification. A Social Democratic victory might have kept a united Germany out of NATO and forced West Germany and its allies to admit a more or less intact East Germany into a new, much weaker, and divided all-German government.

As Gorbachev's domestic position grew weaker, the Bush administration reached out to the opposition, particularly Boris Yeltsin, as well as other dissidents, such as Gavril Popov and Anatoly Sobchak. Baker explained this to Shevardnadze as simply part of the democratic process, actions that the United States would take in its dealing with other democratic countries. Shevardnadze replied that there was no viable political culture in the Soviet Union, and no responsible opposition had developed, only "adventurists in the political arena."[47] Baker thought otherwise, continued contacts with Gorbachev's opponents, and paid little attention to Shevardnadze's warnings, which were prescient. By January 1991, the administration realized that Gorbachev might be brought down by his reforms or be obliged to retrench. Baker identified three developments that caused him and his colleagues to reconsider their approach to U.S.-Soviet relations: the attempt by the Soviet military to take advantage of the negotiations to reduce conventional forces in Europe (CFE) by refusing to count certain military units west of the Urals; Shevardnadze's resignation in December, an occasion he marked by decrying the threat of dictatorship in his country; and brutal actions intended to block Lithuanian independence.[48] Baker typically responded to CIA warnings about Gorbachev's decline with a business metaphor: "What you're telling us, fellas, is that the stock market is heading south. We need to sell."[49] By "sell," Baker meant "to try to get as much as we could out of the Soviets before there was an even greater turn to the right or shift into disintegration. And the way to do that was to maintain our relations with Mikhail Gorbachev until we could successfully prosecute the Gulf War, which we did; finish the [Strategic Arms Reduction] Treaty, which we did in July; and ensure that CFE didn't unravel, while also advancing other unfinished items on our foreign policy agenda, notably progress toward Middle East peace."[50] In other words, despite mounting internal opposition to Gorbachev's reforms the Bush administration would put more rather than less pressure on him to accept the American agenda.

War in the Gulf

After the United States withdrew from Vietnam in 1973, Richard Nixon and Henry Kissinger made Iran a bulwark in the defense perimeter around the Soviet Union. However, a series of upheavals transformed the military and political equation in the Gulf. First, the Shah was overthrown in 1979. Saddam Hussein attacked Iran soon afterward, hoping to take advantage of the weakness and disunity that had followed the Shah's downfall. A bloody stalemate developed that lasted a decade, resulting in the deaths of thousands on both sides, and changed nothing important on the ground. Virtually at the same time, the Soviet Union invaded and occupied Afghanistan. The fall of the Shah and the large and growing Soviet military presence in Afghanistan amounted to a double setback for the United States. The Cold War imperative to block Soviet expansion asserted itself, and the United States took what steps it could to defend its interests in the region. President Jimmy Carter announced the Carter Doctrine—the United States would resist by force any attempt by an outside power to dominate the Gulf. Carter formally made Israel a strategic partner, acquired staging rights in the Horn of Africa and Egypt, and arranged to land aircraft and store war material on Diego Garcia, an island in the Indian Ocean off the southern Arabian Peninsula.

The Iran-Iraq war was a mixed blessing from the American point of view. It locked Iraq, a Soviet client, and Iran, a Muslim revolutionary theocracy, in an exhausting ruinous war. However, the duration and intensity of the fighting were serious problems. If Iraq collapsed, Iran would be the primary beneficiary and could, perhaps, extend its influence deep into the Arabian Peninsula. If Iran collapsed, the vacuum might draw the Soviet Union southward toward Iran's rich oil reserves and the Gulf itself, a globally vital waterway. As the war ground on and Iran's greater population and wealth began to wear down the smaller Iraq, the United States reluctantly sided with Saddam Hussein. The Reagan administration decided to use American technology and sea power—sharing satellite intelligence and providing American warships to convoy oil shipments in the Gulf—in order to make Iran lose the war, but lose slowly. In this way, it was hoped, Iran would be driven to accept a compromise peace before it collapsed. The calculation worked. With his country's resources running out and his people exhausted and demoralized, Ayatollah Khomeini finally accepted a ceasefire. He would rather drink poison, he said, but the war was over.

Iraq and Iran stopped fighting in August 1988. The change of administrations provided a perfect opportunity to reconsider American policy toward Saddam Hussein, but the incoming Bush I administration's strategic review of the Gulf recommended no fundamental changes in American strategy or policy. Within a few weeks, the world was swept into the drama of the end of communism. Caught up in the endgame of the Cold War in Europe and distracted by the Tiananmen crisis in China, the administration simply did not focus on the Gulf.

Saddam Hussein's sudden conquest of Kuwait in August 1990 fooled everyone. No one in Washington saw it coming, nor did Israeli intelligence or any of the Arab governments who claimed to understand Iraqi policy such as Jordan and Egypt.[51] Certainly nothing in the Bush administration's policy review or assumptions about Iraq indicated that anyone in Washington ever dreamed Saddam Hussein would attack another country so soon after the end of the war with Iran. Instead, the Bush administration regarded Saddam as a conventional ruler who made conventional cost-benefit calculations. Acting on that assumption, it chose to continue the Reagan policy of transforming Saddam into a responsible regional and international leader by offering him inducements designed to show that he could have every reasonable thing he wanted—trade, economic assistance, cooperation against Iran—as long as he acted responsibly as defined by Washington.

After Saddam invaded Kuwait in August 1990, the United States quickly sent troops to defend Saudi Arabia. The UN Security Council demanded an Iraqi withdrawal and authorized economic sanctions and the use of force. The administration won a close vote in the U.S. Congress that authorized the president to go to war if necessary to liberate Kuwait, and steadily increased American troop strength in the Gulf. Next, the administration patiently allowed Gorbachev to try to win Iraqi withdrawal, but opposed the Soviet leaders' proposals because they would have failed to produce unconditional withdrawal and Iraqi disarmament. In January 1991, one last fruitless meeting took place between Baker and Iraqi Foreign Minister Tarik Aziz in Geneva. The United States went to war in February, commencing by a long, sustained, and crushing air campaign to disrupt Iraqi communications and decimate forward forces. Schwarzkopf feinted right, suggested an amphibious landing off the Kuwaiti coast, and then unleashed his tanks in a giant "left hook," around the western flank of Iraqi forces. Iraqi opposition was broken in less than 100 hours of ground combat. After consulting with his military and political advisers Bush ordered a ceasefire. Many of the American units that fought in the Gulf came from NATO, where they had trained to fight the Red Army, a much more capable enemy than the Iraqi army marooned in the desert south of Kuwait City without air cover or reconnaissance. Although Saddam's preparations for war had gone unnoticed, the quick, overwhelming victory and the acquiescence of the Soviet Union and China revealed American dominance. Unavoidable questions flew around the world. What would the United States do? What advantages would it seek? How would it choose to exercise its unrivaled power? The same questions haunted policymakers in Washington. The answer came quickly: the Bush administration would act in cooperation with other governments under the aegis of UN resolutions and international law. Bush's restraint when the road to Baghdad lay open became enormously controversial, and above all within the Republican Party. Saddam Hussein remained in power, maintained his hostility to his neighbors, the West, and Israel, and, as was widely believed in the United States and other countries, continued to develop weapons of mass destruction. Had the Sunni military risen against Saddam as the American government hoped, Bush's forbearance would have seemed wise and effective. Washington ought to have known that the Sunnis, a minority in Iraq, saw Saddam as their protector. In reality, the only hope of unseating Saddam lay with the Shia and the Kurds, victims of Saddam's ethnic and religious persecution. The administration and its Gulf Arab allies feared that supporting these two groups would lead to the disintegration of Iraq and the expansion of Iranian influence. When the Shiites and Kurds rose against Saddam, the administration stood aside while they were crushed. Judging from their remarks after the war, none of Bush's senior advisers—certainly not Cheney or Wolfowitz—advocated coming to their assistance or taking the war to Baghdad and overthrowing Saddam. Colin Powell recalled in his memoirs that "[o]ur practical intention was to leave Baghdad enough power to survive as a threat to an Iran that remained bitterly hostile to the United States."[52] Five years later, Paul Wolfowitz put in writing a view that he apparently soon forgot:

> A new regime [in Iraq] would have become the United States' responsibility. Conceivably this could have led the United States into a more or less permanent occupation of a country that could not govern itself, but where the rule of a foreign occupier would be increasingly resented.

Wolfowitz went on to make an analogy between a possible American attack on Baghdad and Douglas MacArthur's blunders in Korea, which turned victory into a "bloody stalemate."[53] Saddam survived to plague the Clinton administration. Ironically, he also became the nemesis of Cheney, Rumsfeld, Wolfowitz, and the radical conservatives. Some of the policymakers who opposed Saddam's overthrow a decade earlier would argue vehemently in favor of it in 2002.

Throughout the crisis, Baker insisted on UN sponsorship for every enforcement measure taken against Iraq. Baker believed that it was essential to obtain UN blessing in order to persuade American public opinion and to prevail in the Congress, as well as to reassure members of the anti-Iraq coalition about American intentions. Baker called his approach to driving Iraq out of Kuwait "coercive diplomacy," an approach that became a major element in the post–Cold War paradigm. Baker's described the steps he would take in this way: "We would begin with diplomatic pressure, then add economic pressure, to a great degree organized through the United Nations, and finally move toward military pressure by gradually increasing American troop strength in the Gulf. The strategy was to lead a global political alliance aimed at isolating Iraq. Through the use of economic sanctions, we hoped to make Saddam pay such a high price for his aggression that in time he would release his Western hostages and withdraw from

Kuwait. If he didn't we would expel him by military force. To pursue this strategy, I had no doubt we needed a coalition of partners. . . ."[54]

Building the coalition began with the Soviet Union, Iraq's long-term arms supplier and patron. Baker knew that if he failed to win Soviet support it would doom the effort to get Iraq out of Kuwait. He was also determined to keep the confrontation from turning into a fight between Iraq and the United States. If that happened, Saddam might succeed in demonizing the United States as a bullying superpower, and potential Arab members of the coalition and even some in the West would not support coercive diplomacy. The aim was to convince Saddam that he was confronting "the entire civilized world."[55] In addition, war would cost billions, and Baker wanted other states to share the cost, notably Germany and Japan, as well as the oil-rich Gulf states. Baker found the political and economic support he wanted through coalition building and allowing the views of other governments to shape the goals of the coalition.[56] The United States had the right to act unilaterally under international law and article 51 of the UN charter, but Baker concluded that this was not an occasion when the United States should act alone. The message from Washington was that the "world's only superpower" would take the needs and interests of other governments into account before it acted. The allies would not only have a voice in American councils but their concerns would alter American policy. Saddam would be forced out of Kuwait, but the American-led coalition army would not advance on Baghdad and destroy his regime. There would be both restraint and proportion to American behavior. If the war led to Saddam's overthrow, so much the better. Prime Minister Thatcher, who was voted out of office by her own Conservative Party before the end of the Gulf War, said it best: "As for Saddam Hussein himself, it would not be a specific objective to bring about his downfall, though that might be a desirable side effect of our actions. We must aim for a situation in which Saddam Hussein had to face his own people as a beaten leader of a beaten army."[57]

It would have been an ideal result, leaving Iraq without Saddam and in the hands of chastened and cooperative Sunni military elite still dominant in the country, avoiding Kurdish secession, which would excite Turkish opposition, and preventing Iran from taking advantage of possible ties to the large Shia population in southern Iraq. For a few weeks after the end of hostilities, it appeared as if the scheme might work. In an emotional outpouring of rage and frustration, the Shia and Kurds rose against Saddam. Angry crowds murdered state officials. Defectors from Iraq's beaten army joined the demonstrators, and the rebels took over towns and villages in the north and south of the country. Without help from the American forces nearby, the revolt in the south sputtered and fell apart under the hammer blows of the Republican Guard, elite forces that Saddam had carefully preserved during the Gulf War. When he had crushed the rebellion in the south, Saddam sent his troops against the Kurds in the north with the same result.[58]

Bush I, the Arabs, and Israel

Despite serious reservations, Baker plunged into a high-profile, time-consuming attempt to build on the progress between the Israelis and Palestinians during the last months of the Reagan administration.[59] "I could either manage the issue," he said later, "or let it manage me. Like it or not, I didn't have the luxury of totally ignoring it."[60] Although he claimed to have been concentrating on U.S.-Soviet relations Baker began his foreign policy initiatives in the Middle East in February 1989 and kept at it for a year. Ostensibly, Baker committed himself to a "moderately activist policy," with no illusions that it would produce results. But once he started, his prestige was involved, and anything less than success seemed a serious setback. When the first round of negotiations failed, Baker's publicly expressed disappointment made it plain that his ego was also engaged. He cared more about his initiatives than he should have if he were simply managing events to keep them from spinning out of control. President Bush was supportive but stayed away from direct public involvement in the negotiations until after the Gulf War. Baker's actions tied up the Palestinians and Israelis in consultations, and at least left the situation no worse than before it began, except perhaps for the hard feelings in Washington against Israeli Prime Minister Yitzhak Shamir. Baker and Ross doubted that conditions were ripe for a settlement among Syria, the Palestinians, and Israel. However, they thought that they could move the parties toward peace and protect American interests in the region by getting them to talk with each other. Their approach was incremental and strongly protected Israeli interests. "We want to take what you have," Baker told Shamir, "and market it with the Arabs. . . . [B]ut you have to give us something."[61] Ross called this "selling." "Selling became part of our modus operandi—beginning a pattern that would characterize our approach throughout the Bush and Clinton years. We would take Israeli ideas or ideas that the Israelis could live with and work them over—trying to increase their attractiveness to the Arabs while trying to get the Arabs to scale back their expectations."[62] Baker made a point of looking at the issues from the Palestinian viewpoint, as will be seen; the Clinton and Bush II administrations took fewer pains to do so.

The plan that Baker and Ross put into play in February 1989 was ingenious. Not long before the administration took office, the Palestinians began a spontaneous uprising, or intifada, in the West Bank and Gaza. Tens of thousands of Palestinians took part without direction initially, at least, from the "Tunisians," leaders of the Palestine Liberation Organization (PLO) who had accompanied Yasser Arafat when he fled to Tunis under American and allied protection after the Israeli invasion of Lebanon. This suggested to Baker's State Department advisers that it might be possible for Palestinians from the territories to negotiate with Israel without the direct involvement of the PLO.[63] They decided to try to persuade Israel to begin talks with the Palestinians on the basis that no official representatives of the PLO would be allowed to take part, ostensibly driving a wedge between Arafat and the rest of the Palestinian movement, long a goal of the Israeli government, comprised of an uneasy coalition of the extreme nationalist Likud Party and the barely more conciliatory Labor Party. The intifada raised serious doubts in the minds of some Labor leaders including Yitzhak Rabin because it meant that two decades of relatively low-cost occupation were over. However implausible it must have seemed to the Palestinians, Baker's plan was to attempt to convene low-level talks and to ask Arafat "to disenfranchise himself: there was no way a Shamir-led government would ever negotiate with the PLO." It wasn't much to go on. It was made even more dubious by Baker's recognition that no Palestinians would participate without Arafat's consent.[64] The plan also called for the help of Egyptian President Hosni Mubarak and an attempt to limit Israeli settlement in the occupied territories.

During talks in Washington in early April 1989, Baker asked Shamir to get things started. Shamir said he would try, but would do nothing that would weaken Israel, and nothing that would help the PLO in any way.[65] Palestinian candidates for office had to announce in advance that they would take part in negotiations for an interim settlement, after which negotiations could be held on a final settlement. How limited the proposal was emerged in the last sentence of the plan. It was still necessary, Shamir said, to talk about "the various questions surrounding the holding of elections." This odd phrasing actually meant that Israel continued to demand that no one associated with the PLO or who lived in Jerusalem could take part in the negotiations or be a candidate in the elections. Rather than what should be done to settle the Israeli-Palestinian conflict, the main subject of the talks became, who could run for elections if elections were ever held? The Americans found themselves having to ask questions like: Could Palestinians take part if they owned a second home in Jerusalem? If this was a turkey shoot, Baker was not the one calling the shots.

On May 22, Baker began by defining some of the parameters of the negotiations in a way that would appeal to the Palestinians and make it easier for Mubarak to help. Speaking before the American-Israel Public Affairs Committee, a leading pro-Israel lobby group in Washington, he said: "For Israel, now is the time to lay aside once and for all the unrealistic vision of a Greater Israel."[66] Israel had to stop creating new settlements in the occupied territories and treat the Palestinians, "as neighbors who deserve political rights." Baker told his listeners that opposition to the use of U.S. funding for new settlements was an important part of the administration's policy, and that President Bush had raised the issue forcefully with Shamir during their talks at the White House. Shamir initially tried to avoid dealing with the issue by saying that it was an internal matter. Bush said no, not when U.S. taxpayers gave Israel more than $1,000 for each of its citizens every year. According to Baker, Shamir then told the president not to worry, that the settlements would not be a problem, and Bush came away from the meeting thinking that Shamir had promised not to build new settlements. Israel's housing minister at the time, Ariel Sharon, had no intention of halting new settlements, and when Bush was shown the results, he lost faith in Shamir and the Likud Party. In September, Mubarak offered a plan to break the stalemate that required Israel to recognize the rights of the Palestinian people, agree to exchange land for peace, halt the settlements, refrain from interference in elections that were to be held under international supervision, and allow Palestinian residents of Jerusalem to participate. The plan made no reference to the political affiliation of the candidates, meaning, presumably, that members of the PLO could take part. Mubarak's plan was unacceptable to the Shamir government.

Contrary to all the evidence from the Israeli side, and with no obvious movement from the Palestinians, Baker and Ross persisted in trying to reduce the differences between the two plans enough to begin negotiations. Baker gave five points to the foreign ministers of Egypt and Israel in September: a Palestinian-Israeli dialogue would begin in Cairo, Egypt would have a role in the dialogue, Israel would attend only if a "satisfactory list of Palestinians" had been agreed, Israel would participate on the basis of Shamir's four-point plan, and the Palestinians could raise whatever issues they thought necessary to make the elections and talks successful including final status issues. To get things started, the foreign ministers of Israel and Egypt should meet in Washington within two weeks. Shamir reacted to the heavy American pressure by publicly rejecting Baker's proposal and pledging never to compromise with the Palestinians, even if this meant his government would fall and there would be bad relations with the United States. Openly defying the Bush I administration, Shamir told the Knesset in January 1990 that a "Greater Israel" was necessary because of the imminent arrival of hundreds of thousands of Soviet Jews.[67] Baker felt betrayed. He had spent a year trying to satisfy Israel's demands in ways acceptable to Israel, and Shamir had not even offered ideas about implementing his own plan let alone responded to Baker or Mubarak. It was just the beginning. Palestinian terrorist attacks on Israel, and Arafat's refusal to condemn them, obliged the administration to stop the U.S.-Palestinian dialogue. Despite all of Baker's efforts, nothing was left of the peace process, exactly the result that Shamir had wanted. Baker left little doubt about who was responsible. On June 11, 1990, he told the House Foreign Affairs Committee that Israel was going to have to give up some of its inflexibility and make a good-faith effort, or there would never be peace. With that, he gave the White House telephone number, 1-202-456-1414, and invited the Israelis to call him when they were ready to talk. Privately, Baker concluded wearily that if peace ever happened, it would take better circumstances, a different Israeli prime minister, and a different secretary of state.[68]

Victory in the Gulf War revealed the United States as the sole surviving superpower and established that it would defend its interests in the Middle East. The quick, decisive victory also finished whatever was left of the myth of Iraqi military power, strengthened the security of the oil-rich Arab states and Iran, Iraq's bitter enemy, and diminished the threat to Israel from Iraq. Before the war, Baker had repeatedly promised to convene an Arab-Israeli peace conference after Iraq left Kuwait. It was his way of avoiding a link between Iraqi withdrawal and the Palestinian-Israeli question. When Saddam was ejected from Kuwait, Baker's promise came alive, and he moved quickly to win agreement from all the parties for a peace conference. Without much evidence, Baker concluded that "the Gulf War had created an unprecedented opportunity to pursue the possibility of peace between Israel and her Arab neighbors."[69] Baker recalled that Ross said, "We've just seen an earthquake. We have to move before the earth resettles, because it will, and it never takes long."[70] Baker found the analogy "particularly compelling."[71] Out of this set of hopes and maybes, Baker and his advisers spun an ambitious, intricate two-track peace plan designed to use progress in one area to create conditions for progress in others, and, in this way, to move ahead on all the aspects of the Arab-Israeli conflict. In practice, the large, unwieldy multilateral conferences that were held in Madrid and Washington amounted to a renewal of Henry Kissinger's step-by-step diplomacy. Once again, process became more important than substance. "Some progress is better than no progress," Baker said.[72] Once again, an American secretary of state was arguing that limited, incremental progress could become self-sustaining by gradually changing perceptions and attitudes, recording small changes, and moving ahead. Major issues, such as Jerusalem, refugees, and borders were to be avoided until greater trust had developed between the parties.

The peace process was actually only one element in what Baker called President Bush's vision for the Gulf after the war. The administration's overall goals were: (1) "new regional security arrangements" that would combine Arab peacekeeping forces and American naval forces; (2) conventional and nuclear arms control agreements for the region; (3) substantial international commitments to economic development, including a bank for Middle East economic development; (4) a revived and expanded peace process; and (5) and a major effort to reduce American dependence on oil.[73] Of these five, only the peace process would amount to anything in the months ahead. Nothing came of the other four.

Baker wanted to put Shamir "in a position in which he could no longer say no to new initiatives."[74] His plan called for Israel and carefully selected Palestinians from the occupied territories who were not formal members of the PLO to renew their dialogue. Formally, they would be members of a Jordanian delegation but the point was to make it possible for them to talk to the Israelis. Direct negotiations would be held between Israel and the other Arab governments attending, something that had been an Israeli goal since the founding of the state forty years earlier. Baker hoped that if the Israelis showed "flexibility" toward the Palestinians, Arab governments could use this as evidence to justify their decision to enter the talks. Both sides could help the process along by simultaneously offering one another "confidence-building measures" as proof of their good faith.

It was an ingenious, complex plan, and Baker promptly began to sell it all over the region. In visits to Egypt, Israel, Kuwait, Saudi Arabia, and Syria, he promised that the United States would be a "catalyst for peace" provided the parties would take "parallel reciprocal steps" to reassure one another in order to get the process started.[75] Baker obtained limited support from the Saudis and a self-interested and even more limited gesture from the Syrians. Both dealt in the hypothetical. The Saudis pledged to recognize Israel if it would agree to a Palestinian homeland. The Syrians pledged to work for a more conciliatory Palestinian leadership if Israel permitted elections in the West Bank and Gaza. Mubarak doubted that Shamir would move, but Baker asked the Egyptian leader to help convince Syria and other Arab governments to attend the conference, and to "fence out the PLO from a formal role in the process." He hoped that the deeper he engaged the Arab governments and Israel in planning for a conference, the harder it would be for them to refuse to take part or to let it fail.[76]

Baker offered Shamir a guarantee of Israel's security. In return, he asked the Israeli leader to relax Israeli pressure on the Palestinians, to meet with Palestinian leaders, to consider a withdrawal from Lebanon within a year, and to think about negotiations with Syria over the Golan Heights. Shamir made no concessions of any kind and repeated his 1989 plan for interim negotiations with Palestinians who were acceptable to Israel, to be followed after three years by talks on permanent status. Shamir insisted that any Palestinians who took part in a conference would have to be members of a Jordanian delegation, and they could not have anything to do with the PLO. Shamir saw no contradiction in saying that Israel wanted peace but had no one to talk to. Somehow, Baker decided that these responses from Shamir demonstrated "a flexibility of spirit." As a committed practitioner of personal diplomacy, he was even more persuaded that Shamir had altered his rigid positions when the Israeli prime minister invited Baker and his wife to dinner at his home.[77] Baker was right about one thing: with the United States openly supporting an international peace conference and Arab states willing to attend, Shamir could not stay away. But it should also have been clear to Baker that Shamir would give absolutely nothing to the PLO. Shamir was interested in transforming the situation between Israel and the Palestinians, not just in blocking American initiatives. In early April, a few weeks before Baker and Shamir were to meet, the Likud government's housing minister, Ariel Sharon, announced plans for the construction of 13,000 new units in the occupied territories by 1994. Baker considered this "a deliberate effort to sabotage the peace process" and asked Shamir to repudiate Sharon's announcement. Shamir said, "I will deal with it." Whatever Baker understood Shamir to mean, apparently it did not mean that he would stop it, and he did not.[78] Shamir kept hammering on the unacceptability of PLO representation, even demanding that any Palestinian who attended the conference submit a letter formally repudiating the PLO and Arafat. Baker refused, and demanded that Shamir say unequivocally whether he would negotiate with Palestinians who said that they represented the PLO.

In September 1990 and again in January 1991, Baker spoke at length with Hafez Assad of Syria about a postwar peace process. At the earlier meeting, Baker argued that "once Saddam's overriding threat to regional instability was removed, all the parties would feel more comfortable in taking risks for peace."[79] To this, Assad flatly said there would be no peace until Israel returned every inch of the Golan. He also refused to halt support for terrorist attacks in the occupied territories. During meetings in March, Assad suggested that Israel should take "parallel reciprocal steps," but that no Arab states should. With calculated ambiguity, Assad said that he would respond seriously to American seriousness about peace. Inexplicably, Baker concluded from Assad's replies that he had in some way made a breakthrough: "After this meeting, I felt, the dichotomy in the Arab world between moderates and radicals had been breached." While still in the Middle East, Baker wrote President Bush that "something potentially significant" was stirring among the Arabs. In another swipe at the PLO, Baker said that perhaps out of all the ferment Palestinians would emerge who could make peace with Israel.[80] Assad bargained as resolutely as Shamir, and Baker thought that Assad's demands were an attempt to force the conference to work according to Assad's own agenda and to have a ready excuse if it failed to come together.[81] To Shamir, who was equally unyielding, Baker said that he needed some help:

> There has to be some procedural flexibility, if for no other reason than to be able to blame the Arabs for failure . . . Shamir and his aides ignored my plea. Instead, they constantly raised procedural roadblocks, debating points, reservations, and new concerns. The haggling seemed endless to me, a calculated exercise in obfuscation to play for time and avoid coming to grips with the hard choices required. My irritation was beginning to get the better of me. By now I had essentially fashioned a process built on Israel's specifications, yet Shamir wasn't satisfied.[82]

Not surprisingly, Baker came away from his meetings with the Syrian and Israeli leaders thinking that the conference would never happen.

Baker's final encounter with Shamir before the Madrid conference was an ugly one, and left a legacy of distrust and hostility on both sides. Shamir had requested that the United States guarantee a $10 billion loan for Israel while simultaneously refusing to pledge that he would not use the money to build new settlements in the occupied territories. Baker knew that the settlements severely damaged his credibility. If he failed to oppose them, what reason would there be for Arab governments and the Palestinians to attend the peace conference, let alone begin serious negotiations with Israel? The disagreement became so serious that Baker considered declaring the Israeli ambassador in Washington persona non grata and forcing his recall. Then Shamir went too far. Apparently, he and his colleagues had concluded they could get whatever they wanted by appealing to Congress over the president's head. In an unmistakable bid for control over American policy, Shamir began speaking publicly in favor of a "Greater Israel" during a visit to the United States. Baker responded by urging members of Congress to refuse the loan guarantee without a commitment from Shamir to stop using American funds for new settlements. President Bush then put an end to the loan guarantee by publicly declaring his opposition to new settlements while the United States was trying to arrange a peace conference. The Labor Party followed up by winning a vote of no confidence in the Knesset and the Shamir government fell. With persistence, imagination, and good timing, the administration had managed to coordinate its diplomacy with the dynamics of Israeli and American domestic politics. However, Shamir was able to stay in office for the coming months as head of a caretaker government by taking advantage of a provision in Israeli electoral law. After losing the election, Shamir publicly said he would never have compromised with the PLO. Time was what he had been playing for all along, he added, time to fill up Judea and Samaria with Jewish immigrants.

Despite all the difficulties, the administration eventually managed to convene international conferences in Madrid and Washington to address the Arab-Israeli and Israeli-Palestinian conflicts. More Arab countries negotiated directly with Israel than ever before in history. Regional study groups were established to consider issues such as the environment and water conservation, and they continued to meet for a time after the conference. However unproductive they proved to be in the longer term, they signaled genuine movement toward acceptance of Israel by the community of nations. The groundwork was also laid for what would be an eventual peace treaty between Jordan and Israel. Nothing changed between Syria and Israel. Shamir's intransigence and the rift with the United States had undermined his government's political position at home, and contributed to his defeat in 1992 and the election of Yitzhak Rabin.

Thinking about the Future

By the time that the Bush administration left office, it had made two attempts to spell out a new post–Cold War strategy for the United States. In the White House, President Bush and his National Security Advisor Brent Scowcroft chose the term "new world order" to describe their hopes to prohibit state-to-state aggression through multilateral cooperation in international and regional organizations. At the Defense Department, another attempt with quite a different focus was made. It called for the United States to remain the dominant world power and to use its might to preclude the emergence of rivals. It was the first appearance of global unilateralism, a critical element in Bush II's version of the post–Cold War paradigm. Although the president opposed unilateralism and decided in favor of the new world order, some of the authors of the Defense Department's proposal would return to high office eight years later and shape the second Bush administration's strategy after 9/11.

Preventing the Emergence of Rivals

The growing weakness of the Soviet Union prompted Secretary of Defense Cheney to order two teams to prepare studies of post–Cold War American foreign policy "at the grand strategic level." One was headed by General Colin Powell, chair of the Joint Chiefs of Staff. The other was a "Team B" team group, including among others Paul Wolfowitz, Undersecretary of Defense for Policy, Lewis Libby, a deputy assistant secretary of defense, Eric Edelman, Cheney's chief of staff, and Zalmay Khalilzad, an academic specializing in South Asia who had joined George Shultz's State Department and then shifted to Defense.[83] Cheney preferred the Team B version, and the president apparently planned to make public at least some of its ideas in a major address on August 2, 1990, at the start of an Aspen Institute Conference in Colorado. Prime Minister Thatcher was scheduled to give a speech to end the conference and flew to Colorado early to be on hand for the president's remarks. Their plans were interrupted by Saddam Hussein's invasion of Kuwait. Instead of continuing on her vacation, Thatcher flew to Washington to coordinate the response to the invasion with Bush.[84] Thus, by coincidence, the two Western leaders most capable of responding to the attack on Kuwait with effective military force were together at the start of the Gulf War. As might be expected, Thatcher strongly urged that Saddam Hussein's aggression be stopped and Saudi Arabia defended. Overshadowed by the invasion of Kuwait, the president's speech triggered no alarms.[85]

The 1992 report, "Defense Policy Guidance for 1994–1999," portrayed the world as a very threatening place, so threatening that the United States must stay vigilant, keep large forces in being, and deploy new generations of more powerful and accurate weapons based on advanced technologies. There was a paradox at the heart of the report. On the one hand, it admitted that the United States "no longer faces either a global threat or a hostile, non-democratic power dominating a region critical to our interests."[86] On the other hand, it insisted that the United States must take up a new, difficult, and vital mission:

> Our first objective is to prevent the re-emergence of a new rival, either on the territory of the former Soviet Union or elsewhere that poses a threat on the order of that posed formerly by the Soviet Union. This is a dominant consideration underlying the new regional defense strategy and requires that we endeavor to prevent any hostile power from dominating a region whose resources would, under consolidated control, be sufficient to generate global power. These regions include Western Europe, East Asia, the territory of the former Soviet Union, and Southwest Asia [the Gulf].[87]

This section produced the greatest outcry. It not only seemed to call for preemptive or even preventive war against any potential rival anywhere in the world, but warned that major allies, such as Germany and Japan, might become opponents of the United States. The report portrayed China as a greater threat than the Soviet Union; the latter was discounted because of its loss of control of Eastern Europe and "continuing dissolution of military capacity." The United States would have to reassure advanced industrial nations that their nondefense needs would be met so satisfactorily that they need not seek a greater regional or global role. The United States would also have to deal with regional conflicts and instability in such a way as to encourage democracy and promote respect for international law.[88] Future coalitions would resemble the Gulf War group, "ad hoc assemblies, often not lasting beyond the immediate crisis, and in many cases carrying only general agreement over the objectives to be accomplished."[89] There were also some quite specific recommendations. The United States should preserve NATO; prevent the emergence of "Europe only" defense arrangements, because they would undermine NATO unity; "discourage Indian hegemonic aspirations" in South Asia; and assure the participation of East European states in Western political and economic organizations.

After some weeks of harsh criticism from Congress and foreign policy specialists, Cheney dropped the most controversial elements of the report. The revised version no longer committed the United States to prevent the emergence of a global or regional rival. This removed Germany and Japan from the spotlight. In its place was a much broader, more familiar task: to "deter or defeat attack from whatever source." The final version called "Defense Strategy for the 1990s: The Regional Defense Strategy," appeared over Dick Cheney's signature in January 1993. In remarks accompanying the text, Cheney portrayed it as nothing more than a sensible attempt to reduce American military forces in a way that preserved their effectiveness and American security along with them. One of the participants in the drafting and redrafting thought that he had preserved the original report's emphasis on maintaining unmatchable U.S. dominance through the use of clever euphemisms. His name was Lewis Libby, and he would become Vice President Cheney's chief of staff in the Bush II administration.[90]

The New World Order

As Brent Scowcroft described it after the administration left office, the new world order was conceived as a limited but promising concept:

> The Soviet Union was standing alongside us, not only in the United Nations, but also in condemning and taking action against Iraqi aggression. . . . If the attack on Kuwait marked the end of forty-odd years of such superpower confrontation, what vistas might open up? The Security Council could then perform the role envisioned for it by the UN framers. The United States and the Soviet Union could, in most cases, stand together against unprovoked interstate aggression. . . . From that point forward, we tried to operate in a manner that would help establish a pattern for the future.[91]

The pattern was based on multilateral cooperation and U.S. global leadership. Scowcroft admitted later that the administration never made any of this public: it "remained distinctly secondary in our public explications of our purposes in the Gulf Crisis." But he insisted on its importance. "Our foundation was the premise that the United States henceforth would be obligated to lead the world community to an unprecedented degree, as demonstrated by the Iraqi crisis, and that we should attempt to pursue our national interests, wherever possible, within a framework of concert with our friends and the international community."[92]

Secretary Baker was quick to make use of the new world order idea as he worked to build a worldwide coalition to oust Iraq from Kuwait. In mid-September 1990 during discussions with President Hafez Assad of Syria, Baker described the Gulf war as the first crisis of the post–Cold War period, and then added, "A new order is going to evolve in an important way out of how we handle this crisis. That is why it is important that Saddam not succeed."[93] In November, he spanned the globe, moving from meetings in Cairo, Ankara, Moscow, and London, to Paris, Bermuda, Geneva (for meetings with African members of the Security Council), back to Paris for signature of the treaty to reduce Conventional Forces in Europe, then Saudi Arabia, Yemen, Colombia, and ending in Los Angeles for a meeting with the Malaysian Foreign Minister, Abu Hassan. At each stop, Baker offered incentives to win the cooperation of other governments: money (from the Gulf states and Germany, Japan, or the U.S. Treasury), prestige in the form of a meeting with the president for the Chinese Foreign Minister Qian Qichen, or debt relief from the G-7. Always there was the drumbeat of Baker's arguments that sanctions would not work and the UN Security Council should authorize the use of force against Iraq. He also stressed the risks of crossing a newly powerful United States. When the Malaysians expressed their unhappiness about the inequity of punishing Iraq without punishing Israel for its bad treatment of the Palestinians, Baker showed the other face of the new world order: "[I]n light of recent world events," he warned, "it might be prudent to consider one's future relations with the United States very carefully. . . ." Baker recalled later that "[s]uddenly, there was a dead silence in the room. You could have heard a pin drop. For the first time, I thought he [Abu Hassan] had absorbed just how serious we were about this."[94]

On November 18, shortly before the end of his coalition-building odyssey, Baker appeared with Shevardnadze at 1:45 A.M. in Paris to brief the press. He was exhausted, but he had the votes the United States needed in the Security Council, and he worried that his relaxed body language and upbeat manner might have given it away. The Soviets wanted to talk to Iraq one more time, but it did not matter. On November 29, 1990, at 5:26 P.M., Baker called for a show of hands in the Security Council. By a vote of 12–2, the Council authorized the use of force against Iraq. Two countries, Yemen and Cuba, voted against, and China abstained. At Soviet insistence, the resolution provided for a "pause of goodwill," during which the Iraqis might comply, and did not explicitly refer to military force. But it set an unmistakable deadline for Iraqi compliance of January 15, 1991, and authorized member-states "to use all necessary means to uphold and implement resolution 660 (1990) and all subsequent relevant resolutions and to restore international peace and security in the area."

The administration was disappointed by the reception that its new world order concept received. From the moment that it became public, the concept generated enormous criticism, not to mention paranoia and bizarre accusations of conspiracy and treason, as even a casual search of the Internet reveals.[95] Scowcroft was annoyed by the distortions, although the president and his advisers were partly to blame for overdramatizing the idea and exaggerating the scope of what had changed and what could be accomplished in the new circumstances. Offended by the excesses, Scowcroft insisted on the narrow limits of the new world order:

> We certainly had no expectation that we were entering a period of peace and tranquility. Indeed the outlines of a very messy world were already perceptible. The phrase, as we thought of it, applied only to a narrow aspect of conflict—aggression between states. A limited aspect of conflict, yes, but one which had been a chief ill of civilization since the beginning of recorded history. The term has subsequently been broadened beyond recognition, mostly to disparage its application. In retrospect, such an outcome was perhaps to be expected, but possibilities for dealing successfully with aggression between states in the current world still look promising.[96]

In an address to the Congress on September 11, 1990, Bush reported on the measures that he had taken in the Gulf and regarding Soviet-U.S. relations. He used the occasion to mention the new world order and, as presidents often do when speaking to the Congress, let his rhetoric get away from him. He did not hold out the prospect of a "very messy world," "or the mitigation of a limited aspect of conflict." Instead, he offered something much grander and far more appealing. A new world order was being born, he said,

> a new era—free from the threat of terror, stronger in the pursuit of justice, and more secure in the quest for peace. An era in which the nations of the world, East and West, North and South, can prosper and

live in harmony. . . . Today that new world is struggling to be born, a world quite different from the one we've known. A world where the rule of law supplants the rule of the jungle. A world in which nations recognize the shared responsibility for freedom and justice. A world where the strong respect the rights of the weak.[97]

The crisis in the Gulf had become the first test of the new order, and Bush called on the Congress and the American people to meet the challenges that lay ahead.

Saving Somalia

The Bush administration's last major foreign policy decision—the intervention in Somalia—was the first post–Cold War humanitarian intervention. It was a foreign policy driven largely by televised pictures of starving Somali children. "Somalia" generated the very same pressures for intervention that would haunt the Clinton administration, the NATO alliance, and the United Nations in Bosnia, Haiti, Rwanda, and Kosovo. A fractured society in a country with little geopolitical importance that was consuming its own citizens' lives at a horrific rate made a very awkward place to apply lessons from the war in Vietnam, but apply them the Bush administration did. The awkwardness appeared most obviously in news photos of dozens of American soldiers in full battle dress lying in defensive positions on the ground with weapons ready while children wandered around them. Identical pictures would come out of Haiti when the Clinton administration intervened to restore order in that country.

The mission of the American troops that President Bush sent to Somalia was defined as narrowly as possible—to feed the people—and the number of troops sent was overwhelming. There was no gap between ends and means, mission and capability. Tens of thousands of lives were saved. And an opportunity was created, however brief, for the restoration of normalcy in Somalia. However, such a narrowly defined intervention left untouched the political and social problems that had caused the starvation in the first place. Saving lives was always worthwhile, but what then? And, what would happen to the American troops in Somalia? The Bush administration never managed to withdraw American troops before its term expired. The answers to these questions would be given by a new president, Bill Clinton.

2

Moses and the Promised Land[1]

In statecraft and strategy paradoxes abound. Almost every achievement contains within its success the seeds of a future problem.

—James A. Baker[2]

Any appraisal of the Bush I administration's foreign policy must begin by recognizing its remarkable achievements. Its imaginative and self-effacing diplomacy during the endgame of the Cold War contributed importantly to a stable and legitimate peace in Europe, and left the world safer and more democratic. It built new international institutions and trade mechanisms to promote Asian Pacific economic cooperation and the North American Free Trade Act. Committing the United States under the "new world order" to prevent state-to-state aggression, restart the Middle East peace process, and cooperate with the United Nations, the administration sent a message that governments around the world saw as strongly positive. These measures not only helped structure the post–Cold War world but reassured other governments and their citizens that the enormous and now unrivalled power of the United States would be used in ways congenial to their interests and that they would be able to shape American foreign policy through consultation, bargaining, and mutual compromise.

If the operational code and strategies of the Bush administration were to be evaluated by these accomplishments alone, they would have to be judged astonishing successes. Of course, these are not the only tests. Every significant international development contains threats and opportunities, and costs as well as potential gains. It is necessary to ask not just whether the administration coped with the problems it faced, but also whether it took full advantage of its strategic opportunities as the Soviet Union weakened and collapsed. This question really has two parts: To what extent did the administration consciously seek to establish American global dominance during the endgame of the Cold War? Did the administration exploit American primacy to achieve its objectives? A second set of questions concerns the administration's handling of the Israeli-Palestinian conflict and Iraq after the defeat of Saddam Hussein in 1991. A third group of questions emerges from the most frequent criticism of the Bush administration's foreign policy: the new world order was of little use in dealing with the issues of the post–Cold War world, particularly ethnic conflict, the environment, and the transition of the Soviet Union away from communism.[3] This is an argument from "reality" to policy, that is, the criticism assumes that the test of success is whether a foreign policy conforms to what are perceived to be decisive external constraints and trends. It is an argument that implicitly denies the possibility of using American power to transform international "reality." No foreign policy can be properly evaluated without reference to its moral content. What moral ends were served? And did the policy cause pointless suffering? It is not always possible to avoid the loss of human life or the destruction of property, but that does not remove all restraints on the exercise of power. Justice requires political and military leaders to accept the responsibility not to cause suffering or loss that goes beyond what is needed to achieve their goals. A number of questions must also be asked about the intrinsic merits of the administration's foreign policy. Did its strategy identify the principal threats to American security and provide effective ways of addressing them? Were ends and means, and intentions and capabilities, in balance within the strategy's own terms? Or was it necessary to introduce some extrinsic method of bringing them into alignment? Were there logical or practical inconsistencies in its strategy?

Ensuring American Primacy

Throughout the tumultuous years from 1989 to 1991, President Bush constantly reassured his Soviet counterpart that the United States was not seeking political or military advantage from the massive changes that Gorbachev had triggered.[4] The reality, of course, was that the changes brought enormous advantages to the United States, including the withdrawal of the Red Army behind Soviet borders, and the appearance of governments throughout Eastern Europe eager to shed their subordination to Soviet rule and join NATO and the European Union. The collapse of the Soviet Union created a unipolar world, and opened a military and political gap between the power of the United States and all other countries. These were the building blocks of American global superiority.

There is considerable evidence that Bush I policymakers understood exactly what was happening and some tantalizing clues that they acted in ways intended to enhance American superiority starting well before the fall of the Soviet Union. For example, after leaving office, national security adviser Brent Scowcroft wrote: "As 1990 began, we were cautiously optimistic. . . . Perhaps we could achieve a fundamental shift in the strategic balance."[5] About the situation a few months later, Scowcroft added:

> The easing of Cold War tensions threw open the fundamental assumptions on which the entire postwar security structures of Western Europe, *and our own strategic planning*, were based: a Soviet threat and a divided continent. . . . We had to rethink the larger strategic picture of European security, of our role in it, and of superpower relations. The events underway across Europe were interrelated in their cause and effect and had to be considered in a collective context as well as individually. *We were witnessing the sorts of changes usually only imposed by victors at the end of a major war* [emphases added].[6]

Gorbachev and Shevardnadze understood that the United States was going to rise at least as far as their country was going to fall. At the same time, they felt obliged by their commitment to reform at home and self-determination abroad and their need for foreign economic assistance to avoid provoking the West. The developing asymmetry was so great that Bush and his advisers often clouded their actions in ambiguity. A good example appeared during an exchange in mid-May 1990 between Gorbachev and Baker about inconsistencies in the American position on Germany. Gorbachev said:

> If a united Germany joins NATO, it will be a huge gain for the United States and a commensurate loss to the Soviet Union. You say it's not a problem, because the Germans have proved themselves and we can trust them. If they are not a threat to anyone, then why do they have to be in NATO? . . . If [the Bush administration] had offered a realistic analysis of Germany's non-membership in NATO as a serious threat to the alliance's infrastructure, [I] could understand. But if you *are* saying that, then there's a problem. Because you are saying you continue to need a bloc even when the other alliance is disappearing.[7]

That was exactly what the Bush administration was saying. Gorbachev said that such a shift in the strategic balance ought to provoke a systematic reassessment of Soviet strategy:

> [O]ne step might be for us to suspend all talks and think about how this development is going to affect our doctrine, how it's going to affect our forces, what effect it should have on our approach to the Vienna [Conventional Forces in Europe] talks.[8]

In other words, the Soviet government should stop coming to terms with the United States in Europe until it found a way to prevent such huge strategic setbacks or at least hold on to some of its advantages. During the Cold War, the Soviet Union had repeatedly and adamantly refused even to contemplate the slightest change in Germany and Eastern Europe or the overall military balance that would have led to any gains for the United States, much less the one-sided gains it now stood to win. But times had changed. Gorbachev was in no position to force the issue. "I think the best way to put it," he concluded forlornly, "is we need some oxygen. . . . What I will say to the President is that we're going to need fifteen to twenty billion dollars to tide us over."[9]

Secretary Baker responded with the administration's constant refrain: there is no attempt to take advantage, and no political games are being played. A united Germany would pose uncertainties and dangers as it had in the past, particularly if it were to become isolated in Central Europe. While true, this was only part of the strategic argument. The United States insisted that a united Germany remain in NATO, because without it the United

States would lose its position in Europe. In the memoir he wrote with President Bush after leaving office, Brent Scowcroft spelled out the private reasons for this insistence without mincing words:

> The lesson we drew from this bloody history [of Europe in the twentieth century] was that the United States had to continue to play a significant role in European security, *whatever developed with respect to the Soviet Union*. The vehicle for that role must be NATO. The alliance was the only way the US could keep forces in Europe as a visible commitment to its security and stability. In addition, a united Germany as a full member of the alliance was key to our presence. Germany held our bases. If it left the alliance, it would be difficult if not impossible to retain American troops in Europe. We needed Helmut Kohl's commitment to keep Germany in the alliance and American troops on its soil. Together, these requirements gave us an enormous stake in the outcome of German reunification, apart from ending the division of Europe.[10]

To have American forces stay in Germany and to have Germany in NATO as the Red Army evacuated its troops was humiliating for the Soviet Union. But what was surely most agonizing to Soviet and perhaps French leaders was that by remaining in Germany as Soviet power was eclipsed, and Germany and a united Europe continued to be militarily ineffective, the United States widened its freedom of action without accepting any restraint or granting compensation to any other country. The *effect* of the changes in Central and Eastern Europe, and especially the collapse of the Soviet Union, was to establish American global superiority. It is clear that this was not the *intent* of American strategists from the very beginning. At first, they reacted cautiously and slowly. But the possibilities clearly did not escape them. Had the Soviet Union remained intact politically, militarily, and economically, and merely withdrawn its forces from Germany and Eastern Europe, the United States would not have become the world's only superpower. Ultimately, the Soviet Union could not keep itself together because its identity was imperial abroad and tyrannical at home. One could not change one without changing the other. The attempt to reform the Soviet Union domestically meant the end of the Soviet empire in Europe, the Caucasus, and Central Asia, and the end of one-party dictatorship at home. Critics attacked the Bush I administration's failure to help restructure the Soviet economy as lacking in vision, and, some say, humanity. Defenders point to the hostility in Congress and public opinion to greater foreign spending, to the recession in the United States, and the likelihood that lavish aid would have been wasted and stolen. More will be said about this in the following section. In retrospect, it seems likely that Bush I's reluctance to rescue the Soviet economy after 1989 proceeded from a harsher strategic calculus than its critics imagined.

American Primacy and the Post–Cold War Paradigm

The influence of the post–Cold War paradigm on the Bush I administration was mixed, partly because the Soviet Union collapsed only a year before the president's defeat in the 1992 elections, and partly because some of its components, such as democratization and globalization, had only begun to attract the attention of policymakers. The willingness of the president and his advisers to work within the boundaries of international organizations, alliances, the United Nations, and international law corresponded with a still nascent globalization and boosted its appeal. In effect, the Bush I administration defined American primacy as the capability to set the global agenda and persuade other states to follow the United States in carrying it out. The administration took advantage of American primacy to undo Saddam Hussein's conquest of Kuwait and advance the Israeli-Palestinian peace process. It expanded the international agenda in ways consistent with the post–Cold War paradigm by initiating talks to establish the North America Free Trade Agreement and helping to create a loosely structured arrangement of regular meetings to foster Asian Pacific economic cooperation. Beyond these modest steps, however, Bush I would not go, which meant terrorism, global environmental issues, and international human rights questions received little attention. The control of the Soviet nuclear arsenal became a major concern when the Soviet Union disappeared, but this did not lead the administration to pay greater attention to nuclear proliferation elsewhere. The last-minute intervention in Somalia reflected some concern about human rights, but it failed to offset the administration's indifference to suffering in the Balkans or Haiti, and in any case seemed primarily motivated by horrifying pictures of starving children shown on television news programs. Coercive diplomacy and economic sanctions formed the heart of the administration's approach to Iraq after the Gulf War. There was some bandwagoning as the administration sought support for the war against Iraq. It also put severe pressure on other governments to follow its lead.

Bush I adopted a carefully bounded definition of America's role in the world and of the significance of the American experience. Bush, Baker, and Scowcroft believed the United States did not need a world that was entirely democratic to be safe, just one that was not mostly totalitarian. Attempting to make the entire world democratic would waste American lives, money, and international opportunities. A decade later, as Bush II struggled with insurgency, terrorism, and ethnic and religious conflict in Iraq, Scowcroft publicly repeated these ideas.[11] By restricting the use of American military force to deterring and defeating state-to-state aggression, the administration sought to avoid interventions in ethnic and religious conflicts. If the United States became entangled in these bitter civil wars, mounting casualties, restrictions on the use of force, and no exit strategy would ruin popular support at home for an activist foreign policy and lead to drastic reductions in defense budgets, which could wreck the ability of the United States to respond to genuinely menacing threats in the future.

The administration used its response to Saddam Hussein's conquest of Kuwait to shape the emerging international order. The expulsion of Iraqi forces from Kuwait with the consent of the UN Security Council acting at the head of a truly global coalition set a hopeful precedent. It also enabled the administration to use its enhanced prestige and new credibility to try to move the Israelis, Syrians, Jordanians, and Palestinians toward peace. The administration's decision not to go "on to Baghdad" to overthrow Saddam Hussein was taken well before the fighting started and helped knit the coalition together. It was especially important to Arab and Muslim countries. Baker's coalition-building efforts were also helped by the worldwide opposition to state-to-state aggression. Most governments around the world agreed with Bush I: if Saddam's aggression were not checked, it would surely encourage other states to attack their neighbors. The president and his advisers reasoned—correctly—that the overthrow of the Iraqi government would saddle the United States with an enormously costly, open-ended occupation of a country that was deeply divided along ethnic and religious lines, and had not been able to establish a decent, stable government for more than a handful of years at any time in the twentieth century. It would expose American troops to terrorist attacks: "another Lebanon" was an all too plausible scenario. It would stir fears in other governments that the United States had begun to operate without any restraints. Bush I decision makers also remembered Korea, where an incautious advance precipitated catastrophe, and the "quagmire" of Vietnam, a war that took 58,000 American lives, and destroyed the domestic consensus about American foreign policy. "Why push our luck?" was their reaction. The administration thought that such a gross humiliation and defeat for Saddam Hussein would trigger his overthrow by the Sunni military establishment. It did not, and Bush I saw its larger goals in the Gulf slip away as Saddam twisted and turned to emerge weakened but solidly in control of his country.

The Ends and Means of the Bush I Strategy

The larger purpose of strategy is its most important but most overlooked aspect. What end does it serve? The usual answer is, "whatever end the political leadership chooses." Strategy may be considered without reference to moral ends, as one might consider a painting or musical composition, but that would be as incomplete a view of strategy as it is of art. In the hands of governments, strategy is a political instrument and cannot be fully evaluated without considering the moral character of the ends it serves, and whether it preserves a sensible balance between gains and losses. On these grounds, the Bush I administration's strategy deserves high praise for its actions in Europe, for the expulsion of Saddam Hussein's army from Kuwait, and the efforts to advance the peace process in the Middle East. The result left Europe and the Middle East safer and, in the case of Europe, more democratic. However, the administration's decision to continue economic sanctions on Iraq turned into a political and moral nightmare. Pinching pennies when more generous assistance might have smoothed Russia's transition away from communism seems shortsighted in retrospect. The failure to intervene early and decisively in the developing ethnic conflict in Yugoslavia surrendered a precious opportunity to prevent genocide. Bush I preserved a balance between commitments and capabilities by limiting what it attempted to do, and assuring that when it tried for ambitious goals, its policies were widely supported by other governments. As a result, even while cutting the size of the American military and reducing the defense budget, the administration found it relatively easy to accomplish its goals and its achievements were generally popular and widely regarded as legitimate. Unfortunately, the ability to balance commitments and capabilities did not carry over into the administrations of Bill Clinton and George W. Bush. Paradoxically, many of the weaknesses of Bush I foreign policy arose from its strengths, notably the emphasis on state-to-state relations, and James Baker's highly personalized and centralized style of running American diplomacy. At the same time, emphasizing nonintervention in the internal affairs of other states meant leaving Saddam Hussein in power after the liberation of Kuwait, with, as it turned out, the vain hope that he would be overthrown. It also meant ignoring the possibility that the post-communist transition in Yugoslavia would turn into genocide. Finally, it kept the administration from focusing on terrorism and especially its subnational causes. Other failures arose from the clash between the administration's fundamental assumptions and a number of concrete situations abroad. There were failures of conception and, in some cases, failure to adjust to radically new circumstances.

Postwar Iraq

The expulsion of Saddam Hussein's armed forces from Kuwait and the manner in which the entire campaign was conducted carried an important moral message from the strong to the weak: the United States together with the most powerful and wealthiest countries in the world would oppose state-to-state aggression, but only within the limits of international law and the charter of the United Nations. The oil-rich Kingdom of Kuwait was hardly the most attractive regime in the world, and guaranteeing the inviolability of national borders runs the risk of making it difficult or even impossible to remedy injustice. At the same time, respect for international law and sovereignty denies dictators the justification of external threat for their oppressions. It also reinforces the security of all nations, and in this way reduces the incentive for unnecessary expenditures on armaments. The decision to stop at the borders of Iraq conveyed another extremely important and positive message to other countries. Although its armed forces had become virtually irresistible in conventional battle, the Bush I administration made clear that it intended to oppose only state-to-state aggression and would take the interests of other governments into account in setting its international objectives. The advantage, particularly in light of the later reaction to Bush II unilateralism, was that the approach helped minimize opposition to American policies. But just as importantly, it revealed a government aware of its country's and its own limitations, uninterested in grandiose projects, and possessed of the confidence and coherence that comes from self-restraint.

These gains were dimmed considerably by the administration's inability to grasp the futility and growing immorality of the economic sanctions imposed on Iraq. Economic sanctions against Iraq and other countries were embraced by the Bush administration and justified as coercive diplomacy, an important element in the post–Cold War paradigm. Economic sanctions made sense as a wartime measure and had been imposed by the UN Security Council after Saddam Hussein's invasion of Kuwait.[12] After the fighting ended, however, the administration insisted on maintaining the sanctions to bring about the overthrow of Saddam Hussein. The policy failed, and imposed enormous suffering on the Iraqi people. The reasons for the failure stemmed from a misunderstanding of the limits of economic sanctions; disagreement among the members of the UN Security Council about the purpose of the sanctions; failure to anticipate Saddam's ability to evade the sanctions and pass hardships on to the Iraqi people; and an inability to grasp the negative impact of the sanctions on Iraqi, Arab, and world opinion.

Economic sanctions are attractive and often irresistible to policymakers because they promise to achieve political and military objectives without war. The same policymakers appear to forget the limits on sanctions as a tool to force other governments to change their behavior. Sanctions are slow-acting and usually succeed only one time in three. Of particular relevance to Iraq, "[s]uccess is more likely when the goals are modest, the nation targeted is small and dependent on supplies from nations participating in the embargo, and there is an active internal opposition that supports imposition of sanctions."[13] None of these conditions applied to Iraq. As a result, Saddam evaded the sanctions, and the suffering fell on the middle and lower classes. A senior official in the State Department during the Bush I administration said:

> You cannot show one government that has changed due to economic sanctions. . . . When the government, the elite and the black marketers are one and the same, the ones that we really want to hurt do well and the common people get hurt. There's really no way to structure an embargo where you don't hurt the common people.[14]

Political support for continuing the sanctions began to crumble within a few months of the end of the fighting. Most members of the Security Council wanted to lift the sanctions once Iraq had complied with the terms set by the council for Iraq's disarmament and payment of compensation for war damage, primarily to Kuwait.[15] The administration disagreed. According to a senior official who spoke to reporters on February 28, 1991, the administration hoped the harsh and deteriorating conditions in Iraq would prompt

Saddam Hussein's overthrow. "We will present Iraqis with the prospect of a future in which this leader will just drag them further and further down."[16] Baker said that Saddam's removal was "a prime goal of the coalition forces," although he regarded it as a political rather than military objective. The breach between the administration and the UN widened when on April 3, 1991, the UN Security Council passed resolution 687 offering to stop all sanctions once Iraq had complied with the UN's terms for ending the war.[17] And on April 30, President Bush in remarks at the White House said that there would not be normal trade with Iraq "as long as Saddam Hussein is in power."[18] A senior White House official recognized that Iraq's recovery under sanctions would be "slow and painful." Likening Saddam to the Romanian dictator Nicolae Ceausescu, who had seemed invulnerable but was overthrown and assassinated in 1989, the official said that in the end those around Ceausescu turned against him. "We hope that the people like that at Saddam's side will look around and say look what he has done to his country, and take the action that's needed."[19] The importance that the administration gave sanctions was ironic: before the war Bush I had insisted that sanctions would not cause Saddam to remove Iraqi troops from Kuwait, a much more limited action than political suicide. Now it sought Saddam's downfall by economic sanctions, an even less likely outcome. The administration's unwillingness to see Iraq as it was, its exclusive focus on state-to-state diplomacy, and its refusal to intervene in the rebellions against Saddam, contradicted and, in the end, defeated any hope that Bush I might have had of removing the Iraqi dictator.

Saddam and his cronies soon learned to twist the sanctions to their advantage, first by smuggling and then from kickbacks and bribes obtained by subverting the UN's oil for food programs. The sanctions impoverished ordinary Iraqis, destroyed the middle class, and prevented the modernization of Iraq's vital oil and water and electricity sectors. Saddam's repressions, made easy by the administration's refusal to aid the Shia and Kurdish rebellions, caused the deaths of tens of thousands. Hundreds of thousands of Kurds became refugees to escape military reprisals, and had to be given military protection and relief supplies mostly by the United States, including the establishment of zones protected by American warplanes, and the beginning of nearly 15 years of constant air patrols. As early as June 1991, barely three months after the war, a team of experts from Harvard University reported that cholera, typhoid, and gastroenteritis had begun spreading at epidemic rates inside Iraq. Bombing had destroyed power, water purification, and sewer facilities, and it was impossible to import replacement machinery. One member of the team estimated that 500 Iraqi children died every day from unsafe drinking water and not enough food. The team predicted that 170,000 Iraqi children would die in the next twelve months, double the normal rate for child mortality. By August, Egyptian President Hosni Mubarak was urging the administration to end the sanctions.

To alleviate the suffering, the Security Council came up with a "food for peace" program designed to allow Saddam Hussein to sell limited quantities of oil and use the proceeds to buy food, medical supplies, and other items to meet the urgent needs of Iraqi citizens. Saddam refused and continued to use the hardships as a lever to force the complete lifting of the sanctions. During the summer of 1993, an internationally known specialist, Dr. Eric Hoskins, reported to the UN children's organization, UNICEF, that sanctions were preventing the rebuilding of Iraq's economy and rendering the Iraqi government unable to provide adequate medical care, education, sanitation, and food. Dr. Hoskins said the sanctions had pushed most Iraqi families into an "economic abyss characterized by poverty, unemployment, hyperinflation and community strain." Most people in Iraq lived on food rations; hospitals and clinics could barely function; antibiotics, anesthetics, and insulin were scarce; malnutrition was widespread; and the death rate of young children had tripled in the past two years.[20]

Fearing another backlash against itself and the UN in the United States, UNICEF suppressed the report. Finally, in mid-April 1995, the Security Council established an "oil-for-food program," allowing Iraq to sell oil for the purchase of humanitarian goods and to fund UN activities regarding Iraq.[21] Saddam refused to cooperate, and more than another year passed before the program finally started in December 1996. The program ended only in November 2003, eight months after the invasion of Iraq. In the fall of 1991, a group of British academics and doctors wrote to the *Guardian* newspaper to protest the economic sanctions against Iraq. Their argument captured the failure of imagination and will that unleashed a tragedy:

> The regime is playing a cat and mouse game with the UN over cease-fire conditions and is likely to continue to do so for an indefinite period. At the same time it seems to be well entrenched and protected by its considerable remaining forces, which devastated the country further in the bloody suppression of popular uprisings. If the US and its allies were serious about ending the Saddam regime they should have

adopted a more positive posture toward these uprisings. Now we have
the worst of all possible worlds, with the regime in control and the
Iraqi people suffering the effects of the sanctions. . . . If the international community is not willing to intervene decisively in Iraq and
impose on the regime UN agencies charged with the distribution of
aid and resources, then let it do the next most decent thing and end the
pointless suffering and death caused by the sanctions.[22]

The suffering caused by the sanctions alienated most Iraqis; they hated
what was being done to them and blamed the United States. The suffering
offended millions of people, not just in Arab and Muslim countries, but also
around the world. Their opposition to sanctions undermined opposition to
Saddam in the United Nations and the United States and weakened the inspections regime. The widespread condemnation strengthened the determination of the governments of France and Russia to end the inspections
and sanctions in order to resume buying Iraqi oil and selling weapons to
Saddam's military. The Bush administration's policy had turned Saddam
Hussein's Iraq into a victim rather than a ruthless dictatorship.

Bosnia

Bush I's failure to intervene in the early stages of genocide in Bosnia was,
above all, a failure to lead. It was true that the U.S. economy was in recession in the early 1990s, and it was also true that "Americans were weary of
the commitments their nation had carried for more than forty years and
eager to share them more fully with others."[23] The failure lay in surrendering to these conditions, in not trying harder to prevent what led to the deaths
of tens of thousands of people and the imprisonment, torture, and rape of
thousands more.[24] Beyond the administration's timidity lay three profound
failures of conception. The first was a failure to recognize the deadly nature of the conflict. It was a failure of intelligence and, even more importantly, a failure by senior officials, particularly National Security Advisor
Scowcroft and Deputy Secretary of State Eagleburger, to alter their fundamental assumptions as circumstances changed. It was also a failure to recognize the corrosive effect that doing nothing to stop the killing would have
on NATO. When the Clinton administration finally acted three years later,
NATO's reputation had been damaged because of the alliance's inability to
take effective action to stop the slaughter. And finally, Bush I failed to take

account of the spiritual damage to Americans' conception of themselves and to what they stood for in the eyes of others. It would have made far more sense for Bush I to intervene in the Balkans than in Somalia. The winner of the Cold War, the world's only superpower, the government whose military crushed Saddam Hussein without breathing hard, somehow found it impossible to halt the murderous downward spiral in the Balkans. The administration should have been able to do more than one thing at a time, that is, manage the endgame of the Cold War, and seek a settlement in the Balkans and the Arab-Israeli conflicts. But it could not act in this way and still follow Baker's highly centralized approach to decision making. There were not enough hours in the day to allow Baker and his handful of aides to accept responsibility for more than one or two problems at a time.

Israel and the Arabs

Unlike its obtuseness about Iraq, the administration displayed considerable finesse in reviving the Middle East peace process, and in outmaneuvering and contributing to the defeat of Israeli Prime Minister Yitzhak Shamir, who opposed all concessions to the Palestinians. Shamir's defeat made possible contacts between Israelis and Palestinians that culminated in the Oslo agreements of 1993. The combination of diplomatic agility and imaginative negotiating proposals is rare at any time, and practically unknown in the Middle East conflict. Although the Bush administration had not started out to bring down the Shamir government, senior State Department officials could not hide their satisfaction when it happened.[25]

Dennis Ross, Baker aide and State Department specialist in the Middle East, recognized that the Madrid and Washington summits were "more about symbolism than practicality," the breaking of a taboo against Arab governments negotiating directly with Israel.[26] It was not a turkey shoot with Baker framing the issues, marshaling concessions on both sides, and finding a mutually acceptable compromise. But the Madrid and Washington conferences broke new ground and undermined Shamir's popular support at home. Even though no immediate breakthroughs occurred among Israel, Syria, and the Palestinians, the Madrid and Washington summits made other important gains. Encouraged by the American victory in Iraq, Jordan reached out to Israel and set in motion a dialogue that would end in a peace treaty two years later. Israel benefited from contact with dozens of nations, and the imaginative idea to hold talks on mundane issues such as the environment and water resources in various capitals around the world helped to take the poison out of the conflict and restore a degree of perspective and normalcy to a scene fraught with nothing but military and adversarial calculations since the early years of the twentieth century. Baker was determined to make good on his promise to Arab and European governments to work for peace after the war with Iraq. He knew that the United States could not sustain its primacy in the Gulf unless it sought and achieved an important measure of progress in resolving the Syrian-Israeli and Israeli-Palestinian conflicts. There had to be a reward for the support of Arab states for drastic military action against Iraq.

The Transition Away from Communism in Europe

The administration's strategy for post-communist economic development in Eastern Europe and the Soviet Union reflected its expectation that a kind of turnkey revolution would occur: hold elections, set up banks and stock exchanges, allow markets to form, and the societies would fix themselves. Some societies survived the U.S.-sponsored shock therapy and prospered, but others faltered, stymied by the legacies of communism. This was one of the most significant failings of Bush I in its dealings with the post-communist states, not only in Eastern Europe and the Soviet Union, but in Yugoslavia as well. Bush, Baker, Scowcroft, and Eagleburger defended their choices by pointing to the absence of support from European governments, particularly over Yugoslavia, and the hostility of the American public and Congress to large international endeavors after the end of the Cold War. But presidential leadership is enormously powerful at home and abroad, as Bush II would demonstrate a decade later in regard to Iraq. Had the president insisted on different policies toward Russia, Eastern Europe, and Bosnia, many people and some governments might have been persuaded. Even if they had not been willing to act during Bush I, the administration's efforts would have eased the way for the Clinton administration to act and saved lives.

At the end of World War II, the United States offered extremely generous aid to all European states, friend and enemy alike. The offer was calculated to put the burden for the division of Europe on the Soviet Union if it chose not to join the Marshall Plan. When Stalin said no, and forced the Eastern European states occupied by the Red Army to refuse, the U.S. government was relieved and made good its pledge, granting nearly $90 billion in aid to Western Europe during the next five years. At the end of the Cold War, the Bush I administration offered aid to the former communist countries, but it was a poor imitation of Marshall Plan assistance. There was little sense in Bush I's 1990 request for small amounts of aid for Eastern Europe—aid that amounted to $2.60 for each citizen of Poland, which was less than 8% of the aid that Germany offered; even South Korea provided more aid to Hungary than the United States.[27]

The problems of a collapsing Soviet Union loomed larger for the future of Europe, and here the failure of leadership is even more glaring. The economic goal that received the most attention was the Treasury Department's effort to oblige Russia to assume responsibility for the debts of the old Soviet Union.[28] Keeping Russia's tens of thousands of nuclear weapons under control preoccupied the president and secretary of state. The administration acted as if post-communist Russia was a normal, functioning society. Adrift from the command economy, its political elite demoralized and sidelined or intent on enriching themselves, Russia was instead at the beginning of a decade of hardship and internal upheaval. The first of the upsets came on August 19, 1991, when Gorbachev was overthrown by a coup d'état. The plotters failed to keep power, and Gorbachev was restored to office, but the already gravely wounded Soviet state lost whatever shred of legitimacy it had retained. It vanished from history four months later when Boris Yeltsin and other politicians from the constituent parts of the Union dismembered it to form the Commonwealth of Independent States. The Bush I administration publicly sided with Gorbachev until the very end. A chicken-and-egg debate stalled action on economic assistance: there would be no money without reform, but it was unlikely that reform could get very far without money.

The coup stirred Secretary Baker into action, and he brought together an international conference in January 1992 to coordinate aid to Russia. The United States granted Russia $645 million in aid for 1992 and set up Project Hope, which delivered nearly $200 million in food and medical supplies by year's end, a good portion of which came from stocks left over after the Gulf War. Stung by criticism from Richard Nixon and candidate Bill Clinton, President Bush announced a $24-billion aid package in early April 1992. The United States pledged about $5 billion, of which $2.5 billion was for debt rescheduling. Most of the money was to come from other G-7 countries. The news of the package helped Russian economic reformers sustain their policies a bit longer, but the donors failed to follow through, partly because the administration had not consulted them in advance.[29] A deep split opened within the administration, with the Treasury Department mindlessly insisting on rigorous reforms before it would support aid. Aid was limited, as well, by widespread popular opposition inside the United States to more foreign burdens and the consensus among the president and his senior advisers that the money would simply be wasted. The chance to help Russia in an important way during the first years of its existence as a post–Cold War state slipped away.

3

Bill Clinton's Brave New World

Foreign policy is domestic policy.

—Bill Clinton[1]

You know, foreign policy issues mark every president's tenure, whether they want it or not. It just happens that way. No American president can avoid it because he's the leader of the free world. They think they can, but they can't.

—Lee H. Hamilton[2]

Bill Clinton won the 1992 election. But it was an odd, misshapen victory. He received a plurality of the votes, some 44.8 million out of 104.6 million, or a little less than 43 percent of the total.[3] George Bush won 38.8 million votes, or 37 percent. The spoiler was the maverick multimillionaire, Ross Perot, whose 19 million votes (19 percent) drew heavily from the Republican base and helped Bill Clinton into the White House. Had Perot's votes gone to Bush in a handful of crucial states, Bush would have won the election. In all but four states, the totals for Bush and Perot were larger than for Clinton.[4] That Clinton was only a plurality president elected during a recession shaped his first four years in office in crucially important ways and cast a shadow over both of his presidential terms.

During the campaign Clinton emphasized domestic issues, especially the economy. The slogan he drummed into his supporters and advisers reflected his focus: "It's the economy, stupid!" Foreign policy was supposed to be Bush's strength, but his success in ending the Cold War and defeating Saddam Hussein turned out to have little carryover with voters. Bush's popularity soared to an 89 percent approval rating after the Gulf War but, under the impact of a faltering economy, fell to a grim 29 percent by July 1992.[5] After he took office, Clinton sent an early signal of the low priority he gave to foreign policy by delegating to Warren Christopher the responsibility for returning congratulatory phone calls from foreign heads of state. He showed little interest in the CIA and rarely saw his first director of central intelligence, James Woolsey. His lack of interest was so obvious that when a deranged man crashed a light plane on the White House grounds, a joke went around CIA headquarters that Woolsey was the pilot and he had been trying to see Clinton. Woolsey was succeeded by John Deutch, then deputy secretary of defense, in 1994. George Tenet followed Deutch in 1996. Tenet managed to survive in office until 2004, despite damaging blunders by the CIA, including the undetected terrorist attacks on September 11, 2001, and mistakes about Saddam Hussein's weapons of mass destruction.

Clinton lacked not only foreign experience, but had never served in Washington at a high policymaking level. He had been a Rhodes Scholar, but had seen his scholarship as a way of advancing his already highly developed domestic political ambitions rather than an opportunity to learn about European politics and foreign policy. Raised in Arkansas, Clinton returned there after law school to teach and run for office, winning election first as attorney general and then as governor. Neither office compared in the slightest with the high-stakes high-wire act of the presidency, an act that plays without a net. No one ever doubted Clinton's intelligence. He listened and talked endlessly, and often translated what he heard and said into effective political initiatives. But his approach to governing reminded many Washington insiders of a bad graduate seminar: anyone who showed up could contribute ideas to what amounted to a meandering bull session. From time to time, Clinton's lack of experience would combine with his over-confidence in his own intellectual superiority to produce a casualness and offhandedness about supremely difficult and risky issues. Sometimes the president and his advisers would delay making a decision, and then take half-measures that combined too little with too late.[6] Early in the first term, political scientist Fred Greenstein detected a pattern: "a no-holds barred style of striving for numerous policy outcomes with little attention to establishing priorities or accommodating political realities and [after criticism or a defeat] a more measured, pragmatic style of focusing on a limited number of goals and attending closely to the politics of selling his program."[7]

Clinton's Team

The men and one woman that Clinton chose to lead his administration's foreign policy team were with one exception less experienced than their counterparts in Bush I. The woman was Madeleine Albright, who was named ambassador to the United Nations. The exception was Warren Christopher, who had served as undersecretary of state in the Carter administration, as well as in Lyndon Johnson's Department of Justice, and had been active in Democratic politics for four decades. Christopher was an unusual choice because no one knew what he thought about foreign policy, or even if he had any independent views at all. His appointment offered the president a number of strengths. Christopher was a man of the center. He had managed to avoid making enemies among the conservative and liberal wings of a party that had bitterly divided during the Vietnam years. By personal inclination and a lifetime spent in the law, Christopher was careful, thorough, and given to persuasion, consensus, and compromise, rather than polarizing boldness. Colin Powell, a carryover from Bush I as chair of the Joint Chiefs of Staff, thought the top Clinton national security group acted not at all like Bush I's "chieftains of U.S. foreign policy" with whom he was used to dealing. At the first meeting of the top national security group, Powell said:

> Tony Lake, as National Security Adviser, sat in the chairman's seat, but did not drive the meeting. Warren Christopher, the Secretary of State, sat on one side of Lake, somewhat passively. . . . Christopher, lawyerlike, simply waited for his client group to decide what position he was to defend. Les Aspin flanked Lake on the other side. He did not try to lead either, and when Aspin did speak, he usually took the discussion onto tangents to skirt the immediate issue.[8]

On the plus side, with Christopher at State, the president could be sure that he would not be upstaged or have to rein in a policy entrepreneur whose international agenda conflicted with his domestic priorities.

> When people told Clinton that Christopher was immensely hard-working, but not necessarily imaginative, and finally quite lawyerlike, a man to be a functionary rather than a leader, that, too, was precisely what the president wanted—a deputy to run State and cause no problems. What did Clinton like most about Christopher? a top administration aide was once asked. "That he did not give off any heat" came the answer.[9]

Someone who gave off "heat"—and was pushed aside because of it—was Richard Holbrooke. Abrasive, hard-driving, brilliant, and experienced, Holbrooke was a natural candidate for a high foreign policy post in Clinton I, but he was denied anything remotely close to what he expected, finally accepting an assignment as ambassador to Germany. Before Clinton left the White House, Holbrooke would find his role as special negotiator of the Dayton Accords, which put an end to the war in Bosnia. He would finish as ambassador to the United Nations, not as high as he had hoped to rise, but a prominent capstone to a distinguished career of public service. Clinton chose Anthony Lake, a contemporary and in a sense competitor of Holbrooke's, as his national security adviser. He did so apparently at the urging of Sandy Berger, a lawyer and Democratic activist, who became Lake's deputy. Berger's advantages were that he got along well with Clinton and was willing to make allowances for his domestic political needs. Berger would succeed Lake as national security adviser at the beginning of Clinton's second term. Lake began his government service as a Foreign Service officer. Singled out early for advancement, he and Holbrooke served in the coveted positions as special assistants to the U.S. ambassador in Vietnam and to the undersecretary of state, Nicholas Katzenbach, in Washington. Lake joined Henry Kissinger's staff in the National Security Council during the first Nixon administration, but resigned after the United States invaded Cambodia in April 1970 to destroy North Vietnamese staging areas. Lake and Holbrooke found important foreign policy positions in the Carter administration, with Lake serving as head of policy planning at the State Department, and Holbrooke as assistant secretary of state for Asia. Lake's service on Clinton's campaign gave him an edge in landing the national security adviser's job.

The post of UN ambassador went to Madeleine Albright. As a woman vying for a top foreign policy (or any other) government post, Albright was a rarity in Washington, and that no doubt helped her win the UN post. Personal wealth from a failed marriage enabled her to move up the social as well as political ladders of Democratic Party politics. Albright paid her dues. She raised money for candidates, held dinner parties for the powerful, and served on the staff of Senator Edmund Muskie and as foreign policy adviser to Michael Dukakis in his losing campaign against Bush. Clinton's top advisers in Washington smirked at her behind her back, but she enjoyed the assignment in New York and managed to stay ahead of her critics. Ultimately, the clash of personalities around Clinton and the allure of choosing a woman to succeed Christopher worked to her advantage, and she became secretary of state for Clinton's second term. Albright had strong opinions but, unlike Henry Kissinger or John Foster Dulles, Dwight Eisenhower's secretary of state, she had not developed an overarching strategy for advancing American interests worldwide before taking office. Albright's hatred for the brutalities that Slobodan Milosevic resorted to in Bosnia led her to take a consistently hard line against him. Putting an end to Milosevic's depredations in Bosnia and Kosovo would turn out to be one of Clinton's toughest foreign policy challenges.

Les Aspin moved from the Congress to the Pentagon, but it was a tragically wrong appointment. Aspin knew the intellectual side of security matters, having specialized in defense and security issues for many years in the Congress. But running the Pentagon requires the ability to wring consensus out of savvy generals and entrenched bureaucrats. Aspin's disorganized intellectual and legislative style could not have been more wrong for the sprawling giant he had been asked to run. He lasted a year, and was forced out by the uproar over the Clinton administration's attempt to allow gays to serve openly in the military and the debacle in Somalia. It was a sad outcome to a fine career. Aspin's deputy, William Perry, succeeded him. An academic who had worked in the high-tech private sector, Perry was widely respected within the Pentagon, and had all the organizational and managerial skills and habits that Aspin lacked. Perry knew how the Pentagon worked. He had been an undersecretary of defense for science and engineering for four years in the Carter administration. Thoughtful, low-key, with a background in defense industry, Perry ended up playing a major role in the administration's attempt to control North Korea's economic implosion and the threat of its nascent nuclear weapons and long-range missile programs.

Clinton and the Post–Cold War Paradigm

During the 1992 campaign, Clinton referred to the speeches that he gave at Georgetown University on December 12, 1991, and at the Foreign Policy Association in New York City on the following April 1, as the best expressions of his foreign policy ideas. As the campaign unfolded, he honed and reordered the ideas in those speeches. By the time he spoke at the World Affairs Council in Los Angeles on August 13, 1992, his foreign policy message focused overwhelmingly on the domestic economy. He took this line of thinking so far that he felt at liberty to describe Bush's lack of attention to the domestic economy as "the administration's most glaring foreign policy failure."[10] In part, this was simply an indication of how much ground that he had gained on his opponent by focusing on economic issues. It was the single most important issue in the minds of voters during a recession. Partisanship aside, Clinton accorded a significance to domestic and international economic issues that was unusual even in a presidential campaign. The salience that he gave them explains much about where he chose to put his emphasis during his two terms as president, and reveals his noninterventionist view of the post–Cold War paradigm.

In the Georgetown speech, Clinton touched all the bases from national security to the environment. An early address by someone asserting his plausibility as a presidential candidate called for no less. Clinton argued that the changes that had taken place since 1989 obliged Americans to respond in creative and imaginative ways that departed from the old Cold War patterns. Three of Clinton's key assumptions reflected an emerging consensus about American foreign policy and were important parts of the post–Cold War paradigm:

- Restore the country's economic strength; it is the key to domestic well-being, international security, and democratic and market reform abroad.
- Take account of the "power of ideas" in the Information Age, especially the spread of democracy and free markets.
- Broaden the definition of national security to include the environment and other global issues.

During the campaign, Clinton outbid the Bush administration in defense cuts: the Bush administration had proposed to cut the defense budget by 21 percent through 1995, Clinton pledged to cut more than one-third by 1997. Arguing from another premise of the post–Cold War paradigm—that democracies do not go to war with each other—Clinton promised to "reinforce the powerful global movement toward democracy."[11] While focusing on the economy, Clinton nonetheless sought to chip away at Bush's foreign policy reputation by challenging his record on human rights, particularly with regard to China and the Balkans. In his speech accepting the nomination, for example, Clinton pledged "an America that will not coddle dictators from Baghdad to Beijing."[12] In areas where he lacked knowledge, such as China, Clinton tended to adopt mainstream views that were prominent among centrist foreign policy experts and liberal members of Congress.[13] Clinton joined them in advocating that renewal of China's mostfavored-nation trading status be made contingent on improvements in human rights, trade practices, and cooperation in blocking nuclear proliferation.[14] Clinton could have advocated lifting an arms embargo imposed by the Bush administration on Bosnia. Milosevic provided the Bosnian Serbs with plenty of weapons, but the poorly armed Bosnian Muslims were unable to defend their isolated communities. Clinton's running mate, Al Gore, was strongly in favor of lifting the embargo, but when the time came to decide, Clinton's inner circle of campaign advisers and the candidate himself backed away. It was too specific, they thought, and might somehow backfire. Instead, the candidate attacked Bush for ignoring human rights and democratic reformers abroad: "Mr. Bush and his secretary of state gave short shrift to the yearnings of those seeking freedom in Slovenia, Croatia, and Bosnia, and ignored warning signs that Slobodan Milosevic was emerging as one of Europe's bloodiest tyrants."[15] The rhetoric on China and the Balkans was politically astute, but it did not add up to a coherent foreign policy. Linking foreign and domestic economic issues and strengthening the hold of the post–Cold War paradigm on his administration's foreign policy, Clinton repeatedly made statements such as "our national security is largely economic," "[o]ur economic strength must become a central defining element of our national security policy," and "[s]o let us no longer define national security in the narrow military terms of the Cold War."[16]

Clinton's campaign speeches retained the mandatory declaration that the United States would act unilaterally if necessary. The formulation he eventually settled on appeared in his speech to the Foreign Policy Association in New York City in April 1992: "together when we can, on our own where we must."[17] This turned out to mean never on our own. Clinton's understanding of the threats facing the country was essentially the same as the previous administration's: disorder in the former Soviet Union, the spread of weapons of mass destruction, regional instability in the Korean peninsula and the Middle East, terrorism, and ethnic conflict. Clinton assigned a higher priority to democratization, the spread of market economies, and global issues. The Pentagon took a distant fourth or even fifth place.[18]

The Clinton administration pulled these themes together in its annual statements on national security strategy required by Congress. Clinton called his a strategy of "engagement and enlargement" of democracy and market economics: engage global issues and important countries such as Russia and China, and enlarge the number of market democracies. The themes struck in Clinton's first national security policy in July 1994 reappeared throughout his two terms and echoed and shaped the post–Cold War paradigm. "The best way to advance America's interests worldwide," Clinton told the Congress, "is to enlarge the community of democracies and free markets throughout the world." The United States must maintain its military strength but Clinton stressed the importance of democracy and market economics: "For America to be strong abroad it must be strong economically at home; at the same time, domestic economic renewal depends on the growth and integration of the global economy." It was a concise description of "interdependence," one of the most important elements of the post–Cold War paradigm. He returned again and again to the peaceful nature of democracies: "Democratic states are less likely to threaten our interests and more likely to cooperate with us to meet security threats and promote sustainable development. Secure nations are more likely to maintain democratic structures and to support free trade." In every statement about national security strategy, Clinton returned to the same themes:

> We believe that our goals of enhancing our security, bolstering our economic prosperity and promoting democracy are mutually supportive. Secure nations are more likely to support free trade and maintain democratic structures. Free market nations with growing economies and strong and open trade ties are more likely to feel secure and to work toward freedom. And democratic states are less likely to threaten our interests and more likely to cooperate with the United States to meet security threats and promote free trade and sustainable development. These goals are supported by ensuring America remains engaged in the world and by enlarging the community of secure, free market and democratic nations.[19]

It was a short step from Clinton's notion that the tide of history was moving the world toward democracy and market economies to Bush II's insistence on regime change.[20] However, Clinton believed that the transforming power of globalization and democratization spared the United States the need for military intervention. The world would take care of itself in a way that would favor the interests of the United States.

Shaped by the post–Cold War paradigm, a number of key geopolitical assumptions accompanied Clinton's determination to spread democracy and market economics:

- The collapse of the Soviet Union frees the United States and its allies from military threats to their survival.
- Security threats to the United States and its allies now come from other sources, such as uncertainty about the future of Russia and China, the spread of weapons of mass destruction, and from "transnational phenomena," such as terrorism, drug trafficking, and environmental degradation.
- The United States must stay in Europe. NATO is the key to this; the alliance must be enlarged and adapted to the new political landscape in Europe.
- The United States is in a position to use its economic leverage on China to bring about major political reforms in that country. There is no inherent conflict between the long-term interests of China and those of the United States.
- No comprehensive settlement is possible for the foreseeable future between Arabs and Israelis. The United States should act as a facilitator and follow an incremental strategy, seeking limited agreements that keep communications open and build trust among the parties.
- The United States should continue to contain Saddam Hussein's Iraq by means of economic sanctions and no-fly zones.
- The United States should continue the containment of North Korea through nuclear deterrence, the South Korea–U.S. military alliance, and a large conventional U.S. military force in South Korea.

Clinton's strategy of engagement and enlargement recognized the need to deter aggressors, and to be prepared "to win two nearly simultaneous major regional conflicts."[21] However, the "nearly simultaneous" wording conceals (as it was intended to) how difficult it had been for the administration to cut the defense budget, coordinate international and domestic political needs, and maintain the ability to fight in the Gulf and Korea at the same time. After he decided to give top priority to reducing the federal budget deficit, Clinton needed even deeper cuts in defense spending than he had promised during the campaign. Les Aspin had believed mistakenly that if he allowed the military services to develop their strategic proposals regardless of cost, it would be possible for him to adjust their requests to the much-reduced funds that were going to be available after the budget was balanced. When they came, the cuts did not go down easily. They embittered senior military officers and exposed the administration to fierce criticism from Republicans and some Democrats in Congress. Only Aspin's resignation and the restoration of several billions for personnel and readiness by his successor, William Perry, brought temporary relief. Ultimately, Clinton had to add $25 billion in additional increases for FY 1996–2000.[22]

Foreshadowing Bush II's "axis of evil," Clinton's national security strategy named North Korea, Iraq, and Iran as likely aggressors capable of endangering neighboring countries and upsetting the regional balance of power.[23] An obligatory reference to the importance of combining military forces and deterrence always accompanied the repeated references to the determining influence of political and economic measures and multilateral cooperation: "Our national security strategy is based on enlarging the community of market democracies while deterring and containing a range of threats to our nation, our allies and our interests."[24] The order of tasks is clear and explains the early attempts to cut the defense budget and avoid foreign intervention. War had not disappeared, but it was highly unlikely. The United States must maintain its military strength, but the real work lay elsewhere: (1) in promoting economic prosperity at home and abroad through such measures as the North American Free Trade Association and the Asia-Pacific Economic Cooperation; (2) in dealing with the spread of weapons of mass destruction, the environment, and population increase; and (3) in promoting democracy in China and the states of the former Soviet Union. Unilateralism was explicitly rejected and multilateralism preferred:

> No matter how powerful we are as a nation, we cannot secure these basic goals unilaterally. Whether the problem is nuclear proliferation, regional instability, the reversal of reform in the former Soviet empire, or unfair trade practices, the threats and challenges we face demand cooperative, multinational solutions. Therefore, the only responsible U.S. strategy is one that seeks to ensure U.S. influence over and participation in collective decisionmaking in a wide and growing range of circumstances.[25]

Terrorism and the threat that terrorists will acquire weapons of mass destruction are mentioned, but they received only a passing reference and a call for improved intelligence cooperation at home and abroad, something that never occurred as the 9/11 attacks revealed.

When and how to deploy American military forces abroad received special treatment. According to Clinton's strategy American troops would go into action only in response to "key dangers," those posed by weapons of mass destruction, regional aggression, and threats to the stability of states.[26] The strategy set strict limits on unilateral military action. If the "survival, security and vitality of our national entity" were at stake, the United States would use decisive force, unilaterally if necessary. But this extreme case was not likely to occur. In every other case—bound to be the overwhelming majority—the United States "as much as possible" would seek the cooperation of its allies or "relevant multilateral institutions."[27] In addition, a number of questions would have to be answered before the United States sends troops into battle:

> Have we considered nonmilitary means that offer a reasonable chance of success? What types of U.S. military capabilities should be brought to bear, and is the use of military force carefully matched to our political objectives? Do we have reasonable assurance of support from the American people and their elected representatives? Do we have timelines and milestones that will reveal the extent of success or failure, and, in either case, do we have an exit strategy? . . . [O]ur engagement must meet reasonable cost and feasibility thresholds. We will be more inclined to act where there is reason to believe that our action will bring lasting improvement. On the other hand, our involvement will be more circumscribed when other regional or multilateral actors are better positioned to act than we are. Even in these cases, however, the United States will be actively engaged at the diplomatic level.[28]

The questions recall the virtual prohibitions of armed intervention developed by Caspar Weinberger and Colin Powell, and they make clear beyond any doubt that the Clinton administration intended to do everything possible to avoid military intervention.[29] The Clinton strategy further hedged peacekeeping operations in accord with the Presidential Decision Directive, "U.S. Policy on Reforming Multilateral Peace Operations," adopted after the deaths of American soldiers in Somalia. To Weinberger's and Powell's stringent conditions, it added the requirement to make "an assessment of the threat to international peace and security, a determination that the peace operation serves U.S. interests as well as an assurance of an international community of interests for dealing with that threat on a multilateral basis."[30] Tragically, these conditions helped block U.S. intervention against genocide in Rwanda.

Like the second President Bush, Clinton was overwhelmingly committed to democratization, or "regime change," in Bush II terms. However, Clinton focused on democratization, not in the Arab and Muslim world, but in the states of the former Soviet Union, the newly democratic societies of Eastern Europe, and implicitly but unmistakably, China: "Thus, we must target our effort to assist states that affect our strategic interests, such as those with large economies, critical locations, nuclear weapons, or the potential to generate refugee flows into our own nation or into key friends and allies. We must focus our efforts where we can have the most leverage. And our efforts must be demand-driven—they must focus on nations whose people are pushing for reform or have already secured it."[31] Clinton saw Russia as "a key state in this regard," along with Ukraine and the other states of Eastern and Central Europe. Although Clinton could not know who his successor would be or whether he would be reelected in 1996, his remarks a year after the release of his first national security strategy show the overlap between his views of the post–Cold War paradigm and those of George W. Bush. Their speeches about democratization are virtually impossible to tell apart. The words that Clinton spoke at Freedom House in October 1995 could have been inserted into George W. Bush's second inaugural address in January 2005, and no one would have noticed the difference:

> Throughout what we now call the American century, Republicans and Democrats disagreed on specific policies, often heatedly from time to time, but we have always agreed on the need for American leadership in the cause of democracy, freedom, security, and prosperity. . . . And let me say one other thing. We have tried to make it a constant refrain that while we seek to engage all countries on terms of goodwill, we must continue to stand up for the values that we believe make life worth living. . . . We must continue to stand up for the proposition that all people, without regard to their nationality, their race, their ethnic group, their religion, or their gender, should have a chance to make the most of their own lives, to taste both freedom and opportunity.

Clinton's remarks at Freedom House also revealed some of the areas of disagreement with his successor:

> Unilateralism in the world that we live in is not a viable option. When our vital interests are at stake, of course, we might have to act alone. But we need the wisdom to work with the United Nations and to pay our bills. We need the flexibility to build coalitions that spread the risk and responsibility and the cost of leadership, as President Bush did in Desert Storm and we did in Haiti. If the past 50 years have taught us anything, it is that the United States has a unique responsibility and a unique ability to be a force for peace and progress around the world, while building coalitions of people that can work together in genuine partnership.[32]

The administration took credit for the Partnership for Peace, a consultative mechanism designed to bring Russia and other former communist states into closer cooperation with NATO. "Enlargement" of democracy was also to be pursued in Asia. The criteria for deciding which states should be helped along the path to democracy were broad and inclusive. All such countries are called "emerging democracies." "This is not a democratic crusade," much as George W. Bush would say after 9/11, "it is a pragmatic commitment to see freedom take hold where that will help us most." And, in the same section: "Our long-term goal is a world in which each of the major powers is democratic, with many other nations joining the community of market democracies as well."[33]

In other words, Clinton and Bush II were Wilsonians. They shared a belief in American exceptionalism, and were convinced that the spread of democracy around the world was a vital security interest of the United States and the key to world peace. There were some important differences, but they were differences over means not ends. Clinton's preferred means were clearly nonmilitary: trade, economic development, the sharing of democratic experience, and financial, legal, and other technical assistance. Just as Bush II would a decade later, and in almost identical language, the Clinton strategy presented democratic values as universal: "[D]emocracy and human rights are not occidental yearnings; they are universal yearnings and universal norms."[34] It is simply true, and not imperialism or ethnocentrism, Clinton argued, to observe that Asians aspire to democracy. To say otherwise, he said, is an insult to the spirit and hopes of those who seek democracy. In other words, the Clinton strategy moved decisively away from the

Bush I formulation that the United States can be secure in a world that is not mostly totalitarian toward the idea that the United States can be secure only if the whole world is democratic. It was a vision of the world and America's place in it that would be shared by George W. Bush.

Despite the emphasis on spreading democracy and market economics, Clinton's actions resembled those of Bush I, notably his extreme caution in using military force and his desire to reduce defense spending. The reasons for Clinton's caution came from his principles—he was a Wilsonian noninterventionist—and his belief that globalization and democratization would solve the country's security problems and lift its economy. Clinton also tried to avoid going to war because of the priority he gave to the domestic economy, as well as his domestic political vulnerability, first as a plurality president and then as a politician wounded by scandal. The first attack on the World Trade Center in New York City occurred in 1993, but it failed to bring down the buildings or cause heavy loss of life. Like Bush II before 9/11, Clinton failed to break decisively with the prevailing notion that terrorists were dangerous but incompetent, required state sponsors, and posed the greatest threat to U.S. interests overseas.[35]

Russia

The Clinton administration believed that the United States had to help Russia complete the transition from communism to market democracy. The president and his advisers thought it would be as difficult as it was important, but they hoped and believed that they and their Russian counterparts would be able to cooperate. Clinton was prepared to invest huge amounts of his time and prestige, but very little money. It sometimes seemed as if Clinton were trading Boris Yeltsin photo opportunities and status symbols, such as Russian "association" with the prestigious Group of Seven heads of industrial democracies, in exchange for Russian concessions on NATO enlargement and the use of force against Serbia. Annoyed, sometimes humiliated and resentful, Russian leaders knew it would be pointless to oppose these measures. They could do nothing effective to stop the United States, and trying would play into the hands of their internal enemies. In the end, it proved even more difficult and complicated than Clinton imagined. Events seemed to conspire against U.S.-Russian cooperation. Many in the now-discredited Soviet elite, as well as a growing number of Russian nationalists, reacted angrily to their country's meteoric fall from global power. These former communists and nationalists, Red-Brown allies, smoldered over what they regarded as the arrogant and dictatorial behavior of the United States toward Russia.[36] The social and especially economic hardships that accompanied the transition away from a state-centered economy and polity gave them a ready audience among the Russian people, and strong representation in the Russian parliament, or Duma. They exploited their legislative prominence, disrupted cooperation with the United States, and sometimes delayed or defeated Russian President Boris Yeltsin's reforms. The reforms and U.S.-Russian relations were nearly upended by Russia's bankruptcy in 1998 and by the lack of central control over the Russian military-industrial complex, whose members could not resist enriching themselves by selling sensitive technologies to Iran. To make matters worse, Russia-U.S. relations became entangled with the Israeli lobby over Russia's sale of missiles to Iran, with Israeli Prime Minister Benjamin Netanyahu touring Capitol Hill to promote sanctions against Russia. The administration's most important assumptions regarding Russia were these:

- The safe disposition of nuclear weapons trumps all other concerns and must command the lion's share of American aid throughout the 1990s and beyond.[37]
- A successfully reformed and stabilized Russian market economy will create wealth, and wealth will bring democracy and a civil society; social welfare, democracy, and institutional reform have a lower priority than economic stabilization and financial reform.
- Speed is of the essence; circumstances favorable to reform may disappear.
- There can be no reform without reformers; the United States has no choice but to support the individuals in the Russian government that it judges most likely to achieve the needed reforms. In practice, this meant tying the administration to Boris Yeltsin.

The weakness and in many instances absence of an array of legal and regulatory institutions in Russia made the U.S.-Russian relationship almost entirely dependent on personalities: Presidents Clinton and Yeltsin; Vice President Gore and Prime Minister Chernomyrdin; and advisers Strobe Talbott and Sandy Berger, and Georgi Mamedev and Andrei Kokoshkin. While this informality often allowed the two sides to act quickly, it was always vulnerable to the political fortunes of the principals, which worsened during the 1990s, and took U.S.-Russian relations along with them. As Yeltsin juggled the Russian political kaleidoscope throughout the 1990s, what was simple early in the decade with Chernomyrdin and his economics adviser Yegor Gaidar grew awkward and slow when Yevgeny Primakov became foreign minister and, later, prime minister, and was never really tried with Primakov's successor as foreign minister, Igor Ivanov.[38]

It was always easier for Clinton to win Yeltsin's cooperation on foreign and security matters than it was for him to help the Russians reform their country and to improve the lives of ordinary Russians. As Strobe Talbott put it, "It was much more difficult to get the Russians to adopt the legal and regulatory structures necessary to attract and retain investment than it was to get Russia to stop selling rocket engine parts to India or even to cooperate with an expanding NATO. In the final analysis, Russia could not prevent Poland from joining NATO. Conversely, however, the U.S. didn't have much influence over whether the Duma passed a new property or tax law."[39]

China

During the 2000 presidential campaign, Clinton pledged that he would require the Chinese government to meet tests of human rights and democratization before China could be granted most-favored-nation trading status. Barely six months after the inauguration, this approach was dead. It was replaced by what was called in Clinton White House terminology a "broader engagement" with China. Despite all the "spin" that his helpers could put on what was an embarrassing defeat, Clinton could do nothing but eat his old words as he described the new approach: "That policy is best reflected in our decision to de-link China's Most Favored Nation status from its record on human rights."[40] To keep China from becoming a security threat in East Asia, the administration would work to bring it into regional security "mechanisms" and to obtain greater cooperation in preventing the spread of weapons of mass destruction.

Clinton's initial attempt to force the Chinese government to behave decently and democratically depended on two assumptions: that there were no fundamental differences between the two countries and that the United States could use its great economic strength to force China to improve its human rights record. When America pushed, China would give in out of self-interest. Both assumptions were wrong. Because the Soviet Union had collapsed, China enjoyed much greater freedom of action and no longer needed to rely on the United States for protection. One of the clearest signs of China's new latitude in foreign policy was the willingness of Chinese leaders to raise the Taiwan issue much more assertively than they would have during the Cold War. They also knew that American corporations were eager not to miss the chance to make money in China.[41] Adding to the administration's difficulties, Taiwan's president, Lee Teng-hui, began to play politics with Clinton's bitterly partisan Republican opposition. This volatile mix exploded two years later in a crisis when China fired ballistic missiles into the waters around Taiwan to demonstrate its determination to prevent Taiwanese independence. In response, the Clinton administration sent warships into the area as a way of signaling its determination to prevent the use of force against Taiwan.[42] Another setback followed when an American cruise missile struck the Chinese embassy in Belgrade during the Kosovo War. The combination of distrust over Taiwan and outrage over what was widely regarded in China as an intentional act of war sent U.S.-China relations reeling. Clinton left office with little more than a chilly correctness existing between the two governments.[43]

Israel and the Palestinians

Although Clinton supported the use of economic pressure to democratize China during the campaign, he criticized its use against Israel, particularly Bush I's decision to tie approval of a $10-billion loan guarantee to a halt in new settlements in the occupied territories. Happily for the incoming Clinton administration, Yitzhak Rabin's victory the previous June and the Bush administration's desire to strengthen the new Israeli prime minister with additional funding had removed that impediment before Clinton took office. Secretary Christopher asked Baker's adviser Dennis Ross to stay on and oversee the administration's Middle East policy. Ross and other political appointees, including Martin Indyk, in charge of Middle East affairs at the National Security Council, favored an incremental approach to peacemaking that essentially left it to Rabin to decide the timing and scope of the administration's initiatives toward Syria and the Palestinians.[44] The low-profile role of facilitator and partner to Israel pleased Clinton. It would keep the Middle East from interfering with his efforts to stimulate the domestic economy and by avoiding pressure on Israel would minimize political costs in the American Jewish community. At the end of his second term after the peace process had collapsed in blood and recrimination, Clinton would spell out the fundamental assumptions behind his approach:

> When the Oslo Agreement was drafted, these things [return of refugees, Jerusalem, borders] were put down as final status issues because the people that drafted them knew it would be hard. And they took a gamble. And their gamble was that if the Israelis and the Palestinians worked together over a seven-year period and they began to share security cooperation, for example, they began to—we had some land transfers and we saw how they would work in a different geographical way, and if they kept making other specific agreements, that by the time we got to the end of the road, there would be enough knowledge and trust and understanding of each other's positions that these huge, epochal issues could be resolved.[45]

The Madrid peace process sparked a number of negotiations on security and territorial issues with Syria, Jordan, Lebanon, and the Palestinians, and about such matters as the region's environment and economic cooperation. However, by the end of the first Bush administration, the Palestinian-Israeli talks appeared to be going nowhere and the multilateral discussions on regional and other issues had gradually died out without achieving anything lasting. Israel and the Clinton administration then began an odd dance. Working together they approached both Syria and the Palestinians. Secretary Christopher went to Syria some two dozen times in four years. The Israeli government sent clear signals to President Hafez Assad of Syria of a willingness to talk and held numerous meetings with the Palestinians. But whenever Assad signaled the slightest interest in talking about a settlement, the Americans and Israelis put the Palestinians on hold to concentrate on Syria. This odd way of proceeding derived from a widely shared view among Israeli strategists that Syria—not the Syria of today, but the Syria of a nightmarish future ruled by Islamic extremists and armed with nuclear weapons—posed an "existential" threat to Israel, while the Palestinians did not. Inevitably, or so it came to seem, the Israeli and American governments would be disappointed, and then try to pick up where they had left off with the Palestinians, who reacted as might be imagined. In August 1993, for example, the Israeli government decided that conditions demanded by Assad would not permit them to enter negotiations on the basis of an exchange of territory for security guarantees on the Golan Heights. Rabin chose instead to focus exclusively on reaching agreement with the Palestinians. Despite Rabin's disappointment with Syria, when Barak became prime minister, he too, put first priority on a peace agreement with Syria.

After his election, Rabin gave official approval for Israel and the Palestinians to negotiate in secret with the help of the Norwegian government. The result was stunning. On September 9 and 13, 1993, Israel and the PLO exchanged letters of recognition and committed themselves to a declaration of principles on interim self-government for the Palestinians.[46] In recognizing Israel, the PLO committed itself to peace and the peace process, renounced the use of terrorism, accepted responsibility for the actions of all parties associated with the PLO, and declared invalid and pledged to repeal all portions of the Palestinian Covenant that denied Israel's right to exist. In return, Prime Minister Rabin recognized the PLO "as the representative of the Palestinian people," and agreed to enter negotiations "within the Middle East peace process."

The wording of the various documents was exquisitely nuanced and reflected in every possible way the incremental, gradual approach to negotiations and a final peace agreement preferred by Rabin and the Clinton administration. For example, the text of the Israeli-Palestinian agreement failed to acknowledge Palestinian sovereignty or the right of the Palestinians to an independent state, but, instead, established "a Palestinian Interim Self-Government Authority (the 'Council'), for the Palestinian people in the West bank and the Gaza Strip, for a transitional period not exceeding five years, leading to a permanent settlement based on Security Council Resolutions 242 and 338." In other words, the Oslo accords were not a peace settlement but an "agreed framework" like the American-brokered Camp David arrangements between Israel and Egypt fifteen years earlier— meaning a process and some guidelines—within which a peace treaty and Palestinian independence might eventually be worked out. The agreement allowed the immediate return of the PLO to Gaza and Jericho. It called for Palestinians to elect a legislative council and to create a police force. Negotiations for a peace settlement ("final status") were to begin within five years. Israel would withdraw its military from Gaza and Jericho.[47] Subsequent agreements concluded within the Oslo framework divided the West Bank and Gaza into zones of Palestinian, Israeli, and mixed control, and called for the gradual transfer of responsibility from Israel to the Palestinian Authority and the continued withdrawal of Israeli military forces.[48]

Despite his willingness to negotiate with the PLO, Rabin remained ambivalent about the future until he died. His refusal to allow any limits on Jewish settlement in the occupied territories to be put into the accords revealed how tightly domestic politics bound his premiership but also his own uncertainty about the future and, perhaps, his hopes that the Palestinians might still one day agree to a merger with Jordan. It was a damaging omission, for during the next decade tens of thousands of Israelis moved into the West Bank and predominately Arab areas in Jerusalem. The burgeoning settlements were a constant reminder to the Palestinians of the futility of negotiating with Israel. If Israel was serious about the creation of a Palestinian state in the West Bank why would it allow so many Jews to settle there? Rabin's assassination and the defeat of Labor candidate Shimon Peres by the Likud Party's Benjamin Netanyahu nearly sank the accords. By strong pressure and direct presidential engagement during negotiations at Wye Plantation outside Washington, the administration managed to move Netanyahu slightly in the direction foreseen in the Oslo agreements. Once back in Israel, Netanyahu seized on a terrorist incident and stopped all progress.

The election of another Laborite former general, Yehud Barak, as prime minister in 1999, revived hopes for peace between Israel and the Palestinians. But Barak put his government together excruciatingly slowly and turned first to Syria. When an agreement with Hafez Assad failed to materialize, Barak turned to the Palestinians. The date for the beginning of final peace negotiations had come and gone, as had many of the Oslo stages for the transfer of control over territory in the West Bank and withdrawal of Israeli forces. Barak inexplicably decided not to resume the schedule of transfers, prisoner releases, and troop withdrawals, which might have reassured the Palestinians. Instead, he insisted that the two sides work out an agreement on the principles of a final peace settlement before any further progress could be made.

The Clinton administration welcomed Barak's election and stepped up its efforts to bring the two parties to the bargaining table. Against Arafat's wishes, Clinton convened a two-week summit at Camp David in July 1999. To overcome Arafat's reluctance, Clinton pledged not to blame him if the talks failed. The administration put Barak's needs and proposals at the center of the talks as it had done for Rabin. It surrendered the prerogative of setting parameters for the negotiations and agreed that Clinton would try to "sell" Barak's ideas to Arafat. Adding to the odd character of the talks, the United States made no written proposals at Camp David or afterward. No single agreed working document was prepared that would have, for example, recorded areas of agreement and disagreement between the Israeli and Palestinian positions and allowed an orderly, systematic attempt to narrow the differences. The administration imposed no penalties on either side for actions that harmed the talks or the possibility of peace, and it offered few rewards for compliance. In other words, the administration was conducting its mediation without carrots or sticks, except for the ultimate gains to the two sides that would result from making peace.

The problems that flowed from surrendering such important means of influencing the talks were compounded by three other developments. Barak acted in what can only be described as a bizarre manner, staying in his quarters for long periods, refusing to negotiate directly with Arafat, and threatening to leave the talks. It is hard to imagine a combination of Israeli presumption and American mistakes more likely to shake the Palestinians' confidence in what they were being offered. In addition, neither the Palestinians nor the Israelis had prepared their peoples for the sacrifices that they would have to make to reach a final settlement. For many Israelis, it meant the end of a cherished dream of a Greater Israel. For Palestinians, it meant taking less than the 1967 boundaries and giving up forever the dream of returning to pre-1948 Palestine. The most generous interpretation of the failure to prepare their peoples for peace is that Palestinian and Israeli leaders hoped to confront their societies with a fait accompli that could not be renegotiated and would be impossible to refuse. Last, the Palestinians refused to accept what were truly unprecedented concessions—the potential return of all of Gaza and more than 90 percent of the West Bank—largely because they were offered in the form of another "agreed framework," a continuation of negotiations without a final settlement. The Palestinians had been living under an agreed framework for the past six years. During that time very few of its most important provisions—such as the expansion of Palestinian control or Israeli troop withdrawals had been carried out—and tens of thousands of Jews had moved into West Bank settlements. It was impossible for the Palestinians to accept another incremental process wrapped in another agreed framework. The administration tried frantically to keep the talks alive, and the president finally issued an American proposal— orally to Palestinian and Israeli negotiators in Washington—in December 2000. At the end of his remarks, Clinton described the settlement that he was proposing:

It gives the Palestinian people the ability to determine the future on their own land, a sovereign and viable state recognized by the international community, Al-Qods as its capital, sovereignty over the Haram, and new lives for the refugees.

It gives the people of Israel a genuine end to the conflict, real security, the preservation of sacred religious ties, the incorporation of 80% of the settlers into Israel, and the largest Jewish Jerusalem in history recognized by all as its capital.[49]

Clinton's final parameters assigned 94 to 96 percent of the land in the West Bank to the Palestinians, and called for a 1- to 3-percent transfer of land from Israel to Palestine to make up the difference. The land occupied by approximately 80 percent of the settlers—essentially those settlements clustered along the "green line" or 1967 border—would be annexed to Israel. Palestinian refugees would be given a choice of destinations, that is, to stay where they were or go to the new Palestinian state or a third country. A very small number could be allowed to return to Israel. An international fund for compensation of the refugees would be established. Security would be provided by an international force that could be withdrawn only by mutual consent. Israel would withdraw most of its military within three years and keep "a small Israeli presence" in the Jordan Valley in fixed bases for another three years. Israel would man three early warning stations for at least ten years; changes would require mutual agreement. Arrangements for "emergency developments" and maps of the areas where there would be access routes would have to be agreed to by both parties. In Jerusalem what is Jewish would be Israeli and what is Arab would be Palestinian, including the Old City. Clinton proposed that the parties choose between two methods of control over the Haram al-Sharif/Temple Mount: the Palestinians would have sovereignty over the Haram and Israel sovereignty over the Western Wall and other adjacent sacred areas in the heart of old Jerusalem with an agreement that there would be no excavation of any kind; or the two would share control over excavation.[50] When he had outlined the terms, Clinton told his audience: "This is the best I can do. Brief your leaders and tell me if they are prepared to come for discussions based on these ideas. If so, I would meet them next week separately. If not, I have taken this as far as I can."[51] Both sides accepted with conditions, but in Clinton's and Ross's judgment, Arafat's conditions amounted to rejection. Clinton, Barak, and Ross reacted angrily and held Arafat responsible for the failure, despite Clinton's promise not to blame him. Time had run out. Ariel Sharon's visit to the Temple Mount in September 2000 ignited a new intifada, and Barak lost to Sharon in elections held in February 2001. It was a bloody and tragic end to a decade of hope.

Iraq

Iraq was never a primary concern during either Clinton term. It always ranked behind assisting Russia's transition away from communism, engaging with China, expanding NATO, making peace between Israel and the Palestinians, and coping with North Korea's nuclear and missile programs. Iraq commanded fewer headlines and the expenditure of far less military and diplomatic capital than Bosnia or Kosovo. Even with the aircraft and support units needed to enforce the no-fly zones, American deployments in the Gulf region remained around 20,000 troops and cost several billion dollars annually. Throughout the Clinton years, the Gulf was a zone where the U.S. military could accomplish its mission and continue to economize on forces.

Saddam Hussein had a nasty way of distracting the administration from the larger issues. More than once Clinton and his advisers found themselves mired in the intricacies of containing and deterring an unscrupulous, brutal regime. During Clinton's first term, Saddam Hussein attempted to assassinate George Bush Sr. and threatened to invade Kuwait. Clinton responded to the assassination attempt with a heavy cruise missile attack, targeting Iraqi leaders and intelligence agencies. When Saddam appeared to be threatening another attack against Kuwait and defied UN demands for weapons inspections, Clinton quickly mobilized division-sized ground forces backed by heavy air and naval support. Saddam backed off, and the administration let the two crises pass without going to war. During Clinton's second term, the Iraqi leader joined with Russia and France in a concerted effort to end economic sanctions without giving up weapons of mass destruction, and in 1998 made their work so unpleasant and dangerous that the UN weapon inspectors withdrew. Although he had gotten rid of the inspectors and, as documents discovered after his downfall revealed, he had illegally extracted billions of dollars from the oil-for-food process, Saddam failed to end the sanctions, which prevented him from rearming and threatening his neighbors.

As each of the crises revealed, the Clinton administration accepted the status quo and the policy of "dual containment" in the Gulf. Iraq and Iran were to be isolated, deterred, and subjected to severe economic sanctions. Everything about the administration's handling of the clashes with Iraq over eight years showed how tenaciously Clinton and his senior advisers clung to this approach. Even when Congress passed a law declaring regime change in Iraq to be the policy of the United States, the Clinton administration sought in every possible way to keep Iraq from interfering with its agenda and the hierarchy of issues that it had established under the post–Cold War paradigm. Iraq's low priority meant that the United States responded to Saddam's increasingly bold attempts to end the sanctions, and as was thought at the time keep his weapons of mass destruction, with *ad hoc* measures cobbled together at the last minute and dedicated to avoiding war and maintaining deterrence and economic sanctions. An early signal of widespread resistance to American policy appeared when the sanctions excited heavy criticism of the United States from other countries. At home, Clinton's rightwing Republican opposition in and out of the Congress continued their denunciations of the administration for failing to get rid of Saddam Hussein.

The Clinton Administration and Small States

In diplomatic and military affairs, a government's manner of dealing with small states often reveals its clumsiness and vulnerabilities. Big countries and important issues command the most time and resources. This is nowhere better illustrated than in the way the Clinton administration dealt with Bosnia, Kosovo, Somalia, Haiti, Rwanda, and North Korea. All fell well below the geopolitical threshold for sustained top-level attention that applied to the future of postcommunist Russia and China, or the domestically and internationally explosive Israeli-Palestinian conflict.

Bosnia

Anthony Lake told the president at the outset that the administration would have to resolve the Bosnia crisis before it could do anything else in foreign policy. The crisis in Bosnia threatened to damage and even destroy NATO, the most important means through which the United States exercised influence in Europe. Preserving the alliance, and expanding and adapting it to conditions in post–Cold War Europe were major goals of the Clinton administration, as of the Bush administration before it. Intervening in Bosnia meant war against the Serbs in one form or another, something that the West Europeans and the Clinton administration preferred not to think about let alone undertake. Not intervening left the Western governments on the sidelines as impotent witnesses to mass murder. It seemed a classic lose-lose situation.

In Bosnia, a gap opened between the horrors diplomats knew were happening and what their superiors would allow them to do and say. The Bush I administration's policymakers had hoped the problem would go away. James Baker quipped: "We don't have a dog in this fight." But Baker and other senior advisers underestimated the killing. "I knew it was going to be violent," Baker's successor as secretary of state, Larry Eagleburger, told dissident Foreign Service officers in November 1992. "I just didn't know it would be this bad."[52] It was his responsibility to know, not least because of his prior service in the country. Bush I also worried that if Yugoslavia fell apart in a bloodbath, the "disease" would spread to Russia. American generals opposed armed intervention and repeatedly asked questions designed to heighten fears of another Vietnam, a "quagmire." In his memoirs, Colin Powell, then chairman of the Joint Chiefs of Staff, says he exploded when a *New York Times* editorial urged the Bush administration at least to "slow the slaughter" in Bosnia, and another accused the administration of refusing to use America's superb armed forces to save lives. In an angry opinion piece based on an even angrier response that he wrote but never sent, Powell said:

> Whenever the military had a clear set of objectives, I pointed out—as in Panama, the Philippine coup, and Desert Storm—the result had been a success. When the nation's policy was murky or nonexistent—the Bay of Pigs, Vietnam, creating a Marine "presence" in Lebanon—the result had been disaster. . . . So you bet I get nervous when so-called experts suggest that all we need is a little surgical bombing or a limited attack. . . . When the desired result isn't obtained, a new set of experts then comes forward with talk of a little escalation. History has not been kind to this approach.[53]

Powell was convinced that the United States had no business fighting in the Balkans in a conflict that he believed to be fueled by "ancient ethnic hatreds."[54] Many who knew something about Yugoslavia disagreed. "Those who argue that 'ancient Balkan hostilities' account for the violence that overtook and destroyed Yugoslavia ignore the power of television in the service of officially provoked racism," wrote Warren Zimmermann, the last U.S. ambassador to a united Yugoslavia. "Yugoslavia may have a violent history, but it isn't unique. What we witnessed was violence-provoking nationalism from the top down, inculcated primarily through the medium of television."[55]

The opposition of the military and the miscalculations of Bush, Baker, Eagleburger, Scowcroft, and Powell, meant that when the first Bush administration expired, an arms embargo was in place against the Bosnian Muslims, and no American or European military action had been taken to stop the slaughter. "So the Clinton people, taking over, found themselves trapped in a self-defeating, hopelessly incomplete policy put in play by the Europeans and the Bush administration, and by their own reluctance to use force. The tangle apparently offered no way out."[56] When Clinton and his team rejected a plan developed by former secretary of state Cyrus Vance and former British foreign minister David Owen to partition Bosnia on the ground that it rewarded Serbian aggression, the country pitched over into genocide. The final settlement three years later differed hardly at all from the terms of Vance and Owen, but more than 200,000 people had been killed in the interim.

European governments shared responsibility for the slaughter. About the British government in late January 1993, the time of Clinton's inauguration, Owen said: "[T]here was no support in the UK government for any more military intervention than the humanitarian support which was currently being undertaken by the UN Protection Force." Regarding the rest of Europe, Owen said:

Over the next few months with other governments I used to try to argue the case for imposing a settlement, but it never won support. All countries preferred to shield themselves behind the ideal of a negotiated settlement agreed to by all the parties, failing in that posture to acknowledge that this gave a veto power to any one of them, which of course they exercised, not just the Bosnian Serbs but also the Bosnian Muslims.[57]

In Washington, European opposition to American air strikes sounded hollow, an attempt to embarrass the administration into putting large numbers of American troops on the ground in Bosnia, something they were unwilling to do themselves. While charges and countercharges volleyed back and forth among Washington, Paris, London, and Moscow, the ethnic cleansing and killing continued. A combination of developments finally brought the slaughter to an end. The Serbs split, the Americans brought the Bosnian Muslims and Croats together in a military and political federation that held and could fight, and the humiliation of European peacekeepers and atrocities against the innocent finally became too much for European and American leaders to stomach.

Kosovo

In many ways, the tragedy of Kosovo was a totally unnecessary replay of what happened in Bosnia. Just as in Bosnia, neither Balkan party was particularly attractive. Kosovar Albanian militants used force to provoke the Serbs, hoping to cause excessive Serb reprisals that would bring in the West. The Serbs obliged. They killed Kosovars, destroyed their homes, and created hundreds of thousands of refugees. As they had over Bosnia, Western governments hesitated. The White House was slow to act in part because the Monica Lewinsky scandal became public just as violence in Kosovo erupted. It led to Bill Clinton's impeachment by the House of Representatives and a vote in the Senate on whether to remove Clinton from office. A deep split also opened between the State and Defense Departments. Secretary Albright was fervently anti-Milosevic. Most senior generals opposed intervention as they had under Bush I, and Secretary of Defense William Cohen agreed with them. The American general commanding NATO and American forces in Europe, Wesley Clark, sided with Albright. Clark had gotten to know Milosevic while working with Holbrooke on Bosnia. He was convinced that force would be needed to stop Milosevic, but that limited force applied early would do the job. Disagreeing, his military superiors and Secretary Cohen grew to distrust and dislike Clark. Despite his management of the victory in Kosovo, they punished him cruelly at the end of the war by allowing his tenure in Europe to run out and denying him the automatic promotion that usually follows the highest military command in Europe.

By August 1998, 200,000 people had fled Kosovo to neighboring countries. The administration and other Western governments feared that Greece and Turkey might intervene on opposite sides, drastically escalating the conflict and mangling NATO. Holbrooke was brought back into the administration to negotiate with Milosevic but nothing stuck. Finally, the United States moved B-52 bombers to England and threatened to use them unless Milosevic stopped the killings and expulsions. NATO granted General Clark an unprecedented "activation order" to bomb Serbia unless Milosevic stopped the killings and expulsions. Facing this threat and because winter was coming, and no doubt to allow differences to fester within NATO and between NATO and Russia, Milosevic cut a deal with Holbrooke in October

1998. Its provisions obliged Milosevic to reduce Serb forces in Kosovo to pre-conflict levels and allow 2,000 unarmed monitors from the Organization of Security and Cooperation in Europe to move freely in Kosovo. Milosevic also pledged to allow NATO reconnaissance flights over Kosovo, the creation of a new police force, the holding of elections within nine months, the return of all refugees, full cooperation with the Hague war crimes tribunal, and negotiations on a political settlement.[58] It soon became apparent that he had no intention of honoring the agreement.

Milosevic's stalling might have worked, but a Serb massacre in mid-January at Racak, a small town in Kosovo, provoked the Western powers in much the same way as the mass murder at Srebrenica had in Bosnia in July 1995. Determined to move beyond what was in effect a very imperfect truce, Albright convened a conference of Serbs and Albanians in Rambouillet, France, on February 6, 1999. A week later, the Republican-dominated Senate failed to convict Clinton, freeing him to go to war in Kosovo. Meanwhile, the Serbs trivialized the talks at Rambouillet, and the Albanians almost backed out. Neither side liked the Rambouillet framework, which offered substantial autonomy to the Albanians within a Kosovo that would remain part of Serbia. Under the terms of the Rambouillet accord, NATO would put a force of 28,000 troops including 4,000 Americans into Kosovo to verify and enforce the agreement."[59]

It sounded too good to be true, and it was. Even to convene the Rambouillet meeting, NATO had been obliged to go right up to the threshold of bombing Serbia.[60] Counting the B-52s and Stealth F-117 fighters that the United States sent to England and Italy, NATO disposed of 325 aircraft, including 150 from the United States. The Albanians signed only under severe American pressure. The Serbs never took the Rambouillet talks seriously and refused to allow a NATO force to enter Kosovo. In response, NATO governments agreed to begin bombing unless the Serbs complied by late March. This time there was no UN Security Council resolution authorizing the use of force because of the certainty of a Russian veto. Holbrooke made a final visit to Belgrade before the ultimatum expired. He found Milosevic uncharacteristically subdued, and left empty-handed wondering whether the Serb leader thought the bombing would be brief and ineffective, as it had been in Iraq the year before. Milosevic had obviously concluded that he could survive and turn the tables on the West. The bombing began on March 24 and lasted until June 10, 1999. NATO aircraft flew 38,000 combat missions to destroy Serbian tanks and artillery when they could be found, and to impose an increasingly severe cost on the Serbs by systematically destroying bridges, power and communications grids, and armaments factories. Once the bombing started, another 300,000 people fled Kosovo, bringing the total number of refugees to more than 800,000. A few days after the bombing campaign got underway, the International Criminal Tribunal for the Former Yugoslavia indicted Milosevic and other Yugoslav and Serbian officials on charges of crimes against humanity, murder, forced deportation, and persecution on racial, political, and religious grounds. After the fighting stopped, Milosevic tried to stay in power. When he manipulated the results of an election, a popular uprising led to his removal from office. Subsequently, he was arrested and sent for trial by the international tribunal that had indicted him.

Serbia's economy was crippled by the months of bombardment. No allied combatants died and NATO reported the loss of three helicopters, thirty-two unmanned reconnaissance drones, and five aircraft. There was little agreement about Serbian deaths. Human Rights Watch put the figure at 500, NATO at a maximum of 1,500, and the Milosevic government at 5,700. The bodies of hundreds of dead Albanians were found scattered around Kosovo. The end of combat and the return of nearly all the refugees were followed by the flight of some 200,000 Serbs out of Kosovo, reducing their share of the population by about 75%. NATO had hung together and gone to war against Milosevic's use of intimidation and violence to empty a province of people who were not Serbs. The provocations of the Albanian Kosovars made it difficult to feel good about either side. NATO had won, but it was an untidy and unstable victory. Only the presence of foreign troops kept the two sides from starting the murders and expulsions all over again.

Somalia

Under Bush I, American policy in Somalia had been to break a famine, to use an oversized American expeditionary force to cow Somali warlords into allowing food to be distributed to the starving, and then to withdraw. It was a recipe for a limited humanitarian success. George Bush planned to withdraw before Bill Clinton took office, but inauguration day came and went and American troops remained in Mogadishu. The Secretary General of the United Nations, Boutros Boutros-Ghali, and the Clinton White House strongly supported by Madeleine Albright in New York looked for something more ambitious. Why not take advantage of American primacy and the willingness of the Clinton administration to work through the UN—the White House favored the term "muscular multilateralism"—to give Somalia a stable government? In March 1993, the UN Security Council passed a resolution calling for national reconciliation and the restoration of the economy and political and civil society institutions of Somalia.[61] The number of American troops in Somalia for what was a vastly more difficult task than famine relief had shrunk from 35,000 to some 6,000, along with 4,000 Pakistanis and a few smaller international contingents. Somalia's domestic political problems were vastly more difficult to address than famine, even as a much smaller number of American soldiers became more and more deeply involved in solving them. Clinton's agenda was more domestic and economic than international and, in any case, Somalia ranked low on the foreign policy agenda. Several of Clinton's senior advisers began to think about ending the mission.

The first American diplomat assigned to oversee the Somalia operation was Robert Oakley who had served in the country in the early 1980s and understood how to work with the warlords. While their weapons were puny compared to the arms available to the American military, they were ruthless and determined to hang on to control of their piece of the country. Oakley's successor, former deputy national security adviser Jonathan Howe, took over in March 1993. Howe lacked Oakley's firsthand knowledge of the country. More importantly, he worked for the UN. The problem was that the UN goal of establishing a decent government in Somalia could not be achieved without breaking the power of the warlords, a task that would require more rather than fewer troops, and would surely lead to American dead and wounded. Albright spoke strongly in favor of the new approach. "Nation building" was now the goal of the UN in Somalia and, by default, the goal of the United States. Few senior officials in the White House or Pentagon were in favor of sending more troops, and fewer still paid much attention to what was happening in Mogadishu.

A preview of what lay ahead came in June when the fighters of one of the warlords, Mohammed Farah Aidid, attacked a Pakistani patrol, killing twenty-four. The UN's and Howe's reaction to Aidid's belligerence was to make Aidid the target. The Security Council passed a resolution authorizing Aidid's capture and trial, and Howe offered $25,000 for information leading to Aidid's arrest. American troops began trying to take him prisoner. "The decision we must make," Albright argued in an article in the *New York Times* "is whether to pull up stakes and allow Somalia to fall back into the abyss or to stay the course and help lift the country and its people from the category of a failed state into that of an emerging democracy.[62] Oakley told a reporter later that he couldn't believe what he was hearing:

> The U.S. had to stay the course. Oakley thought Albright was crazy. *Emerging democracy!* He marveled at the words. Nice people, he thought of the Clinton team, well-intentioned, but no one was really in charge.[63]

What happened next has been told and re-told, notably in the popular movie and best-selling book, *Blackhawk Down*.[64] Rangers and Delta Force troops, among the most aggressive soldiers in the American military, were ordered to Mogadishu in late August, just as an inattentive White House began backing away from what some senior advisers thought was a risky policy. Further evidence of inattention and a wish to withdraw came in late September when the White House turned down a request for tanks and armored personnel carriers. On October 3, a helicopter assault by the Rangers and Delta Force went horribly wrong. Instead of getting in and out quickly, some of the Americans stumbled into a hornet's nest. Aidid's fighters and angry Somalis poured into the street and opened fire. They used rocket-propelled grenades to shoot down hovering choppers. Without tanks and armored personnel carriers, the American troops found themselves pinned down. Before they could be rescued, eighteen were killed and dozens wounded. An American pilot was captured. A dead American was dragged through the streets behind a truck. Anger and opposition exploded in the Congress. The White House reacted by pushing responsibility onto Jonathan Howe and Les Aspin.

After the crisis, the administration worked out a new policy to govern intervention in unstable Third World countries. The United States would stay out, because if it intervened it would become entangled in local civil wars and lose the support of the Congress and the American people. The new policy proved to be irrelevant in Haiti, the next failed Third World country to confront the administration. Worse, the policy made it difficult for the United States to try to stop genocide in Rwanda. In retrospect, it is hard to avoid the impression that the Clinton administration had been trying to engage in nation building and cooperation with the United Nations on the cheap. It was consistent with Clinton's noninterventionist view of the post–Cold War paradigm, but the administration had fumbled a chance to make nation building a success. The failure in Somalia also worsened Clinton's relations with the military; the major regional commanders began to ignore the White House and go their own way.[65] Members of Congress accused the administration of bungling and wasting American lives in a country without geopolitical importance to the United States. Under harsh criticism from all sides, the administration's commitment to Somalia wilted.

Haiti

Barely a week after the shootout in Mogadishu, another Clinton foreign policy fiasco with tragic overtones took place thousands of miles away. The first Bush administration had left office without overcoming the political and economic crisis that had seized Haiti and produced instability, violence, and a flood of refugees trying to get into Florida. Mostly, the previous administration had behaved as if it hoped Haiti and all its problems would just sink into the Caribbean. An elected president, Jean Bertrand Aristide, a populist Catholic priest, had been overthrown. Unsure about Aristide, Bush I had tried reluctantly and halfheartedly to restore him to power. The Organization of American States imposed an economic embargo that hurt the poor more than the rich and powerful, and increased the flood of Haitian refugees, pathetic in their desire to escape, clinging to makeshift rafts and flimsy boats in the open sea, drowning, dying of exposure and thirst, washing ashore dead and alive in Florida, a state important for its electoral votes and conservative Cuban émigré population.

By early October, Clinton's advisers thought that they had persuaded the current military strongman, General Raoul Cédras, to surrender power and leave the country. To help the transfer of authority back to Aristide, they ordered the USS *Harlan County* to Port au Prince. The ship carried several hundred U.S. soldiers who were under orders to assist in retraining the Haitian police and military. But the *Harlan County* never managed to unload. As the ship approached the pier, a crowd of lightly armed thugs sent by Cédras and his supporters waved their weapons and shouted "Somalia! Somalia!" The *Harlan County* sailed away, taking no casualties, and humiliating the administration. It was a stunning example of poor planning and naiveté on the part of Clinton and his advisers. The *Harlan County* episode was exactly what it seemed: a witless attempt to intervene in another country without appearing to intervene, to deal with thieves and murderers as if they were men of their word, and to do good without paying any price whatsoever. A massive landing of American combat troops followed, with Cédras and his supporters in the Haitian elite refusing to back down until the last possible moment, when they were finally convinced that the United States would invade. In the end, Aristide was restored to power.

Coming on the heels of the losses in Somalia, the *Harlan County* episode revealed a damning incompetence.[66]

Rwanda

The failure to stop genocide in Rwanda is the most agonizing of all the Clinton administration's encounters with small states. Hundreds of thousands of people were massacred from April through July 1994. Day after day the killing continued with primitive weapons while the rest of the world stood by and did nothing to stop the slaughter. Tony Lake regretted the administration's failure to act more than anything else that happened while he was national security adviser.[67] Haunted by the failure in Somalia, neither the UN nor the Clinton administration was eager to act when the first reports of the massacre began coming in. The French, Belgian, Italian, and American governments took steps to protect and evacuate their nationals but did nothing for the Tutsis and others who were being murdered. Finally, in mid-May, the UN agreed to send a protection force to Rwanda, but its departure was delayed while diplomats niggled over meaningless details. Incredibly, the Clinton administration played word games, trying to substitute the phrase "acts of genocide" for genocide. Presumably, if there were only "acts of genocide," it would not be necessary to intervene. This unworthy bit of "spinning" included a damning exchange between a State Department spokesperson, Christine Shelly, and a reporter:

Reporter: How many acts of genocide does it take to make genocide?

Shelly: That's just not a question that I'm in a position to answer.

Reporter: Well, is it true that you have specific guidance not to use the word "genocide" in isolation, but always to preface it with these words "acts of"?

Shelly: I have guidance which I try to use as best as I can. There are formulations that we are using that we are trying to be consistent in our use of. I don't have an absolute categorical prescription against something, but I have the definitions. I have phraseology which has been carefully examined and arrived at as best as we can apply to exactly the situation and the actions which have taken place. . . .[68]

The killing continued until Tutsi fighters invaded and stopped it.

North Korea and Nuclear Weapons

The North Korean attack on South Korea in June 1950, undertaken with the approval of Stalin and Mao, posed one of the hardest questions facing the United States as it struggled to recreate a world balance of power and win allies in the Cold War: How important is it to prevent communist success in countries whose destiny cannot influence the outcome of the global struggle with the Soviet Union? The huge and costly American war in Korea from 1950 to 1953 gave the answer: very important. The even bigger intervention in Vietnam a decade later showed beyond doubt that the United States would fight to stop the spread of communism. In the late twentieth century, as one communist government after another fell apart, the North Korean dictator again seized center stage, this time by manipulating the threat—and eventually the reality—of nuclear proliferation in an attempt to win security pledges and economic assistance from the United States, Japan, and South Korea. The timing of the two crises that the Clinton administration faced in 1994 and 1998 probably owed more to catastrophic economic failure in North Korea than anything else. North Korea's leaders proved to be savvy opportunists, and the two encounters with Clinton, as well as the subsequent rounds with Bush II, revealed two things: Kim Il Sung and his son and successor, Kim Jong Il, and their supporters would starve the North Korean people rather than reform; and they believed they would be able to win security pledges and substantial economic aid from the United States, Japan, and South Korea without having to give up their nuclear weapons and long-range missile programs. Just as in the early 1950s, the Korean problem of the 1990s revealed much about the actual working of international politics, especially the limits of great power and the freedom of action of small, determined states.

In the mid-1980s, Kim Il Sung ordered the construction of a five-megawatt nuclear reactor at Yongbyon that would produce the plutonium necessary to build nuclear weapons. Typically, Kim surrounded his action with a smokescreen by signing the Nuclear Non-Proliferation Treaty at the same time. The Non-Proliferation Treaty requires regular inspections of fuel rods and nuclear reactors by the International Atomic Energy Agency. After six years of negotiation, North Korea and the International Atomic Energy Agency failed to reach agreement on inspection procedures. In an effort to move the denuclearization of the North forward, and in keeping with a post–Cold War de-emphasis of nuclear weapons in U.S. strategy, Bush I withdrew all American nuclear weapons from South Korea in late 1991. South Korea followed suit by agreeing with North Korea never to acquire nuclear weapons or the plutonium and uranium production facilities needed for their acquisition. Against this background, North Korea and the International Atomic Energy Agency reached agreement in January 1992, and six inspections were held from June 1992 to February 1993. As a result, the International Atomic Energy Agency discovered that more plutonium had been reprocessed than the 80 grams that North Korea had reported. The North Korean government rejected additional inspections and on March 12, 1993, announced the beginning of the 90-day period of notice for withdrawal from the Non-Proliferation Treaty. The Clinton administration took the threat very seriously. War seemed possible, even likely, unless a way could be found to eliminate North Korea's nuclear weapons program. That seemed doubtful given the nature of the North Korean government and its record of refusing to compromise. There was precious little room for maneuver: a conventional war on the Korean peninsula, while it would end in the destruction of the Kim regime, would be horrendously destructive to South Korea and unacceptable to the South Korean people on national as well as economic grounds. The assumptions that underlay the Clinton administration's policy toward North Korea were:

- Nuclear proliferation by North Korea posed an extreme and unacceptable security threat, primarily because of the risk that dangerous weapons—fissionable material, bomb designs, and missiles—would fall into the hands of terrorists.
- North Korea would not collapse or fall from subversion in the near term, and in any event not soon enough to remove the nuclear threat to the United States and its allies.
- Delay was better than war, provided there was progress toward ending or at the very least "freezing" the threat of North Korean nuclear proliferation.
- However, war could not be ruled out, and the administration strengthened U.S. military forces in and around the Korean peninsula.
- It would be possible to end North Korea's nuclear programs only if the administration used carefully conceived economic and political carrots and sticks (rewards and punishments).

The Kim government "suspended" its withdrawal from the Non-Proliferation Treaty after Clinton agreed to a high-level meeting that was held in

June 1993. However, North Korea continued to refuse to allow International Atomic Energy Agency inspections of the Yongbyon reactor or the 8,000 nuclear fuel rods, which had been removed from the reactor, an essential first step in reprocessing the plutonium for use in nuclear weapons. The Clinton administration then introduced a UN Security Council resolution calling for economic sanctions against North Korea. When China made clear that it would not veto the sanctions, North Korea cleverly invited former President Jimmy Carter to Pyongyang and offered to freeze North Korean nuclear activities.[69] Carter's visit reduced tensions a bit. Responding to the North Korean gesture, Clinton withdrew the sanctions proposal and resumed what became sixteen months of negotiations. Finally, on October 21, 1994, the two parties signed the Agreed Framework, a complex arrangement that promised political, economic, and security benefits to the North in exchange for a total freeze of its plutonium-based weapons program. The United States would provide military assurances, and South Korea and Japan would furnish virtually all the economic assistance called for in the agreement. Weapons based on highly enriched uranium, which would soon become important, were not mentioned. The framework was also silent about the plutonium that North Korea had already taken from the Yongbyon reactor and concealed from International Atomic Energy Agency inspectors, as well as the possibility that North Korea had secretly reprocessed it in violation of the spirit of the agreed framework, a term carefully chosen to indicate the beginning of a process rather than fixed commitments. Specific rewards from the agreement and movement from one phase to the next were contingent on good-faith fulfillment by North Korea of the freeze and its willingness to allow complete and full inspections to proceed.

North Korea's main obligations under the agreement were to:

- Freeze its graphite-moderated reactors and plutonium reprocessing plant.
- Stop construction of two other reactors (50 and 200 megawatts) capable of producing enough plutonium for 30 to 50 nuclear weapons each year.
- Put no new fuel rods in the Yongbyon reactor, store the old fuel rods safely without reprocessing, and allow them to be monitored.
- And, according to administration officials who cited a secret "confidential minute," to construct no new nuclear facilities anywhere in North Korea.

In response, the United States organized a group of nations to finance and build two light-water nuclear reactors capable of producing 2,000 megawatts of electricity. The organization, the Korean Energy Development Organization, whose most important members are South Korea and Japan, was established in March 1995. Work on the reactor buildings began in August 1997 with a target date of 2007 and perhaps much later. South Korea was to pay for the reactors at a cost of approximately $6 billion, with $1 billion coming from Japan and a nominal $76 million from the European Union. Before the construction and installation of the reactors could begin, North Korea and the United States (American companies would build the reactors) would have to conclude a bilateral nuclear cooperation agreement, and the International Atomic Energy Agency would have to certify that North Korea had come into full compliance with all Agency safeguards and would permit all necessary inspections.

To replace lost electrical generating capacity, and for that purpose only, the United States agreed to provide "heavy oil" to North Korea. Initial shipments of 50,000 and 100,000 tons of heavy oil were sent, and the United States pledged to arrange shipments of 500,000 tons a year until the first light-water reactor went into operation. Diplomatic representation was foreseen, initially liaison offices, to be upgraded as important issues were resolved, including North Korean military deployments along the demilitarized zone that divides Korea, and the sale of North Korean missiles to other countries. Barriers to trade and investment would be reduced within three months, and the United States would take initial steps to end the economic embargo imposed on the North during the Korean War.

The conclusion of the Agreed Framework gave the Clinton administration—and the world—a breather. It delayed the production—and potential sale to others—of what might have been dozens of nuclear weapons. The framework tied the benefits available to North Korea so tightly to major and, in the end, unacceptable concessions that Pyongyang began to lose patience. Facing severe food shortages and economic catastrophe, the North Koreans tried another gambit in 1998, and launched a ballistic missile over Japanese territory. The launch came at a time when Washington had already begun to doubt that North Korea was heeding the Agreed Framework. Since 1996, U.S. intelligence had been reporting the existence of a suspected underground nuclear facility at Kumchangri, about twenty-five miles north of Yongbyon. In exchange for a massive emergency shipment of American food, the North Korean government allowed the United States to inspect Kumchangri. No evidence of nuclear activities was found, but stories continued to run in the *New York Times* and *Washington Post* that as many as ten nuclear facilities were operating in North Korea. By 2000, President Clinton was unable to certify to Congress that North Korea was not acquiring enriched uranium for nuclear weapons.

The North Korean missile launch and the disturbing intelligence reports led President Clinton to order a review of U.S. policy toward North Korea in November 1998. As Ashton Carter, an assistant secretary of defense and Secretary Perry's closest associate on North Korean issues, put it:

> President Clinton, I think rightly, concluded that the United States, relieved, I supposed, over the freeze at Yongbyon had moved on to other crises, like Bosnia, Haiti, and so forth; not so the North Koreans. And he [Clinton] judged that the United States had no overall strategy toward North Korea. . . . [He] asked former Secretary of Defense Bill Perry to conduct an overall policy [review] and come up with an overall strategy.[70]

The Perry Report was made public in October 1999. It sustained the main assumptions behind the Agreed Framework. North Korean nuclear proliferation and its missile program posed a major threat to the United States and its allies; war should be avoided; negotiations should proceed on the basis of carrots and sticks—rewards for North Korean agreement, penalties for refusal; North Korea could not be subverted and would not reform its government under pressure and, in any case, not soon enough to remove the threat. The report's findings focused exclusively on plutonium, specifically on preventing the "unfreezing" of the Yongbyon reactor, which it described as "North Korea's quickest and surest path to acquisition of nuclear weapons."[71] The report also endorsed greater emphasis on cooperation among the United States, South Korea, and Japan, which had already begun in the form of three-sided consultations.

In its policy recommendations, the report sketched what it termed a "two-path strategy." The first sought a "complete and verifiable" end to North Korea's nuclear and missile programs. In return, it offered "step-by-step and reciprocal" reduction of what North Korea perceived as threats to its security.

> If the DPRK [Democratic People's Republic of North Korea] moved to eliminate its nuclear and long-range missile threats, the United States would normalize relations with the DPRK, relax sanctions that

have long constrained trade . . . and take other positive steps that would provide opportunities for the DPRK.[72]

As a first step in this direction, the report revealed that during a visit by American negotiators to Pyongyang the previous May, North Korea agreed to halt its long-range missile tests for the duration of the negotiations and the United States eased sanctions against North Korea. If North Korea reneged, there would be no new relationship between the United States and North Korea, and the United States and its allies would adopt "other steps to assure their security and contain the threat."

The virtues of the Perry Report and its recommended strategy were those of the Agreed Framework. A process was established that promised to address the proliferation and missile threats in a comprehensive way and postpone worse developments. But there were two weaknesses at the heart of the Clinton strategy. North Korea gave no sign that it intended to treat the negotiations as anything more than a maneuver to extract desperately needed economic assistance from the United States and its allies. That nothing more could be agreed than freezing Yongbyon and temporarily suspending missile tests for the duration of the negotiations revealed the limited extent of North Korean commitment to the two processes. From the North Korean standpoint, perhaps the greatest tangible gain came in the form of secret "payments" of hundreds of millions of dollars—bribes—by wealthy South Korean industrialists to make possible a North-South summit that was the centerpiece of the South Korean government's new policy toward the North. The North took the money, attended the summit, and made no concessions of any importance to the South. Pyongyang appears to have been confident it could do the same to the United States, Japan, and China by outthinking, outmaneuvering, and outlasting them.

The Clinton administration prided itself on the realism and toughness of its approach. Everything was reversible, and nothing significant would be provided until the North had actually begun to cut into its precious nuclear and missile programs by allowing full and impartial inspections and agreeing to reduce the military threat at the border between North and South Korea. And all the while the plutonium reactors were frozen. If not perfect, it seemed to be at least the best possible way to deal with "the problem from Hell"—a hostile government capable of inflicting enormous damage that the United States had precious little leverage to prevent. But the threat of North Korea's nuclear weapons and long-range missiles remained. Lack of progress on the nuclear questions forced the Clinton administration to focus on long-range missiles instead of nuclear weapons. Clinton had hoped to be able to visit Pyongyang before his term expired to sign a new agreement, possibly limiting North Korea's missile programs, but sent Albright instead, apparently because the value of any understandings that might be reached remained too uncertain. Albright returned without an agreement. It was the last move of the administration's six-year encounter with North Korea, the end of Clinton's eight years as president, and the beginning of an ambiguous foreign policy legacy.

4

An Eight-Year Odyssey

Munich was last year.

—David Owen[1]

There is an elusive quality about Bill Clinton as an individual that his foreign policy shares. Despite personal failings that were incomprehensible in someone so obviously intelligent and politically savvy, most Americans thought well of him and his presidency, and he easily won reelection to a second term. A messy sex scandal that led to impeachment seemed to have little effect on Clinton's popularity or the standing of his administration at home or abroad. It was as if the messier the Monica Lewinsky scandal and the nastier his opponents became, the more support he received. The shortcomings of Clinton's foreign policy were also on display for eight years. From Beijing to Belgrade the list was damning: the pointless and unnecessary deaths of American troops in Somalia, the failure to prevent genocide in Rwanda and Bosnia, the missed opportunities and folly of U.S. policy toward Haiti, the tardy intervention in Kosovo, the busy but oddly ineffectual and even counterproductive dealings with Russia, the failure to conclude an agreement between the Israelis and Palestinians, the disturbing signs of continuing North Korean nuclear proliferation, and the reliance on cruise missile salvoes to deal with challenges from Islamic terrorists and Saddam Hussein.[2] And yet Clinton left the United States in a generally sound international position at the end of his two terms. Relations with key allies in Western Europe and Asia were solid and supportive. The United States was at peace. Its economy had grown to startling heights, even taking into account the bursting of the high-tech bubble in the late 1990s. American global primacy was unchallenged and widely accepted, even welcomed. Despite having failed to prevent great suffering in Bosnia and Kosovo, the United States and Western Europe eventually forced a settlement and preserved the Atlantic Alliance. None of this quieted Clinton's opponents on the right. Conservative Republicans raised a number of issues but offered few practical solutions, and in the end revealed more about the state of mind of the far right in America than about weaknesses in Clinton's foreign policy. They also pointed to far less serious problems than those that arose directly from flaws in the post–Cold War paradigm. Last, because they occupied so much time and energy during the second term, the administration's efforts to help Russia, oversee a final settlement between the Israelis and Palestinians, and stop North Korea's nuclear program must be examined.

Clinton's conservative critics attacked his foreign policy as immoral, dangerous, reckless, and weak. The charge of immorality had two counts: Clinton wrongly accepted the limitations on American freedom of action that resulted from cooperating with multilateral organizations and the United Nations, and he failed to proclaim the moral superiority of democracy and the United States. To conservative and neoconservative critics, the whole idea of multilateralism was a grotesque immoral falsehood. At the United Nations, a majority of nondemocratic governments presumed to dictate to the United States and other genuinely democratic states. Multilateral organizations such as the European Union usurped national sovereignty and engaged in socialism and massive interference with the free market across the continent and the world. If the United States only had the courage to stand up and speak with "moral clarity"—as they alleged Ronald Reagan had done when he demanded that Mikhail Gorbachev tear down the Berlin Wall—other governments and people of goodwill around the world would rally to its side. In reality, Reagan had been assertive but not aggressive. His conduct of U.S. foreign policy was notable for its caution, prudence, and tentative character. The most aggressive actions that Reagan took were to order covert operations in Central America, Africa, and Afghanistan, the invasion of tiny Grenada, and the dispatch of 1,500 Marines to Beirut. These were limited, prudent steps on a very small scale, well within U.S. unilateral capabilities, and easily reversible in case something went wrong, as it quickly did in Lebanon where a suicide truck bomber killed 241 Marines as they slept in an airport building.

There is little doubt that working through multilateral organizations and alliances affects how quickly and decisively action can be taken. Delays and lowest common denominator policies are the norm. Sometimes it is impossible to take action of any kind. No one who looks at the workings of the United Nations and NATO in the Balkans or Rwanda during the Clinton administration can have any doubts on this score. But the delays and failure to act seem much more the result of national decisions rather than an abstract and corrupted multilateral ethos or bureaucratic confusion. It was not the UN but the Western powers' refusal to act that caused the deathly delays in Bosnia, Rwanda, and Kosovo. As for moral clarity, the critics' arguments mixed up principle and policy. A moral course of action is chosen for its own sake not because it will lead to success. Clear moral statements may indeed persuade others to follow and they may not. Neoconservatives lionized Churchill and Lincoln, but seemed to ignore Churchill's failure to rally his country to oppose Hitler or to understand the complex view that Lincoln took of abolitionism and slavery. As became clear after 9/11, George W. Bush's repeated declarations of "moral clarity" about Saddam Hussein and his alleged weapons of mass destruction persuaded very few governments or people outside the United States, and had little effect on the Iraqi dictator. However, they did convince a majority of voters in the United States, which was essential for the administration to be able to carry out its policies.

Conservative Republicans attacked Clinton's policies toward North Korea and Iraq as dangerous because they left vicious dictators free to oppress their people and acquire weapons of mass destruction. Clinton's approach to North Korea was criticized because it froze rather than destroyed Pyongyang's capability to build nuclear weapons. What appeared to be a failure to disarm Saddam Hussein was condemned because the Clinton administration allowed the search for Iraqi weapons of mass destruction to be conducted by multilateral organizations such as the UN, its inspection teams, and the International Atomic Energy Agency. None could be trusted, the conservative critics insisted, and least of all Saddam Hussein. When pressed for alternatives, the conservatives fell back on the transformative effect of moral clarity and some ingenious if scatterbrained options. Paul Wolfowitz, for example, considered encouraging North Koreans to flee into China in a mass exodus, similar to the escapes of thousands that had helped bring down communist governments in Eastern Europe. As for Iraq, Wolfowitz advocated the creation of enclaves protected by American troops from which the Iraqi opposition could subvert Saddam's regime. Most American diplomats, intelligence officials, and generals thought such schemes were far more dangerous than the Clinton administration's policy, which did not always attract their enthusiastic support either. Unhappily, the opposition within the government to the neoconservatives' proposals encouraged a growing suspicion among conservatives that the entire foreign policy establishment—diplomatic, intelligence, and military—was blind, ideologically unreliable, and even treasonous. The deeply harmful effects of this mutual incomprehension would be felt during the Bush II administration, as will be seen in later chapters.

Clinton's critics charged him with recklessness for blundering into "nation building" in Somalia, Bosnia, and Kosovo with what they said were predictably dismal and costly results. There was a tendency to try to have it both ways. Bob Dole, who ran against Clinton in 1996, wanted the United States to provide much stronger assistance to the Bosnian Muslims and attacked Clinton's caution and hesitancy. George W. Bush declared his adamant opposition to nation building during the 2000 campaign. Most conservative critics condemned the idea of nation building as a pointless waste of American lives and money on behalf of people who would not help themselves. Ironically, four years later some of the same critics would support nation building in Iraq on a scale and at a cost in lives and money that dwarfed Clinton's commitments in the Balkans. It was easy to portray Clinton's commitments to Bosnia and Kosovo as reckless and foolish, but Clinton was anything but reckless about intervening in ethnic conflicts. He acted in Bosnia after tens of thousands had died, and then only after he became convinced that inaction would lead to the collapse of NATO. He went to war over Kosovo only after Milosevic's campaign of murder and intimidation had killed hundreds and turned hundreds of thousands of people into refugees, fleeing in icy weather with what they could carry on tractors and in trucks, cars, and their hands. Nothing had been seen like it in Europe since World War II. If this was reckless behavior, it was reckless in a sense completely the opposite of conservative criticisms. The critics also showed little appreciation of the interplay between conflicting interests. Clinton believed that the spread of democracy and market economics would take care of the future. He and his advisers also understood that the Balkans lacked geopolitical importance. Both considerations made the decision to intervene difficult. It became doubly difficult when it was made to turn, as Clinton insisted, on whether the other NATO allies would support the use of force and the follow-on occupations in both countries.

The critics, and especially the neoconservatives, also convinced themselves that Clinton had failed to exploit what they saw as American global hegemony. Everyone took it for granted that the United States was a global hegemon. Why wasn't Clinton using American dominance to transform the world, particularly those dictatorships that were hostile to the United States, such as China, Iraq, North Korea, and Iran? The question assumed an identity between abstract capability and performance that ought to have been more carefully thought through. The big-picture figures comparing defense budgets or weapons systems concealed far more important weaknesses. The U.S. military had fashioned itself into an unstoppable conventional fighting force. There was only one problem: it was designed to fight a more sophisticated version of World War II. Its potency in post–Cold War conflicts was unproven. The demand to put American hegemony to use also assumed that other nations would follow the American lead (bandwagon), an assumption that entirely missed the possibility that balancing and bandwagoning did not exhaust the possibilities.[3] Most governments might prefer to do nothing but watch. In other words, the reaction of other countries depended not just on the structure of the international system (American primacy), but also on their evaluation of the evidence at hand and their calculation of their own interests. That other governments would refuse support was not clear in the late 1990s when neoconservatives made their criticisms. A hypothetical counterargument could be made for every argument the administration offered. Just how wrong the conservative critics were became obvious after the Bush II administration decided to invade Iraq and theoretical arguments turned into thousands of dead and wounded Americans and Iraqis caught in an ethnic and religious insurgency.

Other critics of Clinton's foreign policy argued that he lacked a strategy— that the balancing of ends and means, and indeed the whole apparatus of foreign policymaking, simply did not exist inside the Clinton administration. As journalist and historian David Halberstam saw it,

> Instead, pragmatic at heart, the Clinton people would handle foreign policy issue by issue, with no guidelines—save the constancy of their awareness of the president's domestic fortunes.[4]

William Hyland, a former member of the National Security Council staff, gave Clinton little credit:

> In the absence of an overall perspective, most issues were bound to degenerate into tactical manipulation, some successful, some not. Clinton stumbled from crisis to crisis, trying to figure out what was popular, what would be effective, and what choices would pose the lowest risk to his presidency, and, especially, to his reputation. . . . In 1993, Clinton was the leader of an unrivalled superpower; six years later he was a badly crippled lame duck. . . . The new global order that was emerging was in many ways antagonistic to American interests and designs. A magnificent historical opportunity to shape the international system had been missed.[5]

These criticisms and many others like them missed the point. There was a strategy. It was imaginative and innovative. It was based on the post–Cold War paradigm, particularly on the power of globalization and democratization, and especially the allegedly peaceful nature of democracies to transform the world without war and with very little effort by the United States. Seeing no serious threats to American security, Clinton's strategy identified improving the domestic and world economy as the primary responsibilities of United States. Success in these two actions would do more than any other measure to make the world safer, wealthier, and more democratic. The problem was that Clinton's strategy did not allow for the problems that confronted the administration, particularly ethnic and religious conflict and Islamic terrorism. These were serious shortcomings. They just were not the problems that the critics identified. Most critics also overlooked the domestic opponents of Clinton and his presidency, and the limits that their poisonous assault imposed on his administration's foreign policy. The most serious criticisms of the Clinton strategy arise from the strengths and weaknesses of the post–Cold War paradigm.

Bill Clinton and the Post–Cold War Paradigm

In the 1990s, "globalization" became the darling of Western analysts and political leaders. An acknowledgment of the tremendous acceleration in the movement of goods, ideas, money, and people around the world, globalization ended up being all things to all people. To conservatives, it embodied the triumph of their cherished ideals of free enterprise and democracy. To liberals, globalization and the high technologies that drove it were inherently populist and democratic, capable of empowering the poor and underrepresented. Conservatives and liberals alike believed that globalization would hasten the spread of liberal democracy around the world: globalization offered peaceful change for the better based on rational choice.[6] Looking at a world dominated by globalization and trying to anticipate the trajectory of events, the Clinton administration concluded that democracy and market economics would transform the world in a very short time. As Thomas Friedman argued in his best-selling book, *The Lexus and the Olive Tree*, governments and individuals everywhere would have to put on a "golden straitjacket" of market economics and the rule of law or they would fall hopelessly behind everyone else.[7] In these circumstances, the most sensible course for the United States was to avoid foreign intervention, cut its armed forces, tune up its domestic economy, encourage democratic change within other countries, and try to open their markets to American trade and investment. Throughout the middle years of the 1990s, the bubble economy buoyed by skyrocketing high-technology stocks seemed to support this approach.

The 1990s also saw the birth and triumph of the idea that democracies are peaceful. Based on the dubious insights of a handful of academics and popularized by a largely conservative claque of journalists, the argument was that the twentieth century proved that democracies do not wage aggressive war and do not make war against one another. By definition, the people govern in a democracy, and they will not allow their rulers to waste their lives and money in foolish wars. It followed from the two propositions that the best way for democratic countries to protect themselves was to convert other societies to liberal democracy, elections, market economics, the rule of law, in other words, all the attributes of governance in North America and Western Europe.

In keeping with its domestic focus on economic issues, the administration also put the emphasis on the economy in its national security strategy. As political journalist Joe Klein said at the end of the second Clinton term,

"Even the most intemperate Republicans had to acknowledge . . . that Clinton did leave one permanent, if underappreciated, mark on American foreign policy. He rearranged the traditional priorities, raising economic issues to the same level of importance as strategic affairs."[8] One of the proudest accomplishments of the administration was its passage of the North American Free Trade Agreement, joining Canada, Mexico, and the United States. Taken together, engagement and enlargement and special attention to Russia's transition to a market economy and democracy amounted to an attractive and responsible way of using American superiority. In the eyes of the president and his closest advisers, the absence of any major foreign threats made their approach safe and feasible.

Sadly, Clinton's strategy ran into three serious problems. First, globalization did not work as it was supposed to. It was not truly global, and it took too long to yield the transformations its supporters claimed for it. Exactly the states that caused the most trouble—much of the Arab and Muslim world and nearly all of Africa—remained outside globalization's ostensibly benign embrace.[9] Islamists regarded globalization and democratization as antireligious. The time actually needed for globalization to work in developing countries—decades, at best—went far beyond the eight years available to Bill Clinton and his advisers. Clinton's strategy focused attention on a distant and ever-peaceful future instead of an unruly and increasingly dangerous present. Far from a dynamic strategy of change, engagement and enlargement amounted to a recipe for letting history take its course—in other words, doing nothing.

Second, the strategy so carefully crafted by Clinton administration policymakers often did not apply to the world they faced. A good example of the administration's preferred focus was the updating of the U.S.-Japan security treaty in April 1996. Coming just a few weeks after China's confrontation with the United States in the Taiwan Straits, the new U.S.-Japanese understanding reaffirmed the importance of the security treaty and provided for greater military cooperation between the two allies during crises.[10] There was nothing wrong with drawing the United States and Japan closer together, particularly in light of all the uncertainties about China's future. However, Clinton's main problems were not great power relations, economic growth, and liberal democratic transformation, but extreme nationalism, failed states, ethnic slaughter, religious extremism in the Arab and Muslim worlds, terrorism, and the proliferation of weapons of mass destruction. The leaders of the troubled societies from the Balkans to the Gulf, Central

Africa, and North Korea were unconcerned with democracy and capitalism. They wanted power, resorted to mass killing to get it, and were indifferent to the suffering of their own people or the peaceful objections of foreign governments.

Third, globalization turned into financial collapse in Mexico, Russia, South Korea, and Southeast Asia. Ethnic slaughter erupted in the Balkans and Africa. Religious fanatics trying to turn the clock back a thousand years attacked the World Trade Center in New York City and American forces and embassies abroad. It took enormous efforts and billions of dollars to rescue the economies sent into collapse by globalization and bad policies in the 1990s, and to keep the financial collapse in Asia, Russia, and Brazil from undermining the global economy.[11] There was nothing high-tech or "rational" about suicidal terrorism or ethnic slaughter. The murderers in Rwanda used machetes. The first attack on the World Trade Center in 1993 used explosives made from the chemical ingredients of fertilizer. Milosevic of Yugoslavia, Saddam Hussein of Iraq, and Kim Il Sung of North Korea relied on World War II weapons, and laughed at economic sanctions while their people's lives were devastated. None of this was supposed to happen in the era of globalization. But it did, and time after time the Clinton administration was unprepared for it. Sometimes the administration made things worse by overreacting to failure. Following the deaths of American soldiers in Somalia and a huge outcry in the Congress critical of the president, Clinton and his advisers adopted a policy that made it virtually impossible for the United States to intervene in Third World countries, regardless of the circumstances. Tragically, this attempt to respond to criticism and make policy on the rebound prevented the administration from fashioning a timely response to genocide in Rwanda. Clinton then swung the other way and, after the war for Kosovo, announced that when the United States could intervene in humanitarian crises it should, but it was too late to prevent great human loss. These murderous tragedies only underlined the Clinton administration's failure to use American primacy to shape the international environment in ways that might have stopped the atrocities and made it more difficult for them to occur in the future.

The notion that democracies are peaceful was central to Clinton's strategy and the post–Cold War paradigm. It should strike anyone aware of the history of the past three centuries as dubious and ethnocentric. From the subjugation of Africa, India, and Egypt by Great Britain in the nineteenth century, to repeated interventions by the United States in Africa, Asia, and

Latin America during the Cold War and the invasion of Iraq in 2003, democracies have been as warlike as any of their nondemocratic opponents. That the democracies of Western Europe and North America have not attacked one another in the twentieth century seems as much a geopolitical accident as a result of their intrinsically peaceful nature. Great Britain, France, and the United States faced the same threats from an expansionist Germany and Japan, and an ideologically and militarily menacing Soviet Union. Regardless of the nature of the governments, it would have been idiotic for them to make war on their only possible allies. They certainly made war on virtually everyone else. At best the notion that democracies do not make war on one another is an unproven historical proposition. It is not a theory of foreign policy but a fact that should be explained. Britain and France shared responsibility for the outbreak of both world wars in the twentieth century. Even though they did not attack Germany, Japan, and Italy, Britain was responsible because it withheld its support from its continental allies until too late, and France because of its inability to fashion a lasting understanding with Germany.

By accepting the responsibility for spreading democracy and market economics throughout the entire world, and basing this on a perceived vital national security interest, the Clinton administration—and Bush II after it— took on an enormous task, one that if taken seriously far exceeded even the vast resources of the United States. The disparity between intentions and capabilities was not as great a problem for Clinton as it would prove to be for Bush II, but not because they disagreed over principle. Their primary disagreement was about means. Clinton assigned foreign policy a low priority and attempted to cut spending on foreign aid and the military. Clinton had the luxury of consistency, adopting Wilsonian goals and nonviolent Wilsonian means. He chose to focus his main efforts on Russia and Europe, and to some extent on China and the Israeli-Palestinian conflict. It was the old Wilsonian wine in a new bottle. Wilson put his trust in public opinion. Clinton trusted globalization. Wilson, Clinton—and Bush II— believed that the operation of reason and self-interest in human minds would bring about a global transformation to liberal democracy and peace. The United States would have to do very little. For Clinton, therefore, the imbalance between the truly immense task of democratizing the world and the very limited means of a declining military and shrinking foreign aid went virtually unnoticed but remained unresolved.

Clinton's record in those areas that fit the strategy of engagement and enlargement is solidly constructive. The North American Free Trade Agreement, NATO expansion, and denuclearization of Ukraine, Belarus, and Kazakhstan were Clinton's greatest successes in foreign policy. Free trade was an economic issue that matched the administration's emphasis on the economy and spreading liberal democracy, and NATO expansion was more political than military. The North American Free Trade Agreement negotiated by Bush I hurt organized labor, a strong supporter of the Democratic Party, but the American, Canadian, and Mexican economies were already deeply enmeshed, and it made sense to take the next step toward full integration. All stood to gain in the long run: according to the liberal economic theory of trade, comparative advantage would result in new and greater economic activity, with each country finding new areas in which they could specialize more successfully than the other. The job losses and shifts in investment in the near term were real and significant. They were controversial at the time of the agreement's passage and remained so a decade later, especially in Mexico and the United States where social safety nets were less comprehensive than in Canada.

The expansion of NATO responded to the desire of the newly independent East European states to gain the protection of the United States. During congressional hearings before the new members were invited to join, President Carter's national security adviser, Zbigniew Brzezinski, joked that the United States wanted these states to join because they would never ask the United States to leave. The joke touched the sense of vulnerability of these states as they emerged from the cocoon of Soviet domination into a geopolitically unorganized space, bounded to the east by a deeply wounded Russia and to the west by a newly united and increasingly powerful Germany, their enemies for centuries. Brzezinski's quip underlined the belief among Clinton administration policymakers that it was essential for the United States to remain in Europe and that NATO was the principal means for expressing its interests on the continent. Brzezinski's suggestion that there was a special bond between these new democracies and the United States turned out to be prophetic during the second Gulf War: a number of them supported the American position, notably Poland, Hungary, and the Czech Republic, despite the hostility of France and Germany to American policy, and the ill grace with which their commitment was received in Paris and Berlin. The Clinton administration and NATO responded to Russia's security interests by inviting closer consultative association with the alliance. The purpose was both symbolic and real. The closer ties recognized Russia's importance, even if that was more potential than real, and it gave the Russians a voice at the center of NATO's deliberations. Some American observers wondered whether the new arrangements were too close and could prevent NATO from acting in the face of Russian opposition. Denuclearization claimed most of the funds committed by Clinton to the former Soviet Union. The disproportion between funding of denuclearization and economic aid revealed the urgency of the need to ensure that the vast Soviet nuclear arsenal be kept away from terrorists and rogue states. It was not a flashy or high-profile policy, but it was crucial and, at least in the early years, strongly supported by both parties in Congress.

Beyond the free trade agreement, NATO expansion, and denuclearization, it is difficult to find foreign policy initiatives during Bill Clinton's two terms that did not have mixed or largely negative results. In some cases, such as the Israeli-Palestinian conflict, Clinton helped prolong what Israelis and Palestinians call "the good years," a time when violence subsided and people felt less afraid. Sadly, as the second Clinton administration ended, the peace process collapsed and violence erupted and quickly escalated to unprecedented levels on both sides. In that sense, Clinton left the issue worse than he found it. For others, such as Bosnia and Kosovo, there were positive results, but they came at such a high price as to leave doubts about the effectiveness and humanity of the administration's policies. Iraq turned out to be even more paradoxical. By 2001, Clinton had not succeeded in bringing down Saddam Hussein, but after Bush II occupied Iraq and overthrew Saddam Hussein, inspectors discovered that sometime in the 1990s Saddam had destroyed his weapons of mass destruction. Russia eventually settled down under the heavy-handed presidency of Vladimir Putin to be governed by that strange creature, authoritarian democracy, and its economy began to grow, vigorously at first, then sluggishly. The Clinton administration avoided "losing Russia," and escaped the kinds of attacks on its policies that fell on the Truman administration after Mao's victory in China.[12] But the suffering of the Russian people during the 1990s and Putin's turn toward authoritarianism made the outcome something less than brilliant. Finally, Clinton's attempts to denuclearize North Korea and reduce if not end the risk of war on the Korean peninsula succeeded but only partially. A plutonium-based effort was halted after lengthy and hard negotiations, but North Korea's decision to build nuclear weapons using highly enriched uranium threw the peninsula into turmoil again and no agreement could be reached before Clinton's second term ended. Four years later North Korea would declare itself a nuclear power.

Russia

More than any other international question that he faced during the 1990s, Clinton gave his time, energy, and prestige in an attempt to ensure the success of democracy and market economics in Russia. The economic policies adopted by the Russian government of Boris Yeltsin forced the Russian people through hardships worse than the Great Depression in the United States. In 1998, the same policies, many of them formulated with the advice of American economic advisers and strongly supported by U.S. Treasury officials, particularly Deputy Secretary Lawrence Summers and David Lipton, failed spectacularly when Russia bankrupted itself. At the end of the decade, Russia had recovered its economic balance and its economy was growing. After a wild ride through coups, attempted coups, fascist-communist coalitions, the possibility of canceled elections, and an unending and brutal war in Chechnya, Russia seemed stable under Yeltsin's successor Vladimir Putin and headed down an increasingly authoritarian path. Bill Clinton was unable to win approval of a nuclear arms control agreement with Russia: the communist-controlled parliament, the Duma, blocked ratification until too late in Clinton's second term, and Putin rejected a deal with Clinton on revising the ABM Treaty. NATO expansion and the war in Kosovo, bitterly opposed by the Russian government, contributed to a worsening of relations between the United States and Russia.

The unhappy state of Russia during the 1990s and since—its bankruptcy and social breakdown, the poverty of many in the country alongside great wealth, the corruption and increasingly authoritarian politics—made the Clinton administration's policies toward Russia extremely controversial. Defenders of the administration argued that when they started, no one knew how to transform a former communist superpower into a liberal democracy. It had never been done before. In remarks made on a radio program during the June 2000 summit in Moscow, Clinton defended his administration's policies:

> I have worked hard to help support Russian economic reform, and a large role for Russia in the world. I supported Russia coming into the G-8, to the Asian Pacific economic leaders group; having a special relationship with NATO; working on the ground, our troops, Russian troops side by side in the Balkans. And I intend to support Russia's effort to get a program going with the International Monetary Fund,

with the World Bank. I believe the world needs a strong and prosperous and democratic Russia that respects the rule of law and the differences among its people. And that's what I've worked for.[13]

Members of the Clinton administration admitted that they made mistakes as they operated from these assumptions. As Strobe Talbott put it:

We should have focused earlier, more critically, and more consistently on the damage that the Russian rampage was inflicting on innocent civilians, and on the damage Russia was doing to its chances of democratization and development as a civil society.[14]

But Clinton and his advisers insisted that the errors and excesses came more from the circumstances in Russia and corrupt individuals than from misconceived American policies. Some analysts admitted the difficulties and pointed out the limits on the ability of outside powers to influence events inside another country. They also stressed that the primary national security concerns of the United States lay with denuclearization and Russia's foreign policy.[15] Still, the administration persisted in supporting reforms that inflicted enormous suffering on the poor and middle class, and facilitated the plundering of the country's national assets and resources and an explosion of corruption. These points, interestingly, united liberals, including the Russian historian Stephen Cohen of New York University and conservatives such as Senator Jesse Helms.

What one thinks of Clinton's policy depends mainly on judgments as to what was possible in the chaotic circumstances inside Russia in the 1990s. Conceivably, a different approach at certain critical points—such as a program of massive Western assistance immediately after the dissolution of the Soviet Union—might have made a difference. Better macroeconomic policies from the international lending institutions in the year or two before the Russian default might have averted the bankruptcy that took place. A slower pace of privatization might have reduced the dislocations and hardships experienced by ordinary citizens. Arguably, it was a mistake to personalize U.S.-Russian relations at the most senior level: the president worked with Yeltsin, Gore with Viktor Chernomyrdin, and Talbott with Yuri Mamedov. Some critics doubted that it made any sense for Russia to attempt to become a liberal democracy immediately after the fall of communism. The administration responded predictably: there was no support in the United States or Western Europe for a massive aid program, the macroeconomic policies of the International Monetary Fund and World Bank were based on consensus among prominent international economists and G-7 finance ministers, and it seemed better to privatize too quickly than not at all. The political opponents of reform inside Russia were gaining ground rapidly. Time was a political as well as an economic factor, and no reform was possible without reformers. There was simply no alternative to Yeltsin and the people around him.

The doubts linger, but a number of genuine accomplishments stand out, along with some clear problems and failures. The administration's achievements in denuclearization solved an extremely difficult and dangerous problem in Belarus, Ukraine, and Kazakhstan. Instead of three new nuclear powers with unstable and untried governments, the administration managed to return the weapons to Russia where they could be stored or dismantled. Congress supported denuclearization by passing a brilliant law, known as Nunn-Lugar after its authors, Senators Sam Nunn and Richard Lugar, which funded the Departments of Defense and Energy to conduct denuclearization and to provide critical financial support to Russian laboratories and scientists who might otherwise have been tempted to sell their expertise outside Russia. The extremely large share that denuclearization took out of the total aid given to Russia by the United States revealed the importance that the problem commanded inside the administration. For example, in fiscal year 2001, of $1 billion in total U.S. government assistance to Russia, about $745 million went for programs administered by the Departments of Defense and Energy, mostly for denuclearization.[16] Throughout the 1990s, these programs accounted for half the funding and many, many times the amounts available for institutional reform (40-1) and democracy promotion (25-1).[17]

President Clinton and his closest advisers believed that helping Russia become a working democracy with a market economy was the best way that they could advance the security interests of the United States. A democratic Russia would be peaceful, and Russia's massive remaining nuclear arsenal would pose no threat to the existence of America. Russia's integration into Western-inspired institutions such as the economic and financial Group of 7 or the World Trade Organization would help make the changes irreversible. That the reforms of the 1990s advocated by the United States as well as those initiated by Russians unilaterally ended in such mixed results politically as well as economically should not disguise the good that was achieved along the way. Governments changed and political power was transferred by elections in Russia, a rare accomplishment in Russian history before the 1990s, and however troubled they were by Bosnia and Kosovo, U.S.-Russian relations during the Clinton years were a vast improvement compared to the same during the Cold War.

The Clinton administration approached foreign policy problems with Russia in two ways: by attempting to leave room for Russia to come around to support the new situation, such as NATO enlargement or war over Kosovo, however difficult the process might have been; and to provide concrete material incentives—the chance to join with the United States in space launches, for example—in exchange for Russian cooperation. Coupled with a genuine sensitivity and empathy for Yeltsin's domestic problems, these measures gave the Russian government time to work through its resentment over not being able to stop international developments that it thought harmful, and eventually, to arrive at a position of trying to do what it could to serve Russian interests in the best ways possible. The value of patience, empathy, and incentives showed during the endgame of the Bosnian war, when Russian and American negotiators found an imaginative way to include Russian troops along with NATO forces as a part of the Implementation Force. The Russian government appointed a military deputy to the commander of American forces in Europe, in this way avoiding the domestic political embarrassment of having to serve under NATO command; the difference was formal rather than real, since the same American general also commanded NATO's troops. Both approaches showed when Hungary, Poland, and Czechoslovakia were brought into NATO. Arrangements worth hundreds of millions of dollars to Russia sweetened the deal, and Clinton delayed NATO expansion until after Yeltsin's reelection in 1996.

In some ways, the Clinton administration's engagement in economic and political reform in Russia gave it the worst of both worlds. The extent and depth of its commitment, even including election campaign advice for Yeltsin from Clinton and its intensely personal quality made the United States a party to what happened without giving it the instruments that it needed to ensure the success of reform. Two Russian analysts, James M. Goldgeier and Michael McFaul, argued that the best that can be said about the administration's support for economic and political reform is that American specialists provided technical and political knowledge that had real and enduring influence for the good, however difficult it was to document.[18] The policies of the international lending institutions, especially the International Monetary Fund, hurt Russia's economic stabilization as much as it helped. Western economic policy ideas and billions of dollars were given to a Russia that lacked the institutions and the legal and technical oversight needed to use either wisely. On the surface, a kind of parodying of Western economic forms covered a reality of corruption and abuse. The examples are numerous and painful to recall. Two examples will suffice. Privatization—the central ideal of Western economic theory and practice—was ensured, but in a manner that betrayed the public trust and impoverished ordinary Russians while lavishing obscene wealth on oligarchs and former Soviet political and economic leaders. When the International Monetary Fund demanded that inflation be reduced through "austerity" measures, the Russian government simply stopped printing money and stopped paying its employees and pensioners. What was already a pitiful social safety net collapsed. It would have made sense for the United States to offer aid directly to individual Russians who had suffered the most, but the administration missed the chance.

In his second administration, Clinton attempted to reach agreements on missile defense and the reduction of nuclear weapons. In what turned out to be a vain attempt to control the issue and free the administration to make a deal with Russia, Clinton chose to compromise with the Republicans and allow testing of components of a nationwide ballistic missile defense. He planned to keep control of deployment by a provision in the deal that allowed the president to decide on deployment on the basis of scientific evidence about whether the system would work. Clinton then tried to persuade the Russian government to amend the ABM Treaty in a way that would permit the United States to build a small number of launchers in Alaska. To encourage Russian agreement on the ABM Treaty, the administration offered substantial cuts in American offensive strategic nuclear weapons, down to about 2,500. The Soviet Duma, controlled by the communists until 1999, had repeatedly blocked ratification of START II, an agreement concluded by the first Bush administration in 1992. In effect, the Clinton administration wanted to begin talking about START III before START II had been ratified. Not even this could induce Putin to agree. Presumably, he reasoned that too little time remained before the election to complete an agreement with Clinton and have it ratified by the U.S. Congress and the Duma. Better to wait for the new president, whomsoever it might be. It turned out to be George W. Bush, who had pledged to denounce the ABM Treaty during the campaign and did so within a year of taking office. Two other international problems—Russian nuclear assistance to Iran and the war in Chechnya—complicated U.S.-Russian relations throughout the 1990s. Sensitivity to Russian problems and financial incentives failed to bring an agreement about either. At one point in the deadlock, Yeltsin suggested that he could not control some of the elements of members of the Russian bureaucracy who were determined to continue profiting from nuclear deals with Iran. He certainly never stopped them. It is also possible that the Russian government was using the assistance as part of its own attempt to entice Iran to cooperate against terrorist and Islamist groups in Central Asia.

Israel and the Palestinians

A positive and truly precious thing came from the Clinton administration's engagement with Israel and the Palestinians. Because the American president was directly engaged in peacemaking, both sides extended their restraint of violence longer than would otherwise have been the case. Fewer lives were lost, fewer people wounded during those years, and families and children on both sides lived with less fear. Although violence never stopped, during the "good years" from 1993 to 1999, it was possible for Israelis and Palestinians to work, breathe, and walk around, even sometimes to relax. Had Clinton himself not been visibly and constantly involved in the peace process, the deadly spiral of attack and revenge would have resumed much sooner, probably during the period when Benjamin Netanyahu was prime minister and effectively halted the Oslo process. It is not a trivial accomplishment to save lives and help people to live with less fear and more hope, even for a little while.

The assassination of Yitzhak Rabin damaged the peace process so severely that it never recovered. The assassin, a Jewish religious extremist, took from Israel a warrior-president and statesman in whom most Israelis had complete confidence. The Palestinians lost a negotiating partner whom they respected and trusted to a degree not seen before or since. Narrowly elected on a promise to bring security to Israel, Netanyahu delayed the peace process, blunted its momentum, and reduced American diplomacy to a holding action devoted to keeping the process alive with the fewest possible setbacks. By the time another Labor prime minister, Yehud Barak, took office, opinion among Israelis and Palestinians had shifted ominously toward confrontation. Among the Palestinians, support for the Palestine Liberation Organization had peaked and begun to decline. The absence of much improvement in the Palestinians' daily existence and the steady increase in Israeli settlements in the West Bank and in and around Jerusalem—from a few thousand in the early 1970s to more than 400,000 by 2000—strengthened the appeal of militant Islamic organizations, such as Hamas. Ultimately, Israel and the Palestinian Authority bore the responsibility for the failure to make peace before the Clinton administration left office, but Clinton's negotiating tactics contributed in important ways.

The Clinton administration made four major mistakes in its mediation among Israel, Syria, and the Palestinians. The first was to allow Rabin and Barak to focus so heavily on Syria. The Israelis argued that Syria posed an existential threat because it might end up with an Islamic government and nuclear weapons and must be dealt with first. Barak repeated the demand. Clinton agreed both times. And both times Syria ultimately refused to make peace. Dealing with Syria first meant a delay of months in the start of negotiations with the Palestinians. Rabin's death could not be foreseen, but time was precious, and the momentum and trust that both sides gained from the Oslo accords were dissipating rapidly. Ordinary Palestinians felt all too keenly the lack of significant political and economic progress, and witnessed the continued settlement of the West Bank. They watched the Oslo deadlines for transferring land to Palestinian control pass unobserved. All these shortcomings played into the hands of extremists and undermined the PLO's influence over Palestinian society. Given the much more tenuous domestic political situation on both sides after Barak was elected, it is difficult to understand Clinton's decision not to insist at the very least on simultaneous negotiations with the Palestinians. Given Syria's past refusals to make peace, it would have made more sense to start with the Palestinians. By the time that Barak was certain that nothing could be done with Syria, his domestic support had fallen even further, and little time remained for Israel and the Palestinians to come to an understanding.

The Clinton administration's second error was to surrender its negotiating strategy to Rabin and Barak. This deprived the administration of any standing as a genuine mediator, although it came closer to playing such a role during Netanyahu's than Rabin's or Barak's premiership. Above all, it meant that President Clinton was unable to pressure Rabin, Netanyahu, and Barak as Carter had pressured Menachem Begin and Anwar Sadat during the first Camp David negotiations. The third, and perhaps the worst mistake, was to allow the final Camp David II talks to proceed without parameters established by the United States or a written text that outlined areas of agreement, disagreement, and possible solutions. Barak vetoed both ideas, presumably to enable him to deny to Israeli voters that he had made any concessions on sensitive matters. Clinton declined to override his opposition. This made the Palestinians understandably suspicious and gave an artificial air to the discussions that most likely was not intended by Barak.

Last, the negotiations from the 1993–1996 and 1999–2000 periods touched on the most sensitive possible matters, everything from borders to Palestinian independence, the return of refugees, and the status of Jerusalem. Yet very little was done to educate the Palestinian and Israeli publics about the scope and significance of the talks, the imminence of peace, and the necessity for changing old opinions and habits and beginning to think about one another in new ways. The talks among Israel, the Palestinian Authority, and the United States took place behind closed doors among experts, diplomats, and politicians. It was a rarefied atmosphere, enlivened by what had become if not friendship at least the close acquaintance and sometimes camaraderie that comes to a group of people who have had to work together at the peak of intensity for incredibly long hours for years. It was, in short, about as far away as it could be from the fears and dreams of ordinary Palestinians and Israelis.

Israeli, Palestinian, and American negotiators agreed that the general public on both sides could be expected to accept the huge changes needed for peace only if a final agreement were completely worked out in advance and presented to them on a take-it-or-leave-it basis. While understandable, the method betrayed a deep distrust of the very people who would have to live under the terms being decided by the diplomats and politicians. The Israeli-Palestinian conflict had defined the lives of the leaders on the two sides. Not so the Americans who lived far away and had never had to live with foreign occupation and constant terrorist attacks and reprisals. Clinton's failure to insist on educating the Israeli and Palestinian people was an inexcusable lapse for a mediator, whose primary responsibility was to think about the conditions needed to make peace.[19]

The talks appear to have taken on a life of their own, independent of the results that they achieved. In the process, leaders on all three sides may have been lulled into believing that the air of rationality, compromise, and accommodation that existed behind closed doors also existed in Tel Aviv, Ramallah, Jerusalem, and Hebron. They grew to believe that they were leading events rather than being led by them. It was an illusion. The talks ended late in 2000 with Clinton, Barak, and Dennis Ross blaming the Palestinians, and the Palestinians answering in kind. To overcome Arafat's reluctance to go to Camp David, Clinton had promised that he would not hold him responsible if the talks ended in failure. That was an appropriate promise for a mediator to make, but Clinton had never acted as a genuine mediator, and Arafat correctly foresaw that Clinton would blame him if the talks failed. He was right. Clinton, Ross, and Barak blamed Arafat over and over and over until virtually everyone in Israel and the United States saw it the same way. Arafat had been offered independence, they said, and at least 95 percent of the land of the West Bank. No responsible Palestinian leader could possibly reject such an offer. His refusal meant that he was incapable of making peace, perhaps had never intended to make peace. Here was a man unable to make the transition from revolutionary to statesman. Angry, wounded by his defeat and the failure of the talks, Barak lashed out blindly. Palestinians, and all Arabs, he said, lived in a culture that made no distinction between truth and falsehood. But blaming Arafat did not settle the issue of responsibility for the failure.

First, the settlements: not only before Oslo but throughout the decade afterward, not only under Likud but also Labor, Israeli settlements always expanded. Far from stopping them, the Israeli government provided substantial subsidies and incentives to the settlers to encourage them to move into the occupied territories. Even after Oslo, the pace of settlement never slowed and in some years even accelerated. It was sometimes faster under Labor Prime Ministers Rabin and Barak than under Likud Prime Minister Netanyahu. Why did Rabin fail to stop the expansion once and for all? Why did Barak fail to stop it? If the Israeli leaders genuinely intended for Israel to leave the West Bank, placing a halt on settlement would have clearly demonstrated their sincerity. Because the settlements continued while the Oslo framework was in place, many Palestinians concluded that Israel meant to mire them in another framework for another round of unending negotiations and take all the land. From this perspective, the negotiations were nothing more than a sham to gain time for more settlement. When Netanyahu was out of office, Ariel Sharon and others in Likud made no secret of their view that the settlements justified the presence of the Israeli army in the West Bank and Gaza, and that the presence of the army meant there could be no Palestinian state. The settlements strengthened those Palestinians who had never accepted Israel's existence, such as Hamas, an Islamist movement that resorted to terrorism. The settlements also undermined the credibility of the Palestinians who were willing to compromise with Israel. In the end, the settlements helped create a self-fulfilling prophecy about the impossibility of a genuine peace between Israel and an independent Palestine.

Second, Palestinians were not offered peace and immediate independence, but another negotiating process designed to last for years. The deal was essentially a replay of Oslo with the goal more clearly articulated, and the return to process only served to exaggerate the importance of atmosphere and trust. What did it mean that Barak was unwilling to meet Arafat face-to-face throughout the negotiations? They saw one another at meals and for small talk, but never negotiated. Why not? A text was not produced that recorded agreement and disagreement and indicated areas of possible compromise. Why? And what of the role of the United States? It never acted as an impartial mediator. As Dennis Ross noted in his memoirs, it soon became obvious that the United States was acting as a mouthpiece for Israeli positions. Why? Why did the Americans wait until the very last minute to submit their overall proposal, and then only orally on a take-it-or-leave-it basis? Why did Clinton approve Barak's decision to put negotiations with Syria ahead of Israeli-Palestinian talks? The precious weeks lost during the unproductive talks with Assad could not be recovered at the very end of the Clinton administration. All these actions by the Clinton administration confirm that it never acted as an impartial mediator, but rather as a partner of the Israeli government.

Arafat had never wanted a Camp David summit, but had repeatedly appealed to Clinton not to hold the talks. The time was not right, he said. He and his advisers were not ready. But Clinton insisted, and Arafat gave way, as he had to. What if the Clinton administration had not forced the Palestinians into an all-or-nothing showdown with the Israelis? What if it had recorded the progress in an interim agreement and continued the talks? Barak's position in Israel would have been strengthened. There would have been no justification for Sharon's accusations of betrayal. There would have been time to begin educating the public on both sides. Above all, both sides might have been spared the emotional and political rollercoaster ride that ended in a crushing disappointment. Israelis and Palestinians would also have been spared the charges leveled against Arafat by President Clinton, which only strengthened the opponents of peace. In the final analysis, the Palestinians did not reject a peace settlement. They did not reject an offer of 95 percent of the land. They rejected another process, another framework for negotiations at the end of which 95 percent of the land might be returned and an independent state might be established at some indeterminate time in the future, provided that an agreement could be reached. The Palestinians feared that at the end of the next ten years, another 200,000 Israelis would have moved to the West Bank and all hope of meaningful independence would have been lost. They also knew that Barak's government had lost its mandate to govern. Given these circumstances, what were the odds that the framework's clauses outlined with such detail would be honored and result in genuine independence?

When the deal fell apart, the extremists' resort to terror and Arafat's refusal to stop it were a catastrophe for the people who died and the worst possible choice for the Palestinian national cause. The hatred and fear on both sides that resulted from the terrorist attacks and reprisals together with the extent of Israeli settlement of the West Bank may well have destroyed all hope of an independent Palestinian state ever coming into existence. Morally revolting, founded on revolutionary zeal and a criminally ignorant analogy that compares the Jews of Israel to the French settlers in Algeria, the mindless acts of terror committed against defenseless men, women, and children reached the depths of depravity and folly. The heavy-handed Israeli occupation answered the Palestinians' moral and political errors in kind. The endless delays at Israeli checkpoints, the humiliating searches, the closing of the borders and resulting mass unemployment, and the raids and assassinations all made recruits for the extremists rather than converts for peace. The failure of the Camp David talks, the discrediting of the peace process, the assignment of all blame to Arafat, the terrorism, and the Israeli occupation all had consequences that reached far beyond the Camp David negotiations. Such a complete and public failure cast doubt on the fundamental elements of the peace process as it had existed for the past quarter century: the direct involvement of the American president, the idea of making incremental progress on peripheral issues as a way of building trust while postponing difficult issues until sufficient mutual confidence existed, and the hope of strengthening moderates and isolating extremists on both sides. This was Clinton's legacy to George W. Bush.

The "lessons" that the people who became George W. Bush's senior advisers learned from the failure of Clinton's efforts shaped their decision not to engage in peacemaking, thereby prolonging the agony of Israelis and Palestinians. Among the lessons that they took into office was that the president should not be involved in negotiating with the Israelis and Palestinians; it was a waste of time. In addition, the "peace process" was bankrupt and could never lead to a lasting settlement. The discrediting of Arafat by Barak, Clinton, and Ross also encouraged the next administration to abandon all dealings with him after 9/11 and to try to force regime change on the Palestinians. It was a time more bitter and tragic than any in the century-long struggle between Jew and Arab.

Concluding Observations

Bill Clinton's two terms as president are a marriage of significant accomplishment and appalling failure. If the charge by former Bush I National Security Council staffer Richard Haass—that Clinton's was "the squandered presidency" seems excessive, the claim of second national security adviser, Samuel Berger, that the two Clinton administrations enhanced "not only our power but also our authority" seems complacent and unreasonable.[20] Clinton's political adroitness, his undeniable personal brilliance and self-demeaning flaws, and the giant public rollercoaster aspect of his second term have a hypnotic attraction that makes it difficult to be objective about the man and his record. In the background of all the ups and downs are the memories of the dead and maimed in Bosnia and Rwanda and the failure to reach agreement between the Israelis and Palestinians.

Bill Clinton was the first American president to combine all the elements of the post–Cold War paradigm into his administration's foreign policy. The emphasis on spreading democracy, globalization and market economics, coercive diplomacy, economic sanctions, the faith in American exceptionalism, a frequent disregard of expert knowledge, and a Wilsonian view of the world and the duties of the United States all came together in the Clinton administration's two terms. The results, like Clinton's foreign policy as a whole, were mostly mixed, although there was a very important positive outcome in that an active U.S. foreign policy was sustained. In the early 1990s, American leaders and foreign policy analysts worried that the disappearance of the Soviet threat would deplete popular and congressional support for a constructive American role in world affairs. Clinton's manipulation of the post–Cold War paradigm put an end to their concerns. When Clinton left the White House after eight years, the U.S. government was deeply engaged internationally, and Americans showed little interest in isolation or withdrawal to a fortress America. However, that gain carried a very heavy price. The post–Cold War paradigm locked the Clinton administration into policies and commitments that were unsustainable and pregnant with trouble, not least because some of its elements, especially democratization and American exceptionalism, could be interpreted aggressively, as Bush II would, as well as passively, which was Clinton's preference.

The administration's emphasis on spreading democracy and market economics, what Clinton called engagement and enlargement, made the United States the custodian of world history instead of the protector of a single nation's vital security interests. Clinton not only stretched the country's philosophical and spiritual responsibilities but also imposed a bewildering set of military responsibilities on the American people. Anthony Lake's list of the grounds for using the armed forces abroad reached from protecting the country against direct attack through the defense and expansion of democracy, to combating the proliferation of weapons of mass destruction, terrorism and the international drug trade, and responding to famine and genocide.[21] As German journalist and newspaper editor Josef Joffe observed, this was "rampant historical optimism," a burden so heavy and so far-reaching that "[n]o European, Russian, or Chinese government would ever enunciate an agenda so open-ended. In truth, no U.S. government, certainly not Clinton's, would ever want to be held to it. . . ."[22] The Clinton administration sought relief from these responsibilities by trying to set stringent limits on American foreign intervention and by abstaining whenever it could, sometimes with shameful and horrific results. Ironically, the Clinton administrations and Bill Clinton himself, so despised by Republicans and neoconservatives, foreshadowed Bush II's emphasis on the "universality" of American values. In words that could have been spoken by George W. Bush, Clinton defended his commitment to spreading democracy: "These rights are universal—not U.S. rights, not Western rights, not rights for the developed world only, but rights inherent in the humanity of people everywhere."[23] "[O]ur values and interests are one and the same."[24] The sting in William Hyland's criticism—that democratization was "a witch's brew, too vague to be a guide to practical policy" haunted not just the Clinton administration, but its successor as well.[25]

Despite repeated terrorist attacks, the Clinton administration failed to develop an effective American and allied response to international terrorism. Like the traps of globalization, democratization, and ends and means out of balance, this shortcoming also passed to the Bush II administration. Knowing that 9/11 was coming, it is agony to follow the efforts of Clinton and his advisers to combat terrorism during the 1990s. Those precious, irretrievable years were a time when al-Qaeda might have been destroyed or its plans broken up and its agents killed or taken into custody. Instead, the years slipped away in well-meant and ultimately empty measures of little impact in stopping the coming catastrophe. The core of the problem lay within the American government, particularly the inability to recognize the changing nature of terrorism and the unwillingness of the Federal Bureau of Investigation (FBI) and Central Intelligence Agency (CIA) to cooperate and share information, and the parochial focus of the Justice Department on law enforcement. Rather than closing these critical gaps,

Clinton smothered the problem by doing what was bureaucratically acceptable: spend money on computers. Because of opposition from the U.S. military and his and his advisers' hesitations, the administration failed to destroy al-Qaeda in response to the attacks on American embassies in Africa and a U.S. Navy warship. Above all, the Clinton administration utterly failed to achieve the conceptual and organizational breakthroughs inside the American government, or to put spies in places that might have led to actions capable of sparing the United States and the world at least some of the agony it experienced on and after September 11, 2001.[26]

5

George W. Bush and the World

"We had no plan for catastrophic success."[1]

—Senior U.S. official

George W. Bush won the presidency in 2000 in an even stranger way than his father lost it eight years earlier. A faltering economy and a strong showing by third party candidate Ross Perot cost the first President Bush the election in 1992. Eight years later, his son's opponent, Vice President Al Gore, campaigned in the shadow of Bill Clinton's personal scandals and lost votes to the Green Party, led by Ralph Nader. Even with these strong assists, George W. Bush failed to win the popular vote. Only the hasty and unprecedented intervention by a conservative majority on the U.S. Supreme Court awarded him the contested electoral votes of the state of Florida and the presidency.

Bush's Team

During the campaign, candidate Bush professed a cautious, realist foreign policy. The woman who became his national security policy adviser, Condoleezza Rice, led Bush's foreign policy team. They called themselves Vulcans after the Roman god of fire, the symbol of Rice's hometown, Birmingham, Alabama. On more than one occasion, Bush spoke winningly of the need for humility in the conduct of American foreign policy and disarmingly admitted his lack of experience. He promised to compensate by hiring the best people he could find. A good number of them turned out to have worked for his father and to have strong and conflicting views about what the administration's foreign policy should be. Their clashing viewpoints pushed American foreign policy toward paralysis during the first months of Bush's presidency, but he and his political helpers knew that was not necessarily a bad thing for a domestically oriented administration. Bush's carefully chosen words left him free to begin what he hoped would be a Reaganesque first term that emphasized tax cuts and deregulation and avoided foreign entanglements.[2]

For the top three posts, Bush chose from his father's generation: Dick Cheney for vice president, Donald Rumsfeld as secretary of defense, and Colin Powell as secretary of state.[3] All three were strong-willed, experienced, Washington savvy, and exceptionally successful men who were convinced that they knew what the problems facing the nation were and what should be done about them. As a result, sharp and lasting disagreements began immediately and shook the administration for the next four years. But much more was involved than turf battles and clashing personalities. All the top political appointees were conservatives. They could not have joined the administration otherwise. But within that larger coherence lay a deep incoherence: on one side stood those who believed it was essential that the United States act unilaterally, and on the other were individuals who while not excluding unilateral action as a last resort believed that U.S. interests were best served by a policy of thoughtful multilateralism. The clash of viewpoints might have worked to the advantage of the president by ensuring that he heard all points of view. In practice, and particularly after 9/11, it was impossible to blend the differences in outlook and approach into a coherent whole. Instead, when they could not dominate decision making, as they did regarding Iraq, the unilateralists brought policy to a standstill, especially in regard to North Korea, Iran, and the Israeli-Palestinian conflict.[4]

Vice President Dick Cheney had served as secretary of defense in the first Bush administration. A staunch conservative, Cheney brought the experience of a long career in politics to the vice presidency. He was elected to the Congress for ten years before serving as President Gerald Ford's chief of staff.[5] In 1989, Cheney became secretary of defense and oversaw the invasion of Panama, the ouster of Panamanian dictator Manuel Noriega, and the military victory over Iraq in 1991. Out of office in the 1990s, Cheney went to work as chief executive officer for Haliburton$$$, a self-styled "energy services" company with extensive international operations in the Middle East, Mexico, and Indonesia. Under Cheney's five-year leadership, Haliburton doubled its government contracts—from $1.2 billion to $2.3 billion—and Cheney became a rich man.[6] Donald Rumsfeld had been Richard Nixon's defense secretary twenty-five years earlier; a member of Congress through the 1960s; President Gerald Ford's chief of staff (Rumsfeld brought Cheney to the Ford White House); ambassador to NATO; and a special envoy on a variety of missions for the Reagan administration, including discussions with Saddam Hussein's Iraq during the Iran-Iraq war when U.S. policy was to make Iran lose the war slowly.[7] Rumsfeld left Washington earlier than Cheney and spent his years out of office working for pharmaceutical companies and made a great deal of money.[8] During the 1990s, Rumsfeld reentered the political arena by joining various conservative study groups attacking Clinton's foreign policy and at the very end of the decade headed commissions established by the Republican-controlled Congress to reassess the nation's missile defense and space needs.[9] Rumsfeld occasionally referred to terrorism before 9/11, but he saw it as one of a number of "asymmetrical" threats, ways of attacking the United States without having to confront American forces in conventional battle. Instead of making terrorism a top priority, Rumsfeld initially focused on upgrading the technological capabilities of American military forces, particularly their uses of space and missile defense. He hoped these improvements would make it possible to reduce the size of American combat forces without diminishing their "lethality."[10]

Colin Powell's success is a uniquely American story. He knew this and often referred to his modest upbringing.[11] Powell's parents emigrated from Jamaica, and Powell graduated not from Yale or Stanford but from City College of New York (CCNY), and accepted not a West Point but an ROTC commission in 1958. Powell loved the army and rose rapidly. He stood out from his peers because he found ways to make distinctive accomplishments in virtually every assignment and refused to fight over things that others

turned into matters of principle. "Give the man his shilling" was one of the
maxims he borrowed from his father. As he rose higher, another of Powell's
attributes became more and more important. In each of the "special assistant" posts he received, he quickly made himself indispensable, the man to
whom everyone turned to make things work when all else was failing. Powell's appointments as national security adviser and head of the joint staff
gave him a global perspective and helped accustom him to dealing with foreign political and military officials and the U.S. Congress, as well as the
White House and Pentagon.

As chairman of the Joint Chiefs of Staff, Powell became widely known
as the author of the "Powell Doctrine," a set of rules for the commitment
of American troops abroad:

> Is the political objective we seek to achieve important, clearly defined
> and understood? Have all other nonviolent policy means failed? Will
> military force achieve the objective? At what cost? Have the gains and
> risks been analyzed? How might the situation that we seek to alter, once
> it is altered by force, develop further and what might be the conse-
> quences . . .? When the political objective is important, clearly defined
> and understood, when the risks are acceptable, and when the use of
> force can be effectively combined with diplomatic and economic poli-
> cies, then clear and unambiguous objectives must be given to the armed
> forces. These objectives must be firmly linked with the political ob-
> jectives. . . . Decisive means and results are always to be preferred, even
> if they are not always possible. . . . This is not to argue that the use of
> force is restricted to only those occasions where the victory of Ameri-
> can arms will be resounding, swift and overwhelming. It is simply to
> argue that the use of force should be restricted to occasions where it can
> do some good and where the good will outweigh[s] the loss of lives and
> other costs that will surely ensue. Wars kill people. That is what makes
> them different from all other forms of human enterprise.[12]

Powell spoke for a generation of career officers and enlisted men who
had fought in Vietnam, and thought the war had been handled badly by
civilian and military leaders. His rules revealed a profound distrust of civilian politicians. In an offhand and even insulting manner, the Powell Doctrine assumed political incompetence. Powell insisted that he did not mean
to forbid military intervention, although that is what activist political leaders always claimed. After the failures in Vietnam and Lebanon, Powell's

reservations about American political leadership were not unwarranted, but a much more important problem for Powell as secretary of state was that the "Powell Doctrine" is essentially procedural. The rules identify the conditions that Powell and his fellow officers believed were necessary in order for military intervention to succeed, but they are silent about the goals of policy or the criteria by which to determine them. The lack of substance was appropriate for a military leader in a society that subordinates military to civilian leadership. Procedure without substance is not an appropriate stance for a secretary of state. In his new post, Powell had the opportunity to set the goals of policy, something that neither his procedural orientation, essentially a staff officer's recipe book, nor his "we'll make it work" ethos inherited from years in the military had prepared him for.

Condoleezza Rice broke into the inner circle of the Bush I administration with the help of the man who became George H.W. Bush's national security adviser, Brent Scowcroft, who met her at a faculty seminar at Stanford University in 1984. Scowcroft appointed Rice to the National Security Council as director of Soviet and East European Affairs in 1989. She left after two years to return to her faculty position at Stanford but during that time had become close friends with the president and his wife Barbara. Visits to the Bush compound in Kennebunkport followed where she met George W. Bush. Rice became provost at Stanford—chief academic and budgeting officer—in 1993, and stayed in that position until she joined the 2000 campaign.[13] In keeping with her long-standing *realpolitik* outlook, Rice sharply criticized Clinton's foreign policy during the campaign, especially for wasting lives and resources in such unimportant places as Kosovo and Haiti. She also endorsed an idea dear to Republican conservatives that U.S. military forces should protect "liberated zones" from which the Iraqi opposition could overthrow Saddam Hussein. The scheme horrified U.S. generals, but had apparently become conservative dogma by 2000.[14] Brought together by the Bush family and their joint ambitions, George W. Bush and Condoleezza Rice were an odd couple: the tightly wound, upwardly mobile, middle-class, African-American intellectual female, and the rich recovering alcoholic who had found religion.[15] Because Rice refused to allow even a hint of difference to appear between her and the president, it was difficult to know who influenced whom the most. By embracing Bush's intuitive moralistic activism, Rice cleared the way for a far more ambitious role for the United States—and herself—in shaping the world in the twenty-first century. Bush appointed her secretary of state after he won the 2004 election.

Donald Rumsfeld filled the political offices in the Pentagon with men who had served under Cheney in the first Bush administration, including Paul Wolfowitz, who became deputy secretary of defense.[16] Wolfowitz had held a number of foreign policy appointments over the years: head of the State Department's Policy Planning staff, assistant secretary of state for Asia and Pacific Affairs, ambassador to Indonesia during the Reagan administration, and undersecretary of defense for policy during Bush I. Wolfowitz's background was academic, and when Bush I lost the 1992 election, Wolfowitz became dean of the Johns Hopkins School of Advanced International Studies in Washington. During the 1990s, he frequently criticized Clinton's foreign policy and called for much tougher treatment of North Korea, the overthrow of Saddam Hussein, and an end to pressure on Israel to grant the Palestinians a separate state in all the occupied territories.[17] Wolfowitz repeatedly attacked Clinton's policies toward Saddam as inadequate and pointless, and eventually began to argue for a far-fetched scheme for the United States to invade Iraq and establish "a safe protected zone in the South" of that country, including Iraq's largest oil field, in which a provisional government could be established.[18] Iraqi exiles with whom Wolfowitz and other foreign policy conservatives such as Dick Cheney and Richard Perle were in contact were to form the nucleus of such a proxy state.[19] A former commander in chief of U.S. forces in the Gulf, General Anthony Zinni, said the idea of a safe zone in Iraq was a design for a "Bay of Goats," a disaster like the Bay of Pigs fiasco during the Kennedy administration. What would happen if Saddam decided to attack the U.S.-protected enclave? Wouldn't it be wiser to go to war at a time and in a way of our own choosing? Wolfowitz stubbornly defended his idea against all attacks.[20] Although he had a reputation as a patient and analytical man, Wolfowitz was an activist, preoccupied with the costs of not acting than with the risks of taking a particular step. He was convinced that by exercising its enormous power, the United States could change the world for the better.

Colin Powell's choice for deputy secretary of state was a friend of twenty years, Richard Armitage.[21] A bear of a man, Armitage graduated from the U.S. Naval Academy, served three combat tours with the Navy in Vietnam, worked as administrative assistant for Senator Bob Dole, and performed a wide variety of duties in several Republican administrations in posts at the Pentagon and Department of State. Armitage was one of the Vulcans who advised Bush about foreign policy during the 2000 campaign and validated his credentials among conservatives by serving as head of a working group to examine the Clinton administration's policy toward North Korea. Issued in March 1999, the report was rhetorically critical—it described current policy as "politically unsustainable" and "fragmented," but it offered little that differed in substance from the Clinton policies.[22]

George W. Bush and the Post–Cold War Paradigm

George W. Bush adopted Ronald Reagan's presidency as his model rather than his father's. He and his advisers thought that they had learned the lessons of the first Bush administration's defeat in 1992. There would be no enemies on the Republican right, and the president and his administration would pay attention to the economy. Undaunted by having lost the popular vote, Bush pushed his conservative domestic agenda and downplayed foreign policy.[23] During the months before 9/11, the administration lashed out at international organizations and multilateral and even bilateral cooperation. It refused to take part in the multilateral Kyoto agreements on the environment or the International Criminal Court (ICC), and quickly made clear it planned to denounce the ABM Treaty with Russia and replace the strategic arms reduction treaties with what amounted to a handshake agreement, with no requirements for information exchange or mutual inspections. President Bush was not turning the United States away from international affairs, but a number of senior policymakers and a gaggle of neoconservative commentators were determined to free the country from what they regarded as the immoral and dangerous encumbrances of multilateralism.[24]

Bush II foreign policy differed from Clinton's and Bush I's in many ways, but at its core the post–Cold War paradigm remained a powerful shaper of Bush II's operational code and thus of its strategy. The president and his advisers accorded great importance to what they believed to be American global hegemony and American exceptionalism. They reminded Americans and the world that the United States would act unilaterally because it could, because it had a responsibility to lead, and because it sought no selfish advantage, only the security of the United States and the peace and well-being of the world. The administration embraced Clinton's position that the democratization of other societies was a vital security interest of the United States. Many of the president's speeches on democratization sounded as if they had been written for Bill Clinton. Remove the dates and references to specific events and it would be almost impossible to tell them apart. George W. Bush's willingness to go to war to achieve these goals did not signal a break with the post–Cold War paradigm. Rather, it showed the president to be an interventionist Wilsonian. Like Woodrow Wilson, George W. Bush did not shrink from going to war, while emphasizing that he did so to bring democracy and peace to the world. Bandwagoning also played an important part in the administration's calculations. That so few important countries sided with the United States to overthrow Saddam Hussein surprised and disappointed the president and his advisers.

The Unilateralists

During the Bush I administration, Dick Cheney and Paul Wolfowitz had put together a unilateral strategy of global dominance for the United States. (See Chapters 1 and 2.) They argued that the goal of American strategy should be the creation of "a U.S.-led system of collective security and a democratic 'zone of peace.'"[25] American supremacy would be used to prevent nations such as Iraq, Iran, and North Korea from acquiring weapons of mass destruction, and to make it unnecessary for rising powers such as Germany and Japan to acquire these weapons on their own or become global strategic players. These ideas and many others from the earlier planning surfaced again after 9/11, particularly as the administration prepared to go to war in Iraq.[26] During their eight years out of power, the unilateralists refined their notions of global primacy and preventive war, and returned to power eager to put them into practice.[27] Blocked by the pulling and hauling of bureaucratic politics in the opening months of the administration, the unilateralists seized the opening blasted by the horrific attacks on 9/11 to advance their policies.

Denouncing the Kyoto protocol on global warming, the ICC, and the ABM Treaty with Russia gave opponents around the world ammunition to fire at the administration, but the unilateralists were pleased with the results. They also worked to give Israeli Prime Minister Ariel Sharon a green light to use massive force against the Palestinians. The changes aroused less opposition than might have been expected. The Kyoto and ICC agreements were far from perfect, and were not vital to national security, and Russia was too poor to counter an American missile defense with its own nuclear buildup. Very few members of Congress wanted to fall on their swords over multilateral agreements or missile defense. Those inside the administration with reservations about the unilateralists and their rhetoric preferred to let the noisy challenges go by in order to maximize their influence on issues where the need for caution, multilateralism, and incremental change was clear and widely supported.

While it was easy to support Israel and denounce Kyoto and the ICC, the unilateralists found themselves unable to gain complete acceptance of the assumptions and policies that they hoped would turn American strategy and diplomacy into instruments for global transformation. Thus, before and after the terrorist attacks in Manhattan and Washington, the Bush administration operated with what mounted to two sets of fundamental assumptions about the world, the threats facing the United States, and what might be done about them. Before 9/11, the unilateralists assumed that:

- American global hegemony enables the United States to transform the world; other countries will join the United States (bandwagon), not oppose it.
- Deterrence has been weakened and must be restored.
- The international status quo damages the United States and the cause of human freedom.
- Democracy is possible for all peoples.
- The moral dimension must be restored to American diplomacy and military strategy.
- Time is not on our side; the costs of inaction are greater than the costs of action.

After 9/11, George W. Bush's determination to transform the world was stated explicitly in the arguments that he and his advisers gave in favor of going to war in Iraq. The aim was never simply to disarm Saddam Hussein, but to give Iraq a democratic government. Like Bill Clinton, George W. Bush believed that democracies are peaceful and do not attack one another. Bush and his unilateralist advisers also argued that carrying out regime change in Iraq would lead to the spread of democracy throughout the Middle East and even the Muslim world. In their eyes, the absence of democracy, not poverty or the Israeli-Palestinian conflict, was the source of terrorism. The attacks on 9/11 not only put the unilateralists' assumptions on top, but convinced the president to add global transformation to his already transformational domestic agenda. Changing Iraq turned out to be a huge undertaking, far more difficult and costly than the administration had envisioned, but the problems seemed to encourage rather than discourage the president. In his inaugural address in January 2005, Bush extended de-mocratization to the entire world:

> The survival of liberty in our land increasingly depends on the success of liberty in other lands. The best hope for peace in our world is the expansion of freedom in all the world. . . . From the day of our found-ing, we have proclaimed that every man and woman on this Earth has rights, and dignity and matchless value because they bear the image of the maker of heaven and Earth. . . . Advancing these ideals is the mission that created our nation. It is the honorable achieve-ment of our fathers. Now it is the urgent requirement of our nation's security and the calling of our time.
>
> So, it is the policy of the United States to seek and support the growth of democratic movements and institutions in every nation and culture, with the ultimate goal of ending tyranny in our world.[28]

Just how ambitious the administration's goals were emerged clearly in a discussion between one of Bush's senior advisers and Ron Suskind, bi-ographer of Paul O'Neil, who would lose his job as secretary of the treas-ury partway through the first term:

> The aide said that guys like me were "in what we call the reality-based community," which he defined as people who "believe that solutions emerge from your judicious study of discernible reality." I nodded and murmured something about enlightenment principles and empiricism. He cut me off. "That's not the way the world really works anymore," he continued. "We're an empire now, and when we act, we create our own reality. And while you're studying that reality—judiciously, as you will—we'll act again, creating other new realities, which you can study too, and that's how things will sort out. We're history's actors . . . and you, all of you, will be left to just study what we do."[29]

When he added global to domestic transformation, President Bush made no concessions to "normal" wartime practice. He opposed any increase in taxes to pay for the war, and at the start of his second term began a campaign to cut taxes further and allow participants in Social Security to create private in-vestment accounts by using some of the money that they would previously have paid into the government's retirement program. Estimates of the costs to the government and taxpayers ran into the trillions of dollars.[30]

The unilateralists' overpowering need to act to transform the world arose from a strange compound of confidence and despair. Their belief in American global hegemony gave them confidence bordering on arrogance about their chances of success. Time was precious, and the opportunity to act was fleeting. It would be wrong and dangerous to let it pass without using the now-unrivalled power of the United States to make the world a better place. The unilateralists believed beyond a doubt in their moral rectitude, and the error and even immorality of their opponents. They thought that expressing their ideas openly and frankly and acting forcefully would win governments and peoples to their cause. Curiously, they also dreaded the present and the future. A sense of cultural despair gnawed at the corners of their minds. Perhaps it was too late. What if what they saw as the ravages of modernity had made it impossible to save what was precious in American and Western culture? Miraculously, events had left the United States in a dominant position in the world and brought a genuine conservative to the White House. Such an extraordinary opportunity must be used not only to make the United States more secure but to transform the world's nations into peace-loving market democracies. Everything about the present convinced them that if the moment was not seized and every effort given immediately, the chance to do great and good things would vanish and never come again. The risks of not acting outweighed the dangers of making a mistake. The unilateralists believed that terrorists and rogue leaders had found encouragement in Clinton's unwillingness to destroy those who attacked Americans. The United States had become "risk averse," especially when it came to sending American soldiers into combat. The unilateralists meant to restore deterrence by using American military power decisively and overwhelmingly.

Conservatives and unilateralists alike detested what they saw as a cult of multilateralism. In their eyes, multilateralism was as bad and as much to be resisted as its domestic and what they believed to be essentially socialist equivalent, the Clinton/Blair/Schroeder "Third Way." Murderous dictators hid behind multilateralism to plot against their own peoples and the United States. Multilateralism confused people of good will, elevated governmental authority to a dangerous degree, handicapped and prevented the United States from acting in ways essential to its own vital national security interests, and substituted the judgment of foreign governments for the sovereign judgment of the American government. It was a snare and a delusion. Many governments resented, despised, and opposed everything that the United States stood for. Why bother asking them to cooperate? Ultimately, they were certain to refuse and obstruct U.S. policy. In a world no longer threatened by the Soviet Union, NATO added little to American security and seriously limited American effectiveness and freedom of action.

Echoing Cheney's Bush I study, the unilateralists argued that American primacy could be sustained by maintaining a margin of military superiority so vast that it discouraged other governments from challenging the United States. They believed this would render the international order peaceful and benign. Arms races and wars would be replaced by competition in trade, economic development, and international games such as the Olympics.[31] Relations with the great powers were important to the United States, but they must be founded on the basis of American supremacy and a clear understanding of American interests—in other words subordination to American leadership. The unilateralists opposed an independent foreign policy and military capability for the European Union on the grounds that it would weaken the American position in Europe and interfere with American policy in other regions. China posed the greatest future threat to the United States, and the dangerous nonsense of treating China as a strategic partner must be stopped. China was a long-term enemy, and should be treated in public as a competitor and potential adversary, not a partner.

The emphasis on military predominance seems to be a departure from Wilsonianism and the post–Cold War paradigm, but it is consistent with Wilson's resort to war and his and the unilateralists' interpretation of American exceptionalism and democratization. Like Woodrow Wilson, the unilateralists believed they could use American power to change the world and make it a better place. In a sense, their determination to back American-led global transformation with massive military power corrected a serious shortcoming in Wilson's view of exceptionalism. Wilson recognized that American presidents could not maintain a global foreign policy unless they linked it to the country's perception of itself and its morals, but his proposals failed in part because he lacked a complete view of the causes of conflict—attributing wars to exceptional circumstances or the faults of individual leaders—and because he thought that public opinion and the spread of democracy would provide an adequate foundation for world peace.[32] George W. Bush's version of making the world safe for democracy was based on American military and economic primacy and his willingness to wage preventive war. The American conquest of Iraq ran into problems, but they were not the result of over-reliance on the support of public opinion.

Conservatives and unilateralists associated with Bush II shared the 1990s infatuation with democracy. They believed that democratic states do not make war on one another. For this reason, the single most effective step that could be taken to ensure American security and well-being was to replace rogue dictatorships in Iraq, Iran, North Korea, Syria, and Libya with democratic governments. Echoing Bill Clinton, they believed that to argue otherwise was to patronize peoples from poor countries, and even to fall into racism and religious prejudice. The United States must not shrink from supporting embattled democracies such as Israel, nor should it refrain from pressing for the immediate democratization of friendly states such as Egypt and Saudi Arabia. The unilateralists also believed that morality was forgotten and even spurned in the contemporary world in favor of a soul-destroying moral relativism and ethical ambiguity. The United States must take the moral high ground, and, if necessary, force other nations to accept its views of right and wrong. If the United States acted decisively and told "the truth" about evil in the world, its moral clarity would attract decent governments and rally decent world opinion (the only kind Americans should care about), offend none but the malevolent and those beyond help, and provide an invaluable weapon in the war against Islamic fundamentalism and terrorism. Not to act in these ways only strengthened the "evil doers," confused decent governments and people of good will, and undermined their strength.

The Multilateralists

There was much that united the multilateralists and the unilateralists: a deep and abiding commitment to the well-being of the United States and all that it stands for, a powerful desire to create a decent international order, and a prevailing wish to help the less fortunate. But more divided them. They disagreed not so much over threats as what to do about them. They also differed over the limits of military power, style, and in a deeper sense, personal philosophy and sensibility. The multilateralists held a mixed view of American primacy and exceptionalism. Without denying that the United States played a unique role in the world, they doubted that democracy was a panacea for world problems, and worried about the imbalance between commitments and capabilities that resulted from making the spread of democracy a vital security interest of the United States. Working within the limits of a half-century of American caution and cooperation with allies and international institutions, the multilateralists found it difficult to spell out the reasons behind their approach to foreign policy. It was like trying to make a case for breathing. The multilateralists assumed that:

- American primacy justifies confidence about the future.
- Global trends favor the United States more than any other country.
- Multilateralism is better than unilateralism.
- Democracy has only limited relevance to other countries.
- Introducing morality into public diplomacy can hurt as much as help.

Before 9/11 the multilateralists would have agreed with the Clinton administration that there were no threats to vital American interests that required an immediate all-out military response. American primacy—an overwhelming superiority in military and economic power—made it unnecessary to seek radical international change in the short term. Global trends since 1989 also strengthened their confidence about the future. Globalization, democratization, the spread of information technology, and, until very late in the 1990s, a scintillating American economy, were all changes of greater advantage to the United States than any other country, provided that the right use was made of them. Time was important, but it did not suffocate the multilateralists. As the Bush II administration began, they agreed with the unilateralists that there was no urgent need to put terrorism, the environment, or nuclear proliferation ahead of other problems, such as relations with the great powers or peacemaking in the Middle East.

The multilateralists believed that the United States should continue its vocation as an international institution builder. Working through international and multilateral organizations often led to delays but the gains in burden sharing and international legitimacy more than compensated for the costs. It might sometimes be necessary to act alone or with a few close allies, as was done in the case of Bosnia and Kosovo, but these exceptions did not disprove the general rule favoring multilateralism. In addition to its other benefits, multilateralism generally supported U.S. interests, and in any case, disguised American primacy and made it more acceptable to other governments. The multilateralists were aware of the fragility of democracies imposed on others before they were ready. European decolonization had led to short-lived democratic governments that were quickly replaced by military dictatorships and colossal corruption, and ended in civil war and, in some cases, genocide. Moreover, all the world's full-fledged democracies—those that protected minorities, and allowed the rule of law, free speech, and religious freedom—had a long history of responsible, limited government that preceded and accompanied their transition to democracy.

The multilateralists recognized that the claim to be acting on moral principle was available to anyone who wanted to make it. Some of the worst evils of the twentieth century were committed by Mao Zedong and Stalin, political leaders who claimed to be acting in the name of high moral principle. Certainly many of their early followers believed in the moral rectitude of their cause. Islamic terrorists always claimed to be acting out of sincere religious conviction. The assumption that moral principles ought to be simply and directly translated into policy transported political, religious, and economic differences out of the realm of politics and negotiation into an arena where compromise itself was immoral. When necessity intruded, the result was either hypocrisy—flexibility must be restored in some way—or hyperbolic commitment and unending and needless conflict. Publicly insisting on the unique morality of the U.S. position, and at least implicitly the immorality of others, flirted with self-righteousness and risked equating moral clarity, an essential at every level of politics, with the policies that were required to achieve a morally acceptable and politically constructive outcome. As the clash between Abraham Lincoln and the abolitionists showed, moral clarity does not automatically lead to agreement about what should actually be done, even among those who share the same moral convictions.

9/11 and a New National Security Strategy

The suicidal terrorist attacks of September 11, 2001, destroyed the Twin Towers and a wing of the Pentagon and took thousands of lives. People around the world responded with spontaneous and widespread sympathy and support for the United States. "We are all Americans," a headline in a leading Paris newspaper declared for hundreds of millions of people. The outpouring of concern and support was genuine, spontaneous, and heartwarming. The destruction of innocent life was appalling, all of it shown over and over again on television, unforgettable pictures of giant airplanes striking the towers, the fires, the bodies hurtling downward, the collapsing structures. It took little imagination to put oneself on board a doomed airplane or to imagine the loss of loved ones anywhere in the world in a city struck at random. For the first time in history, NATO invoked Article 5 of the Atlantic Treaty, which calls for the defense of member-states that have been attacked. The administration responded to the attacks by changing one of its fundamental assumptions about foreign policy. Within a month of the attacks, senior officials in the administration spoke of a "nexus" between suicidal terrorists and dictators armed with weapons of mass destruction. Bush declared that the combination threatened the world, and pledged to crush the terrorists and disarm the dictators by any means necessary.[33]

Iraq

Immediately after the 9/11 attacks, the administration focused on destroying the Taliban government of Afghanistan, home to Osama bin Laden, the instigator of the attacks, killing or capturing him, and crushing his organization, al-Qaeda. On October 7, 2001, supported by British, Australian, and Afghan forces from the Northern Alliance, the United States attacked. Barely two months later, the leader of the Taliban, Mullah Mohammad Omar, fled the city of Kandahar, his last stronghold. Other Taliban and al-Qaeda fighters including Osama bin Laden reportedly took refuge in a mountainous region between Afghanistan and Pakistan. Pursued by American forces, bin Laden became a hunted man with a price on his head, his camps destroyed, his followers scattered and killed. The victory in Afghanistan came so quickly and at such a low cost because the administration decided against a conventional invasion and occupation of the country. Instead, U.S. strategists left the social and political structure of the country in place. Its deep fractures along ethnic and religious lines—exploited by regional "warlords"—actually helped the U.S. plan, which was to supply the warlords not with American troops but with U.S. warplanes armed with precision munitions. Four years after the fall of the Taliban, Afghanistan remained an economic and social basket case. The country held national elections successfully, but aid dribbled into the country, security was scarce outside the capital, Kabul, and the new president Hamid Karzai had managed to disarm only a few warlords. The quick victory over the Taliban freed the administration to plan the overthrow of Saddam Hussein. Keeping weapons of mass destruction out of the hands of terrorists had become its first priority.

At the beginning of George W. Bush's first term, Iraq had been one of the places that the administration sought to keep from exploding and derailing its hopes for tax cuts and reductions in government. Although divided about what to do, the administration allowed Colin Powell to take the lead in trying to persuade the international community and Saddam Hussein to agree to "smart sanctions," a reduction in the number of prohibited items, and tougher enforcement of those that remained in exchange for unlimited sales of Iraqi oil. Saddam Hussein refused to cooperate, encouraged in his refusal by government officials and influential individuals in a number of countries, including France, Russia, China, Australia, Canada, Spain, a number of Arab states, and Indonesia, some of whom may have been accepting substantial bribes. The United States and Britain knew about the corruption but declined to stop it because Turkey and Jordan, both friendly countries, benefited handsomely from the legal and illegal shipments of Iraqi oil.[34] Seeing the international community divided and hesitant, the Iraqi leader calculated that in a short while the consensus in favor of sanctions of any kind would evaporate and it would be possible to escape them altogether. It was not his worst miscalculation, but it was a serious error.

After 9/11 the president's rhetoric left little room for compromise short of regime change in Baghdad. Since Saddam Hussein would not leave voluntarily or allow free elections, and he posed no immediate danger to the United States, this meant preventive war. The Bush II administration's strategy for dealing with Iraq was based on these assumptions:

- Saddam Hussein has chemical and biological weapons and seeks nuclear weapons.
- These weapons pose a dire threat to American security because a "nexus" exists between terrorists and rogue dictators that makes it likely that these weapons will be used against the United States, its allies, and friendly countries.
- Deterrence is useless against such enemies.
- Intelligence is severely limited in its capacity to detect the intentions and capabilities of rogue states and terrorists in advance of a catastrophic attack, and must be replaced by the use of logic, historical analogy, and common sense.
- The United States must destroy the nexus composed of Saddam Hussein's Iraq, terrorists, and weapons of mass destruction.[35]
- American global hegemony allows the United States to wage unilateral preventive war if necessary.
- The universal validity of democracy and market economics will make the task of reconstructing and democratizing Iraq relatively quick and easy once Saddam Hussein is overthrown.
- Coercive diplomacy must be applied to the United Nations as well as Iraq; noncompliance will lead to war.

In taking action against the Taliban and in choosing to overthrow Saddam Hussein, President Bush came down on the side of those who wanted to use

American dominance unilaterally, that is, Cheney, Rumsfeld, and Wolfowitz. It is sometimes argued that Cheney and Rumsfeld sought to use force to crush America's enemies and cared little for the transformationist and democratizing ideas of the neoconservatives.[36] It may be true, but in practice it was a distinction without a difference. After having overthrown Saddam Hussein, Cheney and Rumsfeld had no choice but to try to democratize Iraq. The United States has no other model for rehabilitating countries. In going to war in Iraq without explicit UN authorization or the military support of many important allies and Arab states, Bush II relied on all the assumptions of the post–Cold War paradigm: American hegemony (unilateral preventive war), American exceptionalism, democratization (regime change), coercive diplomacy, and bandwagoning.

At least as early as December 2001, President Bush decided to overthrow Saddam Hussein.[37] From February 2002, President Bush spoke repeatedly in public about his determination to remove Saddam.[38] Nearly all the heads of government he talked to agreed about the seriousness of the threat, but most expressed reservations about going to war against Iraq to force disarmament and regime change.[39] Bush responded by equating regime change in Iraq and the global war on terrorism:

> Countering Iraq's threat is also a central commitment in the war on terror. We know Saddam Hussein has longstanding and ongoing ties to international terrorists. With the support and shelter of a regime, terror groups become far more lethal. Aided by a terrorist network, an outlaw regime can launch attacks while concealing its involvement. Even a dictator is not suicidal, but he can make use of men who are.[40]

The administration published its national security strategy in September 2002, a year after the 9/11 attacks, but it had been acting on its precepts since the invasion of Afghanistan in October 2001.[41] The document declared that the United States would maintain American hegemony, a margin of military superiority so great that no rival could hope to challenge it. Asserting the special virtues of the United States, the document stated:

> The U.S. national security strategy will be based on a distinctly American internationalism that reflects the union of our values and our national interests. The aim of this strategy is to help make the world not just safer but better.[42]

The new strategy committed the United States to a "war" against terrorism. National survival was at stake: "In the war against global terrorism, we will never forget that we are ultimately fighting for our democratic values and way of life."[43] The document was comprehensive. It devoted sections to foreign aid and international economic policy in the changed context of global terrorism, but its main purpose was to justify preventive war.

The administration based its assertion of the right to go to war against rogue states and terrorists on a nation's right to self-defense.[44] By calling it preemptive rather than preventive war, the administration sought the cover of long-standing international doctrines of "anticipatory defense" and "imminent threat," and the UN Charter's Article 51, which recognizes "the inherent right of individual or collective self-defense."[45] Virtually no one challenged the right to attack terrorists who had struck a country or its citizens. This clearly applied to Afghanistan, where the al-Qaeda terrorists had lived and trained before 9/11, and helps explain why the American invasion of that country was so widely supported. But the administration was asserting a much broader right to attack not just terrorists but rogue states that it claimed would pass weapons of mass destruction to terrorists. Deterrence was meaningless. Rogue dictators were immune to deterrence because they were indifferent to threats to their peoples and societies that more sensible and humane leaders sought to avoid. Rogue dictators brutalized their own people, disregarded international law, sought weapons of mass destruction, sponsored terrorists, rejected human values, and hated the United States and all it represented. Rogue states not only were pursuing weapons of mass destruction, but with help from their "terrorist clients" they would use them against the United States and its allies. Terrorists were also indifferent to the costs that their actions imposed on themselves, their targets, or their supporters, and thus were immune to deterrence. The danger lay in the combination of technology, intent to harm, and capability to harm America and its allies and friends: "The overlap between states that sponsor terror and those that pursue WMD compels us to action."[46] Safety demanded that the world follow the lead of the United States and recognize that the traditional concept of imminent threat as a justification for preemptive war could not meet the threat posed by rogue states and terrorists. This led inexorably to preventive war. Or, as the national security strategy put it:

> The greater the threat, the greater is the risk of inaction—and the more compelling the case for taking anticipatory action to defend our-

selves, even if uncertainty remains as to the time and place of the enemy's attack. To forestall or prevent such hostile acts by our adversaries, the United States will, if necessary, act preemptively.

Knowing how far this stretched the idea of self-defense, the administration sought to qualify its application. This was nothing new, the national security strategy asserted: the United States had often taken preventive actions in the past. It would not resort to them in every case and would weigh every situation carefully. The U.S. government would strengthen its intelligence capabilities in order to detect emerging threats accurately, and coordinate with other governments to arrive at a common assessment of the threat.[47] Finally, "The purpose of our actions will always be to eliminate a specific threat to the United States or our allies and friends. The reasons for our actions will be clear, the force measured, and the cause just."[48] Unpersuaded, even friendly governments regarded the new strategy as a deeply troubling assertion of American primacy. Critics at home and abroad saw it as American imperialism. The administration ignored them.

Thanks largely to the efforts of Colin Powell, the administration delayed the start of hostilities and took its case against Iraq to the United Nations in the fall of 2002.[49] A compromise UN Security Council resolution 1441 passed unanimously on November 8, 2002. It required Iraq to allow UN weapons inspectors and the International Atomic Energy Agency to return and renew their search for the weapons and programs that had been interrupted when Saddam had managed to force their withdrawal four years earlier. Iraq was given 45 days to report all measures that it had taken to halt production and destroy stockpiles, and was enjoined to grant the inspectors unfettered and safe access at all times anywhere in the country.[50] The resolution's language showed the strains of diplomacy without consensus. To placate the Americans and the British, it implicitly threatened Iraq with war. Iraq was found to be in "material breach" of its obligations, and warned that if it would be in "further material breach" if it failed to fulfill all its obligations to allow inspections and report all its programs and weapons. To accommodate French, German, and Russian opposition to war, the resolution had no trigger authorizing the immediate use of force and created a four-month delay, during which, presumably, some of the war fever in Washington would subside and more conclusive evidence one way or the other about the weapons might be found. Months would be necessary to reconstitute inspection teams, get them into Iraq, and hear back from them. The French and German governments believed that they could use the delay and the inspectors' reports to compel Iraqi disarmament, if that proved to be necessary, and arrange a compromise short of war. Iraq accepted resolution 1441. It could hardly defy all the great powers. While the inspections were underway, the president and some of his closest advisers showed their contempt for the French and German position and for the United Nations by publicly denigrating the inspections and threatening unilateral action if the Security Council failed to authorize the use of force. Hopes for a compromise dwindled. Back came the inspectors to report that they had found nothing significant. There was no "smoking gun," but the absence of results failed to convince the United States and Britain that Iraq had complied with its obligations to disarm.[51]

War began on March 19, 2003, without explicit Security Council approval. In a conscious departure from the weeks-long aerial barrage that had preceded infantry combat in 1991, American commanders launched a stealth bomber and cruise missile attack on the Iraqi leadership and began the ground invasion immediately. Apparently expecting a long preparatory bombing and the time to adapt, Iraqi leaders lost the initiative to the American and British invaders and never recovered. The clash of armies in large-unit fighting ended in less than two months with the decisive defeat of the Iraqi army, the overthrow of the Iraqi government, and the occupation of the entire country. On May 1, 2003, speaking from the deck of an American aircraft carrier off the coast of San Diego, President Bush declared the end of "major combat." His words were literally true, but also deeply misleading and premature. After a lull of two months, a festering insurgency began, fought by former members of Saddam's regime, Sunni nationalists who feared domination by Iraq's majority Shia, and foreign Islamist extremists. Saddam Hussein was eventually captured months later hiding in a hole in the ground near a poor farm in central Iraq and jailed to await trial for crimes against humanity. The first trial began in October 2005 and sought to punish Saddam for the murder of dozens of people whose only offense was that they lived near the site of an attempted assassination of the Iraqi leader.

Cheney and Rumsfeld took the lead in advocating war, and their arguments reveal much about the administration's assumptions and Iraq policy.[52] They constantly warned of the unacceptable risks of not overthrowing Saddam Hussein and the incalculable dangers of waiting until firm evidence of his weapons and intentions had been found. Inevitably, the debate centered on the truth of the administration's allegations about the weapons. Bush, Rumsfeld, and Cheney made few if any references to the long oppression of the Shia and Kurds by the Sunnis that had left so much hatred and division between Iraq's ethnic and religious groups, and few people outside the administration challenged them about the omission. It turned out to be far more important than either the weapons or the conventional fighting that the United States had won so easily. The president and his advisers assumed that the chief problem was to get rid of Saddam. In their minds, democracy, markets, and the capacity of the United States to change the world for the better would take care of the rest. These assumptions were chillingly reminiscent of the assumptions that Bill Clinton and his advisers had made about postcommunist Russia. Cheney and Rumsfeld also assumed that Iraqis would not object to the American occupation because it was obvious that the United States sought only to protect its own security and help Iraq to become a market democracy. This was old-fashioned American exceptionalism, a key element in the post–Cold War paradigm.

Partly in response to criticism from members of Congress that the administration had failed to present a convincing argument for overthrowing Saddam Hussein, Cheney reviewed the reasons for war at a convention of the Veterans of Foreign Wars meeting in Nashville in August 2002.[53] Cheney shared Bush's and Rumsfeld's belief that deterrence and containment were irrelevant in the post-9/11 world, and emphasized his certainty that Saddam Hussein would behave in the future exactly as he had in the past. He underlined the inability of the U.S. intelligence community to penetrate Saddam's veil of secrecy and deception. As for UN inspectors, they could not be relied on to discover anything important in Iraq; their reintroduction into that country would be meaningless. Cheney said that Iraq was "enhancing its capabilities" in chemical and biological weapons and continuing its nuclear program. Documents captured in Afghanistan, he said, proved that al-Qaeda was seeking weapons of mass destruction. "We now know that Saddam has resumed his effort to acquire nuclear weapons," he declared.[54] That was all that Cheney needed to establish a nexus between terrorists and a rogue dictator. Cheney told the veterans that it was certain that Saddam Hussein would acquire nuclear weapons "fairly soon." It was impossible to know with certainty when that would happen, he allowed, but there was no point in trying to find out from American intelligence or UN inspectors. U.S. intelligence agencies could not help: they had repeatedly given inaccurate reports about Iraq's nuclear weapons program in the early 1990s. UN inspectors had "missed a great deal," including "boxes of documents" about Iraq's most secret weapons programs.[55] The return of the inspectors would actually be harmful because it would create a false sense of security when there was no basis in the history of the past twelve years to believe that Saddam would ever give up his quest for weapons of mass destruction. There is no doubt, Cheney added, that Saddam intends to use them against his neighbors, friendly governments in the region, and the United States. "The risk of inaction," he declared, "are [*sic*] far greater than the risk of action." To think otherwise, Cheney said, was to engage in wishful thinking or "willful blindness."[56]

In making the case for war, Rumsfeld sought to force a choice between invasion and horrendous loss. By asserting that Saddam had weapons of mass destruction, Rumsfeld challenged his opponents to prove that Iraq did not have them. By the rules of logic, he was making an argument from ignorance: Iraq's weapons of mass destruction exist because no one has proved they do not exist.[57] By the same reasoning, it is possible to prove that ghosts exist, because no one has proved that they do not. Or, as Rumsfeld liked to say, "Absence of evidence is not evidence of absence." Contradicting logic, Rumsfeld was proclaiming that lack of proof was proof. His repeated claims about the limited value of intelligence cast doubt on all evidence that contradicted what the administration was saying about the weapons and intentions of the Iraqi government. The certitudes Rumsfeld deployed included the following: the increased lethality of terrorist attacks, the certainty that Iraq possessed large stocks of chemical and biological weapons and was actively seeking nuclear weapons—Iraq lacked only fissile material, he argued—the certainty that rogue dictators would pass weapons of mass destruction to terrorists, the certainty that it was futile and a grave and unacceptable risk to continue to seek containment and deterrence, the certainty that intelligence was practically useless for policymaking, the certainty that the old inspections system was bankrupt, and the certainty that without regime change, Iraq would present a great and unacceptable danger to the United States and the world.[58]

Rumsfeld repeatedly used analogies to make his points. It was possible to "know" that Iraq had weapons of mass destruction, he said, by projecting Iraq's past behavior into the present and future. We "know" what Iraq did before Saddam forced out the inspectors in 1998, Rumsfeld said over and over, and the nature of the Iraqi regime certainly has not changed. What reason, he asked, is there now to suspect that has been any reduction in the threat or in Iraqi efforts to acquire weapons of mass destruction and hide them from the world? Iraq and Saddam Hussein had these weapons before, and it is the same Iraqi regime and the same Saddam Hussein in power; therefore, Iraq has the weapons today.[59] Asked if there were any "concrete" differences in the threat posed by Saddam Hussein in Iraq today than there a year earlier, Rumsfeld hammered on projections from past behavior:

> Well, without putting an adjective to it, the short answer is yes there is a difference today from a year ago. When you're dealing with any entity—let's call it the moon—that—(laughter) give credit—give credit where's credit's due—where there—where you know from certain knowledge that the moon has in the past had weapons of mass destruction capabilities and that the moon has been continuing free of inspections and with relatively open borders, with a great deal of dual use capabilities, and has been proceeding aggressively to further develop those capabilities and make them more mature, more robust, with greater lethality, greater distances and greater variety, then one has to say that the situation has changed, and not for the better.[60]

The president, Rumsfeld, and the other senior members of the administration extended this reasoning to include Saddam's invasions of Iran and Kuwait; his clandestine programs to build weapons of mass destruction in defiance of UN prohibitions and sanctions; his support of terrorism; his use of chemical weapons against Kurds and Iranians; his launching of ballistic missiles against Israel, Iran, Saudi Arabia, and Bahrain; and his persecution and oppression of the Iraqi people. The argument in simplest terms was that no one in their right mind would trust such a regime on anything at all, and especially not the construction of weapons of mass destruction or passing them to terrorists for use against the United States.

The claims about Saddam's weapons convinced the U.S. Congress and the American people, and American and British troops overthrew the Iraqi government. But as the summer of 2003 passed into fall, the insurgency grew in intensity, forcing the administration to abandon its plans for a five-year occupation of Iraq and total privatization of the country's economy and accelerating the transfer of sovereignty to an Iraqi provisional government. By October 2005, more than 2,000 Americans had died in Iraq, more than ten times the number killed during the invasion. Estimates of Iraqi civilians killed varied from the 12,000 given by the Iraqi Interior Minister, to between 24,700 and 28,000 as calculated by an independent research group.[61] The ferocity and duration of the insurgency revealed the poverty of the administration's plans for the postwar treatment of Iraq. Throughout the summer and into the fall of 2004, dozens of American soldiers and hundreds of Iraqis were killed every month. The first national elections since Saddam's downfall were set for late January 2005. As the elections approached, the violence escalated first to eighty and then 100 attacks a day in December 2004.[62] The elections for the transitional assembly failed to reduce the violence, which rose again as the October 2005 plebiscite to approve the new constitution came closer. During just three days in September 2005, suicide bombers killed 200 Iraqis and wounded more than 600. The most harmful effect of the widespread insecurity was to lower the January turnout in Sunni areas. Unhappy with the certain decline in their power and deeply opposed to the elections and the American presence in Iraq, many Sunnis boycotted the elections. Others stayed away because they feared reprisals from the insurgents. Whatever their reasons for abstention, they ended up with the worst of both worlds: little representation in the new parliament, which was charged with writing a new constitution, and no end to the occupation. The main Shia party won a slim majority of seats in the interim legislature that was elected to write a new constitution. The Kurds won about 25 percent of the seats, and the Sunnis a bare 2 percent.

As the date for the constitutional referendum neared, U.S. and Iraqi units attacked insurgents in western Iraq to diminish their ability to disrupt the voting.[63] The insurgents answered with more bombings in Baghdad and other cities, and on the eve of the voting damaged the electricity supply to Baghdad and put out the lights.[64] Despite the escalation in fighting and the carnage in the streets, Iraqis approved the new constitution.[65] Shia and Kurdish voters turned out in record numbers and supported it overwhelmingly.[66] Most Sunnis opposed the constitution but were unable to muster the two-thirds majority in at least three of Iraq's eighteen provinces needed to defeat it. Elections for a new Iraqi government in December 2005 gave Sunnis a second chance to gain political influence in post-Saddam Iraq, and the Sunni turnout was very heavy.

The constitution that Iraqi voters approved emerged from months of frantic bargaining and extraordinary pressures brought to bear on Iraqi participants by U.S. ambassador Zalmay Khalilzad, President Bush, and Secretary Rice. Efforts to obtain Sunni support continued until the last possible moment before the vote took place. Some important amendments were added so late that they could not be included in the text distributed by the United Nations to voters and published in Iraqi newspapers. For example, a new Article 1 addressed Sunni fears that Iraq would fall apart: "The Republic of Iraq is a single, independent federal State with full sovereignty. . . . This constitution is the guarantor of its unity." A new Article 3 guaranteed that

Iraq was part of the Arab world, with its Sunni majority, and a member of the Arab League of Sunni-majority states, as well as the Islamic world.

The new constitution created a federal, parliamentary government. Its provisions also reveal that it is very much a work in progress rather than a finished national compact. They combine features of existing democratic systems, such as the French and German, including a president who acts as head of state as well as a prime minister and cabinet. Unlike his French counterpart, however, the powers of the Iraqi president are strictly limited. The prime minister is commander-in-chief of the armed forces and has the power to initiate legislation. In addition, the presidency is plural, that is, the legislature appoints the president and two deputies who together constitute a Presidential Council. The Presidential Council must approve all laws unanimously, or they are returned to the legislature for further action. The plurality of the presidency invites paralysis and plainly reveals yet another concession to ethnic politics, as the positions seem designed to be given to one Kurd, one Shiite, and one Sunni. The constitution contains a number of provisions that are central to democratic self-government. It guarantees citizens' freedom of religious belief, protects them against arbitrary arrest, establishes the independence of the judiciary and the rule of law, and protects freedom of expression within the limits of Iraqi morality. The constitution also shows how hastily it was put together, notably in the failure to delineate the powers of the Federation Council. Sixteen articles are devoted to the powers of the Council of Representatives, the principal legislative body, and only one to the Federation Council. In an attempt to remedy this and other problems, Article 137 offers a process of constitutional amendment. After national elections the Council of Representatives must establish a parliamentary committee representative of all Iraqi society to recommend amendments. The committee must report within four months, and amendments may be approved by a simple majority of the Council and in a general referendum of all voters. The entire document bears witness to Iraq's tormented history. Its preamble refers to the mass murder of Kurds in the Anfal campaign in which Saddam's generals used chemical weapons, to political assassination, to sectarian oppression, and to the need for "defusing" terrorism. Its most important provisions record aspirations rather than consensus, hope rather than social reality. Perhaps the most obvious are the references to Iraqi unity. The most explosive are undoubtedly the articles that govern the control and distribution of Iraq's oil revenues. With the Kurds and Shia in control of Iraq's oil-rich territories, Sunnis understandably worried that they would be left to an impoverished existence in a declining, rump territory. The constitution attempted to reassure them and provide an equitable solution by assigning the ownership of all and gas resources throughout the entire country to the people of Iraq (Article 108). By Article 109, the government received control of the oil industry and was charged with distributing revenues "in a fair manner in proportion to the population." This was a sensible solution to a worrisome problem, but the remaining provisions of Article 109 indicated that trouble lay ahead. For a period to be determined by law in a parliament certain to be dominated by Shiites and Kurds, the government was also required to reserve a portion of the oil revenues and to pass them to "damaged regions" that had been denied a fair share of oil revenues in the past.

The constitution also combines history and hope. A striking example occurs in Article 6: "Transfer of authority shall be made peacefully, through democratic means as stipulated in this Constitution." Article 19(8) provides another and deeply touching example by outlawing collective punishment: "Punishment is personal." Still others outlaw forcing a person to join any organization and ban all forms of torture.[67] The document's preoccupation with detail, such as the use of Arabic and Kurdish as official languages and the requirement for "balancing" in the armed forces, testifies to the lack of consensus.[68] Virtually every key item in the constitution reflects political and religious balancing of a kind that raises serious questions as to whether it can possibly succeed. Last, the constitution establishes Islam as the official religion of Iraq and "a fundamental source of legislation," and prohibits the passage of any law that contradicts "established provisions" of Islam. It also guarantees the Islamic identity of the majority of the people of Iraq and the full religious freedom of adherents of all other religions.[69] Taken together, these aspects of the Iraqi constitution revealed that it came not from shared experience and ideals but represented, at best, the outline of a compact that might one day bind Iraqis together.

Getting to "No!" with North Korea

When the time came to deal with North Korea, the administration found that it was almost as hard to reach an internal policy consensus as it was to negotiate with Pyongyang.[70] Finding consensus was complicated by increasing evidence that North Korea had begun a secret program to produce highly enriched uranium during the Clinton administration. The allegations about uranium enrichment supported those in the administration who opposed engagement and believed that the North never intended to give up its nuclear weapons.[71] The unilateralists quickly made clear they wanted no part of Clinton's missile deal. North Korea is a "major threat," they told reporters. They felt that South Korean President Kim Dae Jung's "sunshine policy" aimed at engaging North Korea in the world had "moved too fast, with too few concessions from the North." "I'm kind of tired of the old pattern," said one of the president's senior aides, "where they shoot off a missile and we send them a bucket of wheat."[72] Secretary of State Colin Powell, on the other hand, announced that he wanted to resume negotiations with the North where the Clinton administration had left off.[73]

The unilateralists and multilateralists agreed that the most worrisome threat was not nuclear or conventional attack, but the possibility that a needy North Korean government would sell fissile material, bomb designs, and missiles to rogue states and terrorists. The unilateralists and multilateralists also agreed that denuclearization and regime change should be the goal of American policy. Beyond this common ground, their assumptions diverged radically. Those in the White House, Defense Department, and the vice president's office who sought to bring down Kim Jong Il's government assumed the following:

- North Korea's government is not only evil and corrupt, it is failing. The United States must accelerate its downfall by isolating Pyongyang and refusing to give economic aid in response to threats; giving in to blackmail is ignoble and never-ending.
- Negotiations are useless; the North will always try to have it both ways—extract concessions and simultaneously build nuclear weapons.
- Coercion of the North poses no greater dangers to the United States or its allies than already exist; the downside risks must be discounted properly and weighed against the much greater risks of not acting forcefully and with "moral clarity."

The efforts of the State Department to open negotiations with North Korea in order to halt its nuclear and missile programs were based on profoundly different assumptions:

- North Korea's government is evil and corrupt, but there is no significant internal pressure for change; the current government will last ten years or longer. Pressure and isolation will accomplish nothing and could well accelerate the North's acquisition of nuclear weapons.

- Negotiations are useful. In 1994, the United States stopped a danger-ous North Korean nuclear program at very little cost; it is worth try-ing again.
- The downside risks and costs of coercion are enormous, including everything from economic collapse in North Korea that crushes Chi-nese and South Korean economic prospects with floods of refugees, to a military coup in Pyongyang and war.
- If North Korea goes nuclear, Japan, South Korea, and even Taiwan may reconsider their non-nuclear status, undermining global efforts at nonproliferation and raising tensions with China.

After the initial stalemate in the spring of 2001, the administration moved toward a consensus led by Deputy Secretary Armitage, but the pol-icy would not stay put. It went through three phases in four years—"more for more," "tailored containment," and multilateral talks led by the Chinese government. All centered on the administration's demand that North Korea first agree to dismantle all its nuclear programs, and all went nowhere.

In his state of the union message on January 29, 2002, President Bush de-clared that North Korea, Iran, and Iraq were part of an "axis of evil," states hostile to the United States that harbored terrorists, were building weapons of mass destruction, and could make these weapons available to terrorists or use them to attack the United States and its allies. The administration justi-fied the accusation because documents captured in Afghanistan revealed that al-Qaeda wanted to acquire nuclear weapons and other weapons of mass destruction, and the three states were potential suppliers.[74] When Pres-ident Bush made a personal attack on the North Korean dictator Kim Jong Il, the rhetoric on both sides had grown so strong that the South Korean gov-ernment began to warn of the possibility of war. In response, the adminis-tration said that it had no intention of invading North Korea. For the first time, it allowed a White House representative to join the middle-level talks in New York that had been underway for some months as a way of signal-ing Pyongyang that the president was interested in serious discussions. When the North Koreans invited the America representative to those talks, Charles L. Pritchard, to go to Pyongyang, President Bush said no—there would be no protracted discussions. It would be more creative and more forceful to "get this over with."[75]

The next step was the formulation of what the administration called its "bold approach" to North Korea. The administration would seek "more for more," echoing the Armitage report: everything would be on the table, including weapons of mass destruction, missiles, conventional forces, intrusive inspections for verification, humanitarian issues, a nonaggression pledge, and lifting the sanctions. The problem was that someone needed to communicate all this to Kim Jong Il. No cabinet minister would go and no deputy would go. Finally, it was decided to send Assistant Secretary James Kelly. He was given a carefully prepared script that had been approved by the National Security Council, where Robert Joseph, a close ally of Undersecretary of State John Bolton, was in charge of nonproliferation policies. Kelly was ordered not to stray from his script. The administration put Kelly's visit on hold when, on June 29, 2002, the North Koreans fired on and sank a South Korean patrol boat. Meanwhile, the intelligence community concluded first that North Korea had a research and development program to produce highly enriched uranium and, in September, that an enriched uranium production program was underway.

Kelly finally went to Pyongyang in October 2002. The North Koreans apparently expected a normalization meeting. When Kelly raised the enriched uranium issue without advance warning, the North Koreans denied everything. After caucusing, they became defiant. "Yes, we have it. So what?"[76] Kelly had brought along another script that contained ideas about ways in which the two countries could move ahead, but he was not allowed to respond to the unexpected revelations. "We had no plan for catastrophic success," said a senior official opposed to engagement.[77] The talks collapsed, and with them any hope for bilateral resolution of North Korea's nuclear problems. South Korea and Japan agreed to American demands to suspend work on the light-water reactors, and the United States also stopped shipments of fuel oil. In mid-January 2003, Pyongyang gave its response: it announced that it was quitting the Nuclear Non-Proliferation Treaty, and said it would remove the fuel rods at Yongbyon for reprocessing and complete construction of its 50- and 200-megawatt reactors, greatly increasing its capacity to produce nuclear weapons.

At this point, the administration's decision to go to war in Iraq began to hamstring its attempt to isolate and coerce North Korea. The administration felt it had to deny that there was a crisis on the Korean peninsula when it was apparent to all that North Korea's nuclear breakout meant a serious crisis existed. If it were to acknowledge the existence of a crisis, then the administration would have to change its policy, something it was unwilling—or unable—to do. The administration also found it difficult to justify a patient strategy of economic and political pressure toward North Korea—which openly violated all its commitments not to produce nuclear weapons—

while it was getting ready to go to war with Iraq, a country where UN weapons inspectors roamed freely and found nothing. Secretary Powell and others made the obvious arguments—Saddam had used chemical weapons, he had attacked neighboring states recently, he was more unpredictable than the North Koreans—but they sounded hollow.[78] In early January 2003, President Bush emphasized that the United States would not invade North Korea. During the next few days, the administration's policy jumped all over the map as it struggled to appear organized and coherent and to keep South Korea and Japan on board. At one point, the administration suggested that it would take the North Korean issue to the United Nations, and then refused to negotiate until International Atomic Energy Agency inspectors were allowed to return and the North had stopped work on all its nuclear programs. Next, the administration offered to talk with the North about how to get rid of its nuclear weapons.[79] There was no graceful way to resolve the contradictions, and the more that they tried, the more that the administration strategists appeared to be running around in circles.

The next move was to cobble together another bureaucratic compromise in Washington, known as "tailored containment." The idea was to increase pressures on North Korea across the board by invoking UN sanctions, intercepting missile shipments, and reducing North Korea's economic ties with its neighbors. It sounded good. The trouble was that none of North Korea's neighbors would agree to this kind of coercion, and China and Russia opposed a UN resolution imposing sanctions on the North. For its part, North Korea demanded direct talks with the United States. The United States refused, and insisted instead that the problem was regional, not bilateral, and that all the countries in the region, especially China, had to help. This step promised much to both sides of the policy conflict in Washington. Those who supported engagement liked the idea of a multilateral diplomatic forum. Surely this would make provide good cover for the U.S. and North Korean governments to start talking. Those who sought North Korea's isolation and downfall accepted the need to spread the responsibility for dealing with North Korea as the United States prepared to go to war in Iraq. Multilateral talks would reassure China, Japan, and South and North Korea, and nothing would happen.

When Beijing offered to convene a three-sided meeting with North Korea and the United States, more divisions appeared inside the administration. Secretary Rumsfeld opposed the meeting as a way of disguising a bilateral U.S.–North Korean negotiation. When he lost that battle, Rumsfeld argued that Bolton and Joseph should head the U.S. delegation instead of Charles L. Pritchard, the special envoy to North Korea. Ultimately, Pritchard was not allowed to head the delegation and resigned. As Pritchard predicted, the North Koreans refused to have anything to do with such a format, and the meetings died after the opening session.

In January 2004, the Kim government allowed a strange replay of Jimmy Carter's mission to the North during the Clinton administration (See Chapter 3.) A delegation of American academics, former officials, congressional aides, and a nuclear weapons specialist (a former head of Los Alamos National Laboratory), was allowed to visit the reactor at Yongbyon to view what the North Korean government called its "nuclear deterrent force." The gesture was apparently meant to support an attempt by China to reconcile North Korean proposals for a freeze on its nuclear program with the demand of the Bush administration for a complete and verifiable dismantling as a basis for any other agreements.[80] The organizers plainly hoped to create the conditions for serious talks, but the issue remained frozen through the 2004 election and into Bush's second term.

After the second term began, it quickly became obvious that the administration had chosen a different course. In part because of Secretary Rice's close relations with the president and in part because the occupation of Iraq continued to falter and narrowed his freedom of action, the president granted American negotiators greater latitude in the six-party talks. In September 2005, a break in the stalemate appeared tantalizingly close with the conclusion of an agreement in which North Korea seemed to renounce its nuclear weapons programs in exchange for pledges of security guarantees and normalization from the United States and economic assistance from the other parties.[81] China's mediation appeared to have borne fruit. However, there were puzzling aspects to the accord. The agreement set no dates for accomplishing its ambitious goals, and North Korea and the United States immediately disagreed publicly as to what they were obliged to do. Regardless, the administration had managed after five years to return to the pattern established by Clinton and Perry a decade earlier.

According to news reports, the chief American negotiator, Christopher Hill, had doubts about the agreement because of the absence of dates for disarmament and the need for the United States "at an appropriate time" to discuss the creation of civilian nuclear power plants in North Korea.[82] Unnamed "senior Bush administration officials" told reporters that the administration had accepted the agreement only after China more or less demanded it, and because China threatened "to go to the press and explain that the United States sank the accord."[83] "They said, 'Here's the text, and we're not going to change . . . , and we suggest you don't walk away.' "[84] Officials of several foreign governments said that other parties to the talks—China, Russia, and South Korea—liked the word "appropriate" because it imposed no binding obligation on the United States. Other officials added that the president was "tied down in Iraq, consumed by Hurricane Katrina, and headed into another standoff over Iran's nuclear program."[85] The accord permitted at least a temporary escape from a confrontation with yet another member of the "axis of evil." By issuing its own interpretation of the talks, the administration covered its relapse into Clintonian diplomacy and made clear its doubts about the future. Putting the best face on the move, the president declared: "They have said, in principle, that they will abandon their weapons programs. And what we have said is great, that's a wonderful step forward, but now we've got to verify whether or not that happens."[86]

The outcome was a defeat for those inside and outside the administration who had argued that the United States must not accept the status quo in North Korea. If American intelligence analyses were correct the agreement allowed North Korea to keep its nuclear weapons and reactors until, at some uncertain date in the future, it decided to rejoin the Nuclear Non-Proliferation Treaty and allow unfettered inspections of all its nuclear facilities. Worse, according to critics, the agreement made no mention of the alleged uranium enrichment program that had caused the breakdown in the nuclear disarmament talks three years earlier. Undoubtedly, one of the least attractive aspects of the agreement was that Iran immediately used it to denounce the Bush administration and the European Union's campaign to stop Iran from developing its own capacity to enrich uranium. At a news conference in Iran, the head of nuclear negotiations for Iran, Ali Larijani, pointed to the agreement with North Korea and said the Bush administration's plan to isolate North Korea had failed: "What was the result of such tough policies?" He added, "After two years they ended up accepting its program, so you should accept ours right now." The newly elected Iranian president, Mahmoud Ahmadinejad, emphasized Iran's rejection of international limits on his country's nuclear program during an address to the UN General Assembly. He condemned the United States and its allies for practicing nuclear "apartheid" against Iran and for their brutal treatment of Iraqis and Afghans. Western countries, he added sought "to impose a climate of intimidation and injustice over the world" while they speak of spreading democracy and human rights.[87] The Iraq invasion and troubled occupation also haunted the North Korean negotiations. "The lesson of

Iraq," a skeptical member of the administration said sourly, "is that we can never confront a country about its weapons unless we show that we have tried every available alternative to disarm it."[88] Jack Pritchard, who was forced out of the talks by hard-liners in the administration, pointed out that North Korea had used the Iranian example, as well. That the talks were taking place simultaneously made coming to terms with the two countries even more difficult: "Having these negotiations with North Korea and Iran take place simultaneously means that both countries use the other's tactics, and I'm sure the administration wished that was not happening."[89]

On a Road to Nowhere with the Israelis and Palestinians

One of the lessons that President Bush and his advisers took into office was learned from the Clinton administration's problems with Israelis and Palestinians: do not let the president or the administration get deeply involved in trying to make peace.[90] Two other assumptions lay at the heart of the Bush II administration's policy: Israel and the Palestinians are unlikely to make peace, and no great harm will come to the United States if the president and the administration play a less direct role in peacemaking than their predecessors. The president and his advisers also assumed:

- U.S. interests in the Middle East are greater than the Israeli-Palestinian conflict and must be viewed in a regional context.
- Israelis and Palestinians must take the responsibility for making the hard choices needed for peace.
- Strong support for Ariel Sharon's government coincides with U.S. interests in the region and will not harm the chances for peace with the Palestinians.
- The onus is on the Palestinians to stop all terrorist attacks; no progress is possible without this.
- Diplomatic simultaneity—political and military steps taken by both sides at the same time—is counterproductive.

The attacks on 9/11 that triggered the decision to conquer Iraq and democratize it added one more:

- The United States will support Palestinian independence, but only if the Palestinians oust Yasser Arafat and democratize their society or, in other words, accept externally imposed regime change.

Taken together these assumptions meant two things: the U.S. government would not use its influence to force the parties to stop fighting and start talking, and there would be no penalties for Israeli noncompliance with American proposals and no immediate rewards or incentives for Palestinian compliance. It is not correct to call the administration's policy "hands-off." There were many initiatives from Washington—in reality, too many initiatives with too little backing. At times, the administration's policy resembled a seminar on conflict resolution techniques rather than an attempt to mediate a desperate and bloody conflict between two peoples struggling to establish their national identities. Bush II's assumptions and the policies that flowed from them sidelined the administration just as violence surged between Israelis and Palestinians.

From February to September 2001, the administration's policy flowed directly from its initial assumptions. President Bush and his advisers took the position that they would "assist but not insist" in peacemaking between Israelis and Palestinians. They suggested combining the recommendations from an international fact-finding commission led by former U.S. Senator George Mitchell with a ceasefire negotiated by CIA director George Tenet. "First Tenet then Mitchell," that is, stop the violence with a cease-fire, and follow it with confidence-building measures leading to peace talks. It was a perfectly reasonable approach except for one thing: if the conditions needed to establish Tenet and Mitchell had existed, neither would have been necessary. Tenet managed to put together a ceasefire, but it was immediately undermined by terrorist attacks and Israeli reprisals.[91] Colin Powell made a personal trip to try to stop the spiraling violence, but his visit failed to bring the parties together, and he came away convinced not to go again until there was a greater chance for a breakthrough. In a statement whose shallowness and naiveté would have been comic if the situation had not been so tragic, a senior administration official said, "We've thrown Tenet at it; we've thrown Powell at it; we're not going to throw anyone else at it."[92] By late summer, violence between Israelis and Palestinians had become so serious that friendly Arab governments, especially Egypt, Jordan, and Saudi Arabia, demanded that the United States take a more active role, and warned that the violence was destabilizing the region and undermining American interests.[93] With these concerns in mind, the president decided that Colin Powell would speak of American support for a Palestinian state from "the sidelines" of the UN opening sessions in September 2001. The attacks on 9/11 stopped the speech. Powell later observed ruefully that it was the most famous speech he had never given.

The terrorist attacks of 9/11 and the decision to overthrow Saddam Hussein had a profound effect on the administration's policy toward the Israeli-Palestinian conflict. On the surface, the changes appeared to respond positively to Arab and European criticisms. The administration brought the European Union, Russia, and the United Nations into a "quartet" with the United States to draft a "road map" to peace, and in June 2002, President Bush made a public commitment to the creation of an independent Palestinian state.[94] The moves made sense as part of the administration's efforts to win wide international support for the war against Saddam Hussein. But the president postponed release of the road map until after the war, and he also made U.S. support of Palestinian independence contingent on regime change: the Palestinians would have to get rid of Arafat and democratize their society. The Palestinians distrusted Bush's support for independence precisely because it depended on regime change.[95] The Israeli government rejected the road map because it aimed at Palestinian independence by 2005 within the 1967 borders of the West Bank. Sharon avoided a clash with President Bush by setting preconditions that made the plan unworkable rather than refusing it outright. Two years and hundreds of deaths later, Deputy Secretary of State Richard Armitage plaintively observed during an interview for Egyptian television:

> We're having a great deal of difficulty. The Administration of Abu Alaa, Prime Minister Qureia, is not able or willing to make any tough stands on the question of security and on the other side the Israelis are intent on not compromising either. So we're at a bit of a stalemate. We haven't given up our efforts. . . .[96]

The Israeli government quickly realized that the 9/11 attacks and the president's demand that the Palestinians agree to regime change had greatly increased its freedom of action. Immediately after the 9/11 attacks, Sharon cancelled ceasefire talks with the Palestinians that might have led to a Bush meeting with Arafat. Then, on September 24, Israeli troops began establishing "closed military zones" up to one mile long along the West Bank border with Israel. Arab residents needed new identity cards to enter the zones. These actions coincided President Bush's public announcement of his support for the establishment of an independent Palestinian state. The Sharon government intended the security zones to become part of a ladder-like structure of Israeli control imposed on the western and eastern sides of the West Bank. Based on a design that Sharon had reportedly shown to President Bush, the western leg of the ladder, from three to six miles wide, ran the length of the border and reached to the east to embrace Israeli settlements in the West Bank and well to the east of Jerusalem. The Israeli government claimed that the extensions were necessary to stop attacks on Israel's heartland. The eastern leg of the ladder, some nine to twelve miles wide, ran parallel to the Jordan River, and amounted, in effect, to a massive anti-tank and anti-invasion barrier. In between the two legs of the ladder, the Israeli government intended to run access roads, establish checkpoints, and provide a means for Israeli forces to reach at will into the occupied territories or a rump Palestinian entity, if one were ever to be established. The Israeli government had established a similar rung-and-ladder arrangement in Gaza.[97]

Sharon had first introduced the plan a quarter-century earlier when he served as minister of agriculture in Menachem Begin's government.[98] But there was a huge difference between then and now. When Sharon first made his proposal, there were 7,000 Israeli settlers in the West Bank and Gaza. Twenty-five years later, more than 400,000 Israelis lived there. To show Washington that he was reasonable and to confuse his Israeli opponents on the left and right, Sharon said he might be willing to accept in principle the idea of a Palestinian state on about 40 percent of the occupied territories, an amount far less than any Palestinian leader could or would accept.[99] After 9/11, President Bush refused to meet with Arafat, and essentially ignored Sharon's decisions to impose a curfew on the entire West Bank, demolish Arafat's compound in Ramallah, and besiege the Palestinian leader in its ruins. On occasion, life imitates art, but no novelist, playwright, or film director would have dared to make such a blatant manipulation of symbolism to portray purpose.

Reeling from the massive shift in American policy, deeply affronted by Sharon's attack on the Palestinian Authority, oppressed by the closures and curfews, Palestinians rallied around Arafat, not necessarily because they admired him but because he belonged to them and, as a result of the siege of his headquarters in Ramallah, suffered just as they suffered.[100] Sharon chose this moment to put his twenty-year-old plan into operation. The Israeli government began constructing what he called a "security fence," actually an elaborate system of high cement walls, fences, detectors, and barriers. They were the legs of the ladder. Presented solely as a security measure that could be undone at any time, the walls and fences alarmed Palestinians because they reached deep into Palestinian territory,

cut Palestinian villages from their farmlands, and separated large Palestinian population centers from one another.

In the weeks that followed Bush's speech, Israeli troops began to re-
occupy the West Bank by imposing military closure on seven of eight of the
most important Palestinian towns. Yielding to American pressure, the
Israeli government ended the imprisonment of Arafat after ten days, but he
chose to stay on in the rubble as a symbol of Palestinian resistance, finally
emerging in May 2002 only to encounter the administration's demand for
his ouster the following month. In keeping with the administration's desire
to deal with regionwide problems, Colin Powell launched the Middle East
Partnership Initiative in December 2002, a program to encourage economic
development and the growth of civil societies throughout the entire Arab
world from the grassroots up.[101] However well-intentioned, the initiative
was so broad, so underfunded, and such a long-term program that its results, whatever they might eventually be, were irrelevant to the ongoing
Palestinian-Israeli crisis. It was not meant to be tokenism, but to many observers its creation seemed a cruel joke.

In its public statements, the administration portrayed the road map and
the Middle East Partnership Initiative as two of the ways to trigger what it
called a "domino theory of democracy." One senior official enthused:

> This is a realistic way of going about regime change—transitions that
> balance introducing democratic principles with short- and medium-
> term stability. We want to see steady change rather than overthrows. . . .
> We want to help traditional societies adapt to the modern world. As
> those societies and Arab thinkers realize the 21st century is different,
> we want to be there to help them take advantage of it. . . . In the past,
> we've separated the peace process and pressing democracy. The idea
> now is a set of principles—of peace, democracy, the rule of law, trans-
> parency and openness across the board and working all the time.[102]

In addition to the "road map" and democratization, the administration intended to advance economic development through bilateral trade and investment agreements, starting with Egypt and Morocco. Jordan already had
a free trade agreement with the United States, and the administration admitted that it would be difficult to find other partners. Last, the "domino
theory of democracy" targeted Iran, and sought to enlist the cooperation
primarily of the European Union and Russia to strengthen measures to stop
Iran from acquiring nuclear weapons.

The administration finally allowed the "road map" to be published on April 30, 2003.[103] It envisioned a three-stage process leading to independence for Palestine, security for Israel, and the conclusion of an overall regional peace settlement. The parties were to move toward peace in three stages: an even more detailed version of Tenet-Mitchell, that is, stop the violence with a ceasefire, and restore mutual confidence followed by two international conferences, one to establish a Palestinian state with provisional borders and involve Lebanon and Syria in peacemaking, and the other to codify the existence of the Palestinian state in international law and conclude a final overall peace agreement within three years that included Syria and Lebanon as well as Palestine. The president and his advisers seemed not to recognize that the road map and the demand for regime change were contradictory. The road map offered negotiations with the Palestinians as they were; the insistence on regime change postponed negotiations until Arafat had been overthrown. Ultimately, the administration squared this contradictory circle by accepting cosmetic regime changes, in the form of a moderate prime minister imposed from the outside who had undefined powers, and was quickly discredited and undermined by the violence and lack of support from Israel, the United States, and Arafat and other Palestinian groups such as the Islamic party Hamas. Commenting on the policy's failure, Martin Indyk, former U.S. ambassador to Israel, said:

> We did nothing. *We* lost Abu Mazen [Mazen, also known as Mahmoud Abbas, was a close associate of Arafat; after serving briefly as prime minister he was elected president of the Palestinian Authority in January 2005 after Arafat's death] . . . and the moral clarity of his saying terrorism is bad. The issue that mattered was giving the Palestinian people the sense that Abu Mazen could deliver—on prisoner releases, on checkpoints, on the dismantling of settlement outposts, on bettering their economic situation. . . . Instead, we just left them to their own devices. And now the Bush Administration is quite satisfied to let the Israelis and Palestinians wallow in their misery— and blame the Palestinians.[104]

Months earlier Sharon had set preconditions that doomed the road map to failure even before it was published. Sharon's preconditions included no progress between or within phases unless there is a complete cessation of terror, violence, and incitement, and the destruction of all terrorist organizations—Hamas, Islamic Jihad, the Popular Front, the Democratic Front, Al-Aqsa Brigades, and all others; no progress until "a new and different leadership" emerges within the Palestinian Authority; all monitoring activities were to be controlled by the American government; no discussion of any kind of Israeli settlements in Judea and Samaria (West Bank), except for a settlement freeze and illegal outposts; no discussion of any official Palestinian presence in Jerusalem; no progress to the next phases until the prior phase has been fully implemented; performance is all, time lines mean nothing; and the right of Palestinian refugees to return must be abandoned forever.[105]

Two summits were held on June 3 and 4, 2003. In attendance at the Arab-U.S. summit at Sharm el-Sheikh were King Abdullah II of Jordan, Crown Prince Abdullah of Saudi Arabia, King Hamid bin Isa al-Khalifa of Bahrain, the new Palestinian Prime Minister Mahmoud Abbas, and President Bush. At Aqaba the next day, Abdullah of Jordan, Sharon, Abbas, and President Bush attended. Everyone said the right thing and a marvelous picture was taken of the Aqaba group standing over a makeshift bridge built on top of a swimming pool expressly for the photograph. No one was impolite enough to point out the image's dubious symbolism. Failure was not long in coming. Within a week, the bridge was down again as a new round of violence erupted between Israelis and Palestinians. "There has been a total breakdown of trust," commented a Western diplomat.[106]

Sharon chose this moment to announce that the "security fence" would cut even deeper into Palestinian territory on the West Bank; approximately 90 percent of Israeli West Bank settlers would be on the Israeli side of the fence, and the Palestinians would be left with about half the territory of the West Bank.[107] In November 2003, Sharon said that Israel would not wait forever, and issued an ultimatum to the Palestinians: begin following the road map or Israel would enact a "disengagement plan." Under its provisions, Israel would accelerate the construction of the fence, unilaterally regroup its settlements, set its own borders, and deploy its military forces along the new borders. "Obviously," Sharon added, "through the 'Disengagement Plan' the Palestinians will receive much less than they would have received through direct negotiations as set out in the roadmap."[108] Sharon refused to accept criticism of the fence, known as a wall by its critics. "I know that people are talking about the fence," he said in January 2004, "You know who built the fence. Terror built the fence."[109]

With government-to-government diplomacy at a complete standstill and an ultimatum facing the Palestinians, public attention shifted to a document negotiated by Israeli and Palestinian citizens, including former Israeli minister and peace advocate Yossi Beilin and former Palestinian minister Yasser Abed Rabbo. The "Geneva Accord" proposed what amounted to a return to the Camp David II arrangements. Although polls reported that roughly a third of both peoples backed the "Geneva Accord," neither the U.S. government nor the Israeli government made any change in their policies. Another exercise in public diplomacy, the "People's Voice" initiative received 100,000 Israeli and 65,000 Palestinian signatures by December 2003. The initiative was led by Ami Ayalon, a retired Commander of the Israeli Navy and former Director of Shin Bet, Israel's internal security agency, and Sari Nusseibeh, who was from a prominent Palestinian family and president of Al Quds University in Jerusalem. The People's Voice plan called for peace between Israel and the Palestinians based on a two-state solution.[110]

One last astonishing and totally unprecedented development in public diplomacy occurred inside Israel during this period. The Israeli Army chief of staff, Lt. General Joshe Yaalon, and four former heads of the Shin Bet, denounced Sharon's policies as counterproductive and ineffective. General Yaalon argued that Israel's policies increased the hatred of Palestinians for Israel, and actually strengthened the extremist organizations that Israel was attempting to destroy. Massive use of force could be effective, he added, only if accompanied by meaningful peace talks.[111] "There is no hope, no expectations for the Palestinians in the Gaza Strip, nor in Bethlehem and Jericho," he said. "In our tactical decisions, we are operating contrary to our strategic interest."[112] Avraham Shalom, who headed Shin Bet from 1980 to 1986 said: "We must once and for all admit that there is another side, that it has feelings and that it is suffering, and that we are behaving disgracefully. . . . Yes, there is no other word for it: disgracefully." "The problem as of today," said another of the Shin Bet directors, Carmi Gillon, who ran the agency in 1995 and 1996, "is that the political agenda has become solely a security agenda. It only deals with the question of how to prevent the next terror attack, not the question of how it is at all possible to pull ourselves out of the mess that we are in today."[113] Like the Geneva Accord and the People's Voice initiatives, the denunciations attracted attention, but made no noticeable impact on the policies of the Israeli and American governments. Arafat's death in December 2004 raised hopes for elections and a new round of negotiations. The elections promised to remove an important obstacle to the democratization of Palestinian society, leaving the United States to face the prospect of having to live up to its promise of Palestinian independence.

Part of Sharon's plan for the occupied territories was to withdraw from Gaza, a move he announced in early 2004.[114] President Bush promptly endorsed Sharon's plans and then, inexplicably, added two other endorsements that had previously been reserved for agreement between the Palestinians and Israelis. Bush committed the U.S. government to support the retention by Israel of land in the West Bank and the repudiation of Palestinians' right of return to what had become the state of Israel. Neither of Bush's unprecedented endorsements departed from what had been proposed by the Clinton administration, and had been accepted by the two sides as part of a peace settlement. What was unusual was the unilateral position taken by the U.S. government. The administration plainly intended to reward and strengthen Sharon for his willingness to give up Gaza. Sharon needed help. He ultimately lost his coalition, had to put another together in order to stay in office, and ended up having to leave Likud and start a new party of his own, Kadima. The Israeli cabinet approved the Gaza withdrawal in principle in June 2004 and authorized it in February 2005. It was finally completed the following September. At the same time, the cabinet approved the annexation of 6 percent to 8 percent of the West Bank along the line of the security fence.[115] The Bush administration's action also struck a further blow at Arafat, who was shown again as unable to protect Palestinian positions from Israel and the United States. The underlying question remained whether the aims of the United States and Israeli governments were identical or simply sometimes coincident. Sharon wanted to escape the responsibility for governing the 1.3 million Palestinians of Gaza, with their average per capita income of $600, with 81 percent of its people living below the poverty line, and unemployment running at more than 50 percent.[116] Sharon also insisted that Israel must retain control of all the land, air, and sea borders of Gaza, although he ultimately conceded control of the western border of Gaza to Egypt and the Palestinians.

Mahmoud Abbas's election as president of the Palestinian Authority in January 2005 appeared to open the way for a new round of peace talks between Israel and the Palestinians. Abbas won words of praise and promises of support from the U.S. and Israeli governments, and from European governments as well, but the pledges were undercut by Sharon's policies. After the withdrawal from Gaza in mid-September 2005, for example, Sharon announced that he would not freeze settlements in the West Bank and would discuss the future of settlements only at the very end of the process envisioned by the road map, which had never begun and, given the "conditions" he had attached to it conceivably would never begin. Sharon continued to demand that Abbas destroy Hamas and other terrorist groups as the price for peace talks with Israel. And, contradicting Bush administration rhetoric about democratization, Sharon added that he would do everything in his power to prevent Hamas from running for office in Palestinian elections. These measures seemed certain to brand Abbas as a collaborator with Israel and to validate Hamas's legitimacy as the only effective nationalist voice of the Palestinians. In order to meet Sharon's demands, Abbas would have to risk civil war and would need large numbers of highly trained and well-armed soldiers and police to defeat Hamas and the other terrorist groups. Neither Sharon nor Bush were about to allow a full-scale arming of the Palestinians. At the same time, they seemed unable to give up their insistence that Abbas "deal with the terrorists." It was easy to put diplomatic and economic pressure on Abbas, but he was weak rather than strong, and growing weaker as Hamas gained in popularity. Allowing Sharon to delay peace talks indefinitely made Hamas still more attractive in Palestinian eyes and undercut leaders such as Abbas who were willing to make peace with Israel.[117]

6

Boldness and Blindness

Reasons existed, but reason itself, discredited by the excesses committed in its name, had been abandoned.

—Michael Dibdin[1]

They were careless people. . . . [T]hey smashed up things and creatures and then retreated back to their money or their vast carelessness, or whatever it was that kept them together, and let other people clean up the mess they had made. . . .

—F. Scott Fitzgerald

The war and insurgency in Iraq exposed the flaws in Bush II strategy and the post–Cold War paradigm more clearly than any other developments. The trouble arose from the administration's misperception of American primacy and the limited relevance of American exceptionalism and democratization to the post–Cold War world. These errors maimed the postwar occupation of Iraq, and distorted the administration's handling of intelligence, the Israeli-Palestinian conflict, and North Korea's nuclear programs.

174

Bill Clinton had also misunderstood American primacy, exceptionalism, and democratization, but his reluctance to go to war and his reliance on multilateralism, especially cooperation with the major European countries, spared his administrations most of the consequences of his mistakes.[2]

Getting Primacy Wrong

The Bush II administration took American primacy for granted. It was an understandable mistake. All through the 1990s, journalists, academics, and politicians had been telling Americans that the United States was vastly superior in every realm, and especially the military. Like most Americans, the president and his senior civilian advisers had begun to believe in American primacy without stopping to ask if the threat had changed or the circumstances in which American troops might be deployed differed from those envisioned during the Cold War. As a result, they failed to grasp the significance of the cuts imposed on the U.S. military after the end of the Cold War, or the degree to which specialization had left American forces unprepared for conflicts other than conventional World War II–style warfare. In 1989, the last year of the Cold War, there were 2.1 million men and women serving in the U.S. military: 767,000 in the Army, 584,000 in the Navy, 579,000 in the Air Force, and 195,000 in the Marines. By 2001 the active-duty military that the United States took to war in Iraq had declined by 33.4 percent to 1.4 million overall. Given the nature of the insurgency in Iraq, the cuts to the Army were most serious, down 37 percent to 485,000. The Navy and the Air Force also fell by 34 percent and 36 percent, respectively, to 385,000 and 370,000. The Marines kept three divisions, but lost 22,000 troops, down 11 percent. The Army Reserve declined by 420,000. Together with the National Guard, the reserve forces lost seven divisions. Although the numbers of the post–Cold War military were still large, the reductions posed an acute problem in Iraq because only one-third of the units available could be deployed at any time. Of the remaining two-thirds, one-third would be preparing for deployment and the other would have just returned. Some relief was obtained by extending the stay of troops past their anticipated date of return.

The cuts made American generals reluctant to go to war in Iraq, but there was another reason for their hesitation. They knew how specialized the U.S. military had become. They had designed the active duty forces and reserves to fight more sophisticated state-to-state versions of World War II, and wanted to stay out of other kinds of conflicts. "No more Vietnams!" was still their watchword. They hoped that new technology—given the name "shock and awe" for the war in Iraq—would compensate for the lack of "boots on the ground." This was surely true as long as enemies were willing to fight a "symmetrical" conventional war against the United States, matching inferior tanks and aircraft and inability to "see" the enemy against superior U.S. tanks, aircraft, missiles, communications, and reconnaissance. Once an insurgency began—particularly one driven by non-Western religious and ethnic motives as in Iraq—the war turned "asymmetrical," with the insurgents' strengths applied against the U.S. military's weaknesses. Beyond its numerical problems, the American military lacked the intelligence capabilities, Arabic-speaking officers and noncommissioned officers, training, and equipment needed for a quick victory over the Iraqi insurgents.[3]

Democratization and Exceptionalism in Action

President Bush and his senior political advisers added to the problems facing the United States by miscalculating the appeal of American exceptionalism and democracy to other countries. What was supposed to have been an easy and more or less automatic transition to democracy in Iraq turned out to be a mammoth task: to fashion a new constitution, new national and local political institutions, new armed forces and police, a new judiciary, and a new national identity for people who had known barely a decade of successful government since the creation of the Iraqi state after World War I. Under the spell of exceptionalism and democratization, the administration ignored the accumulated bitterness of Iraqis toward the United States caused by the ruinous sanctions that it had suffered for thirteen years before the invasion. It also ignored the sentiments of Iraqi nationalists who while glad of Saddam's downfall abhorred the American occupation. American exceptionalism and democratization also allowed the president and his advisers to avoid thinking about these problems before the invasion or to take seriously the risk that extremist Muslims would flood into Iraq to oppose the American presence.[4]

If the administration took Iraq's history of misgovernment and ethnic divisions into account before the war, the president and his senior advisers made little or no public reference to such considerations. Instead, they stressed the universal relevance of democracy to all peoples everywhere. The administration seemed to be expecting Iraqis to be so overcome by the opportunity to have free elections and market economics that they would forget their old enmities and religious differences. The administration's way of addressing this complex problem was to translate it into a false dichotomy: anyone who had even modest doubts about the democratization of Iraq was an unpatriotic bigot. As President Bush said in his 2004 State of the Union address:

> We also hear doubts that democracy is a realistic goal for the greater Middle East, where freedom is rare. Yet it is mistaken, and condescending, to assume that whole cultures and great religions are incompatible with liberty and self-government. I believe that God has planted in every human heart the desire to live in freedom. And even when that desire is crushed by tyranny for decades it will rise again. As long as the Middle East remains a place of tyranny and despair and anger, it will continue to produce men and movements that threaten the safety of American and our friends. So America is pursuing a forward strategy of freedom in the greater Middle East. . . . Our goal is a democratic peace—a peace founded on the dignity and rights of every man and woman. . . . This great republic will lead the cause of freedom.[5]

On the whole, this argument worked well within the United States, putting critics in an awkward position and helping to silence dissent. In Iraq, however, as quickly became clear, Saddam's overthrow did not allow an immediate flowering of democracy. Instead, it opened a new chapter in the Iraq's search for national identity. As journalist Sandra Mackey observed,

> The relentless violence in Iraq thus presents more of a challenge to the U.S.-led occupation than just the guerrilla tactics of former supporters of Saddam Hussein and shadowy foreign terrorists. It also involves a bloody struggle among segments of the Iraqi population for the right to define the Iraqi state, a contest that goes to the core of the constitutional process that will create the new government. . . . With Hussein removed from power, the Iraqis have been free to define themselves, which has caused much of the violence ensnaring U.S. soldiers. . . . The longer it takes to define the Iraqi state, the longer the United States will be in Iraq.[6]

The administration's assumptions about the power of exceptionalism and democratization to transform Iraq also shaped its approach to transferring sovereignty. At the outset, the agent of the occupying powers and the United

States, the Coalition Provisional Authority, behaved as if it alone could determine Iraq's future. The top U.S. administrator in Iraq, L. Paul Bremer's original plan called for Iraq to move slowly toward sovereignty while still tightly controlled by the United States. Iraq was to have a constitution written by delegates chosen in a "partial election" before it became sovereign. In reality, this process was not intended to be a true election at all. Instead, the Coalition Provisional Authority would choose caucuses in Iraq's provinces drawn from local political, religious, tribal, and other established leaders who would then select the individuals to draft the constitution. Several years would pass, that is, enough time to ensure that Iraq would not fall into dictatorship or theocracy. In addition, no one knew how the Shia would react to the freedom to assert their numbers, and the slow movement toward normalcy was supposed to allow time to judge their reaction and guide them toward a constructive role in Iraq and friendly relations with the United States.[7]

Within two months of the defeat of Saddam Hussein, it was clear that democratization and American exceptionalism were not working as expected. Instead, the administration faced mounting resistance to the occupation from Saddam loyalists and nationalist Sunnis, followers of Shia cleric Moktada al-Sadr, and foreign Muslims who began to move into Iraq by the hundreds to fight the U.S. occupation, much as Muslims from around the world had gone to Afghanistan to defeat the Soviet Union's occupation of that country. The number of Americans killed and wounded during the occupation quickly surpassed the totals suffered during the invasion. By March 2005, more than 1,500 Americans had died, and more than 11,000 had been wounded.[8] Frustrated by the ability of American commanders to "harden" or protect their troops against bombs and ambushes, the terrorists struck with sickening effect against unprotected Iraqi government officials, police and army recruits, foreign aid workers, and Iraqis working with the Americans or the interim Iraqi government.

By late summer 2003, Iraq was becoming ungovernable, and the occupation threatened to become open-ended unless sovereignty were returned and returned quickly. Bremer and the Iraqi Governing Council ended up producing four plans from mid-2003 through April of the following year. None produced consensus throughout the country. All were sunk by opposition from the Shia, especially the popular and influential cleric, Grand Ayatollah Ali Sistani, who insisted that Iraq's constitution could be written only by Iraqis chosen in national elections. If there was to be an interim legislature, it too must be elected directly by the people of Iraq.[9] It was ironic and embarrassing, but unavoidably true: the United States was being tutored in democracy by a Shia Ayatollah. Bremer's initial response to Sistani's opposition was to try to make the caucus process "as open, inclusive, and democratic as possible," according to a senior American official in Washington.[10] The result was a system so complex that "some American occupation officials said it was difficult even for them to figure out."[11] Ultimately, the administration accepted Sistani's demands. An interim government was elected on January 30, 2005. Most Sunnis stayed away from the polls out of fear of reprisal by the insurgents or to protest the occupation. The Shia lists favored by Ayatollah Sistani gained a slim majority of seats in the interim legislature, but not enough to dictate the writing of the new constitution. After decades of bitter and costly divisions, the Kurds united for the election and won a quarter of the seats.[12] The administration's attempt to win additional international support failed largely because it was unwilling to allow governments who had not fought in the war to have a say over the way Iraq would be governed.[13]

Postwar Reconstruction

Given control of postwar planning by the president, senior defense officials chose to ignore the State Department's interagency effort that had begun in April 2002 called "The Future of Iraq Project." The project was intended to bring together representatives of all the major Iraq groups opposed to Saddam Hussein regardless of ethnicity or religion. Working groups were established to study every imaginable problem from sanitation and education to democratization and the transition after the overthrow of Saddam Hussein. The goal was not to achieve consensus, but to create a sense of common purpose among Iraqi exiles, and to identify and develop solutions for the problems that lay ahead.[14] The planning was extensive and, although it did not provide detailed guidelines for every contingency, amounted to a prescient and thoughtful review of what would take place. The frequency with which its predictions were confirmed made even more dubious the refusal of the Defense Department to incorporate them into its own deliberations. These started barely six weeks before the invasion and failed to anticipate most of the causes of the chaos in Iraq or the insurgency.[15] The Pentagon barred U.S. officials who worked on the study from serving in Iraq, turned their backs on repeated warnings by intelligence agencies about the likelihood of strong resistance to the occupation, and appointed individuals to crucially important posts who had little or no knowledge or experience of Iraq.[16] Rising casualties and skyrocketing costs quickly revealed the inadequacy of the Pentagon's plans. The country was much more run down than had been anticipated. In estimating Iraq's post-war capacity to contribute to its own reconstruction, Rumsfeld and Wolfowitz ignored or discounted an abundance of evidence about the limitations of Iraq's ability to pay. The resulting shortfall dramatically increased the cost to American taxpayers of the war and occupation, which surpassed $275 billion in March 2005 with no end in sight.[17]

A number of senior civilian officials at the Pentagon had become enamored of the idea of installing Iraqi exiles in power in Baghdad after the war. Ahmad Chalabi, leader of an Iraqi exile organization, was one of the most prominent figures in Pentagon calculations. Chalabi convinced his sponsors that Iraqis would welcome him and his fellow exiles, and that by using a secret network inside the country they could quickly restore order to postwar Iraq. Faced with strong opposition from the CIA and State Department, President Bush ruled against relying primarily on the exiles. Even so, the Pentagon continued to support Chalabi, arranged to fly him and a 700-man militia into Iraq during the war, and made lavish payments of hundreds of thousands of dollars every month. "It was very clear," said retired ambassador Timothy Carney, who worked in Iraq just after Saddam's overthrow, "that there was an expectation that the exiles would be the core of an Iraqi interim [governing] authority." Although Bremer named Chalabi to a temporary governing council he and the other exiles failed to attract a significant public following. The collapse of the exile option left a vacuum: there was no other Defense Department plan. The various studies made before the war were painful to read after the insurgency began. For example, the "Future of Iraq" project recommended that the United States purge the Iraqi armed forces of high-ranking Baathists but warned against alienating soldiers in the ranks and demobilizing hundreds of thousands of them, leaving them without a way to make a living. Iraq would need an army to maintain order and defend the country after the departure of American forces, and the sudden denial of income would cause unrest. Despite this warning, the administration completely disbanded the Iraqi military and security forces. An incredulous Iraqi officer protested: "You can't put half a million people with families and weapons and a monthly salary on the dole. You can't do this in any country. They'll turn against you."[18] Another observer pointed out: "The Bush administration had committed one of the greatest errors in the history of U.S. warfare: It unnecessarily increased the ranks of its enemies. Embittered Arab Sunnis, who had dominated the military establishment, would reemerge to lead the insurgency against U.S. troops in the Sunni triangle."[19]

The lawlessness and disorder that followed shocked the Iraqi people, and likely gave millions of them second thoughts about the occupation. Worst of all, the breakdown of order provided a precious interlude of safety to insurgents who seized the chance to arm themselves with explosives, small arms, and ammunition. There were too few American troops to stop them from looting Saddam's armories. One of the administration's most striking errors had been to underestimate the number of troops required for the occupation. A month before the war, Army Chief of Staff General Eric K. Shinseki suggested that "several hundred thousand" would be required. He was immediately contradicted by both Rumsfeld and Wolfowitz: "Wildly off the mark," Wolfowitz told the House Budget Committee on February 27, 2003, barely three weeks from war. "It's hard to conceive that it would take more forces to provide stability in post-Saddam Iraq than it would take to conduct the war itself and to secure the surrender of Saddam's security forces and his army. . . . Hard to imagine."[20] It was hard to imagine apparently only for those at the highest politically appointed levels in the Pentagon. Shinseki's warning was reinforced by similar concerns expressed by the State Department in its "Future of Iraq" study, the U.S. Army War College, the Center for Strategic and International Studies at Georgetown University, and nongovernmental organizations advising the U.S. Agency for International Development.[21]

Unprotected by Iraqi or American forces, everything of value was looted from government offices, schools, hospitals, and businesses, down to toilets, doors, windows, and copper wire from electrical transmission lines. The United Nations left the country after one of its leading administrators was assassinated in a car bomb attack, and returned only months later to assist in the holding of national elections. Cruelly overstretched, U.S. and British forces struggled and failed to stop the descent into chaos. In the crucial first few months of the occupation, they managed to protect most of the oil wells and pumping systems on which restored prosperity depended, and to provide at least some clean water and sporadic electricity. But the confidence of Iraqis in the new order was badly shaken, and a precious opportunity to make a fresh start was lost.[22] The author of a thorough study of Bush II blunders in Iraq concluded:

The administration will be admired in retrospect for how much knowledge it created about the challenge it was taking on. U.S. government predictions about postwar Iraq's problems have proved as accurate as the assessments of pre-war Iraq's strategic threat have proved flawed. But the administration will be condemned for what it did with what was known. The problems the United States has encountered are precisely the ones its own expert agencies warned against. . . . [T]he ongoing financial, diplomatic, and human cost of the Iraq occupation is the more grievous in light of advance warnings the government had.[23]

Early statements about the occupation revealed the extent of the administration's errors. "I don't think it has to be expensive, and I don't think it has to be lengthy," said a senior administration official. "Americans do everything fairly quickly." The idea was to move Iraq rapidly toward "self-managed economic prosperity with a market-based economy and privately owned enterprises that operate in an environment governed by the rule of law." A White House official added, "It's not because we're doing it on the cheap, but because we don't want to have an overbearing presence there that can damage the longer-term view of the United States in the Arab street." At the Pentagon, senior political appointees were equally optimistic. Not even 75,000 troops would be needed for the occupation, one told a reporter. Revealing a stunning ignorance of the history of ethnic conflict, they insisted that Iraq would not need its own armed forces, but could rely on Kurdish fighters who could be moved to the south by the United States, apparently not realizing that this would trigger civil war.[24] A year after Bush declared the end of "major combat operations," the inadequacy, even absurdity, of these assumptions and arguments finally ended in Iraqification and hasty attempts to assemble Iraqi military and police forces adequate to maintain security.[25]

As the casualties and expense mounted, and the time when American forces might leave Iraq receded into an uncertain future, some conservatives and neoconservatives still sounded a triumphal note, urging the administration to persevere in Iraq and to confront Syria, Iran, and China.[26] But a few conservatives and neoconservatives had begun to have second thoughts. Criticism was awkward. Some had been architects and supporters of unilateralism and preventive war. Many had been severe critics of the Clinton administration's "nation-building" enterprises in Somalia, Bosnia, and Kosovo, all of which were dwarfed by what the Bush II administration had taken on in Iraq and Afghanistan. Still, the signs of failure could not be ignored. One conservative critic pointed to "the failure to find weapons of mass destruction in Iraq, the virulent and steadily mounting anti-Americanism throughout the Middle East, the growing insurgency in Iraq, the fact that no strong democratic leadership had emerged there, the enormous financial and growing human cost of the war, the failure to leverage the war to make progress on the Israeli-Palestinian front, and the fact that America's fellow democratic allies had by and large failed to fall in line and legitimate American actions ex post."[27]

Two Iraqi exiles who had been instrumental in persuading the administration to go to war, Kanan Makiya, a scholar and author then at Brandeis University, and Rend Rahim, former ambassador to Washington of the interim Iraqi government, revealed the anguish they felt as the murderous bombings escalated and a consensus failed to develop among Iraqis about the future. Just before the constitutional referendum at a conference held by the American Enterprise Institute, a conservative research organization strongly supportive of the administration and the war, Makiya spoke of "dashed hopes and broken dreams." He added: "Instead of the fledgling democracy that back then we said was possible, instead of that dream, we have the reality of a virulent insurgency whose efficiency is only rivaled by the barbarous tactics it uses. . . . [The violence] is destroying the very idea or the very possibility of Iraq."[28] Makiya characterized the new constitution as unworkable and a destabilizing and even fratricidal document.[29]

He also confessed that he had made major errors when he began urging the Bush administration to go to war in Iraq. Above all, he had failed to understand just how determined Iraqis were, whether Sunni, Kurd, or Shiite, to make Iraq into a country constituted along sectarian and ethnic lines into powerful regions and a weak central government. In addition, he had insisted on the rapid and wholesale demilitarization of the country, but this had humiliated Sunnis and Saddam loyalists and made enemies of them needlessly. The same end could have been accomplished gradually over a period of three to five years without producing the same humiliation and bitter enmity. De-Baathification [removing prominent officials of Saddam's government and punishing those guilty of major crimes] had been badly conceived and poorly administered, failing, for example, to distinguish among degrees of culpability and overlooking the victims of the regime. Last, Makiya argued that his earlier hopes for Iraq had been premised on the emergence of Iraqi leaders with "a nonselfish, long-term and all-inclusive political vision. That kind of leadership has not yet made its appearance in Iraq."

Rahim's detailed and thoughtful comments on the ambiguities and gaps in the new constitution that she thought could well "spin the state out of control" emphasized the weakness of the institutions of the central government: "Right now in Iraq the only real institutions that have substance exist in Kurdistan. The institutions of the central government are weak and lack not only authority but any implementing capability. Institutions in the regions, in the governorates other than Kurdistan are in fact nonexistent except for the militias." That weakness included control over military force, or as she put it: if the regions have their own national guard, police, and intelligence service, it is far from clear how the central government will find the means to combat terrorism and the insurgency that are tearing Iraq apart. Rahim added that the constitution provided no means for the central government to enforce the many rights and freedoms it guaranteed. As for the powers of the presidency, the three-member presidential council indeed possessed a veto, but it could be exercised only by a unanimous vote of the Council. If only one of the members of the Council agreed with the legislative majority, there could be no effective check on parliamentary power.[30] One could not help wondering if Makiya and Rahim would have been so mistaken about Iraq and Iraqis had they lived there for the past thirty years instead of in Britain and the United States.

Disappointed exiles were not the only problem for the administration's Iraq policy in the fall of 2005. A number of American generals reported pessimistically about the prospects of the occupation and the insurgency. The commanding general of U.S. forces in Iraq, General George W. Casey Jr., told members of Congress that only one Iraqi battalion was capable of fighting without American support, and that number had declined in recent weeks from a total of three.[31] General John P. Abizaid, commander of the U.S. Central Command, told the Senate Armed Forces Committee that it would still be some time before Iraqi troops could assume full responsibility for security in their country. The number and readiness of Iraqi units were increasing, Abizaid and Casey said, but, in Casey's words, "Iraqi armed forces will not have an independent capability for some time."[32] Reports also circulated in Washington that U.S. Army recruiting was at its lowest since the beginning of the volunteer armed forces a quarter century earlier.[33] On top of this mountain of bad news came a worsening of violence in Afghanistan and between Israelis and Palestinians.[34] Not since the invasion in 2001 had so many been killed in Afghanistan as perished in 2005—nearly 1,100 people and more than 50 U.S. soldiers. The evacuation of Gaza had apparently not reduced violence but shifted it to the West Bank. Israeli security officials told reporters that their government was considering denying Palestinians the use of all major roads in that territory.

Public support for the president and the occupation of Iraq continued to fall. A CNN/USA Today/Gallup poll revealed a startling reversal in job approval ratings for the president. In mid-March 2003, just before the beginning of the war in Iraq, 58 percent of Americans surveyed responded favorably and 38 percent unfavorably to the question, "Do you approve or disapprove of the way George Bush is handling his job as president?" Exactly two years later, the figures were reversed: 58 percent of respondents disapproved and 38 percent approved.[35] A poll by the Chicago Council on Foreign Relations reported that most Americans opposed the use of force to impose democracy on another country. And 73 percent of those polled, including 60 percent who were Republicans, said that overthrowing Saddam Hussein in order to establish a democracy was not worth a war. Sixty-six percent said that it was better to cooperate with the United Nations when promoting democracy because it will be more widely regarded as legitimate.[36] Congress began to demand explanations and greater accountability from the administration for its failure to quell the insurgency and to begin withdrawing troops from Iraq.[37] Doubts had begun to grow among allies as well. The foreign minister of Saudi Arabia, Prince Saud al-Faisal, warned publicly that Iraq was facing disintegration. "There is no dynamic now pulling the nation together," he told reporters during a meeting at the Saudi Embassy in Washington. "All the dynamics are pulling the country apart. . . . [U]nless something is done to bring Iraqis together, elections alone won't do it. A constitution alone won't do it."[38]

Seventy-nine percent of Iraqi voters approved the new constitution on October 15, 2005. Overall, about 63 percent of registered voters went to the polls. The constitution received overwhelming support in thirteen of nineteen provinces, and substantial margins in two others. The "yes" vote came from Kurdish- and Shiite-majority provinces in the north and south. Two predominately Sunni provinces in the northwest—Anbar (92 percent) and Salahedeen (82 percent)—heavily disapproved, and 55 percent voted against in a third—Ninevah—but the result was short of the two-thirds majority in three provinces needed to defeat the constitution. Parliamentary elections were scheduled to take place within two months. Although the constitution was ratified, the vote revealed a country deeply split along ethnic and religious lines.[39] Amid the gloom cast by continued bombing and the shadow of impending ethnic conflict, there were signs that at least some Sunni politicians and fighters had decided to take part in the December elections.[40]

In response to the violence and bloodshed and the deeply divided vote on the Iraqi constitution, the president insisted that a premature departure of American troops from would encourage terrorists around the world and turn the country into another Afghanistan. Secretary Rice pointed out correctly that tens of thousands of Sunnis had participated in the referendum and that this represented a broadening of the Iraqi political base. She was joined in her upbeat view of the elections by the U.S. ambassador in Baghdad, Zalmay Khalilzad, who argued that the Iraqi constitution enshrined democratic values and structures and subjected Islam to the tests of democracy and human rights. At the same time, he recognized Iraq's divisions and admitted that the new constitution could be at best only a first step toward national unity:

> Ethnic and sectarian factions rather than truly national forces are dominant. Iraq's leaders differ on fundamental goals and deeply distrust each other. The process for drafting the constitution made progress on bridging the divide between them as they worked to develop a common road to the future. . . . Ultimately Iraqis will need to develop a national compact.[41]

Despite their brave public faces, senior members of the administration told reporters privately that they had begun to reevaluate what could be achieved in Iraq. The approval of the constitution should be not be seen as a victory, they said, but as another chance to avoid civil war and hold Iraq together until a political solution could be found to the country's divisions. One senior official involved in Iraq policy since 2003 told reporters that the administration's original expectations for Iraq had been unrealistic and that it was in the process of "shedding the unreality that dominated at the beginning."[42] Another official put it even more bluntly: "We set out to establish a democracy, but we're slowly realizing we'll have some form of Islamic republic."[43] The insurgency and growing domestic opposition to the war had taken away the time the United States needed to use the constitution-writing process to help Iraqis build consensus and establish a culture supportive of democracy in the country. If anything, Bush II officials were even more pessimistic about defeating the insurgency before American troops had to be brought home. Dismal statistics supported the pessimism.

Since the invasion of Iraq, the number of insurgents had grown from 5,000, mostly Saddam loyalists, to 20,000. The first week of August 2005 was the fourth worst for U.S. combat deaths since the invasion, and during the first two weeks of August more soldiers in the National Guard and reserves had died than in any previous month. U.S. convoys were attacked twice as often as a year earlier, and convoys of supplies from Turkey, Kuwait, and Jordan were attacked about thirty times a week. Six million people had no electricity for days at a time. At 2.2 million barrels per day, oil production had yet to reach the daily pre-war level of 2.67 million barrels. According to U.S. government auditors, Iraq had been forced to pay $300 million a month to import refined gasoline because it had too few refineries. Because of soaring costs for security and losses due to mismanagement and corruption, a "reconstruction gap" in funding had opened. To close it would require the United States to double the funding it had hoped to spend for Iraqi reconstruction in order to come close to the 2003 estimate of $56 billion by the World Bank that would be required for Iraqi reconstruction.[44] Some officials and analysts suggested that the administration had already begun to look for an exit strategy: "We've said we won't leave a day before it's necessary. But necessary is the key word—necessary for them or for us? When we finally depart, it will probably be for us."[45]

The irony was that the Bush II administration had ended by putting themselves and their policies into the hands of its Iraqi allies. It was not certain that those Iraqis would fail, but whether they succeeded or failed was beyond the control of the American government. This was the exact opposite of what the president and his advisers had intended when they adopted unilateralism and preventive war. They had meant to put the United States in charge of its own destiny, not tie the country to the success or failure of democracy in Iraq, a war-torn country with no democratic tradition and deep ethnic and religious divisions.[46]

Mismanaging Intelligence

The Bush II administration was not solely to blame for the massive intelligence blunders that led to 9/11 and the fiasco over Saddam Hussein's weapons of mass destruction. Little was done during the Bush I or Clinton administrations to strengthen U.S. human intelligence capabilities—spies inside enemy organizations, which is the surest way to learn the secrets of terrorists and dictators. While Bush II failed to recognize the changed nature of terrorism until it was too late, so had the administration's predecessors. Bush II's initial focus on domestic issues made it even less likely that the true nature of the threat would be discovered in time.

While these faults began long before 2001, another set of errors and misjudgments are entirely Bush II's own. In some ways they are worse than the earlier errors because they set the American government at war with itself, and substituted the wishes and personal beliefs of political appointees for the experience and judgment of career officials in the military, intelligence, and diplomatic agencies of the U.S. government. The history of American diplomacy is filled with examples of this, and the separation of powers makes it a constant temptation by multiplying the delays and obstacles that hamper the president's capacity to act quickly and decisively.

Senior Bush II officials began to manipulate intelligence at least as early as January 2002 when they began to eliminate nuance and conditionality about Iraq's weapons from their public statements, even though these ambiguities had been present in intelligence reports for years. The president, vice president, and some of his most senior advisers, particularly Cheney, Rumsfeld, Rice, and Wolfowitz, began to say flatly that Saddam Hussein would pass nuclear, chemical, or biological weapons to terrorists, despite his history of never having done so, and the risk that discovery was certain to lead to the destruction of the Iraqi government. In order to persuade Congress, the president and his advisers had to eliminate the gap between what they were saying and existing intelligence estimates. This led to a hastily produced October 2002 National Intelligence Estimate that made a very strong case that Saddam was actively seeking nuclear weapons, and downplayed dissent from the intelligence agencies.[47] Prepared by the National Intelligence Council, National Intelligence Estimates are intended to pull together the best judgments of all the intelligence agencies of the U.S. government about the direction that events will take in the future.[48] It seems likely, as intelligence specialist Thomas Powers suggested, that CIA analysts charged with evaluating Iraq's weapons programs knew that the evidence was thin and of dubious reliability, but "surrendered to pressure from above and hoped to be saved by a miracle—they convinced themselves that something would turn up when the troops got to Baghdad and were free to look in all the nooks and crannies."[49] The miracle never happened.

In addition to pressuring the intelligence community to support the war, the president and his advisers relied heavily on uncorroborated and dubious information from Iraqi exiles and selectively extracted intelligence that supported war (known as "cherry picking") and sent it to key decision makers ("stovepiping") without allowing the broader intelligence community to evaluate it. These kinds of actions appear to have been undertaken by political appointees at very senior levels within the administration, particularly in the Pentagon's Office of Special Plans that reported to Douglas Feith, undersecretary of defense for policy. This operation was reminiscent of earlier conservative efforts to second-guess established intelligence agencies. A special White House Iraq Group coordinated the administration's policy statements in order to present a prowar façade of unity.[50]

Bush II was not alone in its mistakes about Iraqi weapons. Apparently, every major intelligence agency in Europe, Israel, and the United States got it wrong. Prestigious independent think tanks, such as the International Institute for Strategic Studies, joined the parade of error in early September 2002 by publishing a glossy assessment of Iraq's weapons that essentially agreed with the Blair and Bush statements of the case except for greater nuance in regard to nuclear weapons. Opponents of the war such as former National Security Council staffer Morton Halperin argued not that Iraq had no weapons, but that Saddam had been contained and was deterred from aggression.[51] French President Jacques Chirac's sarcastic comment that intelligence agencies feed on each other, and that their views must be discounted, was hardly a firm basis for his all-out opposition to the war. The problem was that the administration meant to go to war on the basis of the reports. An additional problem was that the world looked to the United States for guidance, and expected its information to be reliable. Instead, the administration deceived itself, and was unable to distinguish valid information about Iraqi weapons from "noise," the mass of information that always accompanies anything important.[52] Lost in the private world that they had fashioned out of faulty assumptions, false analogies, logical fallacies, and unreliable information, they found it impossible to penetrate Saddam's ruse. Sometime in the mid-1990s, Saddam destroyed what remained of his weapons and production facilities.[53] He no doubt intended to start them again if he ever had the chance. But they were not where the administration convinced itself they ought to be. In fact, they were not there at all.[54]

The failure to find weapons of mass destruction in Iraq struck directly at the claim of the American and British governments that they acted to forestall an "imminent" threat. Alone among the president's senior advisers, Colin Powell admitted that without the weapons, it was simply not clear whether the United States would or should have gone to war. Despite the evidence to the contrary, Bush, Cheney, and Rumsfeld clung to the idea that the weapons would be found.[55] Rice shifted her reasons for favoring the war and began to stress Saddam's murderous past and the likelihood that he would have resumed weapons production after sanctions had been lifted. Interviews with Iraqi scientists and officials by weapons inspector David Kay suggested that much of the information on which Western intelligence agencies relied was out of date, and was simply extended in a linear fashion into the future based on a worst-case scenario. Daniel Benjamin and Steven Simon, two National Security Council staff members in the second Clinton administration, concluded that no one realized that a widely held assumption—that terrorists were either state sponsored or part of a national liberation movement—was dangerously out of date. Evidence challenging the old assumption was ignored or minimized.[56] The intelligence committees in the House and Senate launched investigations into the failures, but it was too late to influence the decision for war or to prevent the 9/11 attacks. Critics charged that the administration had manipulated intelligence and pressured analysts to produce the "right" conclusions, which would support war with Iraq. It was an extremely serious charge, and the administration flatly denied it. But there was substantial evidence to support the allegation.[57]

The administration's inability to foresee the intensity with which Kurds and Shia would cling to a "winner take all" outlook and the ferocity with which Sunnis would resist the American-led occupation and reconstruction of Iraq mocked its hopes to remake Iraq into a democratic model for the Arab and Muslim worlds. As voters went to the polls to ratify the new Iraqi constitution, it even seemed to some administration officials that this exercise in democracy would intensify the divisions in the country and prolong the terrorism and insurgency rather than diminish them. This insight came despite the administration's long-standing view that terrorism arose precisely from the absence of democracy in the Middle East and South Asia and that the remedy for terrorism was democratization.[58]

North Korea and Nuclear Proliferation

In early 2004, the administration put its North Korea policy on hold for the fall election. According to a U.S. official: "[The] criteria for success was [sic] that the North Koreans don't walk out. . . . The motto is 'Do no harm.' This is a placeholder to get us through the election."[59] The placeholder was regular talks, perhaps working groups to examine a three-phase plan indistinguishable from the Clinton administration's approach: multilateral security pledges in exchange for North Korea's agreement to stop its nuclear programs "verifiably, irreversibly, and completely"; linkage among progress in removing the weapons programs, help for North Korea's energy shortages, and ending North Korea's status as a state sponsor of terrorism; and consideration of normal relations between the two countries, linked, as always, to North Korea's progress on ending its nuclear programs. The meetings convened by China included Russia, South Korea, and Japan, as well as North Korea and the United States. Despite elaborate procedures, the talks went nowhere and were complicated by revelations that a Pakistani nuclear scientist and entrepreneur in selling nuclear secrets had passed nuclear technology to North Korea. The administration emphasized the unwillingness of the North Korean government to discuss its efforts to acquire weapons based on highly enriched uranium, but left open whether a vaguer declaration covering all nuclear programs would suffice to move the process forward.[60]

The inability of the administration either to move the disarmament negotiations ahead or to bring down the regime in North Korea, where the economy showed increasing signs of growth, mocked the unilateralists' insistence throughout Bush II's first term that the Kim regime could be brought down by isolation and diplomatic and economic pressure.[61] Instead, the administration had allowed North Korea to escape all controls and, apparently, to produce more nuclear weapons. The outcome undermined decades of efforts to promote nuclear nonproliferation. North Korea's example also appeared to show that acquiring nuclear weapons was an effective way to keep the United States from overthrowing governments it regarded as hostile. The vague agreement put together by the Chinese government in September 2005 and more or less forced on the administration succeeded by putting off the most difficult questions, such as the dates for North Korean nuclear disarmament or a specific time for stopping the extraction of plutonium from existing reactors. It amounted to significantly less than had been achieved by the Clinton administration a decade earlier.

Israel and the Palestinians

Upon reviewing Bush II policy toward the Israeli-Palestinian conflict, the most striking feature is that all the speeches, road maps, and traveling to and from the region by American officials, including the president, had virtually no impact on the parties. After four years of Palestinian terrorism, Israeli reprisal, occupation, and settlement construction, the two sides found themselves farther apart and as deeply mired in violence as when the administration first began. Robert Malley, a Clinton national security staff member responsible for Arab-Israeli affairs, described the horrific scene in late 2003 in this way:

> Borders—whether physical, political, or moral—are giving way. Palestinian militants routinely strike pre-1967 Israel. They have erased any possible distinction between military and civilian targets. Israel has methodically destroyed the Palestinian Authority, sent troops into territory under the Palestinians' theoretical control and taken steps that condemn large numbers of its inhabitants to misery or worse. Targeted killing has become a matter of course, and Israel publicly considers the assassination of the Arab world's first and only democratically elected president. Even the fence now under construction is well on its way to becoming the first border in history that actually prevents separation, eliminating the possibility of a viable Palestinian state and, with it, of a sustainable two-state solution. . . . In this political vacuum, the only effective constraining factor left is the threat of retribution.[62]

It may have been impossible for the American government to have stopped the descent into brutality. However, Bush II policies denied the administration any chance to influence what the Palestinians and Israelis did to one another or the damage that their conflict inflicted on American security interests in the area. A strong purposeful mediation that held out a clear picture of a final settlement and systematically used American leverage to move toward that goal might have interrupted the violence, but this was precisely what the administration refused. Instead, it aligned its policy with that of Israeli Prime Minister Ariel Sharon and doomed any possibility of Palestinian cooperation in stopping the violence and moving toward peace. It was not that the administration's proposals lacked imagination. If anything, all the posturing showed an excess of imagination: first "assist but not insist," then Tenet, then Mitchell, then a "road map," then regime change for the Palestinians—read the downfall of Yasser Arafat—and then not one but two summits. There were too many plans, too many words, and too little pressure on the parties to perform. The effect was to postpone peace negotiations indefinitely. Senior intelligence analysts concluded that the two-state solution was dead.[63] Delay played into Sharon's hands, because it allowed him time to develop his ideas for strangling any hope that a viable Palestinian state would be created. That Sharon sought this outcome out of his conviction that Israel's very existence depended on it did nothing to ease the suffering of both peoples or to assist the United States in pursuing its larger interests in the Arab and Muslim world.

The best that might have been possible was to tie the two sides up in negotiations, fiercely overseen by the United States, whose victories in Afghanistan and Iraq ought to have multiplied its influence with Israeli and Palestinian leaders. Instead, the administration offered an over-elaborate process and, after 9/11, a demand for regime change. The Palestinians understandably regarded the process warily: during the Oslo negotiations every Israeli government had allowed the number of Jewish settlers in the West Bank to increase steadily until it reached more than 400,000.[64] Giving so much importance to removing Arafat and replacing him with someone who would be more pliable guaranteed that successive candidates would appear as quislings in the eyes of Palestinians and killed the idea before it could be started. One after another, the substitute leaders acceptable to the United States rose and fell with no change in the conflict with Israel or the effectiveness and honesty of the Palestinian Authority. The administration's calls for democratization amounted to a poorly concealed attempt to divide the Palestinian leadership and impose new leaders, apparently without realizing that this had been the goal of Israel's Likud Party since the discredited "village council" scheme of the 1970s. The efforts to humiliate and replace Arafat angered Arab governments friendly to the United States, and ultimately succeeded in making him irreplaceable.[65] The policy failed, in large measure because it made it possible to oppose Israel and the United States merely by supporting Arafat. The avoidance of substance and the insistence on an open-ended democratization process gave Sharon a chance to push his plans for "separation" of Israelis and Palestinians, a term that Palestinians regarded as a euphemism for the continued annexation of Palestinian land and the final defeat of independence and statehood. The unrelieved plight of the Palestinians worsened relations with Arab and Muslim states and, in this way, harmed larger U.S. security interests in the region and in the fight against terrorism. The contradiction in the policy showed clearly after Israel's assassination of Sheik Ahmed Yassin, spiritual leader of the militant Islamist and terrorist organization Hamas. Arab states found themselves forced to postpone a scheduled Arab League summit that had peace with Israel and democratic reform on its agenda.[66]

Bush's attempt to impose regime change on the Palestinians had a strange, "hit-and-run" dimension. There was little follow-up to all the declarations.[67] It was also unworkable at its heart, because Palestinians could not hold democratic elections without an easing of the Israeli occupation, and the administration refused to insist on this.[68] In July 2002, shortly after Bush launched his attempt to replace Arafat, an American journalist interviewed Hamed Shaheen, thirty-eight, a Palestinian man with six children who had lost his job as a gardener because of the intifada and now drove a taxi.

> I was taking my taxi through this road to reach the Kalandia check-point, Shaheen said. "The Israeli soldiers stopped me and ordered me to drive here and took my ID and my keys. I have no choice but to wait here for my ID. The last time it happened to me, 20 days ago, I was kept waiting for 26 hours. Of course I blame the occupation. . . . I blame everybody: America, Israel, and the Palestinian Authority for the situation. We need a solution. It's not a life. If I don't work, I will lose the car and I will have no job. . . . When you blame the Americans it's because they gave the green light to Israel. Israel is responsible for the occupation. . . . I blame the Palestinian Authority for not being able to help us. For the corruption that exists.[69]

Or, as Israeli columnist Akiva Eldar put it: "Once again, we're looking for kosher Palestinians, those who don't appear to be subject to Yasir Arafat." The only solution, he argued, would come from the White House. "Everything else is hot air."[70] Instead of reconsidering its policies, the administration hired a public relations expert to improve its image in the Arab world. She soon resigned without accomplishing any significant change in public opinion. As Bush's first term ran out, the two-state solution seemed further away than ever, even though more than 70 percent of Israelis and Palestinians believed in the possibility and desirability of peace based on an end to violence for the first, and a settlement based on the 1967 borders for the second.[71] Israeli novelist Amos Elon observed:

> In Israel and in Palestine, the center has collapsed. The much talked-about "two-state solution" may no longer be practicable since on both sides all confidence is gone. The extremists of Greater Israel and the extremists of Greater Palestine mutually veto all progress. . . . The bazaar diplomacy of the past ten years has clearly been counterproductive. . . . When force did not work, there was a tendency to believe in using more force, which led, as we are seeing, only to more force. . . . The settlement project has not provided more security but less. It may yet, I tremble at the thought, lead to results far more terrible than those we are now witnessing.[72]

The stalemate and exhaustion of the parties, the harm to American interests that flowed from a failure to resolve the conflict, and the victories in Afghanistan and Iraq provided reason and opportunity for American mediation. Instead, the United States stepped briskly to the sidelines. Whenever Palestinian terrorists set off bombs or Israeli troops invaded villages and closed the occupied territories, the administration announced that progress toward peace waited on Palestinian democratization. Until that day, however far away it might be, Israel had a right to defend itself. It was as close as governments come to an admission of bafflement and irrelevance.

Arafat's sudden death in December 2004 brought a break in the cycle of violence and despair. Elections made Mahmoud Abbas, one of Arafat's longtime associates, president of the Palestinian Authority. Hope revived but remained fragile. Sharon had spent his life opposing the creation of an independent Palestinian state that included all of the West Bank. The poor record of Abbas's party, Fatah, in governing the Palestinian territories and stopping corruption also cast doubt on the future. To make matters worse, Hamas, an Islamist group that frequently used terrorism to attack Israel, boycotted the presidential elections, arguing that their participation would amount to acceptance of the Oslo Agreements and peace with Israel, which the group vehemently opposed. In local elections, Hamas won control of seven of the ten districts that it contested and seemed likely to win dozens of seats in the next round of legislative elections. Abbas's response was to try to co-opt Hamas into accepting a ceasefire and negotiations with Israel.[73] The leaders of Hamas appeared to have calculated that Sharon would soon reveal his intention to deny Palestinian independence, strengthening them and further weakening Fatah and the PLO. Hamas would then resume the struggle against Israel. The one sure result of Bush II policy toward the Israeli-Palestinian conflict had been to strengthen the appeal of the most radical Islamist party in the occupied territories.[74]

Bush repeated his commitment to an independent Palestinian state a few weeks before meeting with Sharon at his Texas ranch in mid-April 2005, and Bush planned to extend an invitation to Abbas to meet with him in the White House: "The world must not rest until there is a just and lasting resolution to this conflict."[75] However, Sharon's plans to suspend Palestinian statehood indefinitely also remained unaltered. An American journalist explained the pessimistic possibilities in this way:

> If all proceeds as planned, [Sharon] will remove Israeli settlements from Gaza and one small part of the West Bank by the end of this

summer [2005]. He will complete construction of the West Bank
fence by the end of this year. Then, having effectively created a new
Israel that includes all of Jerusalem and at least 7 percent of the West
Bank, he will freeze the situation indefinitely. Palestinians will be left
with Gaza and several West Bank enclaves separated from each other
by Israeli roads and settlements; whether that is someday called a
state is a secondary concern for the Israeli prime minister.[76]

Regardless of how one viewed Sharon's intentions, it made sense for
the president to minimize public differences with him over the West Bank
until the withdrawal from Gaza was completed. The "road map" had become irrelevant, as Sharon intended. While U.S. assistance to the Israeli
economy had declined by 10 percent a year for several years, Israel remained heavily dependent on American military and economic aid. In addition, opposition to Israel's policies toward the Palestinians had grown
far more widespread and vocal in Western Europe since 2001. The United
States remained Israel's only trusted international friend. In other words,
the elements of American pressure existed much as they had during Bush I.
The loss of confidence in the United States throughout the Arab and Muslim worlds after the invasion of Iraq actually increased the pressure on the
United States to help Israel and the Palestinians make peace. The stakes
were high, and the possibilities for a successful mediation obvious. Sadly,
the administration's arms-length approach to the conflict during the previous five years suggested that the president and his advisers would find a
way to avoid becoming peacemakers.

Unilateralism and the Allies

Some analysts blamed clumsy diplomacy for the difficulties between the
administration and America's European allies.[77] There was lots of clumsiness on both sides, with the prize stumble no doubt the announcement by
Deputy Secretary of Defense Wolfowitz that only companies from coalition
members would be allowed to bid on new contracts for Iraq's reconstruction just as former Secretary of State James Baker began to visit European
capitals asking for cooperation in reducing Iraq's international debt.[78] But
far more than clumsiness was involved: the administration meant to assert
America's global dominance, and the allies were correct to see the war in
Iraq and the abandonment of allied solidarity as a symptom of American

hegemony.[79] The dynamics of the clash threatened to poison the possibility of future cooperation.[80] Did it make any sense, asked British contemporary historian Timothy Garton Ash, for the administration to be playing a game of dividing the countries of Europe against one another?

> Today, with a single hyperpower and a larger, more complex Europe, the United States could certainly go on pursuing this classic imperial strategy. The question is, does it want to? Is it consonant with the values, history and habits of cooperation that Europe and America share? Is it in the United States' own long-term national interest, when the West as a whole faces such major challenges, in the Middle East and elsewhere?[81]

France's policy of creating a Berlin-Paris-Moscow "axis of refusal" was equally nonsensical: "a crude, reach-me-down version" of De Gaulle's old dream of uniting Europe against "les Anglo-Saxons." It was possible to imagine Europe and the United States refusing to cooperate, but it was impossible to imagine that such a divorce would make any sense.[82]

What made the Europe–United States divorce even more ridiculous was that two months after the administration went to war in Iraq without the support of France and Germany, the European Union began consideration of a common European security strategy that had much in common with American international objectives.[83] The strategy's objectives were constructive and positive, and ought to have provided a strong foundation for cooperation with the United States. That they did not is a measure of the Bush administration's lack of interest in allied cooperation and support, a position that proved to be an extremely costly one in Iraq. The first Bush II term ended with disinterest bordering on contempt in Washington, and stereotyping and posturing in European capitals. At attempt was made early in the second term to repair relations with France and Germany. Bush and Rice made a point of going to Europe within a few days of the inauguration. Bush met with Chirac and the two continued their cooperation to force Syria to withdraw from Lebanon. However, there was little indication that the administration was interested in renewal of broader consultation and compromise, much less a change in the administration's determination to rely on "coalitions of the willing" rather than allies to accomplish its international objectives.

At a more profound level, the rupture between Europe and America took on a tragic dimension. Contrary to their values and aspirations, many

European governments and citizens found themselves opposing the overthrow of a murderous dictator. Their opposition left the Americans without the resources and legitimacy that came from a larger, pluralistic association. Instead of growing stronger from the crisis, with their instinct for
cooperation strengthened by success and mutual admiration, the two sides
emerged wary of one another, their ability to cooperate in the future diminished. Estranged and suspicious, the United States and Europe had
managed to wound one another instead of the terrorists.[84] Only the enemies
of liberty gained. Long before the Iraq war, Hans Morgenthau, an academic
for many years at the University of Chicago and the founder of "American
realism" (foreign policy based on the calculation of interests and power),
suggested that one of the most important tests for foreign policy was to
distinguish between the desirable and the possible:

> Statesmen, especially under contemporary conditions, may well make
> a habit of presenting their foreign policies in terms of their philo-
> sophic and political sympathies in order to gain popular support for
> them. Yet they will distinguish with Lincoln between their "*official
> duty*," which is to think and act in terms of the national interest, and
> their "*personal* wish," which is to see their own moral values and po-
> litical principles realized throughout the world.[85]

At the end of its first term, the Bush II administration had failed Morgenthau's test.

Rhetoric and Practice in Bush II Strategy

A government's international goals may be analyzed by examining the
character of the demands placed on other states, the time in which they
must be realized, and the resources committed to their achievement. A
vital interest must be realized immediately, makes great demands on other
states, and receives abundant political, diplomatic, and military backing.
The Bush II administration's demands on Iraq show all these characteris-
tics. The administration also repeatedly declared that the spread of democracy around the world was a vital security interest. Although the demands
on nondemocratic states were uncompromising, neither the time in which
they had to democratize nor the resources committed by the administration, signaled that the interest was vital. For example, the administration

requested $87 billion in its first supplemental request to pay for the fighting and reconstruction of Iraq after the invasion. It requested $28 million as the first installment on its Middle East Partnership Initiative, a program to foster democracy and market economics in the entire region, an amount smaller by a factor of about 3,000 to 1.[86] The inconsistency between rhetoric and practice contradicted the administration's emphasis on the importance of democratization and invited charges of hypocrisy. The clash was most acute in Bush II's dealings with governments whose cooperation was crucial to the war against al-Qaeda: Egypt, Saudi Arabia, Pakistan, Kyrgyzstan, Uzbekistan, Afghanistan, and Kazakhstan. Indonesia, a major target of Islamic radicals, with its human rights abuses and politicized armed forces, also embarrassed the administration, which nonetheless sought to reestablish military-to-military cooperation.

The tension between democratization and the demands of effective statecraft posed a greater risk than embarrassment. Treating democratization as a security goal invited intellectual and political confusion:

> This . . . tension between democracy as an end versus a means has surfaced in the administration's press for democracy in the Palestinian territories. Bush . . . urged Palestinians to reform, especially through elections, yet at the same time administration officials have made clear that certain outcomes, such as the reelection of Yasir Arafat, [were] unacceptable to the United States.[87]

Presumably, an electoral victory by Hamas would earn the same opposition. A similar problem confronted the administration as it sought to establish democracy in Iraq: democratically determined or not, certain outcomes—the return of Saddam's Baath Party to power, or control of the government by radical Shiite clergy—were not allowed. If friendly authoritarian governments such as Egypt and Saudi Arabia were to embark on deep and thorough reforms, they might all fall into a prolonged period of instability that could end in the seizure of power by radical Islamists. Authoritarian governments with uncertain legitimacy face enormous risks when they try to reform themselves. If they reject reform, they risk alienating more and more members of the society. If they accept reform and move too quickly, they undermine the regime's foundations and the very groups on which the regime depends for its survival. The demand for immediate democratization also ignored the influence of the history and culture of other societies on the outcome of attempts to democratize. Should formal democratization occur suddenly in a few years, the post-reform society is more likely to resemble its predecessor than a long-established democracy such as Great Britain or the United States:

> The experience of other countries where in recent decades the United States has forcibly removed dictatorial regimes—Grenada, Panama, Haiti, and most recently Afghanistan—indicates that post-invasion political life usually takes on the approximate character of the political life that existed in the country before the ousted regime came to power. After the 1982 U.S. military intervention in Grenada, for example that country was able to recover the tradition of moderate pluralism it had enjoyed before the 1979 takeover by Maurice Bishop and his gang. Haiti after the 1994 U.S. invasion, has unfortunately slipped back into many of the pathologies that marked its political life before the military junta took over in 1991. Iraqi politics prior to Saddam Hussein were violent, divisive, and oppressive. And the underlying conditions in Iraq—not just the lack of significant previous experience with pluralism but also sharp ethnic and religious differences and an oil-dependent economy—will inevitably make democratization there very slow and difficult.[88]

The administration claimed the Iraqi elections as a success for its policy, and publicly noted that what had happened in Iraq had been an important factor "shaking up the region" and promoting democratic reforms in Egypt, Saudi Arabia, Lebanon, and among the Palestinians. It had been worth the cost after all, some senior policymakers observed. It was a claim that was impossible to prove or disprove. The huge cost of the war and occupation, and the open-endedness of the American military presence in Iraq, made the crowing sound hollow. To those who were suspicious of the entire notion, democratization, at least as practiced in Iraq, hardly seemed worth doing again in some other country. The doubters agreed with the American diplomat and historian George Kennan:

> [T]o see ourselves as the center of political enlightenment and as teachers to a great part of the rest of the world [is] unthought-through, vainglorious, and undesirable. . . . [T]his planet is never going to be ruled by any single political center, whatever its military power.[89]

As the second Bush II term began, the new secretary of state, Condoleezza Rice, sounded at times as if the troubles in Iraq had never taken place. When asked by reporters about the risk that its pressure for reform would lead to instability in such states as Egypt, Saudi Arabia, and Syria, Rice affirmed that the administration continued to trust in the universal efficacy and relevance of democratization as well as its pacifying tendencies. These countries were already so unstable and in need of reform, she said, that the issue was not whether democratization would cause instability. The problem was that the United States was getting "neither stability nor democracy," and it was being blamed for preaching democracy while supporting dictators. Previously, she said, "stability trumped everything." Now, stability was no longer possible and, in any case, the United States could not design "the perfect counter" that would prevent the lack of democracy in these countries from spawning terrorism: "[T]he only thing the United States can do is to speak out for the values that have been absent, liberty and freedom there, and it will have to take its own course." Rice said the administration hoped reform would not result in extremists taking over from previously friendly governments, as had happened in Iran. She added that the administration thought that the citizens of Egypt, Saudi Arabia, and Syria would not want their children to become terrorists, and that democracy would have a moderating effect in the region. "Can we be certain of that?" she asked her questioners. "No. But do I think there's a strong certainty that the Middle East was not going to stay stable anyway? Yes. And when you know that the status quo is no longer defensible, then you have to be willing to move in another direction."[90] Rice's statements revealed an odd combination of hope in the power of democratization, and despair about the capacity of the United States to influence events in a positive direction. Her words were not backed by any significant increase in economic assistance, and they showed little confidence in the capacities of the governments of Egypt and Saudi Arabia to maintain control while they enacted reforms.

However troubling and ambiguous Rice's statements, they were intended to support and explain the commitments that George W. Bush assumed as he began his second term. During his second inaugural address, Bush went far beyond the democratization of Iraq or even the Middle East and announced his commitment to the democratization of the world:

> So it is the policy of the United States to seek and support the growth of democratic movements and institutions in every nation and culture, with the ultimate goal of ending tyranny in our world.[91]

The words echoed the globalism of the Truman Doctrine that launched America's role in the Cold War. A powerful reaction of surprise and consternation in Congress and from allied governments prompted the White House to deny that the president had outlined a new and more aggressive policy. It was an odd exercise for an administration that had long insisted that George W. Bush said what he meant and meant what he said.

President Bush's ambitions went beyond the global expansion of America's commitment to democratization. In the course of his speech he attempted to rewrite American and world history. The 1990s were not "years of relative quiet, years of repose, years of sabbatical," as the president described them, but a time of genocide from Kigali to Srebrenica. It was a time when precious opportunities were wasted, chances to save lives, stop terrorism, and ease the hardships and poverty that terrorists rely on to justify their crimes. The president's argument that history showed democracy to be the only antidote to tyranny, terrorism, and war was simply not true. Britain, West Germany, and Italy, democracies all, suffered prolonged terrorist attacks throughout the 1970s and 1980s. There have also been many more legitimate monarchies and aristocracies than democracies throughout history. Nor is it self-evident that democracies are intrinsically peaceful. The sole claim that appears to stand up is that during the past century, democratic states managed to avoid attacking one another. As has often been said, this is not a theory of foreign policy but a fact than needs explaining.

Perhaps the gravest historical errors occurred in the president's interpretation of the American founding. According to the president, the United States was founded to spread democracy around the world. But it was French, not American, revolutionaries who called on all the peoples of Europe and the world to overthrow their monarchs. Americans limited their target to George III. French revolutionaries published the universal "Rights of Man." Americans adopted a Bill of Rights as amendments to a constitution that applied exclusively to American citizens and institutions. According to the Constitution, the mission of the American government is to "secure the blessings of liberty to ourselves and our posterity," not the whole world. The most important question that will be asked by later generations of Americans will not be, as the president alleged, whether their government advanced the cause of freedom throughout the whole world, but whether it preserved the liberty, security, and prosperity of Americans, and helped those it was in its power to help.

Postscript on the Elections in Iraq

The large turnout of Iraqi voters in national elections on January 30, October 15, and December 15, 2005, raised hopes in Baghdad and Washington that it would be possible to establish a stable legitimate democracy in Iraq. The administration was quick to take credit for the result. But such arguments missed the point. Arabs had often held elections in the past, many of them more or less free, and those that were free had been conducted in an atmosphere lacking the fear and mayhem of Iraq's insurgency and suicide terrorist attacks. In such circumstances, it will be extremely difficult for the new government that was elected in December 2005 to establish stability and security in the country.

For the sake of argument, let us assume that the insurgents and foreign terrorists are defeated and American and British troops begin to withdraw and Iraq's new democracy begins to function. What would Iraq's future be? The risk is that Iraq will come to resemble Lebanon, not the Lebanon of the murderous civil war of the 1970s and 1980s, at least not immediately—Iraq would have already passed through war and civil strife—but the pre-1975 democratic Lebanon that was the darling of Westerners and many Arabs in the Middle East—a country whose capital Beirut was the "Paris of the Middle East," a financial and trading center, a sophisticated, glittering, and accomplished success. Despite what became known as its "mosaic" society—Christian, Sunni, Shia, and Druze, with a large disenfranchised Palestinian refugee minority—Lebanon seemed to have everything that a good democracy should: a parliament, president, prime minister, regular elections, stability, prosperity, and peace. There were some disturbing oddities. For instance, the offices in the government were distributed on ethnic and religious grounds. The president was always a Christian, the prime minister, Muslim, and so on down the list. Even more oddly, the distribution of posts in the government and seats in the parliament was based on a census taken in the 1930s. The ethnic and religious divisions were so sharp that the country's political leaders decided not to allow a new census for fear that it would lead to a redistribution of political power in favor of the Muslims, and particularly the Shia from southern Lebanon, that would shatter the mosaic. Why ask for trouble? Lebanon's mosaic democracy was a façade behind which the country was governed not by democratic rule-making, but by ethnic and religious group horse-trading based on communal, family, and sectarian loyalties.

There is little doubt that millions of Iraqis and Americans would settle for this outcome. The killing would be over. American troops could come home, and the formalities of democracy would be observed. Whether such a government and society could survive for the long term is unclear. The long-term danger for Lebanon was that it began to lose the race to develop legitimate, effective institutions, especially the presidency, and was overwhelmed by mounting internal and external pressures.[92] When the pressures grew too great and the race was finally lost, Lebanon plunged into a horrific civil war that killed more than 40,000 people, and drew Syrian and Israeli invasion and occupation. Israel withdrew after 18 months, its hopes for a stable friendly Lebanon destroyed, along with the lives of hundreds of Israeli soldiers and thousands of Palestinians and Lebanese. U.S. military forces entered Lebanon briefly to arrange the safe evacuation of Palestinian fighters, and then returned to try to stabilize the Lebanese government and make peace among Lebanon, Israel, and Syria after the murder of hundreds of defenseless Palestinian refugees by gunmen from Christian Lebanese parties backed by Israel. The Reagan administration's attempt to remake Lebanon and gain a peace settlement between Israel, Syria, and Lebanon ended in failure after the deaths of 241 Marines in a suicide bombing, the withdrawal of American troops, and the collapse of its peacemaking initiative. Syria stayed on in Lebanon and was still running the country two decades later until forced to withdraw by American and French pressure.

Iraq will escape a similar fate only if its new rulers learn from Lebanon's example. The country's new institutions must be strong enough to govern effectively, but not so strong as to become tyrannical. They must make room for all ethnic and religious partners in the federation without allowing them to paralyze the government and prevent it from meeting its domestic and international responsibilities. It is a complex task requiring great wisdom, self-restraint, cooperation, patience, compromise, and mutual trust.

7

An American Foreign Policy for the Twenty-First Century

The ways by which people advance toward dignity and enlightenment in government are things that constitute the deepest and most intimate processes of national life. There is nothing less understandable to foreigners, nothing in which foreigners can do less good.

—George F. Kennan[1]

Nations, as individuals, who are completely innocent in their own esteem are insufferable in their human contacts.

—Reinhold Niebuhr[2]

As of this writing, the United States has entered the fourth year of war in Iraq. The insurgency continues killing and maiming, sending a pall over the country as dense as the smoke that marks attacks on Iraqis and Americans. An Iraqi government finally exists, but is still uncertain when American troops can safely withdraw, or whether Iraqis will be able to establish a stable decent society on the ruins of Saddam Hussein's dictatorship. The bombings of the London transit system in July 2005 sustained an uneasy feeling that terrorists might strike at the United States and American citizens at any moment. It would be the easiest thing in the world to allow the enormous importance of what is at stake to blind us to the necessity of subjecting American foreign policy to the most fundamental review. Prescription is not the same thing as analysis, but the subject is too important and the need too great to end a book such as this without offering an alternative way of thinking about American foreign policy.

My hope is that this book will contribute to what must become a national debate about a new foreign policy for the United States. That debate ought to have happened after 9/11 but did not because of the wars in Afghanistan and Iraq. It might have happened during the presidential campaign of 2004, but that proved impossible because the country was still at war and the leading Democrats were too hungry to return to office to take the chance that a frank discussion of what was right and wrong about America's role in the world might offend undecided voters. In the end, the Democrats had the worst of both possibilities: they lost the election without having provided the country new ways of thinking about American foreign policy. The global superiority of the United States may yet be used to make the world a better place as all three presidents since 1989 hoped, but only if new assumptions are found to inform new policies for a world different from the one as perceived through the lens of the post–Cold War paradigm.

A new American foreign policy for the twenty-first century must begin by abandoning American exceptionalism and democratization: profound differences among peoples are normal and generally welcome—the world was not meant to be everywhere the same. A new foreign policy for the twenty-first century should also be based on three other assumptions that are fundamentally different from those at the heart of the post–Cold War paradigm: (1) the economic and military strength of the United States make it *superior* to any other country but *not a global hegemon*; (2) threats to the *survival* of the United States can arise only from states that possess the necessary combination of human, natural, and industrial resources, such as Japan, China, India, Russia, Germany, and Britain; the new terrorism threatens the *safety* of Americans and their property, not the survival of their values and institutions; and (3) the more successfully the United States solves the most perplexing domestic problems it faces, the more powerful and appealing its example will be to the rest of the world. Changing the way that Americans think about foreign policy will not be easy. The ideas and circumstances that underlie the post–Cold War paradigm—especially ex-

ceptionalism, democratization, and American primacy—touch on principles, partisan loyalties, and even personal identity. As hard as it will be to
achieve, it is essential to begin. "If not now, when?"

Beyond Exceptionalism and Democratization

Exceptionalism and democratization distort American foreign policy for
philosophical and practical reasons. The belief that a country possesses
unique and noble qualities is part of what holds it together, and gives its citizens a reason to see themselves as taking part in something larger than
themselves that possesses lasting goodness. In their benign form as patriotism, these beliefs enrich life precisely because they establish difference
and allow the development of a wealth of associations and shared understandings that make life's joys more intense and its losses less difficult to
bear. In their malign form as nationalism, they distinguish between "us"
and "them," and justify the use of force against others and even against
one's countrymen if they are not "sufficiently" one of "us."[3] Regardless of
the form that they take, the unique qualities of American institutions and
values cannot in themselves give the U.S. government the right to impose
it values and institutions on other societies much less the world. The notion that the principles on which liberal democracies are founded may be
generalized for the rest of mankind betrays two philosophical errors. The
first is the notion of human perfectibility, the yearning for the suspension of
politics, and the appearance of the divine on earth that resides in the idea
that a single set of ideals and institutions represents the culmination of all
progress. The second arises from confusion over the relation between ideals
and action.

For thousands of years, prophets, tyrants, politicians, and philosophers
have claimed that a specific society possessed history's best and final institutions. Yet, the passage of time has revealed the impermanence of em-
pires, kingdoms, and republics, and the beliefs on which they were founded.
In thinking about this issue, Aristotle's *Politics* may be of greater use than
Plato's *Republic*. Aristotle examined dozens of constitutions in the ancient
world and concluded that societies and their governments do not develop in
a steady arc that rises from bad to good. Rather, they revolve from government by one, to government by a few, and then many, over and over again.
If the rulers in any one of these forms govern in the best interests of the
entire society, that government is just and legitimate. Aristotle called the
just forms of government monarchy, aristocracy, and constitutional republic,

and recognized that there are unjust versions of each—dictatorship, oligarchy, and mob rule or unrestrained democracy. Much of his writing about politics considers the circumstances and policies that might prevent misrule and injustice. More than two millennia of experience with just and unjust governments have confirmed Aristotle's research and reasoning: it is possible for nondemocratic regimes to act justly in their dealings with their own people and the outside world. In other words, the survival of the United States does not depend on the spread of democracy throughout the entire world. The same pacific qualities that characterize just democracies will occur in societies governed justly by a few people or by one. The issue is the wisdom and justice of other countries' policies not whether they are democratic.

The process by which a society becomes genuinely democratic and enjoys the rule of law and freedom of speech and religion is unknown and perhaps unknowable. It is not racist or patronizing to observe that only a few of today's candidates have a chance to make a successful transition to democracy. More than anything else, the condition of a society after it attempts to democratize resembles its condition before reform started.[4] Instead of guaranteeing peace, democratization has often been accompanied by a pattern of "belligerent nationalism, and war," a pattern that stretches from the French Revolution through Bismarck's Germany, imperial Japan, and Milosevic's Serbia. As they democratize, societies often experience mass politics, unstable coalitions, weak government, and the projection of internal problems outside national borders.[5] Great caution, patience, and care are needed to avoid the pitfalls of democratization and reap its rewards. The peaceful unwinding of the Ferdinand Marcos dictatorship in the Philippines compares favorably to what happened in Iraq after the overthrow of Saddam Hussein. Not a single American soldier died, largely, one suspects, because of a long history of close relations between American and Philippine senior commanders and decades of democratic practice before Marcos became dictator of the country.[6] These considerations make it clear that democratization should be at best a long-term goal of American foreign policy rather than an immediate vital interest linked directly to the country's survival.

The belief in a single set of values as valid everywhere for all people is at least as old as Socrates and the Sophists.[7] Proponents of the idea argue that without such an anchor, all values lose their meaning, human beings fall victim to moral relativism, and the way is prepared for tyranny and genocide. In their eyes, the failure of Weimar Germany, France, and Great

Britain to prevent the triumph of Nazism and communism in the 1920s and 1930s proves the point. A leading twentieth-century philosopher who held these views, Leo Strauss, strongly influenced some senior figures in the Bush II administration, such as Paul Wolfowitz and Richard Perle.[8] A contemporary of Strauss, the Anglo-Russian philosopher Isaiah Berlin, offered another way of thinking about the relations between ideals and action. Berlin argued that human beings disagree about ultimate values and will not allow themselves to be reconciled to a single truth or to one another. The central challenge facing mankind, therefore, is not to impose a single universal truth on all who disagree—to Berlin this was the source of the twentieth century's atrocities—but to find a way to live decently in a world of diverse beliefs. Berlin celebrated human disagreements over fundamental values and defended them against moral absolutism. To Berlin, tolerance was the chief political virtue, but he was not a moral relativist. He was willing to oppose those beliefs and actions that undermined the basis of a decent society.[9] Resolving the conflict between these two schools of thought lies beyond the scope of this book. However, the differences between interventionist and noninterventionist liberals show that agreement on fundamental values is no guarantee that there will be agreement over what constitutes an effective and appropriate foreign policy. Taking a moral stand is not enough to ensure that the best foreign policy will be chosen.

The claim that American values and institutions are universally valid amounts to an assertion of their international legitimacy. But legitimacy cannot be established unilaterally, it must be awarded by others. Legitimacy is in this sense inherently democratic.[10] The insistence that there exists only one good form of government also transports diplomacy and strategy out of the realm of politics into that of morality, out of the domain of clashing interests sometimes amenable to settlement by compromise and into the realm of absolutes, and out of the realm where the claims of competing values must be weighed against one another into one in which compromise of any kind is evil and intolerable. When authenticity and sincerity become the test of reliability and the guarantee of safety and cooperation, a revolutionary age has begun. Conflicts escalate, and wars become unending.

In addition to philosophical errors, exceptionalism and democratization bring a number of practical problems in their train: the equation of success and virtue, the creation of false expectations, the risks of posturing before domestic constituencies and losing control of policy, and overextension and exhaustion. By basing American policy on a claim to virtue and the disinterested and even noble use of power, American leaders link those values to success. When setbacks occur or the American military commits an outrage—and both are part of the current reality—the risk is that the entire base of popular support for policy will be undermined. The American defeat in Vietnam shattered the unity of American virtue and power, breaking the spell of exceptionalism that had been re-created during World War II and the first two decades of the Cold War. In the aftermath, much of the popular support for American policy disappeared. But the Cold War was far from over, and President Jimmy Carter was forced to find a new basis for American foreign policy or see containment collapse. In place of exceptionalism, Carter offered a moral cause for American foreign policy but with a difference: he proposed that the United States act on behalf of universal human rights, rather than specifically American values. "The attraction of human rights was that they were precisely *not* American, despite having a great deal of commonality with traditional American values. With its foreign policy at the service of universal human rights, America could conceivably avoid the charge of cultural imperialism. Significantly, Carter did not reject the exceptionalist tradition but intended rather, by this means, to save it."[11] Carter's presidency failed, and with it the American government's emphasis on human rights, brought down by the Iranian hostage crisis and skyrocketing oil prices. His successor, Ronald Reagan, reasserted the unique virtue of the United States and the universal relevance of its values, a practice continued by his successors in both parties. Perhaps the most striking aspect of the continued use of American exceptionalism in this way is that it reveals a profound distrust of the judgment of the American people. It is as if nothing had changed since the country was a weak neutral that had to be bombed into World War II and scramble to put together an army and navy to fight in Europe and Asia.

Because they assumed that America's conduct was superior to that of other less virtuous countries, Americans found the abuse of prisoners at Abu Ghraib and Guantanamo deeply upsetting. The scandal caused an even greater outcry inside the United States than the mounting casualties of an unexpectedly prolonged and bloody occupation. Here was photographic evidence not of selfless heroism, but of torture and depravity. Instead of the noble liberation of an oppressed people, the American purpose in Iraq suddenly appeared to be tainted by domination and exploitation, motives that made the American mission abroad seem no different from the imperialism of any other great power. Because the Bush II administration cast the war in Iraq as an example of American exceptionalism, when disappointment came it appeared to pose a choice between "*either* virtue *or* power."[12]

False expectations derived from exceptionalism and democratization led the Bush II administration to believe that most Iraqis would accept the virtue and disinterestedness of the United States as self-evident and welcome democratization without protest. Neither turned out to be valid; reality was much more complex. Most Iraqis resented the war and the occupation at the same time that they were glad Saddam Hussein had been overthrown. Iraqis doubted the motives of the administration even as they turned out in large numbers to vote for a constitution and government that might allow them to begin to reestablish Iraqi sovereignty and, ultimately, its identity. Most Iraqis saw the motives of the United States as little different from those of earlier British and Ottoman occupiers who had wanted to control people and natural resources. This volatile mix exploded in a vicious guerrilla war against the American military as well as Iraqis who cooperated with the occupation. In the national elections of December 2005, most Iraqis voted and acted not as unbiased members of civil society open to persuasion on the merits of issues but as members of religious and ethnic groups. The nature of their participation signaled the limited relevance of exceptionalism and democratization and produced a prolonged political stalemate even among those parties and individuals willing to play by the American-inspired postwar rules of the game.

It is difficult to face disappointments of such magnitude, and societies and their leaders often look for ways to avoid having to reassess their view of themselves and the world. One way is to pass over to domination and forget virtue. This is implicit in the numerous appeals to Americans to quit whining and accept imperial responsibilities and the excesses that come with them. Another is to find fault with the world rather than exceptionalism itself and withdraw into a kind of fortress America, selectively engaging with former allies and friends to solve particularly difficult or threatening problems, a course made attractive by the absence of any major threat from other states. A third way is for supporters of a government to explain failure as the work of internal enemies who had betrayed the purity of national purpose and power. None of these options seems adequate to the challenges of the twenty-first century. The last two were tried with disastrous results during the period between the two world wars, known somewhat misleadingly as "isolationism," and the anticommunist witch hunting of Senator Joseph McCarthy after the fall of China to the communists in 1949. Withdrawal from active world leadership would deny the United States and the world the benefit of American power and ideals in preventing and overcoming major problems before they became unmanageable. The

dishonor and folly of scapegoating need no elaboration. There is no need
to sacrifice American ideals in seeking an alternative to exceptionalism as a
basis for American foreign policy. What is needed, instead, is a better understanding of the relation between ideals and action.[13]

A full discussion of the relation between ideals and action would require a book of its own. But it is possible to suggest some generalizations
that can be applied usefully to American foreign policy. First, humane
and civilized ideals are crucial to any government that aspires to act justly.
Human action that cuts itself loose from decency and humanity loses its
way in barbarism and evil. Aristotle observed that outside law and justice
there is only savagery. At the same time, ideals are abstract and inhuman.
Human imperfection prevents their full realization. They can be aspired
to and approached, but never realized in their entirety. They are an irreplaceable standard, but one that must be interpreted with understanding,
wisdom, and prudence. The just leaders of decent governments are en-
trusted with the collective good of their people. They cannot seek the realization of their personal ideals through the exercise of their official powers, but must act as the custodians of the general well-being. The broad
responsibility that is borne by all just leaders, and the reality that the power
of every nation no matter how great is finite rather than infinite obliges
leaders to act prudentially and to choose among the desirable, possible,
and necessary.

Despite the claims of famous twentieth-century realists, such as Hans
Morgenthau, George Kennan, Henry Kissinger, and their even more illus-
trious predecessors Bismarck and Richelieu, no foreign policy ever consists
of value-free action to advance objective national interests. Although
Richelieu and Bismarck insisted that they acted in the national interest
without regard to conservative religious or political values, they dedicated
their lives to the preservation and strengthening of patriarchal, aristocratic,
Christian monarchies. Bismarck used the pride that Germans felt as a result
of German unification and the defeat of Austria and France to strangle Germany's fledgling democracy and graft the Prussian monarchy onto a much
larger and generally resistant society. Richelieu tolerated dissent within
France and took Protestant princes as France's allies, but he left French
Catholicism and the French monarchy far stronger than they were when
he first encountered them.

Three centuries later, George Kennan argued: "The interests of the national society for which government must concern itself are basically those
of its military security, the integrity of its political life, and the well-being

of its people. These needs have no moral quality."[14] Surely the well-being of a people has a moral quality. Moreover, what if the state, which is at least part of what Kennan meant by "national society," is the embodiment of the principle of *thanatos* (death), as was the case in Nazi Germany, the Khmer Rouge's Cambodia, or Rwanda in the 1990s? The interests of such a "society" have a moral quality, and that quality is evil. In fact, the connection between moral values and action is real, and cannot be dismissed so easily. The claim that "security" interests trump moral values actually amounts to a claim that national security is the greatest moral value. Surely that might be allowable if the state were perfect, but such states have never existed and can never exist.

Abraham Lincoln's conduct regarding slavery stands out as a superb guide to prudent and principled action. Lincoln never compromised his belief in the immorality of slavery, but always refused to become an abolitionist. One has a sense that Lincoln's way of reasoning about such profoundly important moral questions would be regarded with contempt by some of today's more doctrinaire conservatives and liberals. Lincoln spoke and acted cautiously because he feared that immediate abolition would destroy the Constitution and with it, perhaps, the cause of democracy in the world, while leaving the slaves with even fewer protections than they experienced under existing laws. Even when ordering the emancipation of slaves in the United States, Lincoln acted only within the limits of his powers as commander in chief in those territories in active rebellion against the United States. He believed that a general end to slavery could come only through a constitutional amendment. In other words, a principled belief in slavery's immorality did not offer a way of choosing between abolition and Lincoln's gradual emancipation. To arrive at a constructive alternative, Lincoln considered other values, such as the preservation of the Union and democracy, and worked with considerable modesty as he tried to bring wisdom and a sense of proportion into his domestic and foreign policies. Lincoln's conduct shows the importance of ideals, the complexity intrinsic to any attempt to derive conduct from them, and the necessity of acting prudently.

To say that they do not travel well does not detract in the slightest from the excellence or the historic importance of the American and Western European democracies. There is no need to remake the world in America's image, and many reasons not to try. Americans should adopt a modest view of the relevance of American democracy and values to other countries and societies. If other societies find them admirable or helpful, they will adopt them. No amount of hectoring or conquest will make it happen sooner or more permanently. U.S. foreign policy should support and protect the independence of other states, not demand or force their democratization.[15] Democracy is only one form of government that has proven to be legitimate throughout history. For American officials to insist that it be adopted by every country in the world confuses personal preference with official responsibility. American leaders know that it is popular to speak of American institutions and values as universal. Claiming that it is not selfish interests that are being defended but eternal laws and the interests of humanity also makes it easier to obtain funding for American foreign policy. The trouble is that such claims turn into self-righteousness, and blind American policymakers and the American people to the realities inside other countries, much as the Clinton and Bush II administrations were misled again and again about the direction of events in Bosnia, Rwanda, Kosovo, and Iraq.

If the U.S. government makes a serious attempt to compel reform, several outcomes are possible, nearly all of them negative. American demands backed up by punishments of one kind or another—the reduction of economic and military assistance or economic sanctions—may demoralize the authorities whose help is most vital to the success of reform. In the ensuing period of growing instability, it becomes anyone's guess as to which antigovernment group will end up in power. The example of Iran remains a worst case scenario to be avoided. If the demand for reforms destabilizes the country, and an anti-American undemocratic government comes to power, the result will have been exactly the opposite of what was intended. Condoleezza Rice's argument that the United States has no choice but to emphasize democratization in its dealings with friendly but unstable governments ignores the importance of pre-reform conditions to the success of democratization, and minimizes the options available to the United States and its allies, particularly through working with civil society organizations. In all these cases, it is difficult to imagine that pressure to reform will make it easier to obtain cooperation in the war on terror or peacemaking in the area. Unscrupulous leaders will not hesitate to play the nationalist card and evoke the opposition of their compatriots to the United States for meddling in the internal affairs of another country. Other leaders who had previously been friendly to the United States seem likely to resent the demand for reform and begin to ignore appeals for cooperation in other areas.

A more sensible and effective approach would be to cherish and defend American values and institutions, but under most circumstances to maintain a decent silence about the governance of other societies. Genocide and massive violations of human rights, as occurred in Bosnia, Kosovo, and Rwanda, or more recently in Sudan, or the harboring of dangerous enemies, as al-Qaeda was given sanctuary by the Taliban in Afghanistan, should be treated as exceptions to this general approach. At its core, any new American foreign policy must avoid seeing the world solely through the lens of American values and institutions. George Kennan, the author of the strategy that won the Cold War, believed that Americans often mixed up apples and oranges when it came to insisting that other countries adopt American values and practices. When other governments act in ways that harm American interests, Kennan argued, Americans were perfectly within their right to complain and take action to secure them. "What we cannot do is assume that our moral standards are theirs as well, and to appeal to those standards as the source of our grievances."[16]

The belief of the Bush II administration that unchallenged American hegemony and its use to spread democracy to every country in the world might somehow usher in utopia, world peace, and the disappearance of tyranny and conflict itself are without any basis in history, philosophy, or human experience. It belongs in the works of the great dreamers of every era, from the self-sufficient isolated utopia of Sir Thomas More to the workers' paradise of Karl Marx, and the "sex, drugs, and rock and roll" of the 1960s. The United States is not automatically threatened by nondemocratic states, but could find itself in mortal danger only in a world in which most states were unjust and aggressive. The link between American ideals and institutions and policies devoted to their *survival* consists of keeping the entire world from becoming nondemocratic not of democratizing the world. As Kenneth Waltz observed, conflict in international politics arises from the condition of anarchy in the international system, that is, the absence of world government, a condition that would continue even if every country in the world were democratic.

Foreign Policy for a New Century

If it is to succeed, American foreign policy in the twenty-first century must meet a number of requirements. It must be based on a sound understanding of the international order. This reveals the threats and opportunities that a country faces. A just society's foreign policy must make accurate judgments about the strengths and weaknesses of the home country as well as friendly and enemy states. It must be rooted in values that are humane and honorable. And it must be expressed in policies that combine interna-

tional understanding, values, tactics, and strengths and weaknesses in ways
that successfully address threats and opportunities and that can be sustained
for years, and even decades.

Recalibrating American Primacy

A nation's military power depends as much on political judgment as it does
on the sum of the proficiency and quality of the leadership, morale, and
weapons of its troops and generals. Analysts and political and military leaders around the world, as well as Americans themselves, engaged in "macro
self-deception," and took their cues about American primacy from the
country's margin over others in big general numbers, such as gross domestic product and defense budget. It was a huge mistake. Here is an example
of macro self-deception that passed for hard-headed analysis:

> If today's American primacy does not constitute unipolarity, then
> nothing ever will. To understand just how dominant the United States
> is today, one needs to look at each of the standard components of na-
> tional power in succession. In the military arena, the United States is
> poised to spend more on defense in 2003 than the next 15–20 biggest
> spenders combined. The United States has an overwhelming nuclear
> superiority, the world's dominant air force, the only truly blue-water
> navy, and a unique capability to project power around the globe. And
> its military advantage is even more apparent in quality than in quan-
> tity. . . . [T]he United States currently spends more on military R&D
> than Germany or the United Kingdom spends on defense in total. . . .
> And the United States purchases this preeminence with only 3.5 per-
> cent of its GDP. . . . America's economic dominance, meanwhile—
> relative to either the next several richest powers or the rest of the
> world combined—surpasses that of any great power in modern his-
> tory, with the sole exception of its own position in 1945 (when World
> War II had temporarily laid waste every other major economy).[17]

It must have seemed impossible that such a country would soon find it so
difficult and costly to pacify Iraq, an ethnically and religiously divided
country of 25 million, let alone transform it into a democracy. The macro-
level analysts simply did not grasp the difference between abstract and
useable military and economic power, potential and actual political influence, and theoretical and practical control of events in other countries, and

among wisdom, foresight, and folly.[18] Contrary to conventional wisdom, the United States lacks the power to act as a global hegemon. It is *superior* in certain large-scale, quantitative indicators to any other nation, but *not globally dominant*. Illusions about global hegemony proved to be extremely costly in American lives and money in Iraq. As a result of the confusion caused by macro-number hypnosis, the Bush II administration did not begin to understand how to handle the postwar occupation until six months after the fall of Saddam Hussein, and even then it was far from clear that the political and military problems revealed by the postwar rebellion in Iraq had been recognized and overcome, much less the country's economic and social difficulties.[19]

The Bush II administration's version of American primacy ignored the peculiar limitations and highly specialized character of the American armed forces. The American military is designed to fight a twenty-first century version of World War II battles, complete with heavy armor and artillery and massive precision air support, smart bombs, faster and bigger tanks, and real-time views of the battlefield. This is a military to add to indigenous forces on the ground who are willing and able to bear the brunt of urban combat and counterinsurgency warfare. At the beginning of the second Iraq War, the U.S. military was not trained or armed to carry out the counter-insurgency tasks itself, and few if any soldiers and analysts had a sure understanding of how to defeat the insurgency that began in Iraq after the overthrow of Saddam Hussein.[20] According to the former commandant of the U.S. Army War College, at the outset of the war to overthrow Saddam Hussein, there were only 60,000 troops in the entire U.S. military with the training to fight in the cities of Iraq and find and destroy guerrilla fighters. Even those 60,000 could not be deployed all at once: while some fought, others rested, and still others were preparing to fight again. Thus, in Iraq, the global primacy of the U.S. military turned out to be about 20,000 specially trained soldiers who could be sent to Iraq at any one time, and these in a country the size of California with a population of 25 million, deeply divided by ethnic conflict and grievances that had accumulated over a hundred years, and by resentment and even hatred of the United States as a result of the sanctions imposed on Iraq during the 1990s. Of course, it was possible for other American units to engage the Iraqi insurgents, and they did. But the result was the overuse of heavy weapons and air power, which stirred further resentment among the Iraqi population. In addition, the U.S. military and especially the reserve forces were stressed severely by the repeated, dangerous, and prolonged deployments to Iraq, and senior

American commanders began to say in public that they feared the Army would break under the strain. The narrow margins of a misunderstood American primacy undoubtedly contributed to the abuse of prisoners in Abu Ghraib prison and elsewhere, as commanders pressed their subordinates for intelligence that would relieve the pressure on the troops and ultimately lead to the undoing of the insurgency.

The lack of preparedness went beyond training and manpower. Technologically advanced helicopters originally designed to fight in northern Europe fared badly in the Iraqi desert. Instead of fast, thickly armored personnel carriers, American troops rode flat-bed trucks and soft-sided jeeps into combat and suffered casualties in ambushes from improvised explosive devices and low-tech rocket-propelled grenades. Journalists "imbedded" with American troops during and after the second Gulf War reported the sad results. One described repeated attempts by the 101st Airborne to use its high-tech Apache helicopters during the campaign. Desert sand tore up the helicopters' rotor blades and pilots became disoriented by dust clouds and crashed as they tried to land. Worst of all, some helicopters were shot down by small-arms fire, and that made it impossible to use them as they were intended to be used—close to the ground in direct support of troops engaged with the enemy.[21] Another journalist rode with the U.S. Marines to a village near the rebellious city of Fallujah northwest of Baghdad in an open truck: "Open cargo trucks in hostile territory seemed like a bad idea. So I asked another officer, a square-jawed character who told me he would be happy killing insurgents for the next 10 years, why we weren't in armored personnel carriers, like the Army uses. 'These trucks are dangerous,' he said. 'But they're all we got.'" A year later, American soldiers still lacked the armored trucks they needed for convoys and patrols.[22]

Bandwagoning was supposed to be one of the results of American primacy.* Bush administration officials embraced the concept, and confidently predicted that when other countries saw that the United States would maintain its military dominance, many would join the U.S. effort. Bandwagoning was supposed to reinforce and legitimate American primacy. It proved to be a huge disappointment for the Bush administration. Other states had plenty of choices when Bush II invaded Iraq, including staying

---

*Bandwagoning refers to the tendency of states to make common cause with a potential attacker or, by analogy, with a stronger country, rather than resist by themselves or join other states in an opposing alliance to maintain the balance of power. The tendency of weaker states to join together to resist the strongest among them is referred to as "balancing."

on the sidelines, which was the path taken by most governments in Western Europe. They did not "balance" the United States, nor did they jump on the bandwagon. They simply waited and watched. Some opponents of the war in Iraq even helped the American military, as Germany did when it allowed over flights to Iraq. The entirely predictable multiplicity of reality escaped Bush policymakers.

One of the unfortunate consequences of the macro approach to American primacy was the further militarization of American foreign policy. It was not a new story. The discrepancy between military and diplomatic/economic budgets was even greater during the Clinton years when foreign aid budgets dropped to record lows. New or old, the problem remained serious.[23] The surest sign of militarization was the enormous budgetary imbalance in favor of the Department of Defense over the Department of State. For fiscal year 2005, for example, the Department of Defense's budget was estimated to be $402 billion, compared to $28 billion for the State Department (which included all foreign aid), a ratio of 14.3 : 1 in favor of the military.[24] Counting the cost of the wars in Iraq and Afghanistan made the difference even greater: the administration had requested $160 billion in supplemental funds to pay for the wars in Afghanistan and Iraq in 2003 and 2004, and proposed an additional $80 billion for 2005.[25] Recognizing the narrow limits of American superiority is the essential basis for reducing the militarization of American foreign policy. The need to cooperate with other nations to solve military problems should enable the United States to abandon the attempt to dominate the world militarily. This in turn would enable it to find additional funds for economic and political development and preventive diplomacy.

Seeking global democracy is a revolutionary, not a conservative goal. Its realization would require the overthrow of most of the world's governments, including many of the friendly governments whose cooperation in the near term is essential to defeat terrorism, respond creatively to militant Islam, stop the spread of weapons of mass destruction, and attend to global equity and threats to the environment. The character and allegiances of whatever governments might replace those that had been overthrown are uncertain at best. By the most optimistic calculation, it will take years, even decades, to achieve such a revolutionary change. It is at best a long-term policy goal, but Clinton spoke as if it ought to be immediate, and Bush II went to war to achieve it. The Clinton and Bush II definitions meant that the United States was seeking absolute security, and absolute security for the United States meant absolute insecurity for every other government in the world. In its interventionist, militarized Bush II form, the strategy alienated and alarmed other governments and led them to refuse to help overthrow Saddam Hussein, not because they admired the Iraqi dictator, but because Bush II unilateralism seemed an expression of American domination rather than necessity. Because he was less interventionist and believed globalization and democratization carried his foreign policy, Bill Clinton was able to maintain cooperation with American allies and friendly governments around the world. Bush II's war of choice in Iraq and outspoken unilateralism isolated the United States internationally, and squandered the support willingly given after 9/11 by governments and peoples around the world.

Survival and Safety in the Twenty-First Century

Americans and their leaders learned a transforming lesson from two world wars and the tragic interlude between them: if its values and institutions are to thrive, the United States must shape its international environment in favorable ways. As the authors of National Security Council directive NSC-68 put it in April 1950 at the outset of the Cold War, "The objectives of a free society are determined by its fundamental values and by the necessity for maintaining the material environment in which they flourish."[26]

Containment, the strategy adopted to achieve this goal, was founded on a geopolitical assumption derived from history and logic: the survival of the United States—the vitality of its values and the future of its institutions and way of life—depends on preventing any single country from dominating Europe or Asia. George Kennan gave this fundamental assumption an elegant twist. There are, he said, only five areas in the world where the human and industrial potential exists that would be great enough to threaten the *survival* of the United States: North America, Great Britain, Germany and Central Europe, the Soviet Union, and Japan. The maintenance of a favorable global environment for the United States required it to prevent the Soviet Union from conquering all or most of these vital areas or winning their allegiance. Since these areas alone held the potential to threaten national *survival*, the United States could safely remain more or less indifferent to the rest of the world. At the time, China was not on the list because it was convulsed by revolution and had yet to undergo industrialization. Inevitably, Kennan's elegant scheme had to be modified, but at least at first, the exceptions that were made were slight and obvious. For example, the oil of the Middle East constituted a great resource, vital to the well-being of the industrial democracies. It would have been a grave loss to allow it to fall under Soviet control. In addition, no nation could shape the international environment in favorable ways without being confident that its security interests were protected in its own backyard—the Caribbean and Central America—and in the narrow waters of the Mediterranean that bordered its European allies.

With suitable amendments—China eventually joined the list—American opposition to hegemony in Europe and Asia formed the basis of national security strategy not only throughout the Cold War, but also during the Bush I administration. Seeing the world in this way helps put the new terrorism of the jihadists in proper perspective. The new terrorism can threaten the country's *safety*, the lives of thousands of its citizens and their property, but not its *survival*. The *survival* of the democratic values and institutions of the United States can be threatened only by adverse developments among the great centers of industrial and human potential.

The world is in infinitely better shape than it was in 1918, 1945, or 1989. An overwhelming preponderance of military and economic capability exists on the side of the United States and its allies in Europe and Japan. That the United States and some of the governments of the European Union sometimes disagree detracts not at all from their preponderance of power and wealth. India may eventually join the group of countries capable of threatening the survival of the United States. However, its economy has only recently begun to achieve sustainable growth, the product in part of wise decisions taken decades ago to strengthen higher education in India, particularly in technical and scientific fields. India shares many economic, political, and strategic interests with the United States. China's burgeoning economy has been of enormous benefit to its own citizens and to the people around the world who enjoy the lower prices of Chinese goods. However, by any standard, China is decades away from global power. It is already clear that nationalism may harm China's relations with other countries, particularly if it becomes entangled with demands for internal political change at home.[27] Only Russia's nuclear weapons give that country more than regional significance. Its military weakness and economic stops and starts have put it on the sidelines. At best, Russia is able to react to events and try to take advantage of unexpected developments. It can barely influence, let alone control the global agenda.

On this evidence, Bill Clinton concluded that the United States did not really need a foreign policy, that he could preside over the passage of the world into a future built by globalization and democratization. On the same evidence, George W. Bush and his advisers concluded that the United States should become a world hegemon prepared to prolong its dominance indefinitely and engage in unilateral preventive war to transform rogue states into democracies. Clearly, the facts did not speak for themselves. It is easy to argue that 9/11 changed everything. But it should be evident that it did not change the conditions that could threaten the *survival* of American values and institutions. Those remain in the hands of countries that possess sufficient industrial and human potential. On the other hand, 9/11 did threaten American *safety*, and measures had to be adopted to deal with the threat. The new terrorists might threaten American survival if Osama bin Laden or his followers took over a state rich in industrial power and human capability. However, states—even revolutionary theocratic states such as Iran—have to calculate costs and benefits, and are susceptible to deterrence. Many problems remain outside these areas, such as protecting the global environment and reducing global poverty. There is every reason for Americans to want to use their great wealth to reduce suffering in other countries.

It might be possible to achieve global hegemony, although the specialized character of the American military, its profound dependence on increasingly reluctant civilian reservists, and its limited effectiveness in Iraq since the overthrow of Saddam Hussein make that seem extremely unlikely. Equally important, it is unnecessary and undesirable. Global dominance is unnecessary because it is not needed to prevent the emergence of a power capable of dominating Europe or Asia. The constant effort to maintain American global hegemony is undesirable because of the costs such an undertaking would impose on those subjected to American power. It is even more undesirable because of the militarization of American life that would have to accompany the constant warfare and intervention of a global hegemon. If the transition in China breaks down completely—for example, if China's leaders increasingly see external expansion as a way of overcoming internal division or failure—the natural recourse of the United States is to seek the support of India, Russia, and Japan to check such a reckless adventure. If against all expectations, Germany or Russia should once more seek dominion in Europe, the same balancing should be well within America's means. The Europe of the early twenty-first century with its dreams of political and economic integration, thriving economies, and stable prosperous democracies is far better prepared to resist such a development than at any time since the defeat of Napoleon at Waterloo.

However "accidental" Rome's empire, there was nothing accidental about the military takeovers of the Roman government that followed in its train. Rome's institutions—complex, inflexible, far too limited for the responsibilities that it had assumed—collapsed into military dictatorship as a result of the burdens of empire. Rome is not a model for the United States any more than Bismarck's ultimately calamitous domestic and international strategies should be. Sharing the responsibility for preventing the domination of Europe and Asia by a single country will allow the United States to economize on its military expenditures and minimize the burdens that fall on the shoulders of American taxpayers, an achievement shared by the architects of the winning strategy in the Cold War. America's goal in the twenty-first century—the path to the preservation of an environment in which its institutions and values will thrive—is to sustain the current circumstances in which no single country can dominate Asia and Europe.

Tactics for a New Foreign Policy

American foreign policy in the twenty-first century should seek and support an international division of labor in order to avoid the astronomical defense expenditures that have been borne by American taxpayers since the end of the Cold War. A new American foreign policy would foster multinational organizations to address transnational problems, such as global health and environmental problems and the issue of global poverty. A new American foreign policy would emphasize a creative and active diplomacy. It would display a constant willingness to negotiate frankly and openly with any country on the basis of mutual interest. It would seek to align its policy with the national interests of other countries, particularly their desire for sovereignty and self-determination, an approach that would seek to make nationalism a friend rather than an enemy of the United States. Finally, it would regard war as a last resort, at best a tool to allow another try to repair the sources of the original conflict, recognizing that the essence of war is destructive, not creative.

Nationalism and Negotiation

The resurgence of Islam in all its manifestations, from those Muslims who wish simply to live life in closer harmony with their faith to the jihadists who believe that the West and what to them are blasphemous Arab and

Muslim rulers must be attacked and destroyed, poses a new challenge to the United States and the world. To date, no persuasive model of an American response to resurgent Islam has appeared. Hasty early efforts to portray extremist Muslims as "new totalitarians" and "Islamofascists," or to suggest that the attacks on the World Trade Center and Pentagon signaled the beginning of World War IV have proven in the end to be unpersuasive. Perhaps the problem lies in the search for a single explicit model that might replace containment. One of George Kennan's strongest objections to NSC-68 was that its codification took away nuance and the recognition of the uniqueness of specific situations. To Kennan, these were the qualities most needed for effective management of the Cold War, and it is precisely nuance and recognition of uniqueness that are needed in fashioning a sensible, effective response to resurgent Islam. At the beginning of the Cold War, Kennan tried and failed to persuade the Truman administration to rely on the power of nationalism to disrupt and weaken the ties among communist states. Instead, President Truman and his successors froze negotiations with the Soviet Union and China, a freeze that lasted with only one or two exceptions throughout the Cold War.

Nationalism is an important ally of the United States in its dealings with Muslim and Arab societies. The world of Islam is hugely diverse. It reaches from the eastern Atlantic to the Pacific Ocean. It includes Africans, Arabs, Persians, Central Asians, Malays, Indonesians, and Filipinos.[28] The states that lie within this enormous orbit differ markedly from one another in geography, language, history, and culture. Islamic diversity is even greater if countries with large Muslim majorities are included. It would be foolish to ignore this diversity, or to imagine that a transnational movement could easily merge these diverse components into a coherent whole capable of endangering the survival of the United States. At present, for example, while there is consensus among Muslim countries about the Israeli-Palestinian conflict, other conflicts remain beyond consensus, such as those between Syria and Iraq, Lebanon and Syria, and Muslims in Kashmir or Nagorno-Karabakh. Should Islamist or jihadist movements actually take control of Muslim or Arab states, their very success seems likely to sow the seeds of disarray, much as Mao's victory in China and Tito's in Yugoslavia led to bitter disagreements with Stalin. Policies of the United States that were seen by these states as compatible with their national interests would have a strong appeal. In order to exploit these differences, the American government would have to understand them correctly and be willing to negotiate on the basis of mutual advantage. This suggests strongly the need to avoid polarizing or moralistic rhetoric in speaking of societies that differ in culture and religion from the United States.

The Cold War embargo on meaningful negotiations with the Soviet Union found its modern form in Bush II's refusal to negotiate with North Korea and Iran. Bill Clinton and his advisers chose to enter talks with Pyongyang and managed to limit the use of plutonium enrichment in North Korea's nuclear program. The Bush II administration's refusal seemed to turn the clock back to the Cold War and the period between World War I and II when the United States made a regular practice of refusing to recognize, much less come to terms with, unpleasant or dangerous changes abroad. In the 1920s and 1930s and during the Cold War, American leaders postured before domestic audiences with high-sounding phrases about peace and economic freedom. The irony then, as in a half-century later, was that in precisely the periods when the United States possessed the greatest military and economic advantages, it was the least willing to negotiate. If the nuclear capabilities of Teheran and Pyongyang cannot be destroyed by military force, then there is no way to put a stop to proliferation without talking to the proliferators. For four years, the hardliners in the Bush II administration apparently persuaded the president that negotiations were a waste of time—Iran and North Korea were going nuclear regardless of what was said or done. Therefore, why bother? That view overlooked the damage to relations between the United States, and Europe, Japan, and China that resulted from the administration's unwillingness to negotiate productively. It also overlooked the ability of the North Koreans to use the administration's hard line as a justification for its production of nuclear weapons. Bush II strategists should not have been surprised by the results, but they were.[29] The United States must always be willing to negotiate with enemies and friends when it can be done on the basis of mutual advantage. Sensible and effective negotiating strategies rely on incentives as well as threats and punishments. Failure to approach conflicts with other governments in this way misses the opportunity to allow an enemy to move away from its mistakes, and may lead to a steady loss of popular support at home and abroad for American foreign policy.

Of Quick Fixes and Dominoes

The maintenance of a domestic and international environment in which American values and institutions will thrive is an unending task: there are no permanent or quick fixes, no single domino whose fall triggers an avalanche of perpetual change for the better, and no permanent end to tyranny on earth. The circumstances that allow a flowering of stability, justice, and hope can be constructed only by painstaking effort over a very long period at great cost and with consummate care. Consequently, the United States must guard against overextension and bankruptcy. Dwight Eisenhower's warning about a "dual threat" is a good guide: what is done in the name of safety and survival must not bankrupt the country and destroy its foreign policy consensus or, one might add, needlessly turn the world against the United States. Interests should define threats, not the other way around, and interests should be defended patiently and shrewdly, tenaciously and un-apologetically, without huge emotional swings between elation and despair, hostility and admiration.

The task is unending because greed and the lust for power cannot be destroyed or human beings permanently altered in ways to make us im-mune to their appeal. To those who are religious, it is impious to imagine that human beings can eliminate tyranny and injustice from this world. That is the work of God. A truly flawless society exists and can exist only in heaven. To those steeped in the history of diplomacy and war, the idea seems simply absurd. Understanding that imperfections in human beings and their institutions cannot be eliminated puts the use of military power into proper perspective, and should lead to an appropriate adjustment in ex-pectations among American citizens and foreign policymakers. At best, war can provide a chance to start over, to try to remedy the faults and wrongs and excesses that triggered war in the first place. The essence of war is de-struction, as Clausewitz noted two centuries ago. It is never creative. It can-not erase the state of mind or the habits of individuals living in the countries that lost and won the war. When the guns stop firing, the truly hard work of building a better domestic and international order begins on both sides.[30] The allure of radical Islam cannot be overcome by force of arms alone. Individual terrorists can be killed and bases can be bombed, but the ideas that lead the jihadists to murder Arabs, Muslims, Israelis, Americans, and anyone else who opposes them, will live on until overcome by more ap-pealing ideas and the patient construction of just societies.

Concluding Observations

The certainty of human imperfection means that differences, including deep fundamental differences, between peoples and governments are not in themselves abhorrent, unnatural, or something to be destroyed or overcome. Much of the zest in life comes from attempts to fathom and understand difference. The differences between peoples and governments also make it possible to learn from one another. This is emphatically not a call for moral relativism. A modest and sensible patriotism—love of one's country—is an expression of difference, and need not become xenophobic nationalism. Americans are entitled to be proud of their country, and differences that would make it impossible to maintain a decent and secure society must be opposed and, if necessary, defeated. The continuation of democracy in America is worth defending. But a healthy pride in one's own society does not logically, philosophically, or in any other fashion justify propagating democracy anywhere else in the world.

The existence of imperfection also calls attention to the current state of American society and the role that it might play in the conduct of American foreign policy. Throughout his long life, George Kennan pleaded with his colleagues and fellow Americans to understand that the most important single thing that the United States could do to advance its own safety and survival and the cause of democracy in the world would be to attend to its own domestic shortcomings, particularly with regard to health care, education, and the over-reliance on petroleum for transportation and other forms of energy. The power of its unassuming example would be immense, far greater than any attempt at "public diplomacy," however lavishly funded or cleverly presented. Sensible people seek out solutions to the grave problems of modern life, and would certainly try to take the best from such an enlightened American example. It is unbecoming, self-righteous, and ultimately counterproductive to hector others and preach to them about morality and the universal validity of American principles and practice without paying attention to the state of one's own society. "Judge not, that ye be not judged . . ." reads the famous verse from Matthew in the New Testament.[31]

Preaching democracy to the world goes down very well at home, but it amounts to striking poses before domestic supporters instead of thinking hard about specific situations in foreign countries. The resurgence of Islam and the risk that societies will fall into horrifying human rights abuses present huge challenges to the United States and the world. Both demand to be treated in their full uniqueness rather than as examples of much broader and more or less monolithic trends. It is crucial to see the quest by Islamists to transform Arab and Muslim countries as individual and unique. The circumstances and opportunities facing Islamists in Egypt differ enormously from those in Turkey, and both have little in common with Morocco or Pak-istan or Indonesia.[32] In addition, there is much that is positive in the ap-pearance of Islamists on the political scene: their idealism and self-sacrifice, their service to the poor, their willingness to work hard and to persevere in the face of very long odds that they will ever see any real change in their home countries. In a similar way, it is possible to develop a broad general policy governing American responses to humanitarian crises in the world's poor countries. But it was precisely such a broad policy, developed by the Clinton administration after the debacle in Somalia, that contributed to the decision not to use American troops to stop the genocide in Rwanda. Each Arab and Muslim country's encounter with Islamists and jihadists, each occurrence of human rights abuse, and each potential genocide, deserves to be seen as the special case that it is and not as a subset of a general pol-icy that wipes out all uniqueness and specificity. Somalia was not Rwanda. Algeria and Lebanon are not Egypt or Syria or Iran. Hamas and Hezbollah are not identical, and both differ from al-Qaeda. The entry of European and American forces into Yugoslavia during the 1990s ought never to have been seen in the same terms as the invasion of the country by Hitler's armies in World War II.

The soundest strategy joins the United States with Europe and Japan in every possible way, to use the astounding magnetism generated by such an Atlantic/North American/Northern Pacific community to pull Russia into its orbit and in this way create a powerful and attractive coalition of strength, wealth, freedom, and common purpose. The economies of this group com-prise the lion's share of wealth and industrial potential in the world, with combined annual gross domestic products of more than $20 trillion, and a combined population of around 860 million. The comparable figures for China are gross domestic product of $5.6 trillion, and population at 1.2 bil-lion. By cooperating with Europe, the United States increases the likelihood of a benign outcome to Russia's difficult and painful political and economic transition. Adding Japan to the Euro-American group enormously strength-ens it, and shows China prosperous, stable democracies conducting their defense and security policies in harmony and cooperation. If Europe and the United States add Russia to their coalition, conflict with China becomes moot. Such a combination would give the greatest possible encouragement for China to stick to economic development and follow a responsible course in relations with its neighbors.

Failure to join the Europeans and Japan surrenders political and eco-nomic potential that cannot be matched anywhere else in the world, support that would assist the United States in protecting its own security without exhausting and isolating itself. Pushing the mistaken view of American primacy even further, the Bush II administration insisted that geopolitics had lost its significance, that since its preferred strategy was unilateral, Bulgaria or Romania would serve as well as Germany and France as a launching point for interventions in Central Asia or the Middle East.[33] The Bush II administration seemed happy to divide continental Europe and play the smaller states against the larger. The long-term prospects of trying to lead Europe by dividing it hardly seem more promising than French President Jacques Chirac's attempt to lead Europe by opposing the United States. But Bush II's indifference to Europe defied even the most elementary examination of economic and military power, both real and potential. Europe remains of enormous importance to the United States in the present, and will remain so into the foreseeable future. It is folly to imagine otherwise. It is worse than folly to allow half-baked notions of differences between Europeans and Americans to divide the two sides of the Atlantic.[34]

The courage, perseverance, foresight, and sacrifices of Americans and their allies during the Cold War won them a precious opportunity to build a better world after 1989. From 1993 onward, working with mistaken assumptions and flawed policies derived from the post–Cold War paradigm, American presidents and their advisors failed to make good on that opportunity. It is time to turn away from their mistakes and take another path forward. On March 4, 1865, with the Civil War nearly won, Abraham Lincoln attempted to lead his country away from the terrible slaughter of a fratricidal war into a better future. The simplicity and modesty of his aims and the clarity with which he expressed them should be the standard against which to measure American foreign policy in the twenty-first century: "With malice toward none," Lincoln said, "with charity for all, with firmness in the right as God gives us to see the right, let us strive on to finish the work we are in, to bind up the nation's wounds, to care for him who shall have borne the battle and for his widow and his orphan, to do all which may achieve and cherish a just and lasting peace among ourselves and with all nations."

Notes

Introduction

1. For explanations of American hegemony based on the country's history, see John Lewis Gaddis, *Surprise, Security, and the American Experience* (Cambridge, MA: Harvard University Press, 2004); Walter Russell Mead, *Special Providence: American Foreign Policy and How It Changed the World* (New York: Routledge, 2002); and Warren Zimmermann, *First Great Triumph: How Five Americans Made Their Country a World Power* (New York: Farrar, Strauss & Giroux, 2002). The condemnations of hubris and error are, if anything, more numerous. Representatives include Chalmers Johnson, *Blowback: The Costs and Consequences of American Empire*, 2nd ed. (New York: Henry Holt, 2002); and Anonymous [Michael Scheuer], *Imperial Hubris: Why the West Is Losing the War on Terror* (New York: Brasseys, 2004).

2. See Robert Kagan and William Kristol, *Present Dangers: Crisis and Opportunity in American Foreign and Defense Policy* (New York: Encounter Books, 2000). See also the website of the Project for a New American Century, at www.newamericancentury .org. In September 2005, a poll conducted by the Chicago Council on Foreign Relations in cooperation with the Program on International Policy Attitudes and Knowledge Networks found that "[a] majority [of Americans] rejects the idea of using military force to promote democracy, whether by overthrowing dictators or threatening countries with military force if they do not institute democratic reforms. . . . A large bipartisan majority says that establishing a democracy was not a good enough reason to go to war in Iraq. The experience in Iraq has made Americans feel less supportive of using military force to bring about democracy. A majority is ready to accept an Iraqi constitution even if it does not fully meet democratic standards, and wants to start withdrawing troops once the constitution is ratified. . . . Americans are not convinced that when there are more democracies the world is a safer place, and are divided about whether democracy undermines support for terrorist groups, or whether democracies are less likely to go to war with each other or more likely to be friendly to the US. . . . A large majority favors the US promoting democracy through diplomatic and cooperative methods including helping emerging democracies with aid and technical assistance in conducting elections, sending monitors to certify that elections are conducted fairly and honestly, and bringing students, journalists and political leaders from a variety of countries to the US to educate them on how democracy works." *Americans on Promoting Democracy*, September 29, 2005, 3–4.

3. For an insightful discussion of the connection among past, present, and future, see John Lewis Gaddis, *The Landscape of History: How Historians Map the Past* (New York: Oxford University Press, 2002).

4. A word about the term "post–Cold War" is necessary, not least because a decade and a half have passed since the Cold War ended. When does the world stop being post–Cold War? The term identifies a period in time and fits my argument that a constellation of beliefs and assumptions was set in place very soon after the disappearance of the Soviet Union. The name itself reflects a sense of impermanence and conveys a negative rather than positive identity—not something in its own right so much as not something else. Many Western and American decision makers, scholars, and opinion leaders believed that a new name would soon appear to take its place, such as the age of globalization, perhaps, or democratization. Hopes for that brave future soon gave way to darker views, clouded by the economic travail of the late 1990s, and the spread of ethnic and religious conflict, genocide, and suicidal terrorism. Now, well into the twenty-first century, no obvious replacement has appeared. It may be that the war in Iraq signals the end of the post–Cold War era. However, I believe the post–Cold War paradigm will lose its significance only if the lessons of the Iraq war are thoughtfully absorbed and acted on. Until that occurs, the term seems as good as any.

5. See Thomas S. Kuhn, *The Structure of Scientific Revolutions*, 3rd ed. (Chicago: University of Chicago Press, 1996).

6. *Strategies of Containment: A Critical Appraisal of Postwar American National Security Policy* (New York: Oxford University Press, 1982), vii. Gaddis attributed the distinction to J.H. Hexter. In fact, Hexter quoted Donald Kagan. See J.H. Hexter, *On Historians: Reappraisals of Some of the Makers of Modern History* (Cambridge, MA: Harvard University Press, 1979), 241–42.

7. Hexter, *On Historians*, 242.

8. Gaddis, *Strategies of Containment*, vii.

9. William B. Quandt, *Peace Process: American Diplomacy and the Arab-Israeli Conflict since 1967*, rev. ed. (Washington, DC: Brookings Institution Press), 387. Quandt was a member of the National Security Council during the Carter administration before taking positions at the Brookings Institution, and later, on the faculty at the University of Virginia. See also James M. Goldgeier, *Not Whether But When: The U.S. Decision to Enlarge NATO* (Washington, DC: Brookings Institution Press, 1999), especially 5–8.

10. Quandt, *Peace Process*, 10.

11. See Thomas E. Rice, "Army Historian Cites Lack of Postwar Plan," *Washington Post*, December 25, 2004, available at www.washingtonpost.com.

12. Initially, Gaddis supported the Bush II version of the post–Cold War paradigm. For his appeal to the administration to make some adjustments, see John Lewis Gaddis, "Grand Strategy in the Second Term," *Foreign Affairs*, January/February 2005, available at www.nytimes.com/cfr/international/20050101faessay_v84n1_ga. Gaddis remains a supporter: his argument is that if Bush changes superficial aspects of his strategy, it will succeed. Such superficial changes include using "better manners," making more careful explanations of policy, and making common cause with other governments to destroy suicidal terrorists. Inexplicably, Gaddis turns to Bismarck for guidance about the conduct of American foreign policy. Bismarck was not a liberal or a democrat, and his foreign policy helped destroy the basis for conservative cooperation in preserving the peace in Europe before World War I. See especially, George F. Kennan, *The Decline of Bismarck's European Order: Franco-Russian Relations, 1875–1890* (Princeton, NJ: Princeton University Press, 1979); and *The Fateful Alliance: France, Russia, and the Coming of the First World War* (New York: Pantheon, 1984).

13. Henry Kissinger, *Diplomacy* (New York: Simon & Schuster, 1994), 45–46, 50.

14. For a helpful examination of the implications interventionist and noninterventionist versions of nineteenth-century liberalism for foreign policy, see Kenneth N. Waltz, *Man, the State, and War: A Theoretical Analysis* (New York: Columbia University Press, 1959), chapters 4 and 5.

15. On illiberal democracy, see Fareed Zakaria, *The Future of Freedom: Illiberal Democracy at Home and Abroad* (New York: W.W. Norton & Company, 2004).

16. For a summary of the argument that this is so, see Joseph E. Stiglitz, *Globalization and Its Discontents* (New York: Norton, 2002), ix–xvi, and 214–52.

17. Robert E. Rubin and Jacob Weisberg, *In an Uncertain World: Tough Choices from Wall Street to Washington* (New York: Random House, 2003), 212–13.

18. A group of scholars, journalists, and political activists have relentlessly argued and worked to put the United States in an imperial role. Among the most vociferous and influential voices are those of William Kristol, who used his newspaper, *The Weekly Standard*, as a mouthpiece for his views; Robert Kagan, and the "ginger group" The Project for a New American Century (a ginger group in British and Australian politics is a small group within a larger one that seeks to persuade the larger to accept its views) (www.newamericancentury.org), and the newspaper columnist Charles Krauthammer. Two books that contain the essence of the argument for American imperialism are Max Boot, *The Savage Wars of Peace: Small Wars and the Rise of American Power* (New York: Basic Books, 2002), and Niall Ferguson, *Empire: The Rise and the Demise of the British World Order and the Lessons for Global Power* (New York: Basic Books, 2003). In his latest book, Ferguson calls on Americans to take up the burdens of empire, but suggests that they will be unable to stomach it. See Ferguson, *Colossus: The Price of American Empire* (New York: Penguin Books, 2004). A helpful review of *Colossus* is Paul Kennedy, "Mission Impossible?" *The New York Review of Books*, 51, no. 10, June 10, 2004, 16–19.

19. Hans Delbruck, *Krieg und Politik* (Berlin, 1918–1919), vol. 2, 187, quoted by Gordon A. Craig in "Delbruck: The Military Historian," in Peter Paret, ed., with Gordon A. Craig and Felix Gilbert, *Makers of Modern Strategy: From Machiavelli to the Nuclear Age* (Princeton, NJ: Princeton University Press, 1986), 348.

1. Bush I and the New World Order

1. George Bush and Brent Scowcroft, *A World Transformed* (New York: Vintage Books, 1998), 564.

2. See in particular, Henry Kissinger, *Diplomacy* (New York: Simon & Schuster, 1994), especially chapter 1.

3. Bush and Scowcroft, *A World Transformed*, 355.

4. See Christopher Hellman, "Last of the Big-Time Spenders: U.S. Military Budget Still the World's Largest, and Growing. Military Spending: U.S. vs. the World, FY '01," Center for Defense Information, available at www.cdi.org.

5. Michael R. Beschloss and Strobe Talbott, *At the Highest Levels: The Inside Account of the End of the Cold War* (Boston: Little Brown and Company, 1993), 3–4, 9–10.

6. After leaving office, Baker admitted that his highly centralized way of working caused opposition within the State Department and grumbling in the media. He recognized that he failed to help bring along the next generation of talented foreign-service officers as well as he might have. But he argued that he was able to get results by work-

ing this way. "In hindsight," he said, "the strength of this organizational concept was that it allowed me to develop initiatives privately and coherently and to use them to break diplomatic deadlocks. So the system was great at offense, but it was not quite as strong at defense—that is, avoiding potential crises. My approach placed a tremendous burden on me and my closest aides, who simply couldn't always focus on every potential crisis. On balance, however, I believe it served me and, more important, the Bush administration, exceptionally well." Baker's terse references to the burdens of centralization were his way of saying that he and his three aides were overworked, so overworked during the final phase of German unification that they could not pay close attention to other important developments, such as the deterioration of relations between Iraq and Kuwait. James A. Baker, with Thomas M. DeFrank, *The Politics of Diplomacy: Revolution, War & Peace, 1989–1992* (New York: G.P. Putnam's Sons, 1995), 32.

7. Ibid., xiii. "I've always known that I was more of a man of action than of reflection." Ibid.

8. Ibid., xiv–xv.

9. Michael Kramer, "Playing for the Edge," *Time*, February 13, 1989, 44, quoted in William B. Quandt, *Peace Process: American Diplomacy and the Arab-Israeli Conflict since 1967* (Washington, DC: Brookings Institution Press, 2001), 292, n. 4.

10. Baker, *Politics of Diplomacy*, 134–35. Characteristically, Baker describes Soviet cooperation during the Gulf War as the result of personal relationships among Bush, himself, Gorbachev, and Shevardnadze: "Throughout the Gulf crisis and the war to liberate Kuwait, we had to rely again and again on the personal relationships the President and I had carefully developed with Gorbachev and Shevardnadze." Ibid., 473.

11. Throughout the Cold War, the United States avoided as much as possible publicly spelling out its determination to use force to ensure the security and stability of oil supplies from the Gulf. After the fall of the Shah of Iran and the Soviet Union's invasion of Afghanistan, President Carter made public that commitment, which became known as the "Carter Doctrine." See Jimmy Carter, State of the Union address, January 23, 1980, available at http://jimmycarterlibrary.org/documents/speeches/su80jec.phtml.

12. On the origins of the Weinberger and Powell doctrines, see James Mann, *Rise of the Vulcans: The History of Bush's War Cabinet* (New York: Viking, 2004), 43–44.

13. Baker, *The Politics of Diplomacy*, 69.

14. Ibid. Baker's words echoed those spoken four decades earlier by Secretary of State Dean Acheson to George Kennan, a career diplomat and Russian expert, and the man who conceived the doctrine of containment. See n. 26.

15. Ibid., 606.

16. Ibid., 609–11.

17. Ibid., 602.

18. Ibid., 636.

19. Ibid., 651.

20. Bush and Scowcroft, *A World Transformed*, 89.

21. Ibid., 105.

22. See especially, Robert L. Suettinger, *Beyond Tiananmen: The Politics of U.S.-China Relations* (Washington, DC: Brookings Institution Press, 2003).

23. Patrick Tyler, *A Great Wall. Six Presidents and China: An Investigative History* (New York: Century Foundation, 1999), 386, 389.

24. Ibid., 387.

25. Ibid., 373. On the damage to U.S.-China relations caused by Tiananmen and Bush's attempts to mitigate them, see 359–74.

26. The doctrine of containment guided U.S. foreign policy throughout the Cold War. It was established by the Truman Administration and continued in force until the Soviet Union collapsed. Its central idea, conceived by George F. Kennan, a senior career Foreign Service officer who headed Secretary of State George Marshall's policy planning unit, was to prevent communist expansion. American policymakers believed this would protect American vital interests and, eventually, lead Soviet leaders to change their definition of the USSR's vital interests, which in turn would lead to normal relations with the United States and its allies. Kennan disagreed strongly with Acheson and Paul Nitze, his successor as head of policy planning, about the implementation of containment. As practiced by Acheson and all American presidents until Richard Nixon, containment called for a massive American and allied military buildup, opposition to all communist governments everywhere in the world, the prohibition of all substantive negotiations with communist governments, and the integration of nuclear weapons into U.S. strategic planning. Kennan believed that these measures increased the risk of nuclear war, militarized American foreign policy, forfeited any chance to use nationalism to move communist governments away from subservience to Moscow, and condemned the United States to a policy of global intervention against communism which, he believed, would confound and exhaust the country. The disagreements became so pronounced that Kennan resigned his position and left the Foreign Service. Acheson dismissed Kennan's objections as exaggerated and of little help to him in his efforts to build a global political, military, and economic alliance against the Soviet Union and, later, China. See in particular, Dean Acheson, *Present at the Creation: My Years at the State Department* (New York: W.W. Norton & Company, 1969); and George F. Kennan, *Memoirs, 1925–1950*, 2 vols. (Boston: Little, Brown, 1967, 1972).

27. For another, less flattering, view of Soviet leaders, see Stephen Kotkin, *Armageddon Averted: The Soviet Collapse, 1970–2000* (Oxford: Oxford University Press, 2002).

28. About the short time before the anti-Iraq coalition unraveled, Baker wrote: "Those arguing for more time to let sanctions work repeatedly underestimated the difficulty of holding the coalition together for an extended period. Eventually, a key partner was likely to bolt, in which case the coalition would likely disintegrate." Baker, *Politics of Diplomacy*, 301.

29. "The vehicle for that role must be NATO," Scowcroft argued. "The alliance was the only way the US could keep forces in Europe as a visible commitment to its security and stability." Germany was the key to any U.S. presence in Europe, because of the location of U.S. bases and troops. If Germany left NATO, the United States would have to leave Europe. To Scowcroft, the United States needed Kohl to keep Germany in NATO and U.S. troops in NATO. "Together, these requirements gave us an enormous stake in the outcome of German reunification, apart from ending the division of Europe." Bush and Scowcroft, *A World Transformed*, 231.

30. "I thought the changing atmosphere warranted a shift in the priority on US attention away from our relations with the Soviet Union, which were focused almost entirely on arms control, to Eastern Europe. Emphasizing Eastern Europe would also remind everyone that the fundamental structure of the Cold War was still in place and Soviet troops still occupied Eastern Europe. My line of thinking had two main elements. The first would be an attempt through agreements on conventional force reductions to get the Soviet Army out, or at least dramatically reduce its stifling presence. That would create a better environment for political evolution there. The second would be to revise our strategy for treating individual East European states." Ibid., 38.

31. Ibid., 42. The group that reviewed European policy as a whole consisted of President Bush, Vice President Quayle, Secretary of State James Baker, Secretary of Defense Dick Cheney, National Security Adviser Brent Scowcroft, Deputy Secretary of State Lawrence Eagleburger, Deputy National Security Adviser (later Director of Central Intelligence) Robert Gates, and Chief of Staff John Sununu.

32. Ibid., 43.

33. Ibid.

34. Ibid.

35. Ibid., 70.

36. See George Bush, *Public Papers of the Presidents of the United States, 1989* [hereafter PPPUS], Book I, 431, 432, 540–41, 603–4. See also Bush and Scowcroft, *A World Transformed*, 51–52, 55.

37. The redefinition of Soviet national interest as best served by cooperation rather than confrontation with the West was what George Kennan had foreseen when he proposed containment four decades earlier. See especially George F. Kennan, *Memoirs*, 2 vols. (Boston: Little Brown, 1967, 1972).

38. Quoted in Beschloss and Talbott, *At the Highest Levels*, 75–76.

39. Bush and Scowcroft, *A World Transformed*, 55.

40. Ibid., 188.

41. Ibid., 300.

42. "It would have been useful had we been more open with our allies on the issue. We pursued it at length with the Soviets, but with our friends there were almost certainly too few occasions where frank discussions took place." Ibid., 300.

43. Ibid., 301.

44. Gates was offered the post of director of Central Intelligence after William Casey's death during the Reagan administration. He accepted but withdrew his name after his nomination stirred strong opposition in the Senate. He was offered the position again by President Bush in May 1991. After long and controversial hearings, the Senate agreed to his nomination. He was sworn in on November 18, 1991.

45. Robert M. Gates, *From the Shadows: The Ultimate Insider's Story of Five Presidents and How They Won the Cold War* (New York: Touchstone, 1996), 514. The title of Hodnett's paper was "Gorbachev's Domestic Gambles and Instability." Gates believes that speculation about a Soviet collapse before 1989 "would have been ignored, if not ridiculed, by decision-makers." Ibid., 564. Gates called his paper for President Bush, "Thinking about the Unthinkable: Instability and Political Turbulence in the USSR." Ibid., 526.

46. Ibid., 564.

47. Baker, *Politics of Diplomacy*, 473.

48. See P. Edward Haley, *Arms Control and the End of the Cold War: An Oral History of the Negotiations to Reduce Conventional Forces in Europe* (Claremont, CA: Keck Center for International Strategic Studies, 2002).

49. Baker, *Politics of Diplomacy*, 475.

50. Ibid.

51. Baker observes, "Even the Israelis believed that Saddam was bluffing to bully the Kuwaitis into economic concessions. Israel's intelligence service, the Mossad, told U.S. intelligence counterparts that Saddam's rhetoric was designed to deter an Israeli attack, not threaten one of his own. As late as July 31 [the day before the invasion of Kuwait], King Hussein and President Mubarak reassured us that Saddam was engaged

in verbal bluster, not literal threats. Ironically, most of our allies privately worried throughout the spring and summer of 1990 that the United States might *overreact* to Saddam's new aggressiveness!" Baker, *Politics of Diplomacy*, 274.

52. Colin Powell, *My American Journey* (New York: Ballantine Books, 1995), 516.

53. Paul Wolfowitz, "The United States and Iraq," in John Calabrese, ed., *The Future of Iraq* (Washington, DC: Middle East Institute, 1997), 107–13, quoted in James Mann, *The Rise of the Vulcans: The History of Bush's War Cabinet* (New York: Viking, 2004), 190, n. 26.

54. Baker, *Politics of Diplomacy*, 277–78.

55. Ibid., 279.

56. The billions Baker obtained for the war from the Saudis included a $4 billion line of credit to help the Soviet government survive the winter. See ibid., 293–95.

57. Margaret Thatcher, *The Downing Street Years* (New York: Harper Collins, 1993), 827. On the day that she resigned as prime minister, Mrs. Thatcher doubled the number of British troops committed to the Gulf, sending the 4th Brigade from Germany, which brought the total number of British forces to more than 30,000. Ibid., 828.

58. For a description of the Shia and Kurdish rebellions and the measures taken by Saddam Hussein to crush them, see Sandra Mackey, *The Reckoning: Iraq and the Legacy of Saddam Hussein* (New York: Norton, 2002).

59. Baker, *Politics of Diplomacy*, 115.

60. Ibid., 116.

61. Ibid., 119.

62. Dennis Ross, *The Missing Peace: The Inside Story of the Fight for Middle East Peace* (New York: Farrar, Strauss and Giroux, 2004), 55.

63. Dennis Ross says this idea came to him from Dan Meridor, minister of justice in Shamir's government, whose father had been a founder of Herut, the predecessor of Likud. See ibid., 56–57.

64. Ibid., 118. "No solution was possible, however, without at least his [Arafat's] private acquiescence to a separate dialogue between Israel and Palestinians from the territories."

65. After talks with President Bush on April 6, Shamir offered a limited and indirect proposal for the Americans to work with. All but one of Shamir's points simply reiterated long-standing positions of Israel: Arab governments ought to make peace with Israel, end their economic embargo, and, using international assistance, ensure decent living conditions for the Palestinians living in refugee camps. The condition of those Palestinians who had left and been forced to leave mandatory Palestine "must be viewed as a humanitarian problem," not a political and national problem. In words calculated to give the greatest offense to Arafat and the PLO, Shamir's fourth point called for elections in the West Bank and Gaza, using the Hebrew terms Judea, Samaria, and Gaza, whose purpose would be to "locate representatives of the Palestinian population" who could in this way be "free of the intimidation and terror of the PLO." The elections would "permit the development of an authentic representation that is not self-appointed from the outside." The Palestinians elected in this way would take part in "negotiations on an interim settlement, in which a self-governing administration will be set up." Available at www.us-israel.org/jsource/Peace/shamirpro.html, 2–3.

66. Baker, *Politics of Diplomacy*, 121.

67. Ibid., 126.

68. Ibid., 131–32.

69. Ibid., 412.
70. Ibid.
71. Ibid., 443.
72. Ibid., 500.
73. Ibid., 412–13.
74. Ibid., 416.
75. Ibid.
76. Ibid., 444.
77. Ibid., 423.
78. Baker quotes the exchange about this at length; see ibid., 446.
79. Ibid., 427.
80. Ibid.
81. Ibid., 447–48.
82. Ibid., 450.
83. The two teams' reports were due on May 21, 1990, and became known as the "five-twenty-one brief." Nicholas Lemann, "The Next World Order," *The New Yorker*, April 1, 2002, p. 42. As one participant in the review put it, "Normally, Dennis Ross would have led this kind of review. But he had become 'too operational.' He was traveling with Baker and contributing to immediate foreign policy decisions. That was good and bad. He had a great deal of influence over policy, but he was too busy to take a reflective look at what had changed and at what the administration should be doing about it. At the National Security Council, Scowcroft came up with 'the New World Order,' an idea we heard that he had talked about with the president during a boat ride at Kennebunkport. It didn't really provide the kind of guidance we needed." That the strategic review was conducted in the Defense Department put a heavily military emphasis on its conclusions, a pattern that was to be continued in Bush II, when once again the Defense Department and many of the people who participated in the 5/21 study dominated the formulation of U.S. foreign policy. From an interview with a senior official then serving on the Bush II National Security Council who participated in the first strategic review by author, September 17, 2002.
84. Thatcher, *Downing Street Years*, 816–20.
85. George Bush, "United States Defense: Reshaping Our Forces," delivered at the Aspen Institute, Aspen, Colorado, August 2, 1990, in *Vital Speeches of the Day*, 676–79.
86. Patrick Tyler, "Excerpts from Pentagon's Plan: 'Prevent the Emergence of a New Rival,'" *New York Times*, March 8, 1992, pp. I1, I14.
87. Ibid.
88. Ibid. See also Patrick E. Tyler, "Pentagon Drops Goal of Blocking New Superpowers," *New York Times*, May 24, 1992, p. I1.
89. This was the precursor of the Bush II administration's famous phrase, "coalitions of the willing."
90. See Mann, *Rise of the Vulcans*, 208–15.
91. Bush and Scowcroft, *A World Transformed*, 400.
92. Ibid.
93. Baker, *Politics of Diplomacy*, 297.
94. Ibid., 320.
95. For example, an Internet search for "new world order" reveals that at www .educate-yourself.org/nwo/, the new world order is described as "a worldwide conspiracy being orchestrated by an extremely powerful and influential group of *genetically-*

related individuals." At www.conspiracy.freewebspace.com/index.htm#new_world_order: "An international climate of fear & chaos is necessary to justify the final, radical social & political changes that will be officially called the New World Order. We believe that epidemics, or bioterror blamed on America's 'war on terror,' present likely routes to this horrifying state of affairs."

96. United Nations Security Council Resolution 678 (Concerning the Implementation of Security Council Resolution 660), S.C. res. 678, 45 U.N. SCOR at 27, U.N. Doc. S/RES/678 (1991), available at www.un.org/documents/scres.htm.

97. Bush and Scowcroft, *A World Transformed*, 370.

2. Moses and the Promised Land

1. See Deuteronomy 34:4.

2. James A. Baker, *The Politics of Diplomacy: Revolution, War & Peace, 1989–1992* (New York: G.P. Putnam's Sons, 1995), 84.

3. Thomas Homestead and Steven R. Rather, "Why Bush Lost," *Foreign Policy*, no. 89 (Winter 1993): 4, available at http://web12.epnet.com. See also Lawrence Freedman, "Order and Disorder in the New World," *Foreign Affairs: America and the World* 71, no. 1 (1991/1992): 2, available at http://web12.epnet.com; and Alvin Z. Rubinstein, "New World Order or Hollow Victory?" *Foreign Affairs* 70, no. 4 (Fall 1991): 8, available at http://web12.epnet.com. See also, Dan Balz, "Kennedy: Administration 'Has No Agenda,'" *Washington Post*, March 7, 1989, at www.lexisnexis.com/academic; Strobe Talbott, "Why Bosnia Is Not Vietnam," *Time*, 140, no. 8, August, 24, 1992, 49; Strobe Talbott, "Journey Without Maps," *Time*, 138, no. 12, September 23, 1991, 34; and Strobe Talbott, "How Not to Break China," *Time*, 140, no. 5, August 3, 1992, 53.

A typical summary of these points follows: "Eventually, of course, policy-makers will have to acknowledge that many issues, like environmental protection, involve non-state actors, the private sector, technical information and domestic implications beyond the traditional scope of international diplomacy. They must also admit that diffused power means not only an end to bipolarity strategically and to American hegemony economically, but also to an end to the imposition of American goals on others. In short, both the US capacity to coerce and the ability to persuade, the hallmarks of American foreign policy since 1945, are diminished. It would follow that working with others in regional or global institutions, especially on functional issues, provides guidance for redefining American objectives." Linda B. Miller, "American Foreign Policy: Beyond Containment?" *International Affairs* 66, no. 2 (1990): 323.

4. George Bush and Brent Scowcroft, *A World Transformed* (New York: Vintage Books, 1998), 4.

5. Ibid., 205.

6. Ibid., 230.

7. Ibid., 272.

8. Ibid.

9. Ibid., 273.

10. Ibid.

11. See Jeffrey Goldberg, "Breaking Ranks: What Brent Scowcroft Tried to Tell Bush," *New Yorker*, October 31, 2005, available at www.newyorker.com.

12. United Nations Security Council Resolution (hereafter UNSCR) 661, August 6, 1990, available at www.un.org/Security.

13. Mark Sommer, "Sanctions Are Becoming 'Weapon of Choice,'" *Christian Science Monitor*, August 3, 1993, available at www.lexisnexis.com/academic.

14. Stuart Auerbach, "Are Sanctions More Harmful than Helpful? Experts Say Embargoes Enrich Targets, Hurt Poor," *Washington Post*, March 28, 1993, available at www.lexisnexis.com/academic. See also Kimberly Elliott and Gary Hufbauer, "Sanctions Can Work, But They Require Luck, Patience, and Planning," *Atlanta Journal and Constitution*, June 7, 1992, available at www.lexisnexis.com/academic; see also, Gary Clyde Hufbauer, Jeffrey J. Schott, and Kimberly Ann Elliott, *Economic Sanctions Reconsidered*, 2nd ed. (Washington, DC: Institute for International Economics, 1990).

15. See Mary Curtius, "Bush Says He Halted War on Time but Calls Iraqi's Ouster a Goal," *Boston Globe*, January 17, 1992, available at www.lexisnexis.com/academic.

16. APINTNEWS, "Secret Strategy for Coup against Saddam," *Courier Mail*, February 28, 1991, available at www.lexisnexis.com/academic.

17. The text of UNSCR 687 is available at www.un.org/Docs/scres/1991/scres91.

18. David Hoffman, "Bush May Oppose Lifting Oil Sanctions against Iraq," *Washington Post*, April 30, 1991, available at www.lexisnexis.com/academic.

19. Lawrence M. O'Rourke, "Sanctions: Saddam's Tenacity Will Take Toll on Iraqi People, Official Says," *St. Louis Post Dispatch*, June 1, 1991, available at www.lexisnexis.com/academic.

20. Rob Edwards, "UN Suppresses Report on Iraq Suffering," *Scotsman*, July 18, 1993, available at www.lexisnexis.com/academic.

21. Text of UNSCR 986 is available at www.un.org/Docs/scres/1995/scres95. See also, John M. Goshko, "U.N. Approves Resolution for Formal End of the Gulf War," *Washington Post*, April 4, 1991, available at www.lexisnexis.com/academic.

22. Letter: "Sanctions and Suffering," by David McDowell, Robert Mauro, Dr. Ken Brown, Dr. Roger Owen, Professor Neil Harding, Dr. Paul Kelly, Dr. David Boucher, and Professor Fred Holliday and others, *Guardian*, November 23, 1991, available at www.lexisnexis.com/academic.

23. David Gergen, "America's Missed Opportunities," *America and the World: Foreign Affairs* 71, no. 1 (1991/1992): 3–4.

24. See the testimony of Cherif Bassiouni, chairman of the United Nations Commission of Experts to Investigate Violations in the Former Yugoslavia before the Commission on Security and Cooperation in Europe, April 4, 1995, Washington, DC, available at www.fas.org/irp/congress/1995_hr/genocideinbosnia. See also, Mark Danner, "The Killing Fields of Bosnia," *New York Review of Books* 45, no. 14, September 24, 1998, available at www.nybooks.com/articles.

25. Interviews with senior officials at the Department of State, January 1989.

26. Ross, *Missing Peace*, 80.

27. Gergen, "America's Missed Opportunities," 4.

28. James M. Goldgeier, *Power and Purpose: U.S. Policy toward Russia after the Cold War* (Washington, DC: Brookings Institution Press, 2003), 11.

29. Ibid., 82.

3. Bill Clinton's Brave New World

1. Bill Clinton, quoted in Joe Klein, *The Natural: The Misunderstood Presidency of Bill Clinton* (New York: Doubleday, 2002), 78.

2. Lee Hamilton, cited in David Halberstam, *War in a Time of Peace: Bush, Clinton, and the Generals* (New York: Scribner's, 2001), 168. Interview with Lee H. Hamilton.

3. *Statistics of the Presidential and Congressional Election of November 3, 1992*, compiled by Dallas L. Dendy Jr. and Donald K. Anderson (Washington, DC: Government Printing Office, 1993), 83. All the 1992 election statistics come from this source.

4. The four states where Clinton's total was larger than Bush and Perot combined were Arkansas, Maryland, New York, and the District of Columbia.

5. Cited in Fred L. Greenstein, *The Presidential Difference: Leadership Style from FDR to Clinton* (New York: Free Press, 2000), chapter 11, "The Highly Tactical Leadership of George Bush," 160.

6. A good example of both was the decision to "consult" with the European allies about lifting the arms embargo on Bosnia and striking the Serb military with U.S. and allied airpower. After three months of deliberation, the administration decided to send Secretary of State Warren Christopher to Europe to try to sell the idea to allied governments. The results destroyed the only option with any chance to avert the slaughter, a plan put together by former secretary of state Cyrus Vance and former British foreign minister, David Owen. "Vance-Owen," as it was known, amounted to a partition of Bosnia along the lines of existing control. This was unacceptable to some of Clinton's closest advisers because it allowed Serbian aggression against the Bosnian Muslims to go unpunished. But if it had been supported by the U.S. administration, it might have prevented further slaughter. Sensing Clinton's lack of commitment and unimpressed with the proposal, which allowed the United States to intervene from the air and left the Europeans stuck with the consequences on the ground, the allies refused. Christopher ended up looking foolish, his reputation damaged. Worst of all, the murderous fighting escalated. The administration ended up without Vance-Owen, without lift and strike, and without a resolution to a worsening crisis that threatened to spread throughout the Balkans, ruining NATO, and possibly dragging Greece and Turkey into a war.

7. Fred I. Greenstein, "Political Style and Political Leadership: The Case of Bill Clinton," in Stanley A. Renshon, ed., *The Clinton Presidency: Campaigning, Governing, and the Psychology of Leadership* (Boulder, CO: Westview Press, 1995), 137–47.

8. Colin L. Powell with Joseph E. Persico, *An American Journey* (New York: Ballantine Books, 1996), 560.

9. Halberstam, *War in a Time of Peace*, 174.

10. President-Elect Clinton's Foreign Policy Statements, December 12, 1991–November 4, 1992, *Foreign Policy Bulletin*, November–December 1992, 13.

11. Ibid., 5.

12. Quoted in James Mann, *About Face: A History of America's Curious Relationship with China, from Nixon to Clinton* (New York: Vintage Books, 1998), 262.

13. Ibid., 274. The legislators wanted China to change its policies on human rights and arms sales before receiving most favored nation (MFN) trading status. Bush vetoed their bill in 1991, and Clinton attacked him during the campaign a year later when he granted renewal of MFN for China.

14. President-Elect Clinton's Foreign Policy Statements, December 12, 1991–November 4, 1992, *Foreign Policy Bulletin*, November–December 1992, 18.

15. Ibid., 14. Clinton also took refuge in procedure. As a press release from his campaign headquarters in Little Rock, Arkansas, put it on July 26, 1992: "The United States should take the lead in seeking UN Security Council authorization for air strikes against those who are attacking the relief effort. The United States should be prepared to lend

appropriate military support to that operation." Quoted in David Owen, *Balkan Odyssey* (New York: Harcourt Brace & Company, 1995), 13.

16. Ibid., 7.

17. Ibid., 11.

18. See Confirmation Hearing for Rep. Les Aspin (D-WI) as Secretary of Defense, Senate Armed Service Committee, January 7, Federal Information Systems Corporation; Confirmation Hearing for Warren Christopher as Secretary of State, of the Senate Foreign Relations Committee, January 13, 1993, Federal News Service On-line, 8, 25.

19. *A National Security Strategy of Engagement and Enlargement*, February 1996, available at www.fas.org/spp/military/docops/national/1996stra.

20. Statement on the National Security Strategy Report, July 21, 1994, Public Papers of the Presidents, William J. Clinton, 1994, vol. 1, available at www.gpo.org. See also the very helpful article on the law requiring national security statements, known after its sponsors as the Goldwater-Nichols Act, together with an insightful commentary on the first Clinton statement by Don M. Snider, "The National Security Strategy: Documenting Strategic Vision," 2nd ed., March 15, 1995, available at www.carlisle.arm .mil/ssi/pubs/1995/natsec.

21. The White House, *A National Security Strategy of Engagement and Enlargement* (Washington, DC: Government Printing Office, July 1994), 5.

22. For an excellent discussion of these and related issues, see the articles by Don M. Snider, Andrew J. Kelly, Paul K. Davis, William M. Arkin, Michael J. Mazarr, Linda P. Brady, Donald M. Snow, Sam C. Sarkesian, John C. Baker, Paul R. Viotti, and Stephen J. Cimbala in Stephen J. Cimbala, ed., *Clinton and Post-Cold War Defenses* (Westport, CT: Praeger, 1996).

23. *National Security Strategy of Engagement and Enlargement*, 7.

24. Ibid., 2.

25. Ibid., 6.

26. Ibid., 10.

27. Ibid.

28. Ibid.

29. Weinberger's "rules" about the use of force follow: U.S. forces should be engaged in combat overseas only if vital national interests are at stake; the decision to commit troops should be done "wholeheartedly, and with the intention of winning"; political and military objectives should be clearly defined, and there should be precise knowledge of how to obtain those objectives; there should be "some reasonable assurance" that the American people and Congress will support the intervention; and the use of force should be the last resort. See Caspar Weinberger, *Fighting for Peace: Seven Critical Years in the Pentagon* (New York: Warner Books, 1990), 441–42. In a 1992 article, while denying that they existed, Colin Powell nonetheless gave some very firm rules for the use of force: "Relevant questions include: Is the political objective we seek to achieve important, clearly defined and understood? Have all other nonviolent policy means failed? Will military force achieve the objective? At what cost? Have the gains and risks been analyzed? How might the situation that we seek to alter, once it is altered by force, develop further and what might be the consequences. . . . When the political objective is important, clearly defined and understood, when the risks are acceptable, and when the use of force can be effectively combined with diplomatic and economic policies, then clear and unambiguous objectives must be given to the armed forces. These objectives must be firmly linked with the political objectives. . . . Decisive

means and results are always to be preferred, even if they are not always possible. . . . This is not to argue that the use of force is restricted to only those occasions where the victory of American arms will be resounding, swift and overwhelming. It is simply to argue that the use of force should be restricted to occasions where it can do some good and where the goodwill outweighs the loss of lives and other costs that will surely ensue. Wars kill people. That is what makes them different from all other forms of human enterprise." See Colin Powell, "U.S. Forces: Challenges Ahead; Enormous Power, Sobering Responsibility," *Foreign Affairs* 71, no. 5 (Winter 1992/1993), available at www.lexis-nexisacademic.com.

    30. *National Security Strategy of Engagement and Enlargement*, 13.

    31. Ibid., 19.

    32. President Bill Clinton, Remarks at a Freedom House Breakfast, October 6, 1995, *Public Papers of the Presidents: 1995*, vol. 2, 1544–51, available at www.gpo.gov/nara/pubpaps/srchpaps.

    33. *National Security Strategy of Engagement and Enlargement*, 20.

    34. Ibid., 24.

    35. On the conventional wisdom about terrorism, see especially, Daniel Benjamin and Steven Simon, *The Age of Sacred Terror* (New York: Random House, 2002), especially chapter 6, "A Paradigm Lost," and Richard A. Clarke, *Against All Enemies: Inside America's War on Terror* (New York: Free Press, 2004), especially chapter 5, "The Almost War."

    36. Red refers to the color preferred by communists around the world as a symbol of revolution. Brown was the color of the uniforms of Hitler's *sturmabteilung*, or stormtroopers, a paramilitary organization of his National Socialist Democratic Party. A Red-Brown alliance is the joining of political extremes of the left and right.

    37. According to James F. Collins, who succeeded Strobe Talbott as ambassador-at-large to the successor states of the Soviet Union (Newly Independent States) and later, ambassador to Russia: "Throughout the 1990s, [we] never got off the old cold war pie chart. If you looked at where the big money, the big programs, the big effort [went], it's all in security and the rest of it always was playing catch-up. Talk about missed opportunities: I always felt that one of the big missed opportunities of the 1990s . . . was that we never got that pie chart to be more balanced. Almost all, I'd say close to 80 percent of that was security, you know Nunn-Lugar [Cooperative Threat Reduction] and [Department of Energy] programs, some aspect of that." Quoted in James M. Goldgeier and Michael McFaul, *Power and Purpose: U.S. Policy toward Russia after the Cold War* (Washington, DC: Brookings Institution Press, 2003), 110.

    38. Talbott described the exchange between Primakov and Larry Summers, deputy treasury secretary, in this way: "In frequent, often gladiatorial encounters with Larry Summers and other visitors from Washington Primakov blamed many of Russia's problems on his predecessors ('your darlings, the young reformers'), on our administration for backing them and on experts from the IMF ('your university boys who come here to teach us as though we were dunces'). . . . It was one more repudiation of the Westernizing theme that Andrei Kozyrev had represented in Russian foreign policy and that Gaidar and Fyodorov had stood for in economic policy. In its place was economic nationalism: Russia would find its own way to a market economy." Strobe Talbott, *The Russia Hand: A Memoir of Personal Diplomacy* (New York: Random House, 2002), 290.

    39. Mann, *About Face*, 284.

    40. Ibid.

41. It is also possible that during his first days in office, Clinton contemplated a deal with China: concessions on human rights in exchange for a scaling back of the strong support for Taiwan that had been given by the Bush administration in its last year in office. Mann, *About Face*, 278.

42. For an insider's account of this crisis, see Ashton Carter and William J. Perry, *Preventive Defense: A New Strategy for America* (Washington, DC: Brookings Institution, 1999).

43. See Robert L. Suettinger, *Beyond Tiananmen: The Politics of U.S.-China Relations, 1989–2000* (Washington, DC: Brookings Institution Press, 2004), especially 87, 231, 416, 418, 422, 435, 439.

44. For valuable insights into the peace efforts of Dennis Ross and other Bush administration policymakers, see William B. Quandt, *Peace Process: American Diplomacy and the Arab-Israeli Conflict since 1967*, rev. ed. (Washington, DC: Brookings Institution, 2001), 293–95. On the Clinton administration's deference to Rabin, see Samuel W. Lewis, "The United States and Israel: Evolution of an Unwritten Alliance," *Middle East Journal* 53 (Summer 1999): 370, quoted in Quandt, n. 7, 458.

45. The text of Clinton's press conference after the failure of the Camp David talks is available at http://usembassy.state.gov/islamabad/wwwhpr58.html.

46. For the texts of the letters of recognition and the declaration of arrangements on interim self-government, see www.usembassy-israel.il/publish/peace/peaindex.htm.#oslo.

47. For the texts of the September 9, 1993, agreement and the working agreements signed in 1994 and 1995, see www.usembassy-israel.org.il/publish/peace/peaindex.htm#oslo.

48. The exchange of recognition between the Israeli government and the Palestine Liberation Organization, the Declaration of Principles on Interim Self-Government Arrangement, and other key documents that stemmed from the breakthrough in Oslo may be found at www.state.gov/p/nea/rt/c9962.htm.

49. For the content of the proposal, see www.fmep.org/documents/clinton_parameters12-23-00.html.

50. Ibid.

51. Ibid.

52. Quoted in Halberstam, *War in a Time of Peace*, 140.

53. Powell, with Persico, *An American Journey*, 544–45.

54. Ibid., 281.

55. Warren Zimmermann, *Origins of a Catastrophe: Yugoslavia and Its Destroyers* (New York: Times Books, 1999), 120–21. Zimmermann was the last U.S. ambassador to a united Yugoslavia. He resigned in early 1994 after having concluded that his arguments in favor of the use of NATO airstrikes against Milosevic were not going to be heeded. See 224–27.

56. Halberstam, *War in a Time of Peace*, 199.

57. Owen, *Balkan Odyssey*, 103.

58. See Robert Siegel and Noah Adams, "Kosovo Deal," in *All Things Considered*, National Public Radio, October 13, 1998, available at www.lexisnexis.com; and Tom Brokaw and Ron Allen, "Peace Deal Made with Yugoslavia Despite Doubts It Will Be Kept," *NBC Nightly News*, October 13, 1998, available at www.lexisnexis.com.

59. "U.S. Policy on Kosovo," Hearing of the Senate Armed Services Committee, February 25, 1999, Federal News Service, Lexis-Nexis Congressional, 1–2. Text of the agreement may be found at www.usip.org/library/pa/kosovo/kosovo/rambtoc.html.

60. An "activation order" had been agreed, which authorized NATO Secretary General Javier Solana to begin air strikes without a further decision by the North Atlantic Council, although he would still have had to consult with member governments before acting.

61. The resolution authorized the Secretary General and the UN mission in Somalia to provide humanitarian assistance, and to assist in rebuilding its political institutions and economy and achieving national reconciliation. See UN Security Council Resolution 814, March 26, 1993, available at daccessdds.un.org/doc/UNDOC/GEN/N93/226/18/IMG/N9322618/pdf?OpenElement.

62. Madeleine Albright, "Yes, There Is a Reason To Be in Somalia," *New York Times*, August 10, 1993, p. A19.

63. Halberstam, *War in a Time of Peace*, 258.

64. Mark Bowden, *Blackhawk Down: A Story of Modern War* (Boston: Atlantic Monthly Press, 1999).

65. Interview with senior Defense Department official by author, Washington, DC, September 2004. At the start of the Bush II administration, Secretary Rumsfeld abolished the title commander in chief (CinC), pronounced "sink," saying that under the U.S. Constitution, there is only one commander in chief, the president.

66. Two of the best books on contemporary Haiti and the United States, and the U.S. invasion, are: Amy Wilentz, *Rainy Season: Haiti since the Duvaliers* (New York: Simon and Schuster, 1989); and Bob Shacochis, *Immaculate Invasion* (New York: Viking, 1999).

67. Private conversation between the author and Tony Lake, Claremont, CA, November 15, 2001.

68. "100 Days of Slaughter: A Chronology of US/UN Action," Frontline, available at www.pbs.org/wgbh/pages/frontline/shows/evil/etc/slaughter.html.

69. For an excellent short summary of these issues, see Larry A. Niksch, "North Korea's Nuclear Weapons Program," CRS Issue Brief for Congress (Washington, DC: Congressional Research Service, April 5, 2002).

70. Ashton Carter, testimony, U.S. Senate Foreign Relations Committee, Hearing on North Korea, February 4, 2003, available at www.lexis-nexis.congressional.

71. "Solving the North Korean Nuclear Puzzle. Appendix 6: Review of United States Policy toward North Korea: Finds and Recommendations ("Perry Report")," Washington, DC, October 12, 1999. An Institute for Science and International Security (ISIS) internet report, available at www.isis-online.org.

72. Ibid. For a more positive view of Clinton's policies, see Stephen M. Walt, "Two Cheers for Clinton's Foreign Policy," *Foreign Affairs* 79, no. 2 (March/April 2000), accessed at http://web2.epnet.com, especially 2–4.

4. An Eight-Year Odyssey

1. David Owen, quoted in David Rieff, *Slaughterhouse: Bosnia and the Failure of the West* (New York: Touchstone Press, 1996), 182; cited in David Halberstam, *War in a Time of Peace: Bush, Clinton, and the Generals* (New York: Simon & Schuster, 2001), 129.

2. For an argument that the evidence of North Korean cheating on the agreed framework was incorrect, see Selig S. Harrison, "Did North Korea Cheat?" *Foreign*

Affairs (January/February 2005), available at www.nytimes.com/cfr/internatinal/ 20050101faessay_v8_n1_ha.

3. For a more complete summary of the other possibilities, see G. John Ikenberry, "Strategic Reactions to American Preeminence: Great Power Politics in the Age of Unipolarity," July 28, 2003, available at www.cia.gov/nic/confreports_stratreact.html.

4. David Halberstam, *War in a Time of Peace: Bush, Clinton, and the Generals* (New York: Simon & Schuster, 2001), 129.

5. William Hyland, *Clinton's World: Remaking American Foreign Policy* (Westport, CT: Praeger, 1999), 203–4.

6. Michael Doyle makes the argument that liberal democracies do not attack one another. See Michael W. Doyle, "Kant, Liberal Legacies, and Foreign Affairs," *Philosophy and Public Affairs* 12, no. 3 (1983): 205–35; "Kant, Liberal Legacies, and Foreign Affairs," part 2, *Philosophy and Public Affairs* 12, no. 4 (1983): 322–53; and "Liberalism and World Politics," *American Political Science Review* 80, no. 4 (December 1986): 1151–69. In a very interesting article on the same subject, Markus Fischer argues that it is the content of liberalism rather than the procedures of democracy that account for the pacifying effect. See Markus Fischer, "The Liberal Peace: Ethical, Historical, and Philosophical Aspects," BCSIA Discussion Paper 2000-7 (Cambridge, MA: Kennedy School of Government, Harvard University, April 2000).

7. Thomas Friedman, *The Lexus and the Olive Tree* (New York: Farrar, Strauss & Giroux, 1999).

8. Joe Klein, *The Natural: The Misunderstood Presidency of Bill Clinton* (New York: Doubleday, 2002), 78.

9. See especially, Nader Fergany and others, *Arab Human Development Report 2002* (New York: United Nations Development Programme, Regional Bureau for Arab States, 2002).

10. See Japan-U.S. Joint Declaration on Security, Alliance for the 21st Century, April 17, 1996, available at www.mofa.go.jp/region/n-america/us/security/security. See also, Mary Jordan and Kevin Sullivan, "U.S. to Return Air Base to Japan; Planes at Futenma to Move; Overall Troop Strength Will Not Be Cut," *Washington Post*, April 13, 1996, available at www.lexisnexis.com/academic; Cameron W. Barr, "U.S. Swaps Okinawa Base Land for Japanese Military Support," *Christian Science Monitor*, April 16, 1996, available at www.lexisnexis.com/academic; John F. Harris and Kevin Sullivan, "U.S., Japan Update Alliance and Upgrade Role for Tokyo," *Washington Post*, April 17, 1996, at www.lexisnexis.com/academic; Mary Jordan and Kevin Sullivan, "For Clinton in Japan, Accord and Smiles; Military Pact Is Major Shift for Alliance; In Major Shift, Japan Reconsiders Military Responsibility," *Washington Post*, April 19, 1996, available at www.lexisnexis.com/academic; and Patrick E. Tyler, "China Cautions U.S. and Japan on Security Pact," *New York Time*, April 19, 1996, available at www.lexisnexis.com/academic.

11. See Robert E. Rubin and Jacob Weisberg, *In an Uncertain World: Tough Choices from Wall Street to Washington* (New York: Random House, 2001), especially chapters 1, 7–10.

12. Interview by author with senior official responsible for U.S. aid programs to Russia, who requested anonymity, Claremont, CA, October 2003.

13. James M. Goldgeier and Michael McFaul, *Power and Purpose: U.S. Policy toward Russia after the Cold War* (Washington, DC: Brookings Institution, 2003), 299.

14. Strobe Talbott, *The Russia Hand: A Memoir of Presidential Diplomacy* (New York: Random House, 2002), 211, quoted in Goldgeier and McFaul, 351, n. 28.

15. Goldgeier and McFaul, *Power and Purpose*, 336–54.

16. Office of the Coordinator of U.S. Assistance to Europe and Eurasia, *U.S. Government Assistance to and Cooperative Activities with Eurasia, FY 2002 Annual Report* (Washington, DC: Department of State, 2002), quoted in Goldgeier and McFaul, *Power and Purpose*, 344–45, Table 14.1.

17. For a clear, brief summary of these programs, see Goldgeier and McFaul, *Power and Purpose*, 108–11.

18. On the transmission of expertise and philosophy, see Goldgeier and McFaul, *Power and Purpose*, especially 351–52 and 361–65.

19. Conversation with Dennis Ross, Claremont, CA, May 2004.

20. See Richard N. Haass, "The Squandered Presidency," *Foreign Affairs* 79, no. 3 (May/June 2000), available at http://web23.epnet.com; William G. Hyland, *Clinton's World: Remaking American Foreign Policy* (Westport, CT: Praeger, 1999); and Samuel R. Berger, "A Foreign Policy for the Global Age," *Foreign Affairs* 79, no. 6 (November/December 2000), 22–41.

21. Anthony Lake, "Defining Missions, Setting Deadlines: Meeting New Security Challenges in the Post–Cold War World," remarks at George Washington University, Washington, DC, March 6, 1996, White House Press Releases (Washington, DC: Office of the Press Secretary, March 7, 1996), cited in Josef Joffe, "Clinton's World: Purpose, Policy, and Weltanschauung," *Washington Quarterly* 23, no. 1 (Winter 2001), available at http://web2.epnet.com, 4.

22. Ibid.

23. President Bill Clinton, "Address to the German Assembly, September 22, 1997," U.S. Information Agency, U.S. Information and Texts, no 0381, September 25, 1997, 3, quoted in Joffe, "Clinton's World."

24. President Bill Clinton, Remarks at a Freedom House Breakfast, October 6, 1995, *Public Papers of the Presidents: 1995*, vol. 2, 1544–51, available at www.gpo.gov/nara/pubpaps/srchpaps. Although Clinton could not know who his successor would be, or even whether he would be reelected in 1996, his remarks show the overlap between his views of the post–Cold War paradigm and those of George W. Bush. For example: "Throughout what we now call the American century, Republicans and Democrats disagreed on specific policies, often heatedly from time to time, but we have always agreed on the need for American leadership in the cause of democracy, freedom, security, and prosperity. . . . And let me say one other thing. We have tried to make it a constant refrain that while we seek to engage all countries on terms of goodwill, we must continue to stand up for the values that we believe make life worth living. . . . We must continue to stand up for the proposition that all people, without regard to their nationality, their race, their ethnic group, their religion, or their gender, should have a chance to make the most of their own lives, to taste both freedom and opportunity." His remarks also spelled out the differences to come: "Unilateralism in the world that we live in is not a viable option. When our vital interests are at stake, of course, we might have to act alone. But we need the wisdom to work with the United Nations and to pay our bills. We need the flexibility to build coalitions that spread the risk and responsibility and the cost of leadership, as President Bush did in Desert Storm and we did in Haiti. If the past 50 years have taught us anything, it is that the United States has a unique responsibility and a unique ability to be a force for peace and progress around the world, while building coalitions of people that can work together in genuine partnership."

25. Hyland, *Clinton's World*, 25.

26. Richard Clarke praised the Clinton administration for the measures it took, at his instigation, to counter the threat from Osama bin Laden and al-Qaeda. He criticized the Bush II administration severely for failing to follow the Clinton administration's example. But even Clark had to admit that the Clinton administration's response was inadequate. "Bill Clinton . . . identified terrorism as the major post–Cold War threat and acted to improve our counterterrorism capabilities . . . but who, weakened by continued political attack, could not get the CIA, the Pentagon, and FBI to act sufficiently to deal with the threat. . . ." Richard A. Clarke, *Against All Enemies: Inside America's War on Terror* (New York: Free Press, 2003), ix; see also, 91–99. See also, Daniel Benjamin and Steven Simon, *The Age of Sacred Terror* (New York: Random House, 2002), 295. In February 2005, the National Security Archive at George Washington University published a memorandum from Clarke to Condoleezza Rice on January 25, 2001 urging the new administration to take action against al-Qaeda. It and an earlier Clarke memorandum on dealing with terrorism are available at www2.gwu.edu/~nsarchiv/NSAEBB/NSAEBB147/index.htm.

5. George W. Bush and the World

1. Glenn Kessler, "U.S. Has Shifting Script on North Korea," *Washington Post*, December 6, 2003, available at www.washingtonpost.com.

2. See Bill Keller, "Reagan's Son: The Radical Presidency of George W. Bush," *New York Times Magazine*, January 26, 2003, available at www.nytimes.com.

3. See Steven R. Weisman, "Division in Past Bush White House Echoes in Current Struggles," *New York Times*, November 24, 2002, available at www.nytimes.com.

4. See in particular remarks by Larry Wilkerson, a retired Army officer who served as Colin Powell's chief of staff in the first Bush administration from 2002 to 2005, at the New American Foundation American Strategy Policy Forum, October 19, 2005, available at www.TheWashingtonNote.com. A shorter version of his remarks, "The White House Cabal," appeared in the *Los Angeles Times*, October 25, 2005, available at www.latimes.com.

5. While a member of Congress, "Cheney . . . voted with the ideologues—against Head Start education funding, against government funding for abortion, against environmental legislation. On some issues, such as gun control, funding for AIDS research, sanctions against South Africa's apartheid government, and aiding the anti-communist rebels in Nicaragua, Cheney voted to the right of many of his party's staunchest conservatives. He backed the defense buildup, production of the multiwarhead MX missile, a newer generation of chemical weapons, and the Strategic Defense Initiative." Matthew Vita and Dan Morgan, "A Hard-Liner with a Soft Touch; On the Rise in House GOP, Cheney Bridged Competing Factions," *Washington Post*, August 5, 2000, available at www.washingtonpost.com.

6. See "All in the Family," *60 Minutes*, September 19, 2003, available at www.cbsnews.com/sections/60minutes. See also Center for Public Integrity, "Windfalls of War: U.S. Contractors in Iraq and Afghanistan," available at www.publicintegrity.gov.

7. See especially, George P. Shultz, *Turmoil and Triumph: My Years as Secretary of State* (New York: Scribner's, 1993).

8. For insight into the lessons that Rumsfeld learned in politics and business, see Donald Rumsfeld, "Rumsfeld's Rules" (December 1, 1974; copyright 1980; revised February 20, 2001), available at www.library.villinova.edu/vbl/bweb/rumsfeldsrules.pdf.

9. See especially, "Report to Congress of the Commission to Assess the Ballistic Missile Threat to the United States," July 15, 1998, available in the CA Public Affairs Collection, available at www.cqpress.com.

10. According to the senior military correspondent for Knight Ridder Newspapers, Joseph L. Galloway, Rumsfeld began his tenure at the Pentagon by trying to shrink the U.S. Army from ten active-duty divisions to eight, and the Army National Guard from eight divisions to four. "In the first part of 2001, the office of the secretary of defense firmly believed that the United States was beginning a 20-year strategic pause, a welcome breathing space that could be used to transform (read: downsize) the Army and gain billions in savings on personnel that would be spent building a strategic missile defense." Galloway, "Defense Mechanisms," *Washington Post Book World*, January 11, 2004, p. 4.

11. Colin L. Powell with Joseph E. Persico, *My American Journey* (New York: Random House, 1995).

12. Weinberger's "rules" about the use of force are these: U.S. forces should be engaged in combat overseas only if vital national interests are at stake; the decision to commit troops should be done "wholeheartedly, and with the intention of winning"; political and military objectives should be clearly defined, and there should be precise knowledge of how to obtain those objectives; there should be "some reasonable assurance" that the American people and Congress will support the intervention; and the use of force should be the last resort. See Caspar Weinberger, *Fighting for Peace: Seven Critical Years in the Pentagon* (New York: Warner Books, 1990), 441–42. In a 1992 article, while denying that they existed, Colin Powell nonetheless gave some very firm rules for the use of force. See Powell, "U.S. Forces: Challenges Ahead; Enormous Power, Sobering Responsibility," *Foreign Affairs* 71, no. 5 (Winter 1992/1993), available at www.lexisnexis/academic.com.

13. Nicholas Lemann, "Without a Doubt: Has Condoleezza Rice Changed George Bush or Has He Changed Her?" *New Yorker*, October 14 and 21, 2002, pp. 164–65.

14. See Zalmay M. Khalilzad and Paul Wolfowitz, "Overthrow Him," *Weekly Standard*, December 1, 1997, available at www.lexisnexis/academic.com. Khalilzad worked on the Cheney/Wolfowitz national strategy document during the first Bush administration, and went to the government-funded think tank, The Rand Corporation, in Santa Monica, California, when the administration lost the 1992 election. At Rand, Khalilzad edited and wrote a number of studies working out the details of the Cheney/Wolfowitz strategy of global primacy. Khalilzad, an Afghan-American, was appointed to the National Security Council at the beginning of the Bush administration, assigned special responsibilities for coordinating Afghanistan's transition to democracy during the war against the Taliban, and then named ambassador to Kabul, and, later, to Baghdad.

15. "Though Rice and Bush would appear to be an unlikely pair, the common ground between them encompasses religious faith and football fandom and a sardonic sense of humor; more broadly, an outsider-inside-the establishment feeling and a tendency to see life in terms of good guys and bad guys; even more broadly, a complete absence of self-doubt." Lemann, "Without a Doubt," 176. Perhaps Lemann's most telling observation was that Rice was someone who had been brought up to believe nothing was impossible; Bush was someone raised to think everything was possible.

16. Bill Keller, "The Sunshine Warrior," *New York Times Magazine*, September 22, 2002, available at www.nytimes.com, accessed October 1, 2002.

17. For an insightful autobiographical sketch, see "Deputy Secretary Paul Wolfowitz, Interview with James Fallows," *Atlantic Monthly*, January 2, 2002, available at www.defenselink.mil, "Transcripts" section.

18. Testimony before the U.S. House of Representatives National Security Committee, reprinted by the Project for the New American Century," September 18, 1998,
available at www.newamericancentury.org/iraqsep1998.htm.

19. For insight into Perle's style, see the report by the Study Group on a New Israeli
Strategy Toward 2000, sponsored by the Institute for Advanced Strategic and Political
Studies, "A Clean Break: A New Strategy for Securing the Realm" (Washington, DC,
July 7, 1996). Douglas Feith was one of the participants in the study group. Among
other things, the report recommended that Israel support efforts by Jordan "to redefine
Iraq," apparently including the creation of a constitutional monarchy in Iraq once again
under a Hashemite king.

20. Testimony, September 18, 1998, available at www.newamericancentury.org/
iraqsep1898.htm.

21. The two men met when both worked at the Pentagon for Secretary of Defense
Caspar Weinberger, Armitage as assistant secretary of defense for international security
affairs, and Powell as Weinberger's military assistant. Both rose extremely early and
were ahead of everyone else by the time the others started their work days. Bob Woodward quoted Powell as saying of Armitage: "I would trust him with my life, my children, my reputation, everything I have." Woodward, *Bush at War* (New York: Simon &
Schuster, 2002), 11.

22. "United States objectives should be maintaining and as necessary strengthening deterrence, and eliminating through peaceful means the military threat posed by
North Korean nuclear, chemical, biological and conventional weapons and missiles. . . .
Washington should table an offer that meets Pyongyang's legitimate economic, security, and political concerns. This would allow the United States to seize the diplomatic
initiative as well as the moral and political high ground. It would also strengthen the
ability to build a coalition if North Korea does not cooperate." Richard L. Armitage,
"A Comprehensive Approach to North Korea," Strategic Forum, no. 159 (Washington,
DC: National Defense University, March 1999), available at http://nuw.ndu.edu/inss/
strforum/forum159.html.

23. "With a slim congressional majority, Bush would have been expected to seek
genuine compromise—under the old rules. But Washington has become so partisan
and Bush [was] so determined to push through a domestic program based almost entirely on tax cuts for the wealthy that a remarkably radical program [was] winning despite the odds against it and lukewarm public support." E. J. Dionne, Jr., "The New
Rules of Politics," *Washington Post*, May 30, 2003, p. A23.

24. The Bush administration focused its opposition to the ICC on European countries, asking them bilaterally never to bring charges against Americans there, threatening to end U.S. participation in UN peacekeeping activities around the world if European
governments refused to waive granting Americans immunity from prosecution, and holding the threat of the loss of U.S. military aid over countries outside NATO and other U.S.
alliances if they did not cooperate. See Peter Slevin, "U.S. Presses Allies on War Court
Crimes," *Washington Post*, August 27, 2002, available at www.washingtonpost.com.

25. Patrick E. Tyler, "U.S. Strategy Plan Calls for Insuring No Rivals Develop,"
New York Times, March 8, 1992, p. 1.

26. Ibid.

27. See various writings by Zalmay M. Khalilzad, who served in the Cheney Defense Department during Bush I and initially held a senior post on the National Security Council during Bush II, especially, Khalilzad, *From Containment to Global Lead-*

ership? America and the World after the Cold War (Santa Monica, CA: Rand Corporation, 1995); and Khalilzad and Ian O. Lesser, eds., *Sources of Conflict in the 21st Century: Regional Futures and U.S. Strategy* (Santa Monica, CA: Rand Corporation, 1998). Khalilzad would subsequently be appointed ambassador to Afghanistan after the American invasion and ouster of the Taliban and then ambassador to occupied Iraq. See also, Paul Wolfowitz, "Statement before the House National Security Committee," in Project for the New American Century, Memorandum to Opinion Leaders, September 18, 1998, and Executive Summary of the Report of the Commission to Assess the Ballistic Missile Threat to the United States (Rumsfeld Commission) July 15, 1998, Pursuant to Public Law 201, 104th Congress, executive summary, available at www.fas.org; Charles Krauthammer, "The Bush Doctrine; ABM, Kyoto, and the New American Unilateralism," *Weekly Standard*, June 4, 2001, available at www.lexisnexis/academic.com.

28. George W. Bush, Inaugural Address, January 20, 2005, available at www.cnn .com/2005/ALLPOLITICS/01/20/bush.transcript.

29. Ron Suskind, "Without a Doubt," *New York Times Magazine*, October 17, 2004, available at www.nytimes.com/2004/10/17/magazine/17BUSH.html.

30. For a good summary of the arguments that Bush sought to undo Franklin Roosevelt's New Deal, see Paul Krugman, "Spearing the Beast," February 8, 2005, available at www.nytimes.com/2005/02/08/opinion/08krugman.html?hp.

31. See in particular, Nicholas Lemann, "The Next World Order," *New Yorker*, April 1, 2002, pp. 42–48; Tyler, "U.S. Strategy," *New York Times*, March 8, 1992, available at www.nytimes.com; Patrick E. Tyler, "Pentagon Drops Goal of Blocking New Superpowers," *New York Times,* May 24, 1992, available at www.nytimes.com.

32. "Wilson's historic achievement lies in his recognition that America cannot sustain major international engagements that are not justified by their moral faith. His downfall was in treating the tragedies of history as aberrations, or as due to the shortsightedness and the evil of individual leaders, and in his rejection of any objective basis for peace other than the force of public opinion and the spread of democratic institutions." Henry Kissinger, *Diplomacy* (New York: Simon & Schuster, 1994), 50.

33. Woodward, *Bush at War*, 73.

34. The amount of money involved in the sale of Iraqi petroleum under the UN-sponsored Oil-for-Food Program from 1996–2003 was huge: $64 billion. Tragically, the program turned out to be thoroughly corrupt. About two-thirds of the total could be traced as payment for food and supplies that were sent into Iraq. Under the Oil-for-Food Program, companies and individuals that were seen as "friendly" or amenable to bribery received contracts for Iraqi oil. The contracts were then sold on the open market, with the seller receiving a commission of from 15 to 50 cents a barrel and paying part of the commission to the Iraqi government. Companies willing to supply humanitarian goods under the program had to agree to overcharge by at least 10% and surrender part of the overage for the private use of Saddam and other Iraqi officials. The suppliers were allowed to keep what was left. The governments of China, France, and Russia benefited more than any others. They were also the most active in seeking an end to sanctions against Iraq. American oil companies paid slightly more than half the kickbacks that went to Saddam. The companies included Exxon, Mobil, ChevronTexaco, and El Paso Corporation. See Paul A. Volcker, chairman, *Independent Inquiry into the United Nations Oil-For-Food Programme*, especially the Third Interim Report, August 8, 2005, available at www.iic-offp.org. Charles Duelfer, who succeeded David Kay as head of

the task force searching for Iraq's weapons of mass destruction after the overthrow of Saddam, observed that the Oil-for-Food Program saved the Iraqi economy from a "terminal decline" caused by the sanctions. See Charles Duelfer, *Comprehensive Report of the Special Adviser to the Director of Central Intelligence on Iraq's Weapons of Mass Destruction*, September 30, 2004, available at www.cia.gov/cia/reports/iraq_wmd_ 2004. Duelfer also observed that Saddam believed he would soon be able to end the sanctions regime and intended to rebuild his weapons of mass destruction with a focus on Iran, but including nuclear as well as chemical and biological weapons. See aso BBC News, "Oil-for-Food Chief 'Took Bribes,'" August 8, 2005, at http://newsvote.bbc .co.uk; Reuters, "Oil-for-Food Investigation Comes Down Hard on UN," *International Herald Tribune*, September 7, 2005, at www.iht.com; and a special report by the French newspaper, *Le Monde*, "Saddam Hussein récompensait 'ses amis' en barils de pétrole [Saddam Hussein paid his 'friends' in barrels of oil]," *Le Monde*, January 27, 2004, at www.lemonde.fr.

35. The National Security Archive at George Washington University has put together an extremely useful collection of declassified and unclassified reports about Iraq's weapons programs. See www.gwu.edu/~nsarchiv/NSAEBB/NSAEBB80/#docs.

36. This is the argument of Ivo Daalder and James Lindsay in *America Unbound: The Bush Revolution in Foreign Policy* (Washington, DC: Brookings Institution Press, 2003).

37. A former senior adviser to the State Department, David Phillips, who was also involved closely in the Future of Iraq project, puts the decision eight months later, at a August 21, 2002, gathering at the president's home in Crawford, Texas, of Bush, Cheney, Rice, Joint Chiefs chairman General Richard Myers, and White House Chief of Staff, Andrew Card. See David L. Phillips, *Losing Iraq: Inside the Postwar Reconstruction Fiasco* (Boulder, CO: Westview Press, 2005), 42.

38. David E. Sanger, "A Nation Challenged: The Debate; U.S. Goal Seems Clear, and the Team Complete," *New York Times*, February 13, 2002, available at www .nytimes.com. Sanger wrote: "Between now and May, Mr. Bush's team plans to create what amounts to an inspection crisis—demanding that Iraq admit into the country the nuclear inspectors it ousted in 1998. Mr. Bush's aides fully expect that Mr. Hussein will refuse outright or feign cooperation in the hope of dragging out the process. Mr. Bush's plan is to use either action as evidence that Iraq is hiding active weapons programs, and use its resistance to justify more forceful action. Whether that takes the form of direct military attack, support for internal rebellions, or other options 'is still up in the air,' a senior White House official said today."

39. Interview with Jacques Chirac, *New York Times*, September 8, 2002, available at www.nytimes.com. During an interview in early April 2002 with ITN television in Britain, Bush said flatly: "I made up my mind that Saddam needs to go." Interview with the United Kingdom's ITV Television Network, April 4, 2002, *Weekly Compilation of Presidential Documents*, available at http://frwebgate.access.gpo.gov.

40. "Remarks Announcing Bipartisan Agreement on a Joint Resolution to Authorize the Use of United States Armed Forces against Iraq," *Weekly Compilation of Presidential Documents*, October 2, 2002, available at http://frwebgate.access.gpo.gov.

41. See National Security Council, "The National Security Strategy of the United States of America," September 2002, available at www.whitehouse.gov/nsc/nss.html.

42. Ibid.

43. Ibid.

44. "We will not hesitate to act alone, if necessary, to exercise our right of self defense by acting preemptively against such terrorists, to prevent them from doing harm against our people and our country. . . . We must be prepared to stop rogue states and their terrorist clients before they are able to threaten or use weapons of mass destruction against the United States and our allies and friends." National Security Council, "National Security Strategy," September 2002, available at www.whitehouse.gov/nsc/nss.html.

45. For a brief and helpful survey of arguments about self-defense, see Steven Mudoch, "Preemptive War: Is It Legal?" *DC Bar*, January 2003, available at www.dcbar.org/for_lawyers/washington_lawyer/january_2003/war.cfm. See also, Michael N. Schmit, "International Law and the Use of Force: The *Jus ad Bellum*," *Connections* II, no. 3 (September 2003): 89–97.

46. National Security Council, National Security Strategy, 2002.

47. On U.S. intelligence about Iraqi weapons programs see the National Security Archive, George Washington University, at www.gwu.edu/~nsarchiv/news/20051013/index.htm.

48. Ibid. See also quote in Steven R. Weisman, "Pre-emption: Idea with a Lineage Whose Time Has Come," *New York Times*, March 23, 2003, available at www.nytimes.com.

49. Interview with Gerhard Schroeder, *New York Times*, September 4, 2002, available at www.nytimes.com.

50. The inspectors were to commence their work within forty-five days and to report to the Security Council not later than sixty days afterward. United Nations Security Council Resolution, S/RES/1441 (2002), adopted by the Security Council at its 4644th meeting on November 8, 2002, available at http://ods-dds-ny.un.org/doc/UNDOC/GEN/NO2/68s/26.

51. Tony Blair's view of the war—that it was the right thing to do—his determination to do it, and his hopes for European support, are well covered in two books: Philip Stevens, *Tony Blair: The Making of a World Leader* (New York: Viking Penguin, 2004), especially 104–12, 119–21, 187–237; and Peter Stothard, *Thirty Days: Tony Blair and the Test of History* (New York: HarperCollins, 2003), especially 86–96, 103–74.

52. Preparing to tour a dozen European and Middle Eastern states, Cheney summarized the reasons that the administration sought the overthrow of Saddam Hussein. "If you were to put together a list of states, clearly that's got to be the one we focus on. Not only do they have a robust set of programs to develop their own weapons of mass destruction; this is a place that's used it. And we know he drove the inspectors out three years ago, and we know he has been actively and aggressively doing everything he can to enhance his capabilities. He has in the past had some dealings with terrorists, clearly. Abu Nidal for a long time operated out of Baghdad. . . . I think if aggressive action is required, I would anticipate there would be the appropriate support for that, both from the American people and the international community." Quoted in Michael R. Gordon, "A Nation Challenged: The Vice President; Cheney Rejects Criticism by Allies over Stand on Iraq," *New York Times*, February 16, 2002, available at www.nytimes.com. Cheney also made clear that only the United States was capable of broadening the campaign against global terrorism to include nations such as Iran and Iraq, and that the administration would persist regardless of criticism and opposition.

53. Remarks by the vice president at the Veterans of Foreign Wars 103rd National Convention, August 26, 2002, available at www.whitehouse.gov/news/releases/2002/08/20020826.

54. Ibid.

55. The basis for the claim was information acquired eight years earlier when Saddam Hussein's son-in-law defected briefly before returning to Iraq where he was murdered. "That should serve as a reminder to all that we often learned more as a result of defections than we learned from the inspection regime itself. . . . A return of inspectors would provide no assurance whatsoever of his compliance with U.N. resolutions." Ibid.

56. Ibid.

57. For a fascinating discussion of argument from ignorance, see Douglas Walton, "The Appeal to Ignorance, or Argumentum ad Ignorantiam" (University of Winnipeg, 1999), available at io.uwinnipeg.ca/~walton/99ignorantiam.pdf. Aristotle identified it as a rhetorical tactic, and Locke advised it as a method of forcing opponents to accept an argument.

58. Rumsfeld, interview, *New York Times* October 12, 2001, available at www.defenselink.mil/news/Oct2001. See also, Rumsfeld interview with Bob Schieffer and Gloria Borger, *CBS Face the Nation*, February 24, 2002, available at www.defenselink.mil/news/Feb2002; Rumsfeld interview on Face the Nation, September 8, 2002, available at www.defenselink.mil/news/Sep2002; Rumsfeld, Media Roundtable with the BBC and Voice of America, September 13, 2002, available at www.defenselink.mil/news/Sep2002; Testimony to House Armed Services Committee, September 18, 2002. For perhaps the most emphatic of all these perorations, see his news conference of February 12, 2002, available at www.defenselink.mil/news/Feb2002; Rumsfeld, Press Conference at NATO Headquarters, Brussels, Belgium, June 6, 2002, available at www.defenselink.mil/news/Jun2002; News Briefing, Secretary Rumsfeld and General Richard Meyers, Chairman, Joint Chiefs of Staff, September 3, 2002, available at www.defenselink.mil/news/Sep2002; Media Roundtable with the BBC and Voice of America, September 13. 2002, available at www.defenselink.mil/news/Sep2002.

59. News conference, February 12, 2002, available at www.defenselink.mil/news/Feb2002.

60. Press conference at NATO Headquarters, Brussels, Belgium, June 6, 2002, available at www.defenselink.mil/news/Jun2002.

61. See www.iraqibodycount.net/database. For U.S. military deaths, see Glenn Kutler, "U.S. Military Fatalities in Iraq: A Two-Year Retrospective," *Orbis* 49, no. 3 (Summer 2005): 529–44, available at www.icasualties.org/oif/Kutler_2Year.htm. The official U.S. Department of Defense statistics on casualties are available at www.defenselink.mil/news/casualties.pdf.

62. See Michael Massing, "Iraq, the Press & the Election," *New York Review of Books* 51, no. 20 (December 16, 2004): 26.

63. See Jonathan Finer, "U.S.-Led Assault in N. Iraq Town Meets Little Insurgent Resistance," *Washington Post*, September 4, 2005, available at www.washingtonpost.com; Ellen Knickmeyer, "Insurgents Seize Key Town in Iraq", *Washington Post*, September 5, 2005, available at www.washingtonpost.com; Jonathan Finer, "U.S. Troops Cordon Part of Iraqi Town to Trap Insurgents: Rebels Have Fled Undetected in the Past," *Washington Post*, September 5, 2005, available at www.washingtonpost.com; Ellen Knickmeyer and Jonathan Finer, "Insurgents Assert Control over Town Near

Syrian Border," *Washington Post*, September 6, 2005, available at www.washington post.com; Maher al-Thanoon, "U.S. Fights in Northern Iraq as Charter Readied," Reuters, September 6, 2005, available at http://news.yahoo.com; Michael Moss, "As U.S. Tries to Secure an Iraqi Town, Insurgents Respond," *New York Times*, September 6, 2005, available at www.nytimes.com; Jonathan Finer, "With Death at Their Door, Few Leave Iraqi City: Civilians Urged to Flee Before U.S. Assault," *Washington Post*, September 7, 2005, available at www.washingtonpost.com; Craig S. Smith, "U.S. and Iraq Step Up Effort to Block Insurgents' Routes," *New York Times*, October 3, 2005, available at www.nytimes.com; "U.S. Launches Second Offensive In Western Iraq," Associated Press, October 4, 2005, available at www.nytimes.com; "U.S. Troops Begin New Offensive in W. Iraq," Associated Press, October 5, 2005, available at www.washingtonpost.com; Kirk Semple, "Roadside Bomb Kills 6 Marines during Offensive in Western Iraq," *New York Times*, October 8, 2005, available at www .nytimes.com; and Andrew Quinn, "U.S. Soldiers Kill 29 in Iraq Offensive," Reuters, October 7, 2005, available at www.news.yahoo.com.

64. See "Most of Baghdad without Power" and "Power Returning to Baghdad," October 14, 2005, available at http://cnn.worldnews.

65. See "3,663 Iraqis Killed in Past 6 Months," October 14, 2005, available at http://news.yahoo.com. According to the Associate Press these deaths occurred in war-related violence. See also, Robert F. Worth, "Attacks Kill 19 Iraqi Soldiers and Policemen," *New York Times*, September 4, 2005, available at www.nytimes.com; Robert F. Worth and Richard A. Oppel Jr., "At Least 20 Killed by Suicide Bombers in Baghdad," *New York Times*, September 15, 2005, available at www.nytimes.com; Ellen Knickmeyer, "Baghdad Toll Nears 200 as Insurgent Strikes Continue," *Washington Post*, September 16, 2005, available at www.washingtonpost.com; "Latest Iraq Blast Targets Shiite Mosque," Associated Press, September 16, 2005, available at www.washingtonpost.com; Jonathan Finer and Fred Barbash, "Five Soldiers Killed in Three Separate Iraq Incidents," *Washington Post*, September 20, 2005, available at www.washingtonpost.com; Richard A. Oppel Jr., and Sabrina Tavernise, "Attacks in Iraq Kill 9 Americans, including State Department Aide," *New York Times*, September 21, 2005, available at www.nytimes.com; Richard A. Oppel Jr., "Bus Stop Blast Kills 6 Iraqis; 3 G.I.'s Die in Other Attacks," *New York Times*, September 24, 2005, available at www.nytimes.com.

66. As many as 99 percent of voters in some Kurdish and Shiite provinces apparently voted. The turnout was so far beyond expectations based on international norms that it triggered an inquiry by the Iraqi Electoral Commission. The commission reported no irregularities. See Dexter Filkins, "Vote Totals under Inquiry in 12 Iraqi Provinces, Panel Says," *New York Times*, October 17, 2005, available at www.nytimes.com.

67. Articles 35(C) and 37(2).

68. Articles 4 and 9. The constitution is unusual also in its description of the nature and duties of Iraq's intelligence service.

69. Articles 2 and 3.

70. Remarks by and interview with Charles L. Pritchard at and after a meeting of the Pacific Council on International Policy, Los Angeles, California, November 14, 2003. Pritchard was the principal U.S. envoy in talks with North Korea until his resignation in April 2003. He resigned because despite having met twenty-five times with his North Korean counterpart, he was not allowed to serve as head of the U.S. delegation to the six-party talks in Beijing; the unilateralists in the administration apparently feared that

his appointment would send too soft a signal to Pyongyang and wanted the control of North Korea policy in the National Security Council and Defense Department.

71. Ibid.

72. David E. Sanger, "It's North Korea. Go Figure," *New York Times*, March 11, 2001, available at www.lexisnexis/academic.com.

73. For an insightful analysis of China's perspective, see Howard M. Krawitz, *Resolving Korea's Nuclear Crisis: Tough Choices for China* Strategic Forum, no. 201 (Washington, DC: Institute for Strategic Studies, National Defense University, August 2003).

74. See Larry A. Niksch, "North Korea's Nuclear Weapons Program," CRS Issue Brief for Congress, updated April 5, 2002, published by the Congressional Research Service, The Library of Congress, Washington, DC.

75. Pritchard, Pacific Council remarks, 2003.

76. Ibid.

77. Glenn Kessler, "U.S. Has Shifting Script on North Korea," *Washington Post*, December 6, 2003, available at www.washingtonpost.com.

78. Michael R. Gordon, "U.S. Readies Plan to Raise Pressure on North Koreans," *New York Times*, December 30, 2002, available at www.nytimes.com.

79. Ashton Carter, assistant secretary of defense for international security policy in the Clinton administration, recommended both the noninvasion statement and the offer to discuss how to dismantle nuclear programs, which implied American economic aid along the lines of "Nunn-Lugar" law that gave economic aid to Russia to help it protect and dispose of nuclear materials in his statement to the Senate Foreign Relations Committee on February 4, 2003. See the text of his statement: "Three Crises with North Korea," and his testimony and responses to questions from committee members, "North Korea Update," available at www.lexisnexis.congressional.

80. Glenn Kessler, "N. Korea Displays 'Nuclear Deterrent,' " *Washington Post*, January 11, 2004, p. A15.

81. The text of the agreement was made available by the Associated Press on September 19, 2005, and may be found at www.nytimes.com/aponline/international/AP-Koreas-Nuclear-Text.html.

82. Joseph Kahn and David E. Sanger, "U.S.-Korean Deal Leaves Key Points Open," *New York Times*, September 20, 2005, available at www.nytimes.com.

83. Ibid.

84. Ibid.

85. Ibid.

86. Ibid. See also Alexa Olesen, "North Korea Vows Not to Give Up Nuke Program," Associated Press, September 16, 2005, available at news.yahoo.com/s/ap/20050916/ap_on_re_as/koreas_nuclear; Lindsay Beck and Jack Kim, "It's Make or Break for North Korea Talks," Reuters, September 16, 2005, available at news.yahoo.com/s/nm/220050916/wl_nc/korea_north; Joseph Kahn, "China Proposes a Deal to End North Korean Nuclear Standoff," *New York Times*, September 17, 2005, available at www.nytimes.com; Joseph Kahn, "North Korea Says It Will Drop Nuclear Efforts for Aid Program," *New York Times*, September 19, 2005, available at www.nytimes.com; Glenn Kessler and Edward Cody, "N. Korea, U.S. Gave Ground to Make Deal," *Washington Post*, September 20, 2005, available at www.washingtonpost.com; Glenn Kessler, "Nations Seek to Hold North Korea to Text of Agreement," *Washington Post*, September 21, 2005, available at www.washingtonpost.com.

87. Joel Brinkley, "Iranian Leader Refuses to End Nuclear Effort," *New York Times*, September 18, 2005, available at www.nytimes.com; and Nazila Fathi and David E. Sanger, "Iran Warns against Referral of Nuclear Issue to the U.N.," *New York Times*, September 21, 2005, available at www.nytimes.com. For further information about the Iranian position, see Paul Taylor, "Europeans Plead with Iran to Reconsider Proposals," Reuters, September 15, 2005, available at new.yahoo.com/s/nm/20050915/wl/nm/ nuclear_iran; Dafna Linzer and Colum Lynch, "U.S. Agenda on Iran Lacking Key Support: Push to Curb Nuclear Program Set Back," *Washington Post*, September 16, 2005, available at www.wahingtonpost.com.

88. David E. Sanger, "Yes, Parallel Tracks to North, But Parallel Tracks Don't Meet," *Washington Post*, September 20, 2005, available at www.washingtonpost.com.

89. Fathi and Sanger, "Iran Warns against Referral of Nuclear Issue."

90. One famous example of a "lesson" of this kind is Vice President Cheney's comment when the budget deficit began to grow: "Reagan proved deficits don't matter." I took the quote from an interview of Ron Suskind, author of *The Price of Loyalty: George W. Bush, the White House, and the Education of Paul O'Neill* (New York: Simon & Schuster, 2004). Suskind was quoting O'Neill on "The News Hour with Jim Lehrer," during an interview with Ray Suarez, available at www.pbs.org/newshour/bb/ politics/jan-june04/loyalty_01-15.html.

91. Text of the Mitchell Plan available at www.yale.edu/lawweb/avalon/mideast/ mitchell_plan. Text of the Tenet Plan is available at www.yale.edu/lawweb/avalon/ mideast/mid023.

92. Jane Perlez, "Taking a Breather on the Mideast," *New York Times*, July 5, 2001, available at www.nytimes.com.

93. The foreign policy adviser to President Hosni Mubarak of Egypt, Osama el-Baz, reportedly told American officials that the administration's "policy of inaction" was damaging American vital interests, alienating Arab public opinion, and enhancing the appeal of extremists in moderate Arab countries. According to *New York Times* reporter, Serge Schemann, Prince Abdullah sent Prince Bandar al Sultan, former ambassador to Washington, to Condoleezza Rice with a warning that the violence had brought U.S.-Saudi relations to a crossroads. Bush quickly replied to the Saudis that the solution lay in establishing a Palestinian state. Jane Perlez, "Warning on Mideast Inaction," *New York Times*, August 19, 2001, available at www.nytimes.com; Serge Schemann, "Quickly, a Saudi Peace Idea Gains Momentum in Mideast," March 3, 2002, available at www.nytimes.com.

94. See "A Performance-Based Roadmap to a Permanent Two-State Solution to the Israeli-Palestinian Conflict," Press Statement, Office of the Spokesman, Washington, DC, April 30, 2003, available at www.state.gov/r/pa/prs/ps/2003/20062.htm.

95. The operative passages of Bush's speech made clear the administration's decision to try to force democracy on the Palestinians, regardless of their views: "I call on the Palestinian people to elect new leaders, leaders not compromised by terror. I call upon them to build a practicing democracy based on tolerance and liberty. If the Palestinian people actively pursue these goals, America and the world will actively support their efforts. If the Palestinian people meet these goals, they will be able to reach agreement with Israel and Egypt and Jordan on security and other arrangements for independence." The administration's new policy insisted not just on democratization but a certain, very specific kind of democratization as the main precondition for U.S. support for independence. All this was necessary not to achieve independence but provisional sovereignty over some undefined part of the disputed territories. "And when the

Palestinian people have new leaders, new institutions, and new security arrangements with their neighbors, the United States of America will support the creation of a Palestinian state whose borders and certain aspects of its sovereignty will be provisional until resolved as part of a final settlement in the Middle East." The president left no doubt as to the scope and fundamental nature of the reforms: "True reform will require *entirely* new political and economic institutions, based on democracy, market economics and action against terrorism." Palestinian finances must become transparent and subject to independent auditing, the rule of law must be established based on a "truly independent judiciary," Palestinian authorities must stop inciting violence, denounce "homicide bombings," take all possible steps to prevent terrorism. All of this and a final peace settlement could be accomplished within three years. The president asked Israel to respond only as the Palestinians displayed "real performance on security and reform." Just who would define "real progress," and how its achievement would be judged was left unspecified. See "President Calls for New Palestinian Leadership," June 24, 2002 available at www.whitehouse.gov/news/releases/2002/06/print/20020624-3.

96. Richard L. Armitage, Deputy Secretary of State, Interview on Egypt TV with Mohamed Satouli, Washington, DC, January 22, 2004, available at www.state.gov/s/d/rm/28439.

97. Interviews with American intelligence analysts. See also James Bennet, "Hopes Are Modest as Israelis and Arabs Await Bush Plan," *New York Times*, October 12, 2001, available at www.nytimes.com.

98. "The Likud Plan proposed settling Jews in areas of Arab habitation and for numerous settlement points as well as large urban concentrations in three principal areas—a north-south axis running from the Golan through the Jordan Valley and down the east coast of Sinai—a widened corridor around Jerusalem; and—the populated western slopes of the Samarian heartland of the West Bank. The last wedge of Jewish settlement was of prime concern to Likud strategists, particularly Sharon, who was intent upon establishing Israeli settlements to separate the large blocs of Arab population on either side of the Green Line north of Tel Aviv." See "Israeli Settlements in the Occupied Territories: A Guide," Special Report of the Foundation for Middle East Peace, March 2002, available at www.fmep.org. The study describes Sharon's and Likud's intentions as an effort "to preempt the possibility of a territorial division of the land and to strike at the basis of potential Palestinian sovereignty by destroying the continuity of Palestinian-controlled territory. . . ."

99. The Foundation for Middle East Peace (FMEP) maintains useful maps and summaries of Israeli settler population totals for the West Bank and Gaza. See FMEP home page, available at www.fmep.org/charts.

100. James Bennet, "Israelis Conclude that Arafat Has Tightened Grip on Power," June 11, 2002, available at www.nytimes.com.

101. See Middle East Partnership Initiative home page, available at http://mepi.state.gov.

102. Ibid.

103. "A Performance-Based Roadmap to a Permanent Two-State Solution to the Israeli-Palestinian Conflict," April 30, 2003, available at www.state.gov/r/pa/prs/ps/2003.

104. Connie Bruck, "Back Roads: How Serious Is the Bush Administration about Creating a Palestinian State?" *New Yorker*, December 15, 2003, p. 96. The article also

gives details about the role of Eliot Abrams in shaping the administration's policy toward the Israeli-Palestinian conflict.

105. "Israel's Road Map Reservations, May 27, 2003, *Haaretz*, available at www .haaretz.com/hasen/objects/pages/PrintArticleEn.jhtml?itemNo=297230. During the mediation at Camp David by Bill Clinton the two sides had essentially agreed on a solution to the refugee problem. See chapters 3–4.

106. Alissa Rubin, "'Map' of Uncharted Territory," *Los Angeles Times*, June 8, 2003, available at www.latimes.com.

107. Bruck, "Back Roads," 93.

108. Ariel Sharon, "Prime Minister's Speech at the Herzilya Conference," *Haaretz*, accessed December 22, 2003, available at www.haaretz.com.

109. Quoted in James Bennet, "Overnight, a Towering Divide Rises in Jerusalem," January 12, 2004, *Washington Post*, available at www.washingtonpost.com.

110. Texts of the two initiatives are available at www.fmep.org.

111. "Sharon, Army at Odds over Palestinians," Associated Press, October 30, 2003, available at www.nytimes.com.

112. Quoted in Greg Myre, "Israel's Chief of Staff Denounces Policies against Palestinians," October 20, 2003, *New York Times*, available at www.nytimes.com.

113. Molly Moore, "Ex-Security Chiefs Turn on Sharon," November 15, 2003, *Washington Post*, available at www.washingtonpost.com.

114. Rumors circulated for months before anything authoritative appeared in public. Among the earliest stories are: "Sharon Hints at Gaza Pullout," *New York Times*, January 14, 2004; and Greg Myre, "Peace Gestures by Palestinians and Israelis," *New York Times*, April 1, 2004, both available at www.lexisnexis/academic.com.

115. See Ramit Plushnick-Masti, "Israeli Cabinet OKs Settlement Withdrawal," Associated Press, February 20, 2005, available at www.washingtonpost.com.

116. See Central Intelligence Agency, *The World Factbook*, available at www.cia .gov/cia/publications/factbook/geos/gz.html#Econ. The figures for Gaza on the CIA website are 2003 estimates for unemployment and per capita income, and a 2004 estimate for the percentage of people living below the poverty line. Comparable figures for the Palestinians on the West Bank are $800 per capita income (2003 estimate), 27.2 percent unemployment (a 2004 estimate that includes Gaza), and 59 percent of the people living below the poverty line. The CIA estimates that 100,000 of 125,000 Palestinians who once worked in Israel have lost their jobs as a result of the closure of Israel's borders. The website was last updated on August 30, 2005.

117. See "Hamas Vows to Continue Attacks on Israel," Associated Press, August 20, 2005, available at www.nytimes.com.; Glenn Kessler, "If Hamas Participates, Sharon Says Israel Won't Aid Palestinian Elections," *Washington Post*, September 17, 2005, available at www.washingtonpost.com; Joel Brinkley, "Israel to Disrupt Palestinian Vote if Hamas Runs," *New York Times*, September 17, 2005, available at www .nytimes.com; and Nidal al-Mughrabi, "Hamas Gunmen Defy Abbas with Rare Show of Force," Reuters, September 18, 2005, available at news.yahoo.com/s/nm/10050918/ wl_nm/mideast_hamas. By January 2006, news reports from Jerusalem indicated that Sharon intended to negotiate Israel's eastern border, not with the Palestinians but with the United States, and to carry out another unilateral withdrawal, this time from the West Bank. See Amnon Danker and Ben Caspit, "Alternative to Road Map," *Ma'ariv*, January 2, 2006 at http://groups.yahoo.com/group/IPCRI-News-Service.

6. Boldness and Blindness

1. Michael Dibdin, *Medusa* (New York: Pantheon Books, 2003), 65.

2. In the Balkans, for example, Western Europeans contributed a major portion of the combatant forces and most of the postwar occupation forces. Their presence posed a serious problem for any insurgents: serious opposition meant the indefinite exclusion of Serbia from the European Union, a daunting prospect for any dissident Serbs.

3. In light of what had happened in Iraq, news reports in early 2005 about the U.S. Army's plans for the future were not reassuring. The Army apparently planned to rely even more on advanced technology at great cost and with dubious relevance to suppressing ethnic and religious conflicts in poor countries. See Tim Weiner, "An Army Program to Build a High-Tech Force Hits Cost Snags," *New York Times*, March 28, 2005, available at www.nytimes.com. See also Fred Kaplan "The Army, Faced with Its Limits," *New York Times*, January 1, 2006, at www.nytimes.com.

4. As the occupation entered its third year, the U.S. commander in Iraq, John Abizaid, warned that foreign fighters constituted an increasingly large portion of the resistance, which he estimated at 12,000 to 20,000 "hard-core insurgents." See Robert F. Worth and Christine Hauser, "At Least 10 Killed in Iraq as Concern Mounts about Unrest," *New York Times*, March 28, 2005, available at www.nytimes.com.

5. George W. Bush, State of the Union Address, United States Capital, Washington, D.C., January 20, 2004, available at www.whitehouse.gov/news/releases/2004.

6. Sandra Mackey, "Iraq's Dangerous Identity Crisis: Turning Over Power to People Who Lack a Sense of National Unity Won't Work," *Los Angeles Times*, November 16, 2003, available at www.losangelestimes.com. See also Amy Chua and Jed Rubenfeld, "Never Underestimate the Power of Ethnicity in Iraq," *Washington Post*, January 4, 2004, p. B4.

7. See Joseph Curl, "White House Mulls New Iraq Plan," *Washington Times*, November 14, 2003, available at www.washingtontimes.com.

8. For exact casualty figures, see http://icasualties.org/oil_a/CasualtyTrends.htm. See also Dexter Filkins, "Some Iraq Areas Unsafe for Vote, U.S. General Says," *New York Times*, January 7, 2005, available at www.nytimes.com. See also Eric Schmitt and Thom Shanker, "Rumsfeld Seeks Broad Review of Iraq Policy," *New York Times*, January 7, 2005, available at www.nytimes.com. The article by Schmitt and Shanker focused on the poor performance of Iraqi military forces.

9. See Edward Wong, "Occupation Politics; Direct Election of Iraq Assembly Pushed by Cleric," *New York Times*, January 12, 2004, available at www.nytimes.com.

10. Quoted in Steven R. Weisman, "Bush Team Revising Plans for Granting Self-Rule to Iraqis," *New York Times*, January 13, 2004, available at www.nytimes.com.

11. Ibid.

12. See Patrick Cockburn, "Shia and Kurds Poised to Dominate Iraqi Government," *The Independent*, February 8, 2005, available at http://news.independent.co.uk/world/middle_east/story.jsp?story=608872.

13. E.J. Dionne, "An Offer of Help on Iraq," *Washington Post*, April 2, 2004, available at www.washingtonpost.com.

14. A very helpful insider account of the Future of Iraq Project may be found in David L. Phillips, *Losing Iraq Inside the Postwar Reconstruction Fiasco* (Boulder, CO: Westview Press, 2005). The National Security Archive at George Washington University has put together a number of official U.S. government documents about the Future of Iraq Pro-

ject. They are available at www.gwu.edu/~nsarchiv/NSAEBB/NSAEBB163/. See also, Frontline, "Truth, War, and Consequences," Interview with Richard Perle, October 9, 2003, available at www.pbs.org/wgbh/pages/frontline/shows/truth/interviews/perle.html.

15. One of the most harmful oversights was the inadequacy of postwar management. According to the special inspector general for Iraq reconstruction, Stuart Bowen, there were "no comprehensive policy or regulatory guidelines" for choosing people who would manage the reconstruction of Iraq. See also George Packer, *Assassins' Gate: America in Iraq* (New York: Farrar, Straus, and Giroux, 2005).

16. See Rowan Scarborough, "U.S. Rushed Post-Saddam Planning," *Washington Times*, September 3, 2003, available at www.washingtontimes.com. According to David Phillips, an American analyst involved in postwar planning, of the 1,147 Americans hired by the Coalition Provisional Authority, only 34 were Foreign Service officers. Phillips, *Losing Iraq*, 163.

17. The findings of a Pentagon study portrayed Iraq's oil industry as so badly damaged that its production capacity had fallen by more than 25 percent. It would be unable to pay for Iraq's reconstruction for years. Amy Meyers Jaffe, an oil expert and U.S. government consultant at the James A. Baker III Institute for Public Policy in Houston, Texas, told reporters that the Institute's December 2002 study of Iraq's oil industry predicted that "oil revenues would not be enough and that the expenses of reconstruction would be huge." Even without war damage, the Baker Institute study predicted annual revenues of $10 billion to $12 billion. By contrast, Wolfowitz told the Congress that "we are dealing with a country that can really finance its own reconstruction." To the House Appropriations Committee on March 27, 2003, Wolfowitz said: "The oil revenues of that country could bring between $50 billion and $100 billion over the course of the next two or three years." Senior administration officials including Vice President Cheney predicted revenues of $20 to $30 billion a year. In September 2003, however, the Iraq administrator L. Paul Bremer reported to Congress that Iraq's oil revenues for the next two years would not be greater than the amounts Iraq needed to cover its basic daily expenses. See Jeff Gerth, "Report Offered Bleak Outlook about Iraq Oil," *New York Times*, October 5, 2003, available at www.nytimes.com. See also Eric Schmitt and Joel Brinkley, "State Department Study Foresaw Trouble Now Plaguing Iraq," *New York Times*, October 19, 2003, available at www.nytimes.com.

18. Quoted in David L. Phillips, *Losing Iraq: Inside the Postwar Reconstruction Fiasco* (Boulder, CO: Westview Press, 2005), 152.

19. Phillips, *Losing Iraq*, 153. See also chapters 7 through 9, and 12 to 16, which cover U.S. relations with Ahmad Chalabi, the U.S. attempt to bring Iraqi exiles together, some of the main accomplishments of the Future of Iraq project, the various plans for occupation and de-Baathification, and the failure of the Coalition Provisional Authority to maintain political control of Iraq.

20. When asked to give a range for the number of troops that would be needed for a successful occupation of Iraq, Shinseki's exact words were: "I would say that what's been mobilized to this point, something on the order of several hundred thousand soldiers, are probably, you know, a figure that would be required. We're talking about post-hostilities control over a piece of geography that's fairly significant, with the kinds of ethnic tensions that could lead to other problems. And so, it takes significant ground force presence to maintain safe and secure environment to ensure that the people are fed, that water is distributed, all the normal responsibilities that go along with administering a situation like this." United States Congress, Senate, Armed Services

Committee, Hearing, February 25, 2003, available at www.lexis-nexiscongressional
.com. Wolfowitz's exact reply was: "I am reluctant to try to predict anything about
what the cost of a possible conflict in Iraq would be, or what the possible cost of reconstructing and stabilizing that country afterwards might be. But some of the higher-
end predictions that we have been hearing recently, such as the notion that it will take
several hundred thousand U.S. troops to provide stability in post-Saddam Iraq, are
wildly off the mark. First, it's hard to conceive that it would take more forces to provide stability in post-Saddam Iraq than it would take to conduct the war itself and to
secure the surrender of Saddam's security forces and his army. Hard to imagine." U.S.
Congress, House, Budget Committee, Hearing, February 27, 2003, available at www
.lexis-nexiscongressional.com. See also Bernard Weinraub with Thom Shanker,
"Rumsfeld's Design for War Criticized on the Battlefield," *New York Times*, April 1,
2003, available at www.nytimes.com.

21. See also James Dobbins, John G. McGinn, Keith Crane, Seth G. Jones, Rollie
Lal, Andrew Rathmell, Rachel Swanger, and Anga Timilsina, *America's Role in Nation
Building from Germany to Iraq* (Santa Monica, CA: Rand Corporation, 2003). A two-
year report on U.S. intelligence failures, led by Richard J. Kerr, a former deputy director of the CIA, pointed out an irony in the interaction between the administration and the
intelligence community. Kerr observed that Bush administration policymakers paid
close attention to intelligence on Saddam's weapons, "where the analysis was wrong,
but apparently paid little attention to intelligence on cultural and political issues (post-
Saddam Iraq), where the analysis was right." The report added that policymakers did not
so much reinforce intelligence about Saddam's weapons they agreed with as defer to the
expertise they assumed it was based on. A further irony, Kerr observed, arose because
the intelligence community's analysis of post-Saddam Iraq was not based on hard evidence, but "was informed by strong regional and country expertise developed over time,
and yet was on the mark. Intelligence projections in this area, although largely accurate, however, had little impact on policy deliberations." "Intelligence and Analysis on
Iraq: Issues for the Intelligence Community," dated July 29, 2004, released in mid-
October 2005 in the CIA's journal, *Studies in Intelligence* 49, no. 3, (October 2005),
available at www.gwu.edu/~nsarchiv/news/20051013/kerr_report.pdf.

22. Rumsfeld's response was to compare Iraq's travail to the situation confronting
the fledgling United States found in 1783. Apparently Rumsfeld believed that the
"tyranny" of Great Britain in the eighteenth century was no different from the "tyranny"
of Saddam Hussein, and that the condition of a "free and civil society" in North America in the eighteenth century was identical to that in the Gulf in the twenty-first. See
Remarks as Prepared for Delivery by Secretary of Defense Donald H. Rumsfeld, New
York, May 27, 2003, available at www.defenselink.mil/speeches/2003.

23. James Fallows, "Blind into Baghdad," *Atlantic Monthly*, January/February 2004,
available at www.theatlantic.com/doc/print/200401/fallows. Fallows emphasizes that
Rumsfeld distorted the perception of the problem by opposing all attempts to dispel some
of the uncertainty about what would happen in Iraq. Fallows quotes Douglas Feith, the
undersecretary of defense for policy, who was responsible for postwar planning: "If you
tried that, you would get thrown out of Rumsfeld's office so fast—if you ever went in
there and said, 'Let me tell you what postwar Iraq is going to look like in the future,'
you wouldn't get to your next sentence." Ibid. Other problems that the administration was
advised about and ignored: a much higher estimate of the cost of the war and occupation;
warnings from nongovernmental organizations and the U.S. Agency for International

Development about the possibility of a breakdown of law and order after the fall of Saddam, and the responsibilities of the occupying power under the Geneva Convention; from the Army War College about methods of de-Baathification, and other postwar problems; from a number of generals about the need for a large force in Iraq after the overthrow of Saddam Hussein; and the importance of limiting damage to Iraq's electrical grid.

24. Jonathan Weisman and Mike Allen, "Officials Argue for Fast U.S. Exit from Iraq," *Washington Post*, April 21, 2003, available at www.washingtonpost.com; and David E. Sanger and Eric Schmitt, "U.S. Has a Plan to Occupy Iraq, Officials Report," *New York Times*, October 11, 2002, available at www.nytimes.com.

25. See Patrick J. McDonnell and John Hendren, "U.S. Officials and Iraqis Agree That Conflict Will Get Worse: As the Insurgency Grows More Sophisticated, Bloodier Attacks Are Foreseen. The Coalition Remains Confident of Victory," *Los Angeles Times*, December 14, 2003, available at www.latimes.com; Ian Fisher, "More Violence for U.S. Troops in Pro-Hussein Heartland," *New York Times*, December 16, 2003, available at www.nytimes.com; and Rajiv Chandrasekaran, "Attacks Force Retreat From Wide-Ranging Plans for Iraq," *Washington Post*, December 28, 2003, available at www.washingtonpost.com.

26. See in particular, Charles Krauthammer, *Democratic Realism: An American Foreign Policy for a Unipolar World* (Washington DC: American Enterprise Institute, 2004). Krauthammer offered strawman versions of competing international outlooks and argued that "[t]here is not a single, remotely plausible, alternative strategy" for dealing with the threat of terrorism and the turmoil and oppression in the Arab and Muslim world than that of the Bush II administration (16–17). The neoconservative newspaper the *Weekly Standard*, regularly makes the same points. To Krauthammer, the spread of democracy and liberty are "the ends and means of foreign policy."

27. Francis Fukuyama, "The Neoconservative Moment," *National Interest*, Summer 2004, available at www.findarticles.com/p/articles/mi_m2751/is_76/ai_n6127311. Fukuyama's article was written in response to Krauthammer's lecture. A conservative think tank, the American Enterprise Institute, published Krauthammer's arguments in the book, *Democratic Realism*.

28. Jackson Diehl, "Iraqi's Broken Dreams," *Washington Post*, October 10, 2005, available at www.washingtonpost.com. See also, Guy Dinmore, "Conservatives and Exiles Desert War Campaign," *Financial Times*, October 11, 2005, available at www .ft.com.

29. Diehl, "Iraqi's Broken Dreams."

30. For the transcript of Makiya's and Rahim's remarks, see the proceedings of the conference on "Remarking of Iraq: Success, Failure, and the Foundation of A New State," held at the American Enterprise Institute, October 5, 2005, available at www.aei .org/events/filter.all,eventID.1120/transcript.asp. For a more positive view of the elections, see Condoleezza Rice, "The Promise of Democratic Peace: Why Promoting Freedom Is the Only Realistic Path to Security," *Washington Post*, December 11, 2005, at www.washingtonpost.com; and Zalmay Khalilzad, "After the Elections," *Washington Post*, December 15, 2005, at www.washingtonpost.com.

31. Josh White and Bradley Graham, "Decline in Iraqi Troops' Readiness Cited," *Washington Post*, September 30, 2005, available at www.washingtonpost.com.

32. White and Graham, "Decline in Iraqi Troops' Readiness."

33. Robert Burns, "Army in Worst Recruiting Slump in Decades," Associated Press, September 30, 2005, available at http://news.yahoo.com.

34. "Militants Gun Down Afghan Official, Headmaster," Reuters, October 19, 2005, available at http://news.yahoo.com; and Liz Sidoti, "Rice to Meet with Congress over Iraq," Associated Press, October 19, 2005, available at http://news.yahoo.com.

35. See The Polling Report Inc., "President Bush—Overall Job Rating," November 2005, available at www.pollingreport.com, and "Iraq," November 2005, available at www.pollingreport.com/iraq.htm. The Polling Report site also has extremely interesting graphic representations of poll results. See, for instance, www.pollingreport.com/gallery.

36. "Americans Oppose Use of Force to Promote Democracy," Agence France Presse, September 29, 2005, available at http://news.yahoo.com.

37. Mark Sappenfield, "Military Strategy in Iraq: What Is It?" *Christian Science Monitor*, October 17, 2005, available at www.csmonitor.com. See also, Liz Sidoti, "Rice to Meet with Congress over Iraq," Associated Press, October 19, 2005, available at http://news.yahoo.com.

38. Joel Brinkley, "Saudi Minister Warns U.S. Iraq May Face Disintegration," *New York Times*, September 23, 2005, available at www.nytimes.com.

39. Figures for the election are from "Iraqi Election Results, by Province," *New York Times*, October 25, 2005, available at www.nytimes.com. See also, John Ward Anderson, "Draft Constitution Approved by Iraqi Voters," *Washington Post*, October 25, 2005, available at www.washingtonpost.com; and Edward Wong, "Final Tally Shows Iraqi Voters Approved New Constitution," *New York Times*, October 25, 2005, available at www.nytimes.com. See also, Robert H. Reid, "Sunni Ambush Kills 14 al-Sadr Militiamen," Associated Press, October 27, 2005, available at http://news.yahoo.com.

40. See Ghaith Abdul-Ahad, "The New Sunni Jihad: 'A Time for Politics,'" *Washington Post*, October 27, 2005, available at www.washingtonpost.com; Mariam Karouny, "Shiite and Sunni Lines Drawn for Iraq Vote," Reuters, October 27, 2005, available http://news.yahoo.com; Alastair Macdonald and Mariam Karouny, "Iraq Election Shapes Up as Ballot Closes," Reuters, October 28, 2005, available at http://news.yahoo.com; and Mariam Karouny, Shi'ite and Sunni Lines Drawn for Iraq Vote," Reuters, October 27, 2005, available at http://news.yahoo.com.

41. Zalmay Khalilzad, "Politics Break Out in Iraq," *Washington Post*, September 4, 2005, available at www.washingtonpost.com. See also, Steve Hadley, "Iraq's Democratic Determination," *Washington Post*, October 15, 2005, available at www.washingtonpost.com.

42. Robin Wright and Ellen Knickmeyer, "U.S. Lowers Sights on What Can Be Achieved in Iraq," *Washington Post*, August 14, 2005, available at www.washingtonpost.com.

43. Ibid.

44. Seth Borenstein, "Billions of Dollars Short, U.S. Must Scale Back Iraqi Reconstruction," Knight Ridder Newspapers, October 18, 2005, available at http://new.yahoo.com. See also, Seth Borenstein, "Agency Charged with Spending Oversight Left Country in '04," Knight Ridder Newspapers, October 17, 2005, available at www.news.yahoo.com.

45. Ibid. See also Ian Herbert, "Are British Troops at Breaking Point in Iraq?" *The Independent*, October 18, 2005, at www.independent.co.uk.

46. The administration had been warned. During the months before the invasion, the CIA and other intelligence agencies repeatedly advised that the war would be the easiest part of the campaign, and that the occupation and reconstruction would be the most

dangerous and toughest parts of the entire effort. "In particular, the agencies predicted that Hussein loyalists might try to sabotage U.S. postwar efforts by destroying critical economic targets. . . . One analysis warned that Iraqis 'would probably resort to obstruction, resistance and armed opposition if they perceived attempts to keep them dependent on the United States and the West.'" The warnings had little discernible effect on policy. Peter Slevin and Dana Priest, "Wolfowitz Concedes Iraq Errors," *Washington Post*, July 23, 2003, available at www.washingtonpost.com.

47. Bob Droggin, "Iraq Had Secret Labs, Officer Says: Goal Was to Someday Rebuild Chemical and Biological Weapons, General Alleges," *Los Angeles Times*, June 8, 2003, available at www.latimes.com.

48. See www.cia.gov/nic/NIC_about.html.

49. Thomas Powers, "Secret Intelligence & the War on Terror," *New York Review of Books* 51, no. 20 (December 16, 2004): 52.

50. See remarks by Condoleezza Rice, assistant to the president for national security affairs, to the Chicago Council on Foreign Relations, Chicago, Illinois, October 8, 2003, available at www.whitehouse.gov. See also, Seymour M. Hersh, "The Stovepipe: How Conflicts between the Bush Administration and Intelligence Community Marred the Reporting on Iraq's Weapons," *New Yorker*, October 27, 2003, p. 77. See also, Hersh, "Selective Intelligence," 45, 49. The two most embarrassing incidents connected with the intelligence bungling occurred when faulty charges were made by the president during his State of the Union address in January 2003 that Iraq was attempting to acquire uranium ore from Niger, and by Colin Powell in his presentations to the UN Security Council in February, especially the charge that Iraq had acquired thousands of aluminum tubes designed for use in centrifuges to enrich uranium for nuclear weapons. Before the war, one of the world's foremost experts on centrifuge technology told administration officials that the notion that the tubes could be used for such a purpose was nonsense, but his conclusion was discounted. As to why there were so many tubes, some 60,000, a former Iraqi general admitted after the war that there were too many tubes to be used as artillery. The excess, he said, was the result of corruption: "We did not need this many tubes. Someone did this to steal the money." See Droggin, "Iraq Had Secret Labs, Chemical and Biological Weapons, General Alleges," *Los Angeles Times*, June 8, 2003, available at www.latimes.com. In the end, the Niger uranium may have been the most embarrassing blunder. The claim may have originated as part of a British disinformation campaign designed to stir up concern about Saddam Hussein. Although the documents on which the accusation was based were suspect and shown later to be forgeries, the administration chose to use the information during one of the most public and prestigious of all presidential appearances. It would have been laughable if the results of such colossal self-deception had not been war and the deaths of thousands of American and allied troops and Iraqis not closely associated with Saddam Hussein. See Hersh, "Who Lied to Whom?" and Hersh, "The Stovepipe," 78–79.

51. Morton H. Halperin, "A Case for Containment," *Washington Post*, February 11, 2003, available at www.washingtonpost.com.

52. On the hunt for WMD, see Judith Miller, "A Chronicle of Confusion in the Hunt for Hussein's Weapons," *New York Times*, July 20, 2004, available at www.nytimes.com. On the attempt to get UN cover for Pakistani, Turkish, and Indian troops, see Edith M. Lederer, "Powell: U.S. Seeking New U.N. Draft," Associated Press, August 21, 2003, available at www.yahoo.com; David E. Sanger, "Bush Looks to U.N. to Share Burden on Troops in Iraq," *New York Times*, September 3, 2003, available at www

.nytimes.com; Barry Schweid, "U.S. Offers to Share Iraqi Role with U.N.," Associated Press, September 3, 2003, available at www.yahoo.com; Mike Allen and Vernon Loeb, "U.S. Wants Larger U.N. Role in Iraq," *Washington Post*, September 3, 2003, available at www.washingtonpost.com; Peter Slevin and Colum Lynch, "Diplomats Say U.N. Pact Still Is Feasible," *Washington Post*, September 17, 2003, available at www.washingtonpost.com; Evelyn Leopold, "Annan Rejects U.S. Proposals for U.N. in Iraq," Reuters, October 2, 2003, available at www.yahoo.com; Colum Lynch, "Three Countries Give U.S. a Key Iraq Concession," *Washington Post*, October 15, 2003, available at www.washingtonpost.com; Glenn Kessler, "A Solid Vote that Buttresses 'Made in USA': Resolution on Iraq Note Expected to Attract Contributions of Troops and Aid from U.N. Members," *Washington Post*, October 17, 2003, available at www.washingtonpost.com. On the inadequacy of U.S. troop levels in Iraq, see Esther Schrader, "Allies May Pick Up Slack in Iraq: Pentagon Wants Other Nations to Contribute Troops So U.S. Can Send Some of Its Forces Home," *Los Angeles Times*, June 6, 2003, available at www.latimes.com; Thom Shanker, "Officials Debate Whether to Seek a Bigger Military," *New York Times*, July 20, 2003, available at www.nytimes.com; Reuters, "Powell, Myers Dismiss Report on Iraq Decision," September 4, 2003, available at www.nytimes.com; U.S. Congressional Budget Office, "An Analysis of the U.S. Military's Ability to Sustain an Occupation of Iraq" (Washington, DC: Congressional Budget Office, September 3, 2004); Steven R. Weisman, "Bush Foreign Policy and Harsh Reality," *New York Times*, September 5, 2003, available at www.nytimes.com. On the effect of developments in Iraq on presidential politics at the time, see Todd S. Purdum and Janet Elder, "Poll Shows Drop in Confidence on Bush Skill in Handling Crises," *New York Times*, October 3, 2003, available at www.nytimes.com. On the dubious situation in Afghanistan, see Ahmed Rashid, "The Mess in Afghanistan," *New York Review of Books*, February 12, 2004, pp. 24–27, and Seymour M. Hersh, "The Other War: Why Bush's Afghanistan Problem Won't Go Away," *The New Yorker*, April 12, 2004, pp. 40–47. On Libya's renunciation of WMD, see Ray Takeyb, "The Rogue Who Came in from the Cold," *Foreign Affairs* 80, no. 3 (May–June 2001): 62–72; Glenn Frankel, "'A Long Slog' Led to Libya's Decision," *Washington Post*, December 21, 2003, available at www.washingtonpost.com; Robin Wright and Glenn Kessler, "Sanctions, Isolation Wore Down Gaddafi," *Washington Post*, December 19, 2003, available at www.washingtonpost.com.

53. See James Risen, "Ex-Inspector Says C.I.A. Missed Disarray in Iraqi Arms Program," *New York Times*, January 26, 2004, available at www.nytimes.com; and Droggin, "Iraq Had Secret Labs."

54. On the Office of Special Plans, cherry picking, and stovepiping, see Seymour M. Hersh, "Selective Intelligence: Donald Rumsfeld Has His Own Special Sources. Are They Reliable?" *New Yorker*, May 12, 2003, pp. 44–51; Jim Wolf, "U.S. Insiders Say Iraq Intel Deliberately Skewed," Reuters, May 30, 2003, available at www.yahoo.com; and Greg Miller, "CIA May Have Been Out of Loop: Top Democrat on the Senate Intelligence Panel Says Some Officials in the Administration Appear to Have Bypassed Agency in Gathering Data," *Los Angeles Times*, October 25, 2003, available at www.latimes.com. On the reliance on unverified information, see "Tenet Says Official Wanted Iraq Claim," Associated Press, July 17, 2003; Richard Leiby and Walter Pincus, "Ex-Envoy: Nuclear Report Ignored; Iraq Purchases [of uranium] Were Doubted by CIA," July 6, 2003, available at www.washingtonpost.com; Dana Priest and Walter Pincus, "Bush Certainty on Iraq Arms Went beyond Analysts' Views," *Washington Post*, June

7, 2003, available at www.washingtonpost.com; Vicki Allen, "Powell, Rice Defend U.S. Intelligence on Iraq," *Reuters*, June 8, 2003, available at www.washington post.com; James Risen, David E. Sanger, and Thom Shanker, "In Sketchy Data, White House Sought Clues to Gauge Threat," *New York Times*, July 20, 2003, available at www.nytimes.com; Michael R. Gordon, "Weapons of Mass Confusion," *New York Times*, August 1, 2003, available at www.nytimes.com; Walter Pincus, "Bush Team Kept Airing Iraq Allegation," *Washington Post*, August 7, 2003, available at www .washingtonpost.com; Barton Gellman and Walter Pincus, "Depiction of Threat Out-grew Supporting Evidence," *Washington Post*, August 9, 2003, available at www .washingtonpost.com; Walter Pincus, "Intelligence Report for Iraq War Was 'Hastily Done,'" *Washington Post*, October 24, 2003, available at www.washingtonpost.com; Dana Priest, "Inquiry Faults Intelligence on Iraq from Saddam Hussein Was Over-stated Senate Committee Finds," *Washington Post*, October 24, 2003, available at www.washingtonpost.com; and Carl Hulse and David E. Sanger, "New Criticism on Prewar Use of Intelligence," *New York Times*, September 29, 2003, available at www.nytimes.com. On the failure of U.S. inspectors to find weapons of mass destruc-tion after the war, see Bob Droggin, "Banned Weapons Remain Unseen Foe: Frustra-tions Grow as One False Lead after Another Sends Teams of U.S. and Allied Arms Hunters across Iraq," *Los Angeles Times*, June 15, 2003, available at www.latimes.com; Walter Pincus, "U.N. Inspector: Little New in U.S. Probe for Iraq Arms," *Washington Post*, December 14, 2003, available at www.washingtonpost.com; Douglas Jehl, "U.S. Withdraws a Team of Weapons Hunters from Iraq," *New York Times*, January 8, 2004, available at www.nytimes.com; "Outgoing Iraq Inspector Testifies before Senate Panel," Associated Press, January 28, 2004, available at www.nytimes.com. On the role of Iraqi defectors and exiles in the administration's perceptions of Saddam's weapons and production facilities, see Bob Droggin and Greg Miller, "Iraqi Defector's Tales Bol-stered U.S. Case for War: Colin Powell Presented the U.N. with Details on Mobile Germ Factories, Which Came from a Now-Discredited Source Known as 'Curveball,'" *Los Angeles Times*, March 28, 2004, available at www.latimes.com.

55. Dana Milbank and Walter Pincus, "Cheney: Weapons Search Needs Time," *Washington Post*, January 23, 2004, available at www.washingtonpost.com.

56. Daniel Benjamin and Steven Simon, *The Age of Sacred Terror* (New York: Random House, 2002). For a stunning example of the way the administration reasoned about Iraq's weapons, see Condoleezza Rice, "Why We Know Iraq Is Lying," *Wash-ington Post*, January 23, 2003, available at www.washingtonpost.com. In an October 2002 National Intelligence Estimate (NIR), which represented the agreed position of all the government's intelligence agencies, the Bureau of Intelligence and Research (INR) dissented from the view that Saddam Hussein was urgently seeking nuclear weapons: "The activities that we have detected do not, however, add up to a compelling case that Iraq is currently pursuing what INR would consider to be an integrated and com-prehensive approach to acquire nuclear weapons. Iraq may be doing so, but INR con-siders the available evidence inadequate to support such a judgment. Lacking per-suasive evidence that Baghdad has launched a coherent effort to reconstitute its nuclear weapons program, INR is unwilling to speculate that such an effort began soon after the departure of UN inspectors or to project a timeline for the completion of activities it does not now see happening. As a result, INR is unable to predict when Iraq could acquire a nuclear device or weapon." "Key Judgments [from October 2002 NIR], Iraq's Continuing Programs for Weapons of Mass Destruction," available at

www.washingtonpost.com. See also, Sonni Efron and Greg Miller, "Intelligence Veteran Faults Iraq Arms Data," *Los Angeles Times*, October 29, 2003, available at www.latimes.com. The article quotes the head of INR at the time, Carl W. Ford Jr., as follows: "[The entire intelligence community] badly performed for a number of years . . . and the information we were giving the policy community was off the mark." Although there were dissenters, their views were ignored, Ford said. "The majority view prevailed, and that [view] was wrong." The Department of Energy also dissented in the October 2002 NIE, arguing that aluminum tubes which the administration insisted were being used to produce fissile material for nuclear bombs were not part of a nuclear program. See Joseph Cirincione, Jessica T. Mathews, and George Perkovich, with Alexis Orton, *WMD in Iraq: Evidence and Implications* (Washington, DC: Carnegie Endowment for International Peace, 2004), 23.

57. The Carnegie Endowment study strongly supported the charge of pressuring intelligence analysts. The authors made two accusations. Even though no new evidence had been acquired, the National Intelligence Estimate (NIE) of October 2002 differed markedly from its predecessors in all four critical areas: nuclear, chemical, and biological weapons and ballistic missile construction. Regarding the difference in NIEs, before September 2002, the consensus was that Iraq had probably not reconstituted its nuclear program, but was continuing low-level research. David Kay's inspectors were able to confirm after the war that Iraq had no substantial nuclear weapons program. But the administration and the October 2002 NIE insisted that Saddam had reconstituted his nuclear program and would have a nuclear weapon within a decade, and much sooner if he acquired enriched uranium. Pre-2002 intelligence assessments thought it only possible that Iraq had large stocks of chemical weapons. The October 2002 assessment said with "high confidence" that it had, a charge repeated by senior administration officials. Kay's inspectors found no chemical weapons and no evidence that Iraq had a major centrally directed program after 1991. The same transformation of "maybe" and "probably" to unqualified assertion—and the same failure of inspectors to find any confirmation—occurred with regard to biological weapons and missile and delivery systems. These changes were accompanied by Vice President Cheney's repeated visits to the CIA, demands for "raw" intelligence, and the creation of a separate intelligence analysis section in the Pentagon, named the Office of Special Plans and staffed with neoconservative political appointees, whose task was to find evidence that supported Iraq's possession of WMD. The Carnegie report also charged that in addition to slanting the National Intelligence Estimate, administration officials also misrepresented intelligence findings by joining chemical, biological, and nuclear weapons all together in one form as WMD, when there were substantial differences in Iraqi capabilities in each category of weapons. See also, Deputy Secretary Wolfowitz Interview with *Fox News*, February 17, 2002, available at www.defenselink.mil/news/Feb2002; and Linda D. Kozaryn, "Wolfowitz: World Must Act Now to Prevent Evil," available at www.defenselink/news/feb2002.

58. Tyler Marshall and Louise Roug, "A Central Pillar of Iraqi Policy Crumbling," *Los Angeles Times*, October 9, 2005, available at www.latimes.com. See also, David E. Sanger, "Administration's Tone Signals a Longer, Broader Iraq Conflict," *New York Times*, October 17, 2005, available at www.nytimes.com.

59. Glenn Kessler, "Hopes Lowered for U.S.–North Korean Talks: Diplomacy Appears to Be a Priority," *Washington Post*, February 20, 2004, available at www.washingtonpost.com.

60. Jonathan Ansfield and Jack Kim, "South Korea Unveils Plan to End Nuclear Crisis," Reuters, February 23, 2004, available at www.yahoo.com; and Steven R. Weisman and David E. Sanger, "U.S. Urges North Korea to End Nuclear Work," *New York Times*, February 20, 2004, available at www.nytimes.com.

61. Personal conversation about the North Korean economy with U.S. intelligence official, who asked to remain anonymous, Washington, DC, September 2003.

62. Robert Malley, "Without a Road Map, No Rules, Just Fear," *Washington Post*, October 13, 2003, available at www.washingtonpost.com.

63. Personal conversations with U.S. intelligence officials who requested anonymity, Washington, DC, September 2003.

64. The Israeli newspaper *Maariv* reported in August 2004 that the Sharon government intended to begin closing the gap between a large Israeli settlement on the West Bank, Maale Adumim, and Jerusalem. The Israeli government denied the reports. See Ken Ellingwood, "Israel Denies It's Planning Major Settlement Project," *Los Angeles Times*, August 6, 2004, available at www.latimes.com.

65. See Elaine Sciolino, "Don't Weaken Arafat, Saudi Warns Bush," *New York Times*, January 27, 2002, available at www.nytimes.com.

66. See Neil MacFarquhar, "Summit's Collapse Leaves Arab Leaders in Disarray," *New York Times*, March 29, 2004, available at www.nytimes.com.

67. See Serge Schmemann, "A Departure, But to Where?" *New York Times*, June 30, 2002, available at www.nytimes.com.

68. See Todd S. Purdum, "Bush's Mideast Consultations Proceed, Quietly," *New York Times*, July 12, 2002, available at www.nytimes.com.

69. Serge Schmemann, "Palestinian Voice: A Deep Despair," *New York Times*, July 14, 2002, available at www.nytimes.com.

70. John Kifner and Todd S. Purdum, "Flurry Precedes Mideast Meeting in New York," *New York Times*, July 16, 2002, available at www.nytimes.com.

71. See the poll conducted by the Program on International Policy Attitudes (PIPA) of the University of Maryland. The poll was commissioned by Search for Common Ground, a nongovernmental organization devoted to conflict resolution, and released in Jerusalem on December 10, 2002.

72. Amos Elon, "Israelis and Palestinians: What Went Wrong?" *New York Review of Books*, December 19, 2002, available at www.nybooks.com.

73. The situation recalled developments in Algeria in the 1980s when Islamist groups won local elections. The Algerian government suspended the elections and attempted to crush its opponents. Some 60,000 people died in what was an even bloodier civil war than occurred in Lebanon.

74. See Molly Moore, "Democracy's New Face: Radical and Female," *Washington Post*, January 29, 2005, available at www.washingtonpost.com. See also John Ward Anderson, "Hamas Dominates Local Vote in Gaza: Radicals Deal Blow to Abbas' Party," *Washington Post*, January 29, 2005, available at www.washington post.com.

75. Quoted in Jackson Diehl, "Sharon's Gamble Rides on Bush," *Washington Post*, April 11, 2005, available at www.washingtonpost.com.

76. Ibid.

77. See John Lewis Gaddis, *Surprise, Security and the American Experience* (Cambridge, MA: Harvard University Press, 2004); and Jackson Diehl, "The Lesson of Turkey," *Washington Post*, March 10, 2003, available at www.washingtonpost.com.

78. See International Staff, "U.S. Allies Condemn Decision on Iraq Contracts," *New York Times*, December 10, 2003, available at www.nytimes.com; Peter Finn and Peter Baker, "U.S. Decision on Iraq Contracts Irritates Excluded War Critics," *Washington Post*, December 11, 2003, available at www.washingtonpost.com; David E. Sanger and Douglas Jehl, "Bush Seeks Help from Allies Barred from Iraq Deals," *New York Times*, December 11, 2003, available at www.nytimes.com; "Baker to Seek Iraq Relief among Allies," Associated Press, December 11, 2003, available at www.washington post.com; Molly Ivins, "A Model of Rectitude—That's Us," Creators Syndicate, December 21, 2003, available at www.dfw.com/mld/dfw/news/columnists/molly_ivins. For a different view, see Charles Kupchan, "The Atlantic Alliance Lies in the Rubble," *Financial Times*, April 10, 2003, p. 13.

79. See James Mann, "Bush Wanted His Doctrine and the Allies, Too," *Los Angeles Times*, March 26, 2003, pp. B1, B3. Critics of the administration in Europe and elsewhere salted their disagreement with U.S. policies with a stereotype of President Bush as a shallow poorly educated "cowboy." The handful of French supporters of the administration answered that their countrymen had adopted the "nationalism of imbeciles," and, to their shame, had taken no part in liberating Iraq from an odious dictatorship. See Pascal Bruckner, André Glucksman, and Romain Goupil, "La faute [The Mistake]," *Le Monde*, April 14, 2003, available at www.lemonde.fr.

80. In the summer of 2004, the UN contemplated a return to Iraq to assist in the formation of an interim assembly, and to aid in writing a new constitution and holding national elections. However, the continuing violence forced the postponement of the conference at which the new assembly was to be chosen and made the UN's planned return to Iraq risky. See Maggie Farley, "U.N. Sending Political Advisors to Help Set Up Forum," *Los Angeles Times*, August 7, 2004, available at www.latimes.com. See also, Pamela Constable, "Three Hundred Militiamen Killed in Iraqi South; Three U.S. Troops Slain; Clerics Call for Uprising," *Washington Post*, August 7, 2004, available at www.washingtonpost.com; John F. Burns, "Marines Pushing Deeper Into City Held by Shiites," *New York Times*, August 8, 2004, available at www.nytimes.com; Henry Chu, "Fighting Intensifies in Iraqi Cities; Toll Rises," *Los Angeles Times*, August 7, 2004, available at www.latimes.com.

81. Timothy Garton Ash, "Are You With Us? Are We Against You?" *New York Times*, May 30, 2003, available at www.nytimes.com.

82. See Dominique Moisi, "Europe's Essential Role in Winning the Peace," *Financial Times*, March 10, 2003, available at www.ft.co.uk.

83. In particular, the draft European Security Strategy held that Europe must play a major world role in countering the threats of weapons of mass destruction, terrorism, and failed states. "International terrorism is a strategic threat [and] . . . Europe is both a target and a base for such terrorists," the document started. "WMD and missile proliferation puts at risk the security of our states, our peoples and our interests around the world. Meeting this challenge must be a central element in the EU external action. . . . Our objective is to deter, halt and, where possible, reverse proliferation programmes of concern worldwide." The document also emphasized multilateralism and the creation of "a rule-based international order," a phrase particularly dear to French President Chirac. See "A Secure Europe in a Better World: Draft European Security Strategy Presented by the EU High Representative for the Common Foreign and Security Policy, Javier Solana, to the European Council, 20 June 2003 in Thessaloniki, Greece," Council of the European Union, Brussels, available at http://ue.eu.int.

84. By huge margins, public opinion around the world turned against the administration and its foreign policy. "Abroad, almost everyone considers this war unjust and unnecessary. Even in Britain, 60 percent of adults disapprove of President Bush's foreign policy, reported an early March [2003] poll by the Pew Global Associates Project. Elsewhere, disapproval rates approach unanimity: 87 percent in France, 85 percent in Germany, 83 percent in Russia, 79 percent in Spain, and 76 percent in Italy. Polls in Asia and Latin America find similar hostility." The French government led European opposition, arguing that no single power should be allowed to dominate the world, and that a united Europe must balance the "hyperpower." Robert J. Samuelson, "The Gulf of World Opinion," *Washington Post*, March 26, 2003, available at www.washington post.com.

85. Hans J. Morgenthau, *Politics among Nations: The Struggle for Power and Peace*, 5th ed., rev. ed. (New York: Alfred A. Knopf, 1978), 4–15, available at www .mtholyoke.edu/acad/intrel/morg6.htm. Recalling the Vietnam War, Morgenthau also observed: "The experience of the Indochina War suggests five factors [that] such a theory [of foreign policy realism] might encompass: the imposition upon the empirical world of a simplistic and *a priori* picture of the world derived from folklore and ideological assumption, that is, the replacement of experience with superstition; the refusal to correct this picture of the world in the light of experience; the persistence in a foreign policy derived from the misperception of reality and the use of intelligence for the purpose not of adapting policy to reality but of reinterpreting reality to fit policy; the egotism of the policy makers widening the gap between perception and policy, on the one hand, and reality, on the other; finally, the urge to close the gap at least subjectively by action, any kind of action, that creates the illusion of mastery over a recalcitrant reality. According to the *Wall Street Journal* of April 3, 1970, "the desire to 'do something' pervades top levels of Government and may overpower other 'common sense' advice that insists the U.S. ability to shape events is negligible. The yen for action could lead to bold policy as 'therapy.'"

86. It was later renamed the Middle East Partnership Initiative. See home page at http://mepi.state.gov/mepi/. The administration claimed to have provided $293 million over four fiscal years.

87. Thomas Carothers, "Promoting Democracy and Fighting Terror," *Foreign Affairs* 82, no. 1 (January 2003–February 2003), available at www.foreignaffairs.org/ 2003/1.html. See also, "Glenn Kessler and Robin Wright, "Arabs and Europeans Question 'Greater Middle East' Plan," *Washington Post*, February 22, 2004, available at www.washingtonpost.com.

88. Carothers, "Promoting Democracy."

89. Richard Ullman, "The US and the World: An Interview with George Kennan," *New York Review of Books*, August 12, 1999, at the website of Transnational Foundation for Peace and Future Research, available at www.transnational.org/features/ kennaninterview.

90. See "Secretary of State Condoleezza Rice at the Post," *Washington Post*, March 25, 2005, available at www.washingtonpost.com. For evidence that at least some officials had second thoughts about destabilizing Egypt and other friendly Muslim states, see Jonathan Wright, "Islamist Gains in Egypt Give U.S. Pause," Reuters, November 22, 2005, at www.news.yahoo.com/news.

91. George W. Bush, Inaugural Address transcript, January 20, 2005, available at www.cnn.com/2005/ALLPOLITICS/01/20/bush.transcript.

92. See in particular, Michael C. Hudson, *The Precarious Republic: Political Modernization in Lebanon* (New York: Random House, 1968).

7. An American Foreign Policy for the Twenty-First Century

1. George F. Kennan, *American Diplomacy: 1900–1950* (Chicago: University of Chicago Press, 1951), 112.

2. Reinhold Niebuhr, *The Irony of American History* (New York: Scribner, 1952), quoted in Arthur Schlesinger Jr., "Forgetting Reinhold Niebuhr," *New York Times,* September 18, 2005, available at www.nytimes.com.

3. See especially, Michael Ignatieff, *Blood and Belonging: Journeys into the New Nationalism* (New York: Farrar, Straus & Giroux, 1994); and Leah Greenfeld, *Nationalism: Five Roads to Modernity* (Cambridge, MA: Harvard University Press, 1992). Greenfeld makes the fundamental distinction between civic nationalism, or loyalty to an idea of government, and ethnic nationalism, which recognizes citizenship only on the basis of birth.

4. Thomas Carothers, "Democracy without Illusions," *Foreign Affairs* 76, no. 1 (January/February 1997), accessed at http://web17.epnet.com.

5. See the exceptionally fine article on democratization's problems by Edward D. Mansfield and Jack Snyder, "Democratization and War," *Foreign Affairs* no. 3 (May/June 1995): 79–88.

6. Radical conservatives learned the opposite lesson. The easy overthrow of Marcos and the successful democratic transition taught Paul Wolfowitz and others that democracy could succeed just about anywhere. All that was needed was for Americans to stand up for what they believed and take decisive action. See James Mann, *The Rise of the Vulcans* (New York: Viking, 2004), 127–37.

7. An accessible study of the Western philosophical tradition is Richard Tarnas, *The Passion of the Western Mind: Understanding the Ideas that Have Shaped Our World View* (New York: Ballantine, 1993).

8. See in particular, *Natural Right and History* (Chicago: University of Chicago Press, 1953); *Liberalism, Ancient and Modern* (New York: Basic Books, 1968); *On Tyranny* (New York: Free Press, 1991); and *What Is Political Philosophy? And Other Studies* (Chicago: University of Chicago Press, 1988). See also, Anne Norton, *Leo Strauss and the Politics of American Empire* (New Haven, CT: Yale University Press, 2004).

9. A useful and wide-ranging collection of Berlin's writings is found in *The Crooked Timber of Humanity* (New York: Knopf, 1991). See also, Henry Hardy, ed., *Against the Current: Essays in the History of Ideas* (New York: Viking, 1980); Henry Hardy and Roger Hausheer, eds., *The Proper Study of Mankind: An Anthology of Essays* (New York: Farrar, Strauss & Giroux, 1998); and Henry Hardy, ed., *The Roots of Romanticism* (Princeton, NJ: Princeton University Pres, 2001). On related issues, see J.W. Burrow, *The Crisis of Reason: European Thought, 1848–1914* (New Haven, CT: Yale University Press, 2000); and Mark Lilla, *The Reckless Mind: Intellectuals in Politics* (New York: New York Review of Books, 2001).

10. Francis Fukuyama made the point about legitimacy being given rather than taken or commanded with regard to American hegemony in his "The Neoconserva-

tive Moment," *National Interest* (Summer 2004), available at www.findarticles.com/ particles/mi_m2751/is_76/ai_n6127311. About the legitimacy of Bush II policies, he wrote: "Failure to appreciate America's own current legitimacy deficit hurts both the realist part of our agenda, by diminishing our actual power, and the idealist portion of it, by undercutting our appeal as the embodiment of certain ideas and values. . . . Legitimacy is important to us not simply because we want to feel good about ourselves, but because it is useful. Other people will follow the American lead if they believe that it is legitimate; if they do not, they will resist, complain, obstruct or actively oppose what we do." Ibid.

11. John Kane, "American Values or Human Rights? U.S. Foreign Policy and the Fractured Myth of Virtuous Power," *Presidential Studies Quarterly* 33, no. 14 (December 2003): 797.

12. Ibid.

13. A thoughtful German observer, Josef Joffe, suggested that the United States should follow what he took to be the nineteenth-century German statesman Otto von Bismarck's strategy of remaining on better terms with other states than they are with one another. Bismarck's was a strategy, according to Joffe, of "permanent entanglement," of creating "a universal political situation in which all the powers except France [Germany's irreconcilable enemy] need us and, by dint of their mutual relations, are kept as much as is possible from forming coalitions against us." In more prosaic terms, Bismarck advised his successors as follows: "Try to be in a threesome as long as the world is governed by the precarious equilibrium of five great powers. This is the true protection against coalitions." Leaving aside Clinton's indifference to foreign policy and Bush II's complete rejection of multilateral entanglements of any kind, Joffe's picture of American diplomacy has three shortcomings: it makes a false analogy between the world in the twenty-first century and nineteenth-century Europe: as Joffe acknowledges, Bismarck's Germany was the most powerful European state, but nowhere near as powerful as the United States a century later; the United States does not fear Europe combining against it as Bismarck's Germany feared its European neighbors; and the purpose of Bismarck's diplomacy was to preserve a conservative social order in Germany, not to shape the world in Germany's image. Bismarck entirely lacked a world vision, much less the appetite to carry it out. See Josef Joffe, "How America Does It," *Foreign Affairs* 76, no. 5 (September/October 1997), accessed at www.web18.epnet.com.

14. Ibid.

15. The literature on the balance of power is legion. One of the most cogent descriptions of it by a political leader is that given by Winston Churchill as Hitler worked to create the conditions he would need to conquer Europe. See Churchill, *The Gathering Storm*, vol. 1 of *The Second World War* (Boston: Houghton Mifflin, 1948).

16. George F. Kennan, *At a Century's Ending: Reflections, 1982–1995* (New York: W.W. Norton, 1996), 272.

17. Stephen G. Brooks and William C. Wohlforth, "American Primacy in Perspective," *Foreign Affairs* 81, no. 4 (July–August 2002), accessed at Academic Search Elite. To their credit, Brooks and Wolhforth argue for magnanimity and restraint by the United States in exercising its supposed world domination.

18. See Barbara W. Tuchman, *The March of Folly: From Troy to Vietnam* (New York: Knopf, 1984).

19. Thom Shanker, "A New Strategy Document Calls Attention to the Transition between War and Peace," *Washington Post*, May 22, 2004, at www.nytimes.com.

20. The struggle against "non-state actors" has become known as "fourth-generation warfare." For a definition of fourth-generation warfare, see Jonathan Raban, "The Truth about Terrorism," *New York Review of Books* 52, no. 1 (January 13, 2005): 22–26. Raban quotes from an article by William S. Lind and four Army and Marine Corps officers, "The Changing Face of War: Into the Fourth Generation," *Marine Corps Gazette*, October 1989, pp. 22–26.

21. See Rick Atkinson, *In the Company of Soldiers: A Chronicle of Combat in Iraq* (New York: Henry Holt & Company, 2004).

22. Jeffrey Gettleman, "Into the Heart of Falluja," *The New York Times Magazine*, May 2, 2004, at www.nytimes.com. See also, Michael Moss, "Bloodied Marines Sound Off about Want of Armor and Men," *New York Times*, April 25, 2005, available at www.nytimes.com.

23. See also George F. Kennan, *Memoirs, 1925–1950* (New York: Pantheon Books, 1967), especially 405–414, 462–476.

24. For these numbers, see "President Bush's FY 2005 Budget," February 2, 2004, available at: www.whitehouse.gov/infocus/budget/index.html; and "Congressional Budget Justification—FY 2005," last updated January 14, 2005, available at: www.usaid.gov/policy/budget/cbj2005/.

25. See "Estimated Costs of Continuing Operations in Iraq and Other Operations of the Global War on Terrorism" (Washington, DC: Congressional Budget Office, June 15, 2004), available at: www.cbo.gov/publications/byclasscat.cfm?cat=38.

26. See "United States Objectives and Programs for National Security, NSC 68," April 14, 1950, *Foreign Relations of the United States, 1950*, vol. 1 (Washington, DC: Government Printing Office, 1977), 386, 389, 392. The full text may be found at www.fas.org/irp/offdocs/nsc-hst/nsc-68.htm.

27. See Norimitsu Onishi, "Tokyo Protests Anti-Japan Rallies in China," *New York Times*, April 11, 2005, available at www.nytimes.com; and Edward Cody, "New Anti-Japanese Protests Erupt in China: Thousands Descend on Consulate in Shanghai; Beijing Remains Calm," *Washington Post*, April 16, 2005, available at www.washingtonpost.com.

28. For a slightly different classification, see M.H. Tavuz, "Is There a Turkish Islam? The Emergence of Convergence and Consensus," *Journal of Muslim Minority Affairs* 24, no. 2 (2004): 1–22.

29. David E. Sanger, "Steps at Reactor in North Korea Worry the U.S.," *New York Times*, April 18, 2005, at www.nytimes.com.

30. Ibid., 392.

31. Matthew, 7:15.

32. See in particular, Monte Palmer and Princess Palmer, *At the Heart of Terror: Islam, Jihadists, and America's War on Terror* (Lanham, MD: Rowman & Littlefield, 2004); and Steve Coll, *Ghost Wars: The Secret History of the CIA, Afghanistan, and Bin Laden, from the Soviet Invasion to September 10, 2001* (New York: Penguin Press, 2004).

33. Interview by author with Douglas Feith, undersecretary of defense for policy, September 2003.

34. Of all the books and articles written to emphasize the differences between Europe and the United States, the most destructive was Robert Kagan, *Of Paradise and Purpose: America and the New Europe in the New World Order* (New York: Knopf, 2003).

Index

Abbas, Mahmoud: as president of Palestinian Authority, 169, 170, 172–73, 195
Abizaid, John P., 184
ABM Treaty, 117, 121, 137, 138
Abu Hassan, 45
Abu Mazen. *See* Abbas, Mahmoud
Acheson, Dean, 17, 235n26
Afghanistan: national elections, 146; Soviet invasion and withdrawal from, 22, 29; U.S. invasion and defeat of Taliban regime, 146, 250–51n27; violence and casualties in, 184
Agency for International Development, 181
Ahmadinejad, Mahmoud, 163
Aidid, Mohammed Farah, 94
Albright, Madeleine: Kosovo conflict, 91, 92; North Korean visit and negotiations, 104; as Secretary of State, 69, 91; Somalia, UN intervention in, 93–96; as UN ambassador, 67, 69
allied cooperation: Bush II administration "coalitions of the willing," 197; and Bush II administration unilateralism, 196–98; U.S. relations with European allies, 3, 8, 106, 114. *See also* North Atlantic Treaty Organization (NATO)
al-Qaeda [terrorist network], 146, 248n26
American Enterprise Institute, 183
American exceptionalism, 2, 5, 9, 12, 77, 128, 137, 143, 152, 174, 175, 206, 211–12
American global hegemony, 109, 137, 141, 196–97, 215, 217, 222, 231n1, 272–73n10
American imperialism, 150, 233n18
American-Israel Public Affairs Committee, 36
American primacy/superiority, 2, 5, 6, 9, 37, 49, 206; bandwagoning, 218; Bush II administration and, 150, 174, 175–76;

Clinton administration failure to use, 106, 109, 112, 113, 175; ensuring or sustaining, 50–53, 142; and military troop strength, 175; multilateralists' views on, 143, 144; and post–Cold War paradigm, 53–55; recalibrating, 216–20
American realism: in foreign policy, 198
American values and institutions, 207, 209–10, 214–15, 222, 225
Arab-Israeli conflict, 17, 38, 73
Arab-Israeli peace conferences, 37–38, 41, 61
Arab League, 156, 193
Arabs: Middle East peace process, 34–41
Arab-U.S. Summit (2003), 170
Arafat, Yasser: attempts to replace, 164, 166–68, 192–94; Bush (George W.) refusing to meet with, 167; Camp David summit (1999), 84–86, 124–27; death of (2004), 171, 195; in exile in Tunis, 35; Israeli bombing of headquarters and imprisonment of, 167, 168; Israeli-Palestinian settlement rejected by, 86
Aristide, Jean Bertrand, 96
Aristotle, 207–8, 212
Armenia, conflict with Azerbaijan, 27
Armitage, Richard: Middle East peace negotiations, 166; North Korean negotiations, 159; political profile and experience, 136, 250n21
arms control. *See* Conventional Forces in Europe (CFE); nuclear arms control
Ash, Timothy Garton, 197
Asia: democratization of, 77; financial crisis, 7
Asia-Pacific economic cooperation, 12, 18, 48, 53, 74, 117
Aspin, Les: resignation of, 74; as Secretary of Defense, 67, 69, 74, 95

275